the Eco-Design Handbook

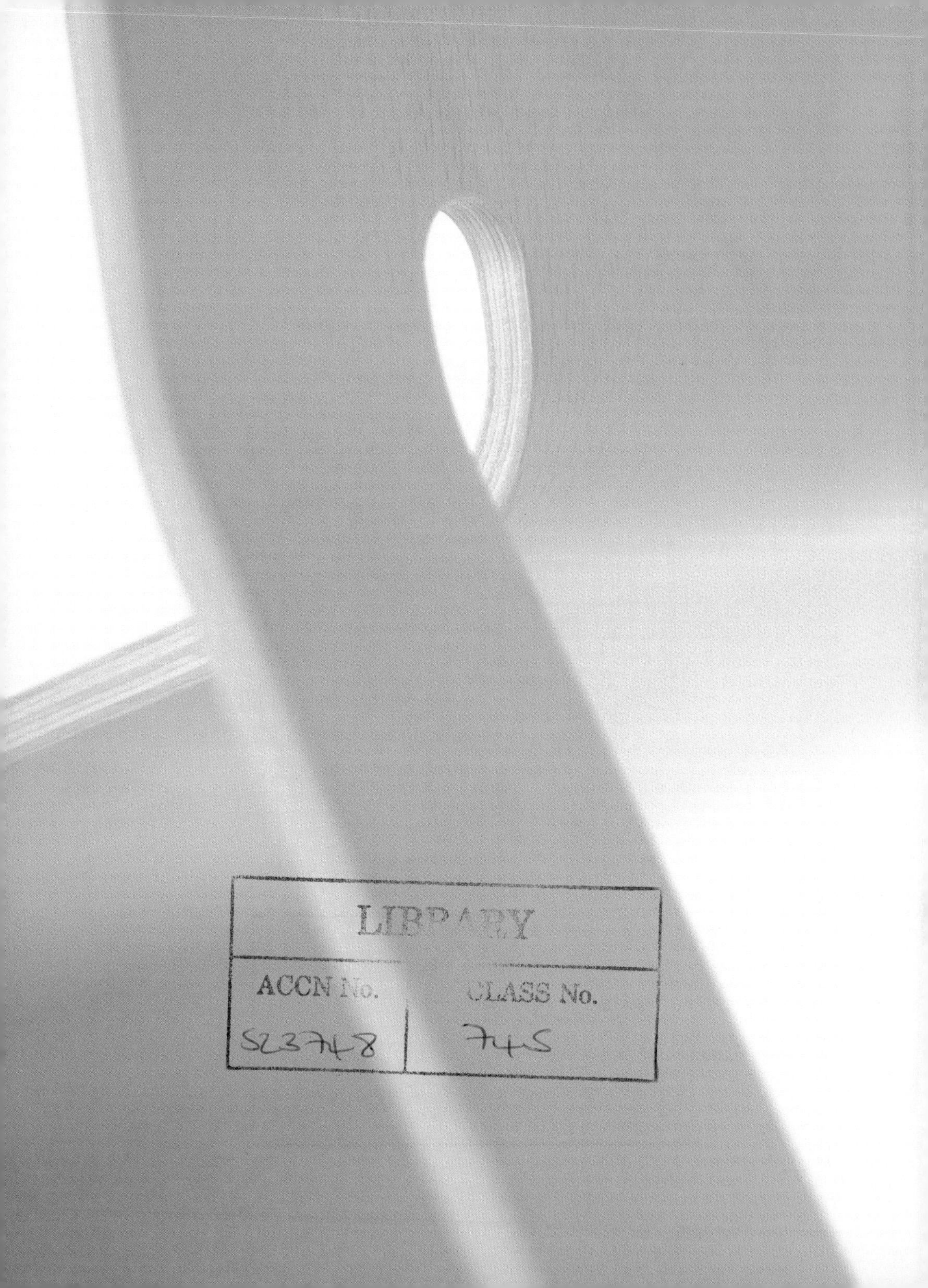

Alastair Fuad-Luke

the Eco-Design Handbook

A Complete Sourcebook for the Home and Office

With 750 illustrations, 690 in colour

Thames & Hudson

Acknowledgments
Researching and compiling this tome was a demanding process in between a busy working life. This process was greatly facilitated by the kindness and assistance of many people. In particular, I would like to thank Lucas Dietrich at Thames & Hudson, whose faith in the project kept me going; Ingrid Cranfield, whose light but firm touch massaged my raw script and whose accurate editing brought clarity to the work; Aaron Hayden at Thames & Hudson for the huge task of preparing and editing the photographic material; and my wife Dina for her encouragement and steadfast support.

Special thanks go to all the designers, designer-makers, manufacturers and other organizations who supplied information and photographic or illustrative materials, without whose kindness this book would not have been possible. Certain individuals provided invaluable support in sourcing material including: Tom Johnson, International Design Resource Awards (IDRA), USA; Ralph Wiegmann and Gabriele Hoffmann, Industry Forum Design Hannover e.V. (iF), Germany; Isabelle Bigler, Design Prize Schweiz, Switzerland; Jacqueline Janssen, Design Academy Eindhoven, Netherlands; Steven Blackman, Design Sense, Design Museum, UK; Philippa Bellhouse, Granta Design Ltd, UK; Tamara Caspersz, Viaduct Ltd, UK; Jackie Dehn, Johnathan Chapman and Anne Chick, Rematerialize database, Kingston University, UK. Thanks are extended to all those who responded to my continuous stream of queries and requests for information.

I dedicate this book to all those who have contributed by their designs and products herein to inspire us towards a more sustainable future.

First published in the United Kingdom in 2002 by Thames & Hudson Ltd, 181A High Holborn, London WC1V 7QX

British Library Cataloguing-in-Publication Data
A catalogue record for this book is available from the British Library

ISBN 0-500-28343-5

Printed and bound in China by Midas Printing

The book was printed on 130 gsm Munken Pure paper, produced by the Swedish mill Munkendals, which has a long tradition of environmental responsibility. Papers are created to minimize the impact on the environment. For example, they have not been subject to chlorine bleaching, pulp is taken from sustainable forests, and production processes have been developed to reduce harmful effects and effluents.

Preface

This book is intended to stimulate new ways of thinking by illustrating an eco-pluralistic approach to design that encourages people to tread more lightly, so that future generations may inherit a healthy planet. This eco-pluralism is reflected in the diverse solutions realized by designers and manufacturers represented in this book from over thirty countries worldwide. Certain solutions reveal an awareness of the adaptive strategies of nature and the cyclic activity of the biosphere (the living parts of the earth). Still others acknowledge the value of materials and products that originate in the technosphere (the parts of the earth that have been synthesized by human technological expertise). Other solutions combine the best of the biosphere and of the technosphere in products and materials that can be easily disassembled and returned to their rightful 'sphere' at the end of their lives. Green designs are as diverse as the people who create them, partly because of human individuality and partly because of such factors as geographical location, habitat, culture, socio-politico-economic system, availability of natural resources including water and other regional or local peculiarities. An eco-pluralistic approach to design, which offers myriad solutions, therefore seems more fitting than the dictatorial 'one-model-fits-all' philosophy of so many design movements from the twentieth century. Eco-pluralism is evolution and revolution. Eco-pluralist designs range from those that embrace minor modifications of existing products (such as the use of recycled rather than virgin materials), through radical new concepts to the complete dematerialization of existing products (making products vanish into services).

The selection of products and materials for this book is entirely personal, arguably idiosyncratic and representing a mere fraction of reality as viewed at a particular time. But a universal thread unifies all the chosen products and materials. Each is an attempt to improve on the status quo, in small or large increments, by reducing the inherent impact of products and materials on our planet and to improve our social well-being. In this book the future is already shown. Unfortunately this future is unequally distributed. It is hoped that this book will help to distribute this better, 'greener' future more equably.

How to use this book

Each product or material is accompanied by a caption and a line box with all or some of the following icons:

The name and nationality of the designer/designer-maker (see pages 304 to 311), or manufacturer and country if the products/materials are designed in-house (see pages 312 to 327).

The name and country of the manufacturer (see pages 312 to 327) or designer-maker (see pages 304 to 311).

The main materials and/or components (see pages 278 to 301 for examples of materials with reduced environmental impacts, i.e., ecomaterials).

The main eco-design strategies applied to the design of the product (see pages 328 to 331).

Important design awards recognizing eco-design (see pages 333 to 334).

The page numbers in the line boxes permit rapid cross-referencing and enable the reader quickly to find designers/designer-makers, manufacturers, materials and eco-design strategies.

Contents

Design for a Sustainable Future

Nearly forty years ago Rachel Carson, in her seminal book *Silent Spring*, documented the devastating effects of pesticide use on mammals and birds in the USA. Today traces of organo-phosphorus pesticides are found in organisms throughout the globe, including in human beings. At the 1967 UNESCO Intergovernmental Conference for Rational Use and Conservation of the Biosphere, the concept of ecologically sustainable development was first mooted. Paul Ehrlich's 1968 book, *The Population Bomb*, linked human population growth, resource degradation and the environment and pondered the carrying capacity of the planet. By 1973 the Club of Rome, in its controversial report, *Limits to Growth*, was predicting dire consequences for the world if economic growth was not slowed down. This report accurately predicted that the world population would reach six billion by the year 2000, although its more frightening predictions of the exhaustion of resources such as fossil fuels were less accurate. Such warnings were, by and large, ignored, with the result that during the last thirty years people have continued to poison the planet with pesticides and other toxic chemicals, which has led to the destruction of ecosystems and the extinction of many species. More recently people have realized that they too are now threatened by human actions. Unfettered use of the internal combustion engine and the burning of fossil fuels to generate electrical power have catalyzed action on climate change. Significant minorities in different places around the globe face the real risk that the land on which they depend will be inundated by rising sea-levels.

In 1950 the world car fleet numbered fifty million vehicles and global fossil fuel use was 1,715 millions of tonnes of oil equivalent. Today there are over five hundred million vehicles and consumption of fossil fuels exceeds 8,000 million tonnes of oil equivalent. For all the individual freedom it confers, the car is making a huge collective negative impact on the environment, specifically the balance of gases, particulate matter and carcinogens in the atmosphere. For every one of the millions of products we use to 'improve' the quality of our lives there are associated environmental impacts. While some products have a small environmental impact, others consume finite resources in vast quantities.

The ultimate design challenge of the twenty-first century is to avoid or minimize the adverse impacts of all products on the environment. Like all challenges, this constitutes both a demand and an opportunity – to steer the debate on more sustainable patterns of production and consumption. Designers need to be an integral part of the debate rather than remain on the fringe or be subject to the whim of the political and commercial forces of the day.

A brief history of green design

Green design has a long pedigree and before the Industrial Revolution it was the norm for many cultures. Goods such as furniture and utility items tended to be made locally by craftsmen such as blacksmiths, wheelwrights and woodland workers, from readily available local resources. Innovation in farming machinery in Europe, particularly Britain, destabilized the natural employment structure of rural areas and in the first half of the nineteenth century almost half of the rural population in Britain migrated to towns to work in factories. Throughout the twentieth century this pattern was repeated around the world as countries industrialized and created new urban centres.

The founders of the British Arts and Crafts movement (1850–1914) were quick to note the environmental degradation associated with the new industries. Their concerns about the poor quality of many mass-manufactured goods and the associated environmental damage prompted them to examine new methods combining inherently lower impact with increased production. For various social and technical reasons, only a small section of society reaped the benefits of the Arts and Crafts movement but the seeds were sown for development of the early modernist movements in

Plaky table designed by Christopher Connell (see p. 56)

Europe, notably in Germany (the Deutsche Werkbund and later the Bauhaus), Austria (the Secession and the Wiener Werkstätte) and the Netherlands (De Stijl). The modernists insisted that the form of an object had to suit its function and that standardized simple forms facilitated the mass-production of good-quality, durable goods at an affordable price, thus contributing to social reform.

Economy of material and energy use went hand in hand with functionalism and modernism. Marcel Breuer, an eminent student at the Bauhaus between 1920 and 1924, applied new lightweight steel tubing to furniture design, arriving at his celebrated Wassily armchair and B-32 cantilever chair. Breuer's 1927 essay, 'Metal Furniture', conveys his enthusiasm for the materials and reveals his green credentials. He saw the opportunity to rationalize and standardize components, allowing the production of 'flat-pack' chairs that could be reassembled (and so save on transport energy) and were durable and inexpensive (and so help improve the lives of the masses).

The early proponents of organic design promoted a holistic approach, borrowing from nature's own model of components within systems. In the USA the architect Frank Lloyd Wright was the first to blend the functionality of buildings, interiors and furniture into one concept. In the 1930s the Finnish architect and designer Alvar Aalto also achieved a synergy between the built environment and his curvilinear bent plywood furniture that evoked natural rhythms. At a landmark competition and exhibition in 1942, entitled Organic Design for Home Furnishings, organized by the Museum of Modern Art, New York, the winners, Charles Eames and Eero Saarinen, firmly established their biomorphic plywood furniture as a means of satisfying the ergonomic and emotional needs of the user. These designs often incorporated laminated wood or plywood to obtain more structural strength with greater economy. With the rapid evolution of new materials such as plastics in the 1960s and 1970s more ambitious expressions of biomorphism were achieved.

Ironically, one of the early advocates of a more sustainable design philosophy, Richard Buckminster Fuller, originated from the USA, a country renowned for both prolific production and consumption. One of Buckminster Fuller's early ventures, the Stockade Building System, established a method of wall construction using cement with waste wood shavings. Building inspectors of the day did not approve of this innovation and the venture faded. Not easily to be deterred, he soon set up a new design company, 4-D, whose name makes reference to the consequence (to humanity) of 3-D objects over time. 'Dymaxion' was the term he coined for products that gave maximum human benefit from minimal use of materials and energy. His 1929 Dymaxion house, later developed as a commercial product in the metal prefabricated Wichita house (1945), and 1933 teardrop-shaped Dymaxion car were both radical designs. The car had a capacity of up to a dozen adults, fuel consumption of 10.7km/litre (30mpg) and the ability to turn within its own length thanks to the arrangement of the three wheels. Remarkable as it was, the car was plagued with serious design faults and never became a commercial reality. The Wichita house could have been a runaway commercial success as nearly forty thousand orders poured in but delays in refining the design led to the collapse of the company. Buckminster Fuller persevered and in 1949 developed a new method of construction based on lightweight polygons. The geodesic dome was suitable for domestic dwellings or multipurpose use and its components were readily transported, easily erected and reusable. His legacy inspired new endeavours such as the Eden Project, near St Austell in Cornwall, UK (2001), in which the world's largest biomes house eighty thousand plant species from tropical to temperate climates.

From 1945 to the mid-1950s most of Europe suffered from shortages of materials and energy supplies. This austerity encouraged a rationalization of design summed up in the axiom 'less is more'. The 1951 Festival of Britain breathed optimism into a depressed society and produced some celebrated designs including Ernest Race's Antelope chair, which used the minimum amount of steel rod in a lightweight curvilinear frame.

During the 1950s European manufacturers such as Fiat, Citroën and British Leyland extolled the virtues of the small car. Economical to build, fuel-efficient (by standards of the day) and accessible to huge mass markets, these cars transformed the lives of almost nine million owners. By contrast, the gas-guzzling, heavyweight, shortlived Buicks, Cadillacs and Chevrolets of America may have celebrated American optimism but were the very antithesis of green design.

The hippie movement of the 1960s questioned consumerism and drew on various back-to-nature themes, taking inspiration from the dwellings and lives of nomadic peoples. Do-it-yourself design books sat alongside publications such as *The Whole Earth Catalog*, a source book of self-sufficiency advice and tools that is still produced annually. Out of this era emerged the 'alternative technologists' who encouraged the application of appropriate levels of technology to the provision of basic needs such as fresh water, sanitation, energy and food for populations in developing countries. And within Europe young designers experimented with new forms using recycled materials and examined alternative systems of design, production and sales.

In 1971 the rumblings of the first energy crisis were felt and by 1974, when the price of a barrel of oil hit an all-time high, the technologists began designing products that consumed less energy and so decreased reliance on fossil fuels. This crisis had a silver lining in the form of the first rational attempts to examine the life of a product and its consequent energy requirements. Lifecycle analysis (LCA), as it became known, has since been developed further into a means of examining the 'cradle to grave' life of products to determine not only energy and material inputs but also associated environmental impacts.

In his 1971 book, *Design for the Real World*, Victor Papanek confronted the design profession head on, demanding that they face their social responsibilities instead of selling out to commercial interests. Although he was pilloried by most design establishments of the day, his book was translated into twenty-one languages and remains one of the most widely read books on design. Papanek believed that designers could provide everything from simple, 'appropriate technology' solutions to objects and systems for community or society use.

By the 1980s three factors, improved environmental legislation, greater public awareness of environmental issues and private-sector competition, ensured that 'green consumers' became a visible force. In the UK in 1988 John Elkington and Julia Hailes wrote *The Green Consumer Guide*, which was purchased by millions of people keen to understand the issues and exercise their 'consumer power'. Designers and manufacturers applied themselves to the task of making their products 'environmentally friendly', not always with genuine zeal or success. Unsubstantiated claims on product labels soon disillusioned an already sceptical public and green design got buried in an avalanche of market-driven, environmentally unfriendly products from the emerging capitalist-driven 'global economy'. Then the pendulum swung back, resulting in more stringent environmental legislation, greater regulation and more uptake of eco-labelling, energy labels and environmental management standards.

Against the grain of the high-tech, matt-black 1980s, a few notable designer-makers blended post-modernism with low environmental-impact materials and recycled or salvaged components. In London Ron Arad produced eclectic works ranging from armchairs made from old car seats to stereo casings of reinforced cast concrete; while Tom Dixon created organic chair forms using welded steel rod covered with natural-rush seating, a design that is still manufactured by Cappellini SpA, Italy, today.

The green design debate gathered momentum following the publication of the Brundtland Report, *Our Common Future*, prepared by the World Commission on Environment and Development in 1987, which first defined 'sustainable development', and also as a result of collaborative work between governments, industry and academia. Dorothy McKenzie's 1991 book, *Green Design*, reported initiatives by individual designers and the corporate world to tackle the real impact of products on the environment.

In the early 1990s in the Netherlands, Philips Electronics, the Dutch government and the University of TU Delft collaborated to develop lifecycle analysis that could be widely used by all designers, especially those in the industrial sector. Their *IDEMAT* LCA software provided single eco-indicators to 'measure' the overall impact of a product. *IDEMAT* was rapidly followed by three commercial options, *EcoScan*, *Eco-It* and a higher-grade package, *SimaPro*. Today there are tens of different LCA and lifecycle inventory (LCI) packages, which can help designers minimize the impact of their designs from cradle to grave.

Over the last ten years academic communities around the world have evolved new terminology to describe particular types of 'green' design, such as Design for environment (DfE), DfX – where X can be assembly, disassembly, reuse and so on – eco-efficiency, ecodesign and EcoReDesign. (Refer to the Glossary for full definitions of these terms.)

Along with the sustainable-development debate has come the concept of sustainable product design (SPD). Most definitions of SPD embrace the need for designers to recognize not only the environmental impact of their designs over time but their social and ethical impacts too. Buckminster Fuller and Papanek would recognize the issues but perhaps wonder why it took so long for the design community at large to take them up.

Our imperilled planet

Twenty-five per cent of the world's population of six billion people account for eighty per cent of global energy use, ninety per cent of car use and eighty-five per cent of chemical use. By 2050 there may be up to twenty billion people on the planet, ten times more than at the beginning of the twentieth century. Scientists estimate that human activities to date have been responsible for increases in atmospheric temperature of between 1.5 and 6 Celsius degrees (2.9–10.8 Fahrenheit degrees). Global warming on an unprecedented scale has melted ice caps and permafrost, with consequent rises in sea-level by up to 60 centimetres (2ft).

It is not an equable world. A typical consumer from the developed 'North' consumes between ten and twenty times more resources than a typical consumer from the developing

'South'. Both types of consumer can sustain their lives but the quality of those lives is substantially different. Almost one billion people suffer from poverty, hunger or water shortages. At present rates of production and consumption the earth can sustain two billion people at 'Northern' standards of living. Could it support twenty billion people at 'Southern' standards of living? Or is there an urgent need to address the way 'Northern' populations consume and examine the true impact of each product's life?

The impact of global production and consumption

Between 1950 and 1997 the production of world grain tripled, world fertilizer use increased nearly tenfold, the annual global catch of fish increased by a factor of five and global water use nearly tripled. Fossil-fuel usage quadrupled and the world car fleet increased by a factor of ten. During the same period destruction of the environment progressed on a massive scale. There was a reduction in biodiversity. For example, the world elephant population decreased from six million to just 600,000 and total tropical rainforest cover decreased by twenty-five per cent. Average global temperature rose from 14.86°C to 15.32°C (58.75–59.58°F), largely owing to an increase in carbon dioxide emissions from 1.6 billion tonnes per annum in 1950 to 7 billion tonnes in 1997. CFC (chlorofluorocarbon) concentrations rose from zero to three parts per billion, causing holes in the protective ozone layer at the North and South poles.

In the North ownership of such products as refrigerators and televisions has reached almost all households. More than two in three households own a washing machine and a car. The North is indeed a material world. It also generates huge quantities of waste. According to *The Green Consumer Guide*, even back in 1988 an average British person generated two dustbins of waste each week, used two trees a year in the form of paper and board and disposed of 90 drinks cans, 70 food cans, 35 petfood cans, 107 bottles and jars and 45kg (99lb) of plastics. By 2000 local authorities in Britain were recycling on average only twenty-five per cent of domestic waste and such valuable resources as glass, metal and plastics were shamefully neglected by disposal in landfill sites or incineration. Furthermore, landfill sites generate methane and contribute to the accumulation of greenhouse gases and rising global temperatures.

The big environmental issues

In 1995 the European Environment Agency defined the key environmental issues of the day as: climate change, ozone depletion, acidification of soils and surface water, air pollution and quality, waste management, urban issues, inland water resources, coastal zones and marine waters, risk management (of manmade and natural disasters), soil quality and biodiversity. Recognition that the planet was fast reaching a perilous state galvanized 172 governments to gather in Rio de Janeiro, Brazil, in 1992 for the United Nations Conference on Environment and Development. The achievements of the 'Earth Summit' were considerable. The Rio Declaration on Environment and Development set forth a series of principles defining the rights and responsibilities of states, a comprehensive blueprint for global action called Agenda 21 was published, guidelines for the management of sustainable forests (Forest Principles) were set and the UN Convention on Biodiversity and the UN Framework on Climate Change (UNFCC) were ratified. The conference set the foundations for establishing the UN Commission for Sustainable Development (UNCSD), which produces annual progress reports, and adopted the Precautionary Principle, which states that 'lack of full scientific certainty shall not be used as a reason for postponing cost-effective measures to prevent environmental degradation'.

Europe's cutting-edge environmental legislation

In 1972 the then members of the European Economic Community (now the European Union), recognizing that environmental damage transgresses national boundaries, agreed that a common transnational policy was required in Europe. Since then the European output of legislation and regulatory measures to combat environmental degradation has been prolific.

Regulations passed by the European Council become effective law for all member states immediately, whereas directives, which are also legally binding, do not come into force in the member states until carried into national law by individual governments. Important legislative advances include the Directive on Conservation of Wild Birds 1979, the Directive on the Assessment of the Effects of Certain Public and Private Projects on the Environment 1985, the Directive on the Conservation of Natural Habitats and Wild Flora and Fauna 1992 and the Directive on Integrated Pollution Prevention and Control (IPPC) 1996. A range of other directives is of great relevance to manufacturers and designers, including on vehicles, electronic equipment, toxic and dangerous waste and packaging and packaging waste. The effect of these regulations is felt well beyond Europe, as transglobal companies manufacturing cars, electronic goods, packaging and chemical products have to meet these stringent standards.

Europe's collaborative efforts to introduce environmental legislation and regulation provide a model to other regions of the world for international cooperation, for example, North America and the 'Tiger' economies of South-east Asia (ASEAN).

The real lives of products

Freedom and death

The car is the ultimate symbol of personal freedom for the twentieth century. It confers unending choices for the user but condemns many to death, directly as accident victims and indirectly as the recipients of pollutants causing asthma (from particulate matter), brain damage (from lead) and cancer (from carcinogens). It also contributes towards climate change via emissions of carbon dioxide, marine pollution in the event of oil tanker spillage or accidents, and noise pollution. Most societies feel that the personal freedom outweighs the collective price but recently several European cities such as Paris and Milan have banned cars on selected days.

One-way trip

Some products lead short, miserable lives, destined for a one-way trip between the retail shelf and burial in a landfill site. Packaging products are the prime example of one-trip products but there are many others – kitchen appliances, furniture, garden accessories and all the paraphernalia of the modern world.

Everyday products quietly killing

Quietly humming away in the corner of millions of kitchens worldwide is the humble refrigerator. It protects by keeping food fresh, but it is a killer too. Coolants using CFCs (chlorofluorocarbons) or HCFCs (hydrochlorofluorocarbons) are the main culprits in precipitating rapid degradation of the layer of ozone gas, which keeps out harmful radiation from space. Not only are there substantial seasonal holes in the ozone layer at the North and South poles but the layer has thinned considerably in other parts of the world. Thus inhabitants receive higher doses of radiation with an increased risk of contracting skin afflictions and cancer.

Everyday inefficient products

The efficiency of products that have become a way of life needs to be challenged continually. The European eco-label for washing machines lays down threshold values for energy consumption of 0.24 kWh per kilogram and water consumption of 15 litres per kilogram of clothes (1.5gals/lb). Yet only a few companies apply for this eco-label and many European retailers sell machines that do not meet the standards, even though they obviously have the technological means to do so. Failure to apply the best technology available means unnecessary daily consumption of massive quantities of electricity and water.

Occasional use

The developed world's preoccupation with DIY home improvements means that each household owns specialist tools, such as electric drills and screwdrivers, which are rarely used.

Novelties and gimmicks

Many of the products available through mail order catalogues are in fact gimmicks that will do no more than provide temporary amusement.

Small but dangerous

Many small electronic devices, such as personal stereos and mobile phones, have a voracious appetite for batteries. While more devices are offered these days with rechargeable batteries, the older models still consign millions of batteries to landfill sites, where cadmium, mercury and other toxic substances accumulate.
In the European Union the disposal of certain battery types is illegal but in many parts of the world it continues unabated.

Industry visions and reality

Although the wastage of resources associated with the planned obsolescence in the US car industry in the 1950s is no longer tolerated, the lifetime of the average family vehicle remains less than ten years. Furthermore, the global car industry is geared up to keep adding to the existing five hundred million cars worldwide at the same level of production. More fuel-efficient cars that can be disassembled at the end of their lives have been produced and some are already on the market, but many manufacturers will not roll out this technology into new models until they have extracted the returns on their capital investment in current models. Moreover, most are concerned to maintain their market share by providing customers with choice, often in the form of fuel-inefficient, prestige or luxury cars.

Both hardware and software companies are obsessed with doubling the speed of personal computers every eighteen months as chip technology continues its meteoric development. Users are seduced into buying faster machines even though they use only a small fraction of the computing power available. Basic functionality, such as being able to adjust the height of a monitor or arrange a keyboard to suit individual needs, remains inadequate. Yet the computer industry conjures up a vision of a future in which we can programme our house to cook the dinner before we arrive back from work, of a wired-up 'information age' in which everyone has access to the Internet. The reality is that ninety-four per cent of the world's population does not have access to the Internet. The building of ever bigger and faster networks and workstations involves considerable consumption of finite resources and the use of toxic substances during manufacture and disposal.

The brand thing

Companies with internationally recognized brands aspire to increase their market share in individual nations in order to claim world dominance. Expectation, in the form of the brand promise, often delivers a transient moment of satisfaction for the purchaser. Whatever happened to products that were guaranteed to 'last a lifetime'? Where is the long view in the companies that sell these brands? The big brands have the potential to reduce the environmental impact of their activities, but not if they persist in encouraging their customers to consume more, not less.

Moving commerce toward sustainability

Evolving environment management systems (EMS)

The flagship international standard that encourages organizations to examine their overall environmental impact arising from production (but not the impact of their products during usage) is ISO14001 compiled by the International Standards Organization in Geneva, Switzerland. Companies that achieve this independently certified EMS have integrated management systems into their business to reduce environmental impacts directly and have agreed to publication of an annual environmental report from an audited baseline, so reductions in impact can be measured. Other independently certified standards exist, such as the Eco-Management and Audit Scheme (EMAS) for companies in EU member states.

Sustainable production and consumption

In 1995 the World Business Council for Sustainable Development (WBCSD), a coalition of 120 international companies committed to the principles of economic growth and sustainable development, published a report entitled *Sustainable Production and Consumption: A Business Perspective*. It defined sustainable production and consumption as 'involving business, government, communities and households contributing to environmental quality through the efficient production and use of natural resources, the minimization of wastes and the optimization of products and services'. The United Nations Commission on Sustainable Development (UNCSD), formed at Rio in 1992, sees the role of business as crucial since it requires the integration of environmental criteria into purchasing policies (green procurement), the design of more efficient products and services, including a longer lifespan for durable goods, better after-sales service, increased reuse and recycling and the promotion of more sustainable consumption by improved product information and by the positive use of advertising and marketing. This represents an important change in the way businesses operate.

Model solutions

WBCSD members are encouraged to adopt measures to improve their eco-efficiency, that is, greater resource productivity, by maximizing the (financial) value added per unit of resource input. This means providing more consumer performance and value from fewer resources and producing less waste. Amory Lovins *et al* of the Rocky Mountain Institute in the USA proposed the concept of 'Factor 4' – a doubling of production using half the existing resources, with a consequent doubling of the quality of life. Researchers at the Wuppertal Institute in Germany find Factor 4 inadequate to deal with the expected doubling or trebling of world population by 2050 and so propose 'Factor 10' as a more appropriate model for the developed North to achieve equable use of resources for populations in the North and developing South.

Another model that is finding favour with business is called 'The Natural Step' (TNS). It sets out four basic 'system conditions' for businesses to adopt. First, substances from the earth's crust, the lithosphere, must not be extracted at a greater rate than they can reaccumulate – thus there must be less reliance on 'virgin' raw materials. Second, manmade substances must not systematically increase but should be biodegradable and recyclable. Third, the physical basis for the productivity and diversity of nature must not be systematically diminished – renewable resources must be maintained and ecosystems kept healthy. Fourth, we must be fair and efficient in meeting basic human needs – resources should be shared in a more equable manner. Companies as diverse as carpet manufacturers, water suppliers and house builders have taken up TNS.

Early adopters and new business models

International companies from Europe, the USA and Japan are exploring new business models that take a long view enmeshed with the concept of sustainable development. For example, Mitsubishi considered the ecology of the tropical rainforest system, which is highly productive in terms of biomass on a fixed amount of nutritional resources. Waste becomes other organisms' food in the rainforest. Mitsubishi mimic this ecology by ensuring their industrial system meets eco-efficient parameters. Where possible waste should be consumed within the company. This model could be extended to ensure that materials are returned to the manufacturer at the end of their lives, keeping the materials in a closed loop and ensuring that the manufacturer retains control of these resources. At the same time, consumers should be discouraged from buying products and instead encouraged to lease product services.

Philips Electronics in the Netherlands produced two publications, *Vision of the Future* (1996) and *La Casa Prossima Futura – The Home of the Near Future* (1999), the latter being also the title of an exhibition at the Milan International Furniture Fair in April 1999. Among factors considered were the role of electronic equipment, the introduction of networks and wireless equipment in the home, changing social needs and interactive products. Ecodesign is integrated into existing design, production and development and innovation processes.

Similarly, the UK-based international oil company, British Petroleum plc, once a company whose revenue derived solely from fossil-fuel products, has now repositioned itself as one of the world's leading energy companies and is a key manufacturer of solar panels and solar-powered systems.

Designers save the earth

Designers actually have more potential to slow environmental degradation than economists, politicians, businesses and even environmentalists. The power of designers is catalytic. Once a new, more environmentally benign design penetrates markets its beneficial effects multiply. Businesses spend less on raw materials and production and so realize better profits, users enjoy more efficient, better-value products, governments reduce spending on regulatory enforcement and the net gain is an improved environment and quality of life. The vivid examples in this book demonstrate the capability of design, and hence designers, to shape the future and save the earth.

A robust tool kit

Today's designer has a powerful array of tools to assist him/her to meet the challenge of reducing environmental impacts at the design stage, such as simple checklists, impact matrices, lifecycle matrices, eco-wheels, Lifecycle Inventory (LCI) and Lifecycle Analysis (LCA) software. Checklists can be found in the publications included in Further Reading (p. 346) and a full list of organizations and agencies offering information and software to assist designers is given in the Green Organizations section (p. 332).

A manifesto for eco-pluralistic design ... designs that tread lightly on the planet

The thoughtful designer of the twenty-first century will design with integrity, sensitivity and compassion. He/she will design products/materials/service products that are sustainable, i.e. they serve human needs without depleting natural and manmade resources, without damage to the carrying capacity of ecosystems and without restricting the options available for present and future generations. An eco-pluralistic designer will:

1. Design to *satisfy real needs* rather than transient, fashionable or market-driven needs.
2. Design to *minimize the ecological footprint* of the product/material/service product, i.e., reduce resource consumption, including energy and water.
3. Design to *harness solar income* (sun, wind, water or sea power) rather than use non-renewable natural capital such as fossil fuels.
4. Design to *enable separation of components* of the product/material/service product at the end of life in order to encourage recycling or reuse of materials and/or components.
5. Design to *exclude the use of substances toxic or hazardous* to human and other forms of life at all stages of the product/material/service product's lifecycle.
6. Design to *engender maximum benefits to the intended audience* and to educate the client and the user and thereby create a more equable future.
7. Design to *use locally available materials and resources* wherever possible (thinking globally but acting locally).
8. Design to *exclude innovation lethargy* by re-examining original assumptions behind existing concepts and products/materials/service products.
9. Design to *dematerialize products into services* wherever feasible.
10. Design to *maximize a product/material/service product's benefits to communities.*
11. Design to *encourage modularity in design* to permit sequential purchases, as needs require and funds permit, to facilitate repair/reuse and to improve functionality.
12. Design to *foster debate and challenge the status quo* surrounding existing products/materials/service products.
13. *Publish eco-pluralistic designs in the public domain* for everyone's benefit, especially those designs that commerce will not manufacture.
14. Design to *create more sustainable products/materials/ service products for a more sustainable future.*

1.0 Objects for Living

Living or Lifestyles

In a media-driven world, where brands promise a lifestyle guaranteed to satisfy your desires, it is difficult to step back and honestly appraise your real needs for living. The word 'lifestyle' implies not just a way of life but also choice. For many people around the globe lifestyle choices are simply not available, as the basic needs of life – clean water, clean air, sufficient food, shelter and medical care – are absent. In today's global economy international brands, such as Coca-Cola soft drinks and Nike trainers, rub cheek by jowl with locally or nationally made products. Designers need to reappraise their role in the production of fashionable lifestyle products or at least strive to minimize the impact of these ephemeral goods, by concentrating on durable, multi-user, multi-purpose designs.

Essential products

The car has become the ultimate symbol of our freedom to move around, yet this 'impact-use' product, which only twenty per cent of the world's population own, impinges on the collective freedom of all people to enjoy clean air and unpolluted water. Over the last twenty-five years the fuel efficiency of the average car has improved only eighteen per cent. The car is a classic example of design innovation lethargy. Only a paradigm shift in the design of cars will remove the environmental burden of this product. But this must also be accompanied by more innovation in alternative modes of mobility. Improvements in personal modes of transport – the push scooter, bicycle and motorbike or scooter – must be accompanied by radical improvements in systems of public transport, such as the provision of flexible mobility paths for individual and group users.

With increasing reliance on electronic equipment and networks to deliver information, to control third-party equipment remotely and to entertain, it is possible to reduce mobility needs. Yet again a small proportion only of the world's population is wired in to the information networks such as the Internet or cable TV. Furthermore, building and maintaining the infrastructure of the information superhighway requires vast physical resources, including metals, chemicals and electricity. Virtual moments may provide some of the needs for some of the world's population for some of the time but the real cost to the environment and societies still needs computing.

Each individual requires different products to sustain life. Aside from the essential physical resources, humans need 'comfort' products to achieve a level of emotional, spiritual and social well-being. These products may permit or provide improved mobility, specialist recreational activities, communal meeting-places or spiritual contemplation. Since comfort products tend be used over a longish time, rather than being ephemeral, the design parameters can embrace durability and therefore judicious use of resources.

Living lightly – a sustainable day

As the products in this section illustrate, it is possible to tread more lightly on the planet, to consume and waste less, yet to maintain or even improve the quality of life. A double responsibility falls on the developed countries of the North. The North must rapidly evolve more sustainable patterns of consumption and production. Further, the North must offer the South the assistance and the means to avoid bad practice and reap the benefits of a more sustainable way of life, sooner rather than later.

A sustainable day in 2025 might involve the following products...

Spin and Oasis chairs

Designing a chair remains the quintessential test of any furniture designer. The imaginative form of the Spin/Oasis chair carefully models itself like a prosthesis, supporting and caressing the seated body. Rigid seat and arms are made from one type of polypropylene to which is clipped a more flexible polypropylene forming the comfortable backrest.

Easily disassembled into component parts, the PP and metal frames can be recycled.

✏	*Ross Lovegrove, UK*	308
⚙	*Driade, Italy*	315
▬	*Polypropylene, metal*	295, 341
♺	• *Improved ergonomics* • *Disassembly and recyclability*	328

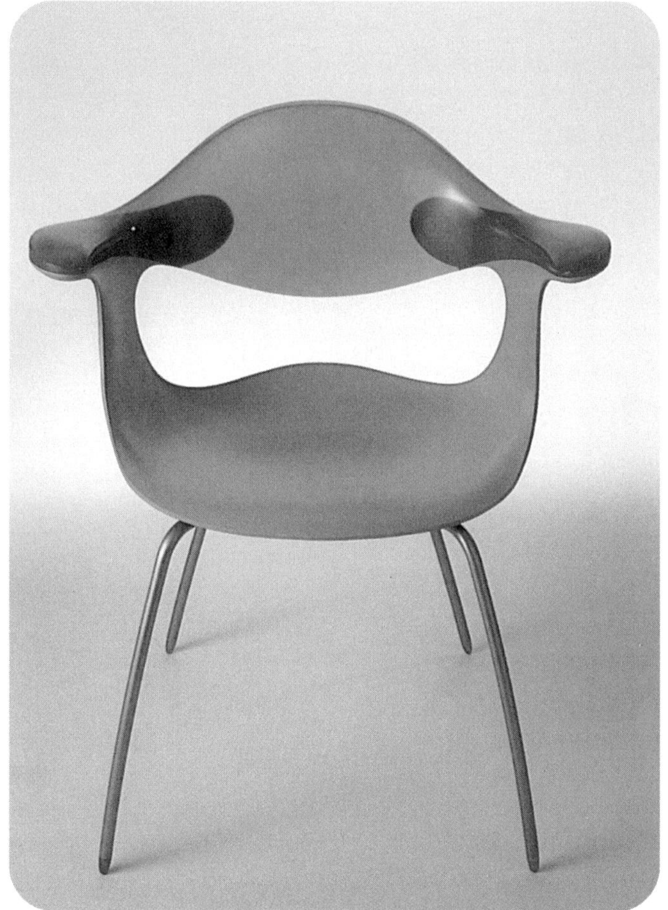

Agatha Dreams

Pillet's elegant chaise longue combines the eclecticism of craft with the technical skills of the workers at Cecotti's factory, a labour force with a long history of 'craft technology'. Renewable materials are bought to a state of refinement that will encourage the owner(s) to cherish this design and confer a degree of longevity. High-quality manufacturing using nature's materials will always be a sustainable business model, as long as raw materials are procured from managed forests.

✏	*Christopher Pillet, France*	309
⚙	*Ceccotti Collezioni, Italy*	314
▬	*Layered timber, solid cherry wood*	339
♺	• *Renewable materials*	327

Chair

Foam rubber has long provided padding for furniture, but Alfons Broess has explored new fillings made from waste wood chips, which cushion and adapt to individual body shapes. The soft fill is enclosed in the rigid synthetic shell.

✎	*Alfons Broess, graduate, Design Academy Eindhoven, Netherlands*	305
⚙	*Prototype*	
▬	*Waste wood, synthetic shell, metal*	293-5 339
♻	• *Reduction of waste production* • *Renewable material*	327

Slick Slick

Stackable, injection-moulded, polypropylene chairs are produced by numerous manufacturers for the contract furniture market. Unfortunately ugliness is often the common design denominator of this genre. Starck rescues the concept with this elegant design requiring a minimum of materials, creating a chair suitable for conference/office seating and domestic use.

✎	*Philippe Starck, France*	310
⚙	*XO, France*	326
▬	*Polypropylene*	341
♻	• *Single recyclable material* • *Multifunctional indoor/outdoor furniture*	327, 329

	Colin Reedy and Renaldi Hutasoit, USA	309
	Meta Morf, Inc., USA	320
	Gridcore or post-consumer plastics, steel	295, 341
	• *Recycled materials* • *Minimal materials usage*	327
	IDRA award, 1996	332

Sprocket

Two types of shell are available for this lightweight, steel-framed lounge chair: Gridcore, which is a reinforced sheeting made from recycled paper, or used plastic sheeting.

Big Legs

Interlocking cutouts of 100 per cent-recycled HDPE plastic panels create sculpture and visual excitement in this three-legged chair. New plastic recyclates offer different properties from the plywood that would have been the usual choice of material for this design. Thus the potential outcomes are different too.

	Henner Kuckuck, USA	308
	One-off	
	HDPE recyclate	341
	• Recycled materials	327
	IDRA award, 1995	332

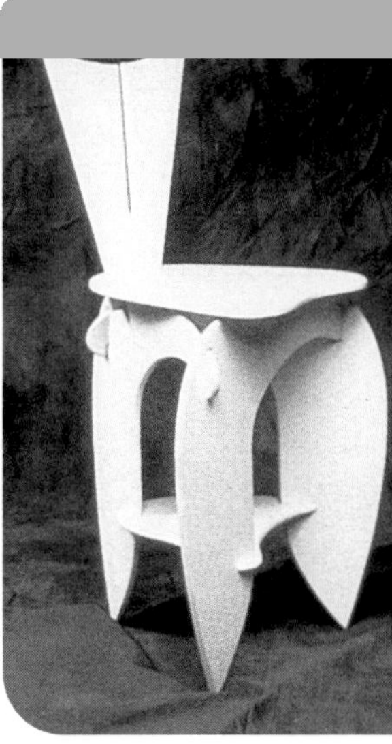

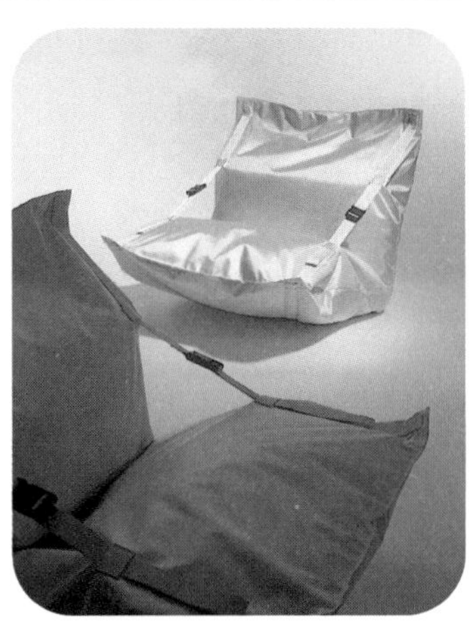

Airbag

Since the 1960s inflatable chairs have come and gone but Suppanen and Kolhonen have added an extra comfort dimension by placing balls of EPS inside the nylon outer cover, at the same time as allowing the chair to be deflated when not in use. Nylon is tough and resists puncturing better than other polymers.

	Ilkka Suppanen and Pasi Kolhonen, Finland	310
	Snow, Finland	324
	Expanded polystyrene, nylon	341
	• Low weight of materials • Reduced energy used during transport	328

Bastian

Brown wrapping paper and softwood, both inexpensive renewable materials sourced locally, are hand-crafted into a lightweight chair with matching footstool. Clean lines reinforce the simplicity of the construction technique and materials, borrowing from the long tradition of Far Eastern wood and paper manufacturing, but in harmony with a Western design ethos.

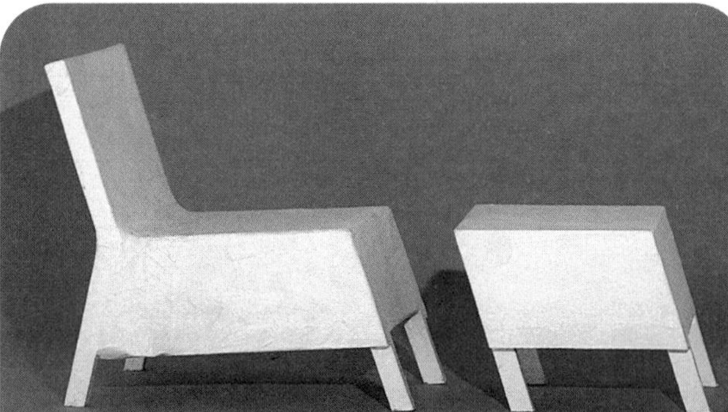

	Robert A Wettstein, Switzerland	310
	One-off/small batch production, Robert A Wettstein	310
	Paper, wood	288-9 339
	• Renewable, low-embodied energy, materials and construction	340

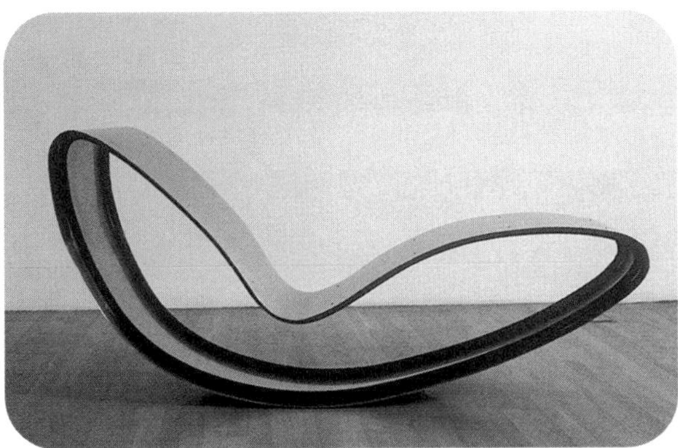

Blotter

'Keeping it simple' is the message delivered by this bent-steel chaise longue with its soft, cushioning skin of rubber to keep out the cold.

✎	*Marre Moerel (Netherlands), USA*	312
⚙	*One-off*	
▮	*Stainless and mild steel, rubber*	295, 283
♻	*• Recyclable materials • Economy of materials usage*	327

Body Raft

Local wych elm is bent with steam to create a curved frame to which further curved lathes are attached. This organic shape is visually appealing. Hand-crafted furniture of this kind can contribute to sustaining local economies.

✎	*David Trubridge, New Zealand*	311
⚙	*Prototype*	
▮	*Wych elm wood*	339
♻	*• Renewable materials*	327

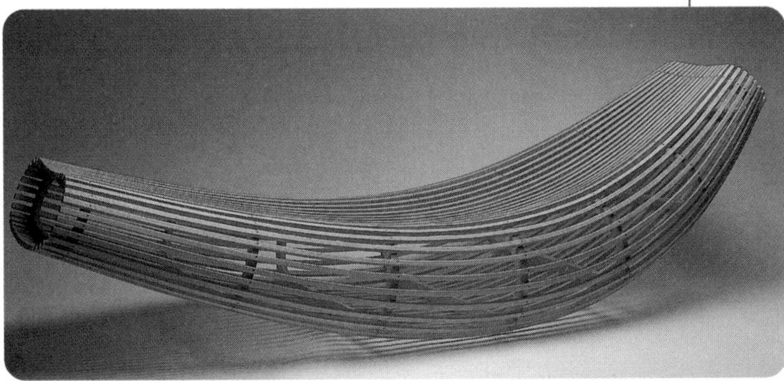

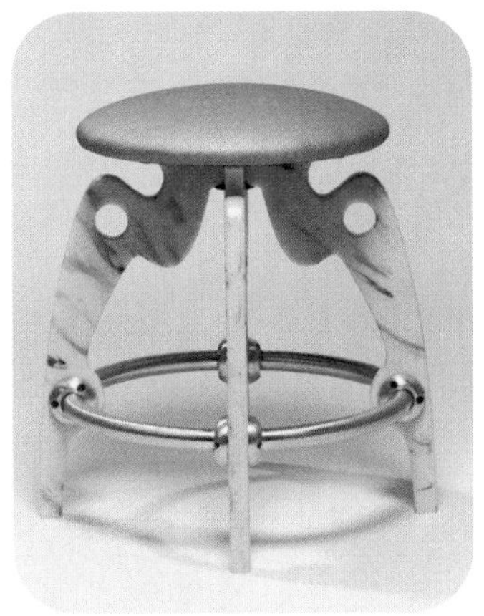

The Bottle-Top Stool

This flat-pack stool is designed for disassembly and is 100 per cent recyclable. Legs and seat are made from R-MOW recycled plastic sheet and the bottom rails from aluminium tube and die-cast fixings. Plastic recyclate replaces the traditional wood and can help increase the amount of the plastic retained in the recycling loop.

✎	*Damian Williamson, UK*	311
⚙	*One-off*	
▮	*R-MOW recycled plastic sheet, aluminium*	292, 339
♻	*• Recycled and recyclable materials • Design for disassembly*	328
✪	*IDRA Award, 1997*	332

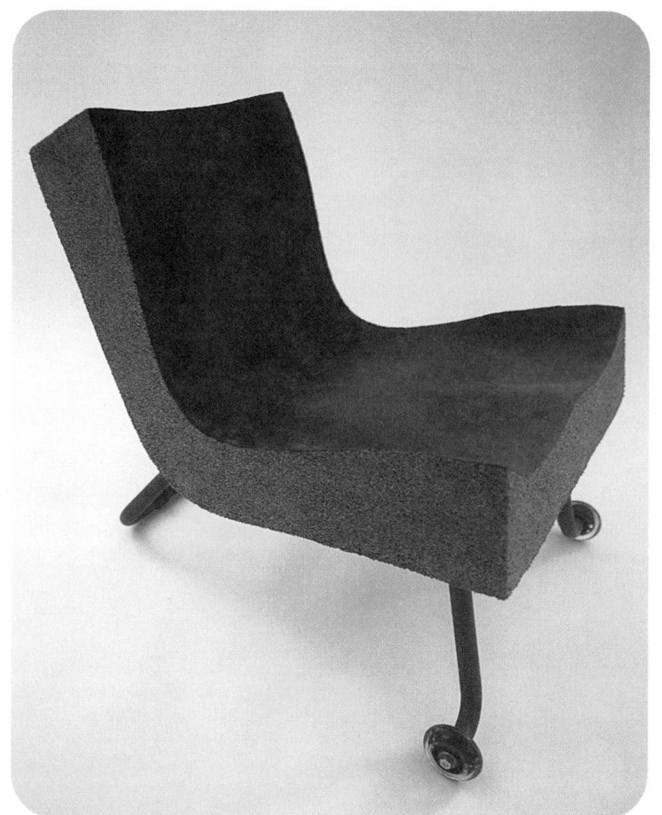

Miss Ramirez

Granular waste from the cork manufacturing industry in the Iberian peninsula is mixed with synthetic rubber to create a durable material suitable for cold moulding. This material can be formed into well-defined shapes but retains some elasticity. Roberto Feo creates an appealing and comfortable-looking lounge chair. The materials look familiar yet strange, creating a heavy chair that is actually easily moved around using the front wheels. This is an economical, functional, ecological and modern design.

	Roberto Feo, El Ultimo Grito, Spain	306
	One-off or small batch production, El Ultimo Grito, UK	306
	Cork waste, synthetic rubber, metal, plastic	283, 295
	• Recycled and recyclable materials *• Cold, low-energy manufacturing*	328

Garden bench

Bey brings nature indoors by taking plant waste from the garden and using high-pressure extrusion containers to generate benches of dried grass, leaves and woody prunings. Durability and longevity of the seating depend on the extent of use and the inherent strength of the compressed raw materials. At the end of its natural lifespan the furniture can be broken up and left to rot on the

garden compost heap. Perhaps Bey's designs represent the current best practice in biodegradable furniture?

Designer	*Jurgen Bey, Droog Design, Netherlands*	304
Manufacturer	*One-offs, Droog Design/ DMD, Netherlands*	304
Materials	*Plant waste, resin*	339
Eco-features	*• Waste materials from renewable sources* *• Compostable*	327

Bucket Seat

Adding a ready-made steel and wood bucket handle to this traditional seating design makes the stool easily portable, which in turn is a feature the user can enjoy. A dash of wit revitalizes craft traditions and helps bring this type of furniture back into living and work spaces.

Designer	*Carl Clerkin, UK*	305
Manufacturer	*Small batch production*	
Materials	*Ready-made steel, wood*	295, 328
Eco-features	*• Renewable and recyclable materials* *• Use of ready-mades*	327

Model 290F

For over 150 years the manufacturer Gebrüder Thonet has mass-produced elegant bentwood chairs espousing good design with economical use of local (European) materials, modular 'flat-pack' designs facilitating distribution and basic, yet customizable options. In 1849 at Michael Thonet's factory in Vienna 'Chair No. 1', the Schwarzenberg chair, made of four prefabricated components that could be reassembled in different configurations, was the precursor of a design ideally suited to industrial production. Thonet chairs graced many a café and restaurant from Paris to Berlin and London in the late nineteenth and early twentieth centuries and created the definitive archetype for the café chair. 'Chair No. 14', later known as the 'Vienna coffee-house chair', was one of the most successful products of the nineteenth century and probably remains the world's best-selling chair, with over fifty million sold in 1930 alone. The roll-call of iconic designers, such as Mies van der Rohe, Mart Stam, Marcel Breuer and Verner Panton, ensured that Thonet always explored designs driven by new movements and schools of thought. Yet Thonet remain aware of their traditions and currently produce modern variants using well-tested principles and materials such as steamed and bent solid beechwood. Model 290F epitomizes the Thonet philosophy: the designers, Wulf Schneider and Partners, use three pieces to create a robust, durable and repairable chair. A single piece of solid bent beech forms the front legs and back stay, a cut-and-drilled, moulded, laminated beech forms the back legs and back rest, both pieces being fixed to the laminated seat with cast-aluminium angled brackets and screws. Nineteenth-century examples of Thonet chairs turn up in the prestigious sale rooms of Sotheby's, Christies and Bonham, attesting to their durability. It is quite likely that Model 290F will in time become a sought-after antique, validating it as a good and green design.

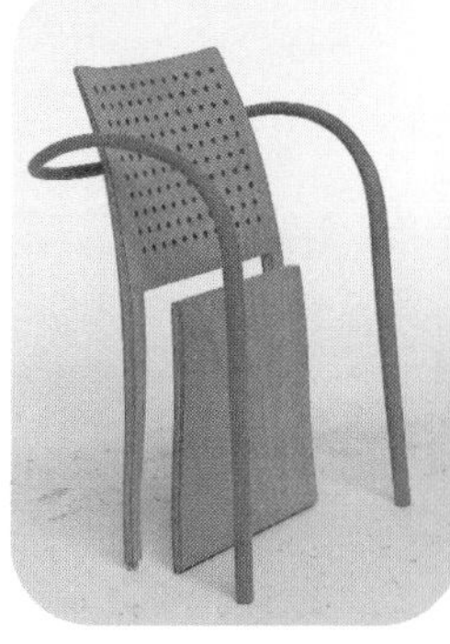

✎	*Prof. Wulf Schneider and Partners, Germany*	310
⚙	*Gebrüder Thonet GmbH, Germany*	317
	Beechwood, aluminium	295, 339
	• Renewable materials *• Low-energy transport and assembly*	327, 329
	iF Ecology Design Award, Germany, 1999	332

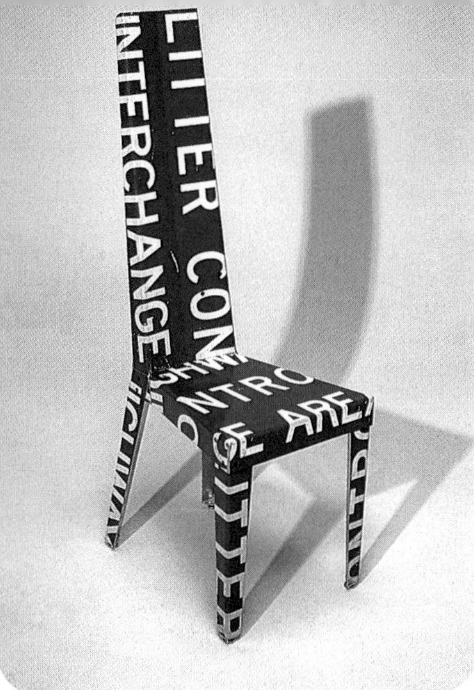

Transit Chair

The familiar graphical language of road signage adds significant character to this chair fabricated from redundant aluminium signs from the Pennsylvania Department of Transportation. Available as a flat-pack, self-assembly kit, the chairs are a good example of reuse and and potential further recycling at the end of their lives.

✎	*Boris Bally, Atelier Boris Bally, USA*	304
⚙	*One-off, limited batch production*	
▬	*Recycled road traffic signs*	341
♻	*• Reuse of materials*	327
✪	*IDRA award, 1997*	332

Seating system

It is clear to anyone who works in a modern office that the paperless office is still a figment of the futurologists' imagination. Paper consumption is increasing worldwide, so opportunities to remanufacture paper into new materials deserve exploration. Martijn van Maanen believes locally generated waste paper can be converted into new seating and suggests that government tax offices might be a good place to start such a scheme!

✎	*Martiijn van Maanen, graduate, Design Academy Eindhoven, Netherlands*	311
⚙	*Prototype*	
▬	*Paper*	288
♻	*• Materials recycled at source*	327

Gallery

This moulded plywood stool is a module that functions in its own right or can be joined to others to form a continuous bench or rows of seats. Efficient use of materials is achieved through simplicity and strength of form.

	Hans Sandgren Jakobsen, Denmark	307
	Fredericia Furniture A/S, Denmark	316
	Plywood	339
	• *Economy of materials usage* • *Renewable materials* • *Dual-function seating*	327, 329
	iF Design Award, 2000	332

Impression

The sculptural possibilities of HDPE recyclate are explored by cutting and shaping sheets. This demonstrates how new materials stimulate innovations in the design process.

✎	*Philip Looker and Plastics f'th Industry Ltd, UK*	308
⚙	*Plastics f'th Industry Ltd, UK*	322
▤	*Recycled HDPE*	341
♲	*• Recycled material*	327

How Slow the Wind

Simplicity of construction can stimulate economy of materials use, permit easy assembly and disassembly and contribute to a reduction in the energy needed for fabrication. Yamanaka uses one sheet of recyclable polypropylene, cut and bent to slide over a swivelling base made of MDF and covered with leather. The result is a dynamic yet pleasing line and a comfortable easy chair equally adaptable to living or working spaces.

✎	*Kazuhiro Yamanaka, Japan*	311
⚙	*Prototype*	
▤	*Polypropylene, leather, MDF*	285, 341
♲	*• Renewable and recyclable materials • Low-energy manufacturing*	327, 340

Maggi

Hinting at an imminent (environmental) meltdown, Bär and Knell's chair is formed of plastic packaging waste, dyed black then surface finished with Maggi plastic carrier bags. The branding lives on but not as the marketeers intended. This chair was made in 1995 but the design partnership experimented with many variants from 1993 to 1997, including sofas and furniture for children. Their playful yet deliberate exposure of the raw-waste medium contrasts with the highly controlled, stylized injection- or blow-moulded designs of the 1960s and 1970s. This reincarnation poses the question, 'How can we throw away such a useful resource?'

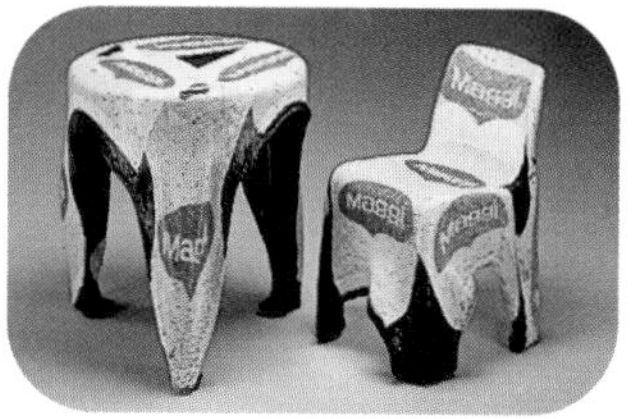

	Beata and Gerhard Bär and Hartmut Knell, Germany	304
	One-off, limited batch production	
	Packaging waste	327
	• Recycled materials	327

Marilyn, I Can See Your Knickers

A single sheet of polypropylene is pre-formed, then fixed to a simple square-section steel frame. Components are easily assembled with low-energy production techniques, materials usage is kept to a minimum and easy disassembly permits recycling.

	El Ultimo Grito, Spain	306
	El Ultimo Grito, UK	306
	Polypropylene, steel	295, 341
	• Economy of materials usage and production	327

Origami Zaisu

A single sheet of plywood is bent and cut to form a simple floor seat. In Japanese culture sitting on the floor is the norm but perhaps the practice should be adopted more widely, since the omission of legs that form a conventional chair saves materials and energy.

✎	*Mitsumasa Sugasawa, Japan*	310
⚙	*Tendo Co. Ltd, Japan*	325
▤	*Plywood*	339
♻	• *Economy of materials usage* • *Renewable materials*	327

Mirandolina

Reviving a technique first used by the designer Hans Coray, with his pressed-aluminium 'Landi' chair designed in 1938, Pietro Arosio has produced an economical yet elegant stacking chair from a single sheet of aluminium. Cut and pressed into its final form, the Mirandolina shouts efficiency. The use of one material, aluminium, facilitates recycling of the waste offcuts and ensures it is easy to recycle or repair.

✎	*Pietro Arosio, Italy*	304
⚙	*Zanotta SpA, Italy*	326
▤	*Aluminium*	295
♻	• *Recyclable single material* • *Efficient materials usage and recycling during manufacturing*	327, 328

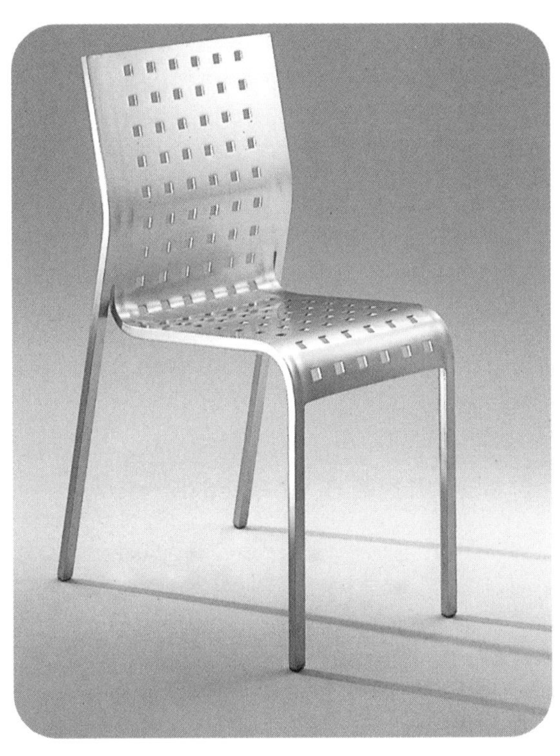

Box

Originally designed in 1975, the Box chair has now been reissued with an injection-moulded polypropylene back as well as seat. Tubular metal legs and back frame are easily assembled and disassembled, facilitating repair, refurbishment and recycling of any of the components. The flat pack and low weight reduce distribution costs and total transport emissions, reflecting Mari's design philosophy of 'reductionism'.

✎	*Enzo Mari, Italy*	308
⚙	*Driade SpA, Italy*	315
	Metal, polypropylene	295, 341
	• *Design for disassembly* • *Economy of materials usage*	328

C1 Recliner and Footstool

Utilizing steam-bent English ash wood allows economical use of materials without sacrificing strength and ensures a low-embodied energy of manufacturing. The chair frame is adjustable to three positions and is cushioned with padded linen. An alternative version, using rattan, is available. Trannon merge the traditions and durability of bent ash with a fresh aesthetic and a green policy for the procurement of raw materials.

✎	*David Colwell and Roy Tam, UK*	305
⚙	*Trannon Furniture Ltd, UK*	325
	Solid ash wood, linen or rattan	290-1, 339
	• *Renewable materials with stewardship sourcing* • *Low-energy construction techniques*	327, 328

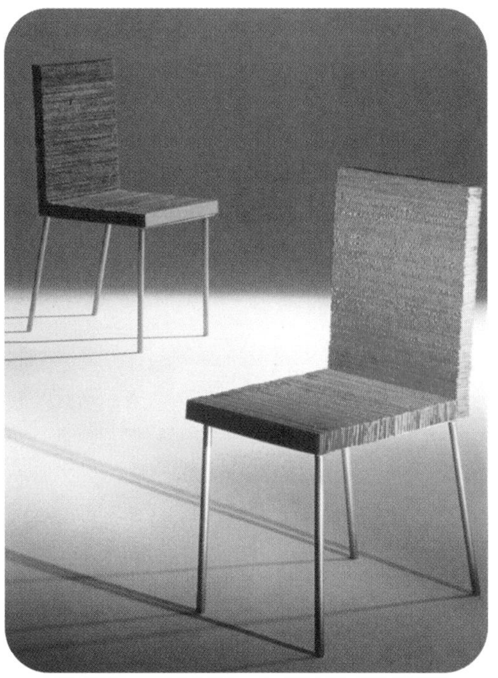

Cardboard Chair

Letting the materials deliver the (environmental) message is a theme common to furniture designers around the world using recycled or recyclable materials. So Jane Atfield (UK) speaks with plastic, Frank Gehry (USA) with cardboard and Lièvore (Spain) with maderon. The Campana brothers combine a robust, solid, iron-rod frame with a laminated cardboard seat and back to create a dining chair that demonstrates how unpretentious materials can encourage a healthy hybrid of modernism and craft.

✎	*Fernando and Humberto Campana, Brazil*	305
⚙	*Limited batch production*	
▬	*Iron, cardboard*	288-9, 295
♻	*• Renewable, recyclable materials*	327

Conversation Chair

Locally crafted wooden furniture is a good model for sustainable manufacturing and Guy Martin's individually made chairs, seating, tables and bookshelves maintain that tradition. Using a classic 'nail and stick' technique, more often found in the Appalachian mountains in the United States than in south-west England, the frames are formed from green ash wood obtained from locally managed woodlands. The willow withies are grown in commercial fields near by in the Somerset levels and waste wood or shavings are used to generate heat and electricity to power the workshop. When craft skills are merged with contemporary designs the results can be refreshingly surprising compared with mass-produced furniture. Martin represents the young designers who could become the 'green' manufacturers of the new millennium, echoing the practices of Europe's largest steamed-beech furniture manufacturers, Gebrüder Thonet of Vienna, in the 1840s.

✎	*Guy Martin, UK*	308
⚙	*One-off and small batch production*	
▬	*Ash wood, willow*	339
♻	*• Renewable and compostable materials • Low-energy manufacturing • Locally sourced materials*	327, 328

The Porcelain Stool

Hella Jongerius hijacks materials associated with a traditional process or product and reapplies them to a totally different function. Such flexible thinking is essential for the future. Porcelain, long noted for its fragility and delicate qualities, is moulded into a robust, organic-shaped stool.

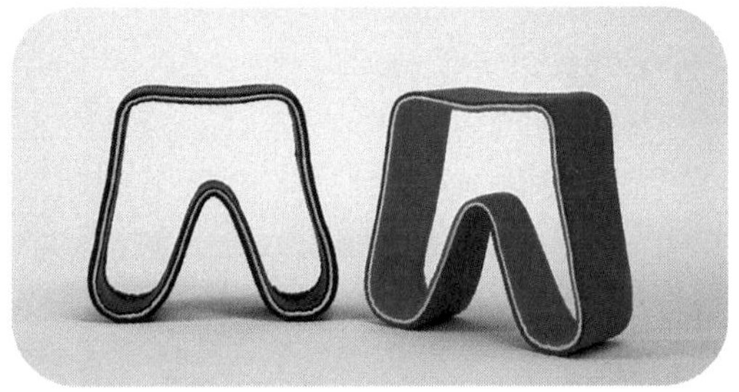

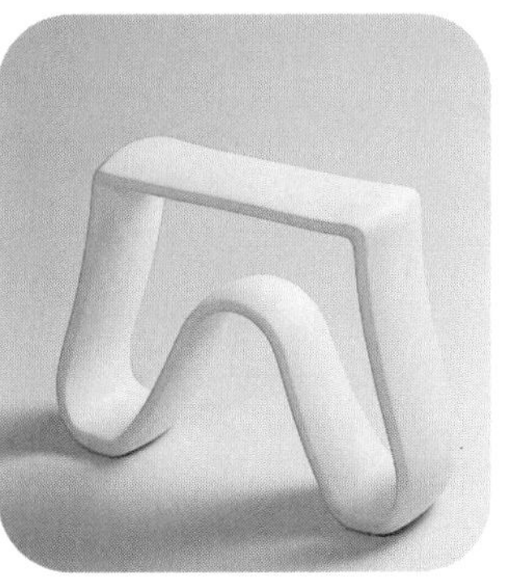

Designer	*Hella Jongerius, Netherlands*	307
Manufacturer	*Cappellini SpA, Italy*	314
Material	*Porcelain*	295
Eco	• *Economy of materials usage* • *Material with low embodied energy*	327, 340

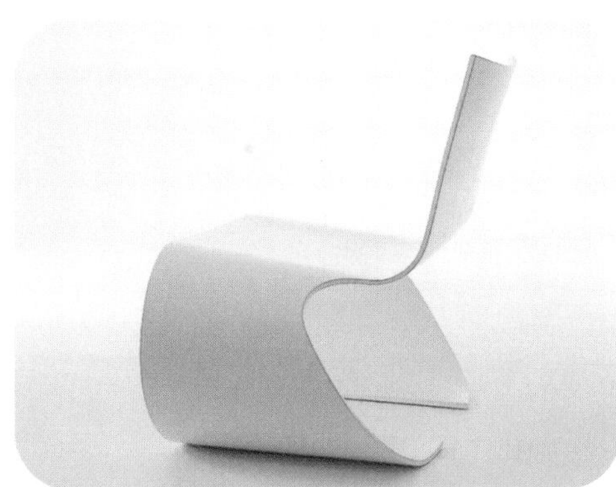

Designer	*Peter Karpf, Sweden*	308
Manufacturer	*Inredningsform/Iform, Sweden*	318
Material	*Laminated beechwood*	339
Eco	• *Single, renewable material* • *Low-energy manufacturing*	327, 328

OTO

Cut and bent from a single sheet of laminated beech, Karpf's graceful chair avoids the need for any other components, keeping the production process efficient and reducing waste.

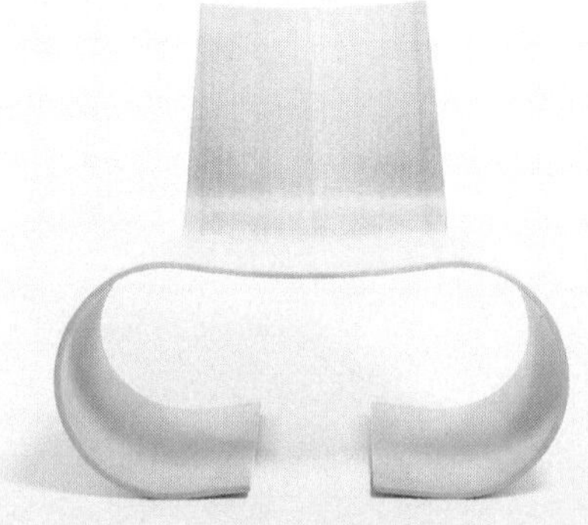

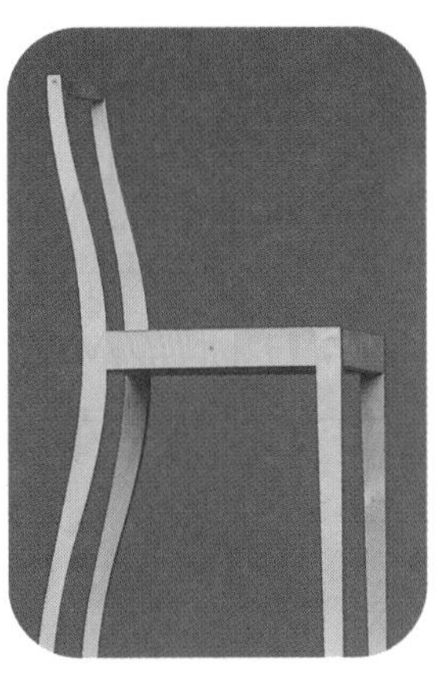

Ply Chair

Avoiding excessive usage or wastage of materials should be a guiding principle of any design in the twenty-first century. The Ply Chair is the latest answer to the 'Superleggera', demonstrating restraint, grace, economy, strength and character.

✎	*Jasper Morrison, UK*	309
⚙	*Vitra AG, Germany*	326
	Aeronautical-quality plywood	339
	• Economy of materials usage	327

Plyboo

In late nineteenth-century London there were over thirty manufacturers making furniture from imported bamboo. Following a theme of her earlier designs using recycled plastics, Atfield lets the materials of Plyboo give character to the object, contrasting the random natural characteristics of the bamboo with the processed, standardized, manufactured look of the birch plywood. Steel rods are used to reinforce the bamboo at critical points. The result is durable seating that may well revive the fortunes of bamboo as a material for the new millennium, casting off the unwanted associations between bamboo furniture and colonial verandas, conservatories and swimming pools. Bamboo is here again. It is modern, renewable, recyclable and toxin-free and is a ferocious producer of biomass in the right climate.

✎	*Jane Atfield, UK*	304
⚙	*Prototype, Float Up VP, UK*	316
	Bamboo, plywood, steel	295, 339
	• Renewable materials	327

Deck Chair

The structural properties of recycled plastic sheet have been thoroughly exploited in this combined chair and ottoman, which can also be used as a deck chair. This material is highly malleable when heated, enabling complex bending to produce results similar to pre-compressed wood.

	Colin Reedy, USA	309
	Meta Morf, Inc., USA	320
	Recycled plastic, steel	283, 295
	• Recycled and recyclable materials	327
	IDRA award, 1996	332

Daybed

This company has been manufacturing furniture, using special techniques for weaving twisted paper, since the beginning of the twentieth century. This daybed combines a contemporary shape with a traditional material by making the most of the manufacturer's extensive experience with this medium.

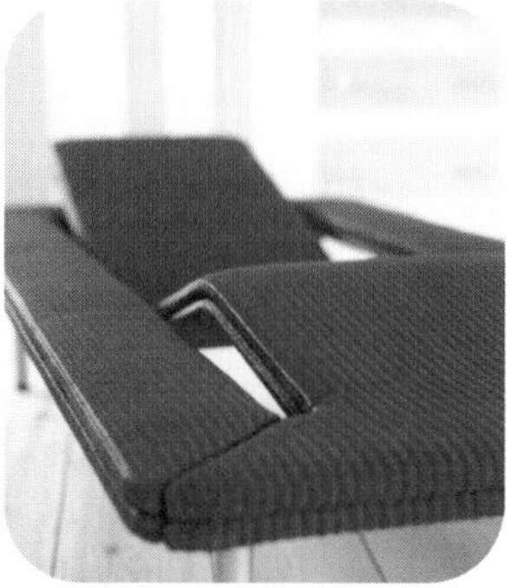

	Nigel Coates, UK	305
	Limited batch production by Lloyd Loom of Spalding, UK	319
	Twisted paper and steel wire	288, 295
	• Renewable and recyclable materials	327

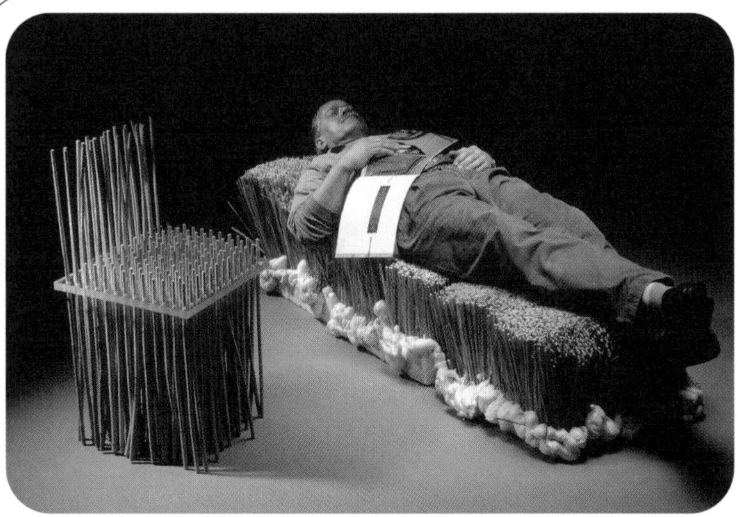

Diva (n) Paradox

Rushes harvested from freshwater reed-beds are inserted and set into a simple frame containing polyurethane foam. Organic materials of natural and synthetic origin are juxtaposed in a visually arresting form. Both materials are quite durable and when no longer serviceable could be incinerated or shredded for reuse as fill material.

Designer	*Pil Bredahl and Liselotte Risell, Denmark*	304
Manufacturer	*One-off*	
Materials	*Rushes, polyurethane*	276, 341
Eco-strategy	*• Encouraging use of historic renewable material*	327

Earth Chair®

This simple sphere of stitched denim is despatched from the manufacturer empty and filled by the buyer with once-used plastic shopping bags or similar pliable plastic fill. The designer-makers claim that it requires 9kg (20lb) of such fill. Perhaps the item would be 'greener' if, instead of plastic bags, the filling were made of renewable or compostable materials.

Designer	*Earth Chair, USA*	315
Manufacturer	*Earth Chair, USA*	315
Materials	*Denim*	290
Eco-strategy	*• Low-energy fabrication includes self-assembly*	328

Spring

Modular components can be used to assemble a range of furniture from chairs to chaises longues, fashioned from wood, wool and leather. Natural compounds such as water-based paints and oils and waxes provide protection for the wooden parts, while the leather originates from a tannery that uses vegetable-based products. Easy assembly and disassembly facilitate repair and extend the life of the products.

(designer)	*Galleri Stolen AB, Sweden*	317
(manufacturer)	*Galleri Stolen AB, Sweden*	317
(materials)	*timber, wool, leather, natural finishes*	276, 327
(environmental benefits)	*• Clean production • Modular design facilitating repair, reuse and longevity*	327
(awards)	*Design Sense awards, Shortlist, 1999*	332

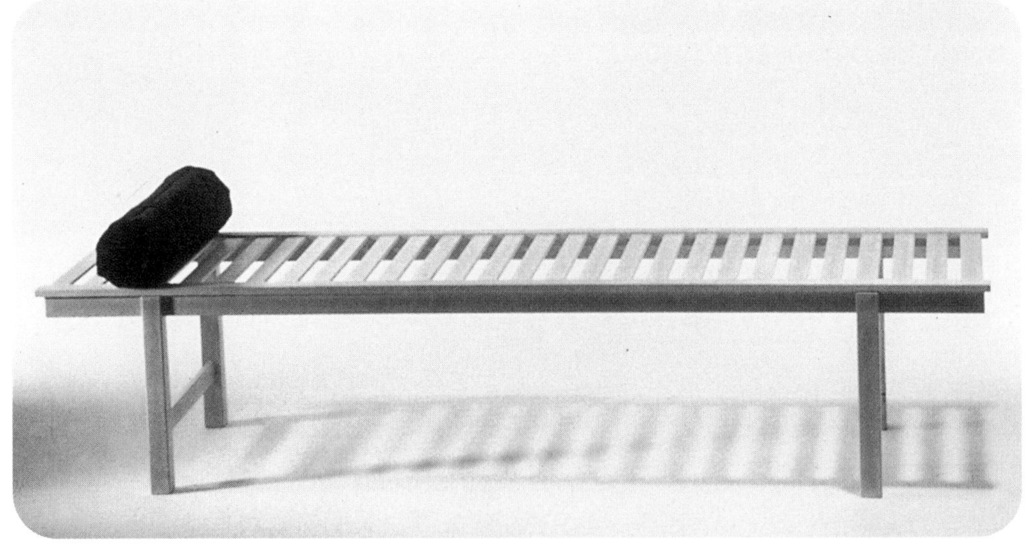

Pouffe

Moore explores the sculptural possibilities of recyclates, in this case HDPE sheet, treating them as new materials ripe for experimentation. The result is an eye-catching take on an old theme and an economy of materials use.

	Isabell Moore, UK	309
	One-off	
	HDPE recyclate, maple plywood	339, 341
	• Recycled and recyclable materials	327
	IDRA award, 1996	332

	Julienne Dolphin-Wilding, UK	306
	One-off/small batch production	
	Yew wood	339
	• Recycled and renewable material *• Durability*	327

100-piece-kit armchair

Durable, richly patterned, native British yew wood offcuts and salvaged pieces have been reworked into a series of interlocking blocks, which, once assembled, form an armchair with considerable presence. Dolphin Wilding breathes new life into waste that would have been burnt or despatched to landfill.

Eco

These stackable chairs are cut from a single piece of veneer-faced ply and follow in the Scandinavian tradition of working with bent ply, as were the designs of Gerald Summers for the firm of Makers of Simple Furniture based in London in the late 1930s. Simplicity, economy and functionality meet in this award-winning design.

	Peter Karpf, Sweden	308
	Inreningsform/Iform, Sweden	318
	Plywood	339
	• Renewable materials *• Economy of materials usage and low-energy production*	327, 328
	Winner of the iF Ecology Design Award, 2000	332

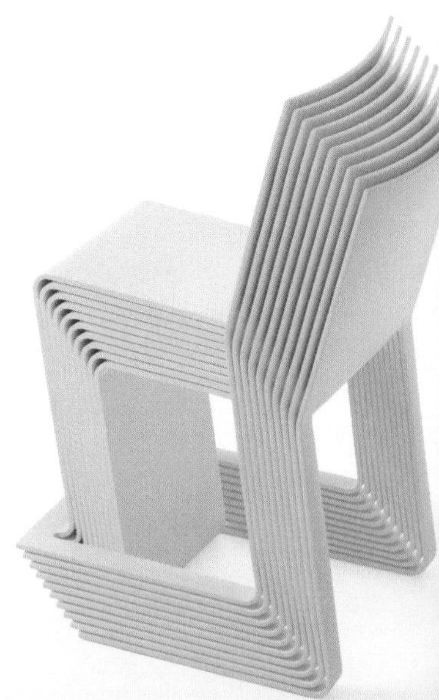

Eraser Chair

The innards of most chairs are hidden from view but Culpepper has chosen to celebrate the inner secrets of the Eraser Chair, which raises the value of recycled materials by bringing them to the attention of the viewer. Laid bare is the structural fabric of this design, which consists of 95 per cent-recycled wood felt attached to a rigid frame.

	Michael Culpepper, USA	305
	One-off	
	Recycled wood felt	339
	• Recycled and recyclable materials	327
	IDRA award, 1995	332

Eric

Cardboard is combined with laminated and painted plywood to produce an armchair requiring low-energy input to manufacture. Wettstein emphasizes the corrugated construction of the cardboard and joins a distinguished list of designers such as Gehry and the Campana brothers, who also make the most of the strength of this laminated material.

	Robert A Wettstein, Switzerland	311
	One-off/small batch production	
	Cardboard, plywood	339
	• Renewable materials	327

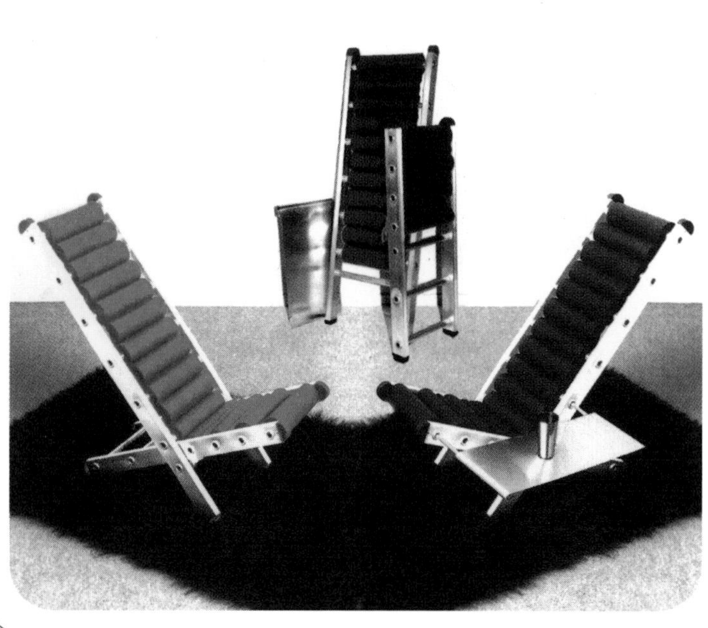

q-bac

A striking and comfortable easy chair has been created using ready-made components, such as aluminium ladder sections and rubber, with minor modifications. Existing manufacturing plant and capacity are utilized more efficiently to introduce new products. At the end of their lifespan, the components can be easily disassembled for recycling or reuse.

✎	*Gabriele Ackon, David Zyne Productions, UK*	315
⚙	*David Zyne Productions, UK*	315
▮	*Aluminium ready-mades, rubber*	283, 327
♻	*• Use of ready-made components*	327

Ragchair

Waste rags and pieces of cloth are bound over a wooden frame using steel bands, mimicking the process of binding bales of recycled textiles, to create a comfortable yet unique easy or lounge chair. Remy has observed the textile industry recycling its products and neatly translated the idea into eclectic furniture that boldly states its origins.

✎	*Tejo Remy, Droog Design, Netherlands*	306, 309
⚙	*DMD, Netherlands*	315
▮	*Textiles, steel*	290-1, 295
♻	*• Recycled materials* *• Low-energy manufacturing*	327, 328

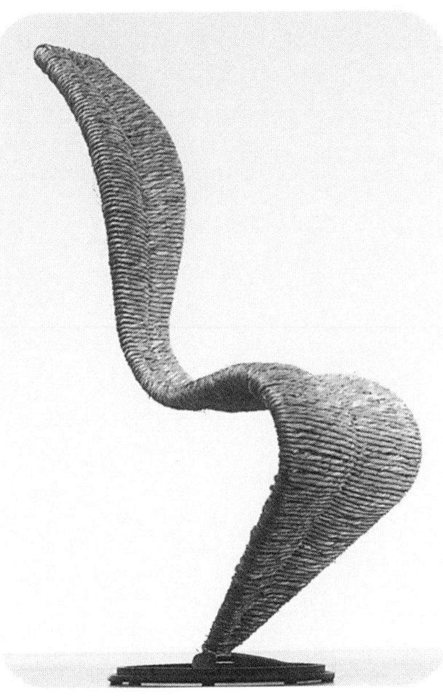

S chair

Following his experimentation in the 1980s with one-offs using salvaged materials, Tom Dixon designed this elegant cantilever chair. A steel frame is wrapped with woven rushes, creating a sculptural form. At the end of the chair's life materials are easily separated for recycling (steel) or composting (rushes).

✎	*Tom Dixon, UK*	306
⚙	*Cappellini SpA, Italy*	314
▦	*Steel, rushes*	276, 295
♻	*• Economy of materials usage • Renewable and recyclable materials*	327

RCP2

In 1992 Atfield created the RCP2 chair with a simple but robust construction technique using a radical material challenging the ecological awareness of designers and the public alike. New techniques for recycling HDPE waste created a new sheet-like material whose constituents readily divulged their origins. The rawness of the early work of designers such as Atfield and Bär and Knell contrasts with the more sophisticated use of recycled sheet HDPE in Bopp-Leuchten's lamps in the late 1990s. Further innovation in manufacturing using recycled plastics can be expected over the next decade as attempts are made to close the plastic recycling loop.

✎	*Jane Atfield, UK*	304
⚙	*One-offs and small batch production*	
▦	*High-density polyethylene (HDPE)*	341
♻	*• Recycled and recyclable materials*	327

Trinidad No.3298

'Industrial craft' production will undoubtedly prosper in the twenty-first century if the workmanship and graphical form of this ash chair are a measure of the output of today's furniture manufacturers.

	Nanna Ditzel, Denmark	306
	Fredericia Furniture A/S, Denmark	316
	Ash wood, metal	295, 339
	• Renewable material	327

Flying Carpet

A steel frame with supporting rods suspends stiffened felt in mid-air to create a seat that sways as the user moves around. Economy of materials use combines with ease of separation into pure-grade waste streams for recycling the materials at the end of the product's life. This imaginative design explores new applications of wool felt to furniture.

	Ilkka Suppanen, Finland	310
	Cappellini SpA, Italy	314
	Steel, felt	290, 295
	• Economy of materials usage *• Renewable and recyclable materials*	327

Ghost

Purity of form and function can often be achieved by focusing on the exclusive properties of one particular material. Cini Boeri and Tomu Katayanagi have taken a single piece of 12mm-thick (c. 1/2-inch) toughened glass and cut and moulded it into an extraordinary object. They juxtapose the contradictory characteristics of the material – its fragility and toughness – and create a durable, rather timeless design. Ghost provides food for thought on how other familiar materials can be modified or mutated to fit new forms and functions. Being composed of a single material facilitates recycling at the end of the product's life and encourages closed-loop recycling, where the manufacturer uses its own recycled materials to produce new goods.

✎	*Cini Boeri and Tomu Katayanagi, Italy and Japan*	305
⚙	*Fiam Italia SpA, Italy*	316
▬	*Glass*	295
♺	*• Recyclable single material* *• Durability*	327

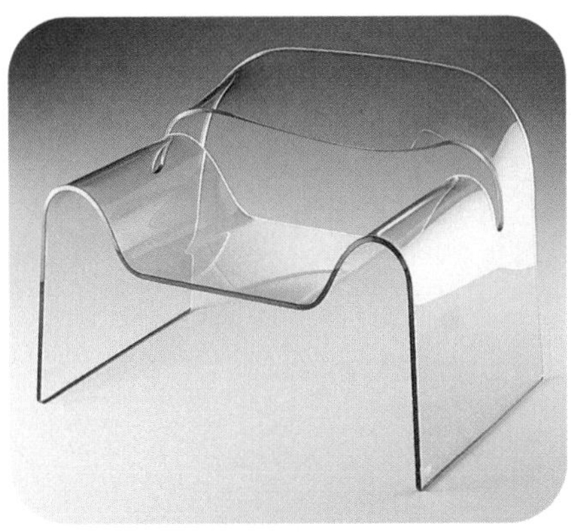

Chair and ottoman

Slabs of heavy-grade industrial felt, typically used for noise insulation in military vehicles, are bolted together to create an archetypal armchair. An ottoman emerges from the offcuts. The original felt slabs are transformed from the utilitarian to the purposeful, yet retain their honesty of origin. Like the Danish designer Niels Hvass, who has made a similar chair from used newspapers, Atfield reminds us to keep it simple and create zero waste.

✎	*Jane Atfield, UK*	304
⚙	*One-offs*	
▬	*Felt, steel*	290, 295
♺	*• Economy of materials usage* *• Zero waste production*	327, 328

IKEA a.i.r./MUJIAIR sofas

IKEA are peering into the future and testing the way forward for sustainable product design. This example by Jan Dranger sets the stage for manufacturing furniture using recyclable plastics and interchangeable covers, as wear and tear or fashion decrees. As resource scarcity bites in the twenty-first century, manufacturers will have not only to use recyclable materials but also to develop business models that ensure that product take-back keeps materials in a closed recycling loop.

✎	*Jan Dranger, Dranger Design AB, Sweden*	306
⚙	*News Design DfE AB for IKEA, Sweden*	321
▮	*Plastics, nylon or polyester, cotton*	283, 291
♺	*• Recyclable materials • Economy of materials usage • Low-energy transport and assembly*	327, 328

Bench

In a imaginative turn-around, paper from trees is recycled in a 100 per cent-waste-paper material called 'Shetkaboard' to become a substitute for sawn timber in this indoor/outdoor bench. Why cut down more trees when waste paper will do the job nicely?

✎	*Stanley J Shetka, USA*	310
⚙	*One-off*	
▮	*Shetkaboard*	280
♺	*• Recycled, renewable materials*	327
✪	*IDRA award, 1995*	332

Chair

This knock-down chair uses lightweight Gridcore, made of 100 per cent-recycled paper honeycomb sandwiched between laminated paper surfaces, for the sides and back. Solid cherry wood is used for the arms and rear leg. The furnishing fabric comes from DesignTex, a US company known for reducing the environmental impact of its textile range.

	Janice Smith, USA	310
	One-off	
	Gridcore, cherry wood, furnishing fabric	290-1 339
	• *Recycled and recyclable materials* • *Self-assembly* • *Design for disassembly*	327 328
	IDRA award, 1997	332

Chair

Discarded industrial pallets are the raw material for this chair. After machining, the individual wooden lathes are held together using steel bolts. The chair is easily disassembled for repair or recycling.

	James Varney, USA	311
	One-off	
	Recycled pallet wood	339
	• *Recycled and recyclable materials*	327
	IDRA award, 1998	332

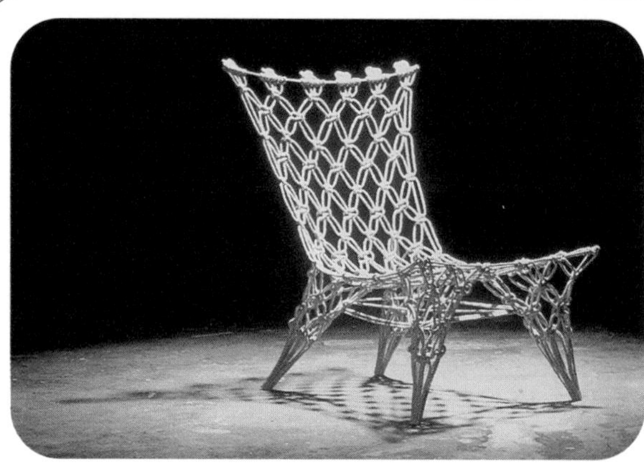

Knotted chair

A loose, flexible, macramé form of aramide fibre braid is dipped into a solution of epoxy resin. The resin is hardened by drying at high temperatures to produce the necessary rigidity for the purpose. This remarkable chair is a blend of imagination and technology, which fits the Factor 4 philosophy of 'doing more with less'. However, a few reservations surround the technosphere materials. Epoxy resins need careful handling during production and the resultant aramide reinforced with epoxy resin is a composite that could prove difficult to recycle.

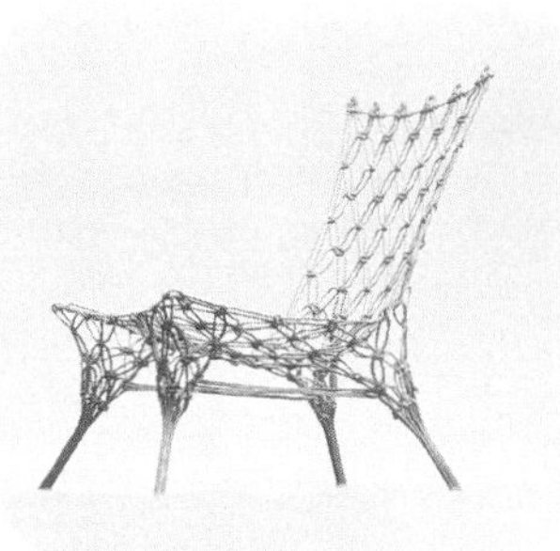

✎	*Marcel Wanders, Netherlands*	311
⚙	*Cappellini SpA, Italy*	314
▮	*Aramide fibre braid, epoxy resin*	284
♺	*• Economy of materials usage*	327

Kids furniture

The confetti-like colours and patterns of the recycled plastics in these furniture items are tailor-made for creating a stimulating learning environment for the young child. Demonstrating this material's versatility for making robust, fun furniture, Reedy introduces some nice touches such as the hand holds for carrying the chair and rounded edges for safety.

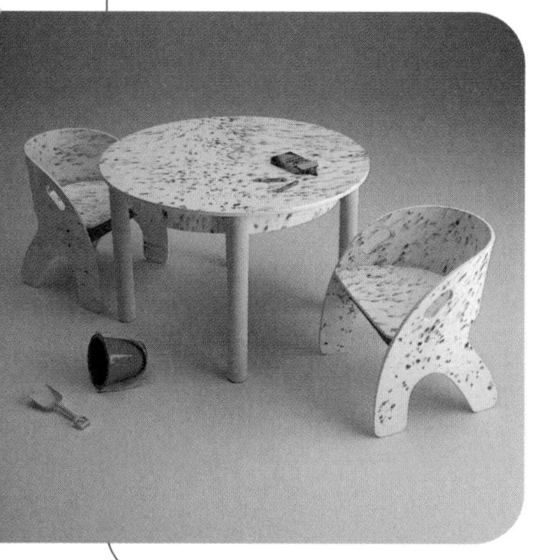

✎	*Colin Reedy, Meta Morf, Inc., USA*	309
⚙	*Meta Morf Inc., USA*	320
▮	*Recycled plastics, steel*	283, 295
♺	*Recycled material*	327
✪	*IDRA award, 1997*	332

Krogh chair

The single-piece back support and arms are made of pre-compressed wood. Many types of wood will respond to pre-compression treatment. The process involves mollifying the fibres with steam and then compressing them, which causes the fibres to adopt an accordion-like zig-zag structure. This results in an overall shortening of the wood by 20 per cent, which reduces to 5 per cent when the compressing force is removed. The wood is malleable at this stage and can be bent before being allowed to dry. Once dry it maintains its original strength and flexibility.

✎	*Erik Krogh Design, Denmark*	306
⚙	*One-off*	
▬	*Pre-compressed wood*	339
♺	*• Renewable material with improved characteristics*	327

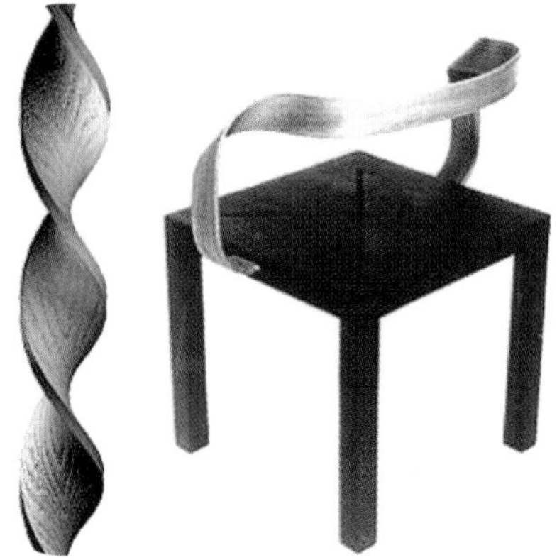

Leg Over

The colourful, circular polypropylene seat clips over the powder-coated steel frame to provide a versatile, stackable stool or footrest. It is economical in its use of materials and stylistic language.

✎	*Sebastian Bergne, UK*	304
⚙	*Authentics artipresent, Germany*	313
▬	*Recyclable polypropylene, metal*	295, 341
♺	*• Recyclable materials • Design for disassembly • Minimal use of materials*	327, 328

Little Beaver

Part of Gehry's 'Experimental Edges' limited edition for Vitra, the Little Beaver comprises offset layers of thick cardboard with large corrugations, glued and stood on end. Both the material and the construction technique reveal numerous permutations for working these materials and contrast with his earlier furniture work with cardboard in the Wiggle series of 1972, now being produced again by Vitra.

✎	*Frank O Gehry, USA*	306
⚙	*Vitra AG, Germany*	326
▬	*Cardboard, glue*	287, 299
♺	*• Renewable and compostable materials*	327, 330

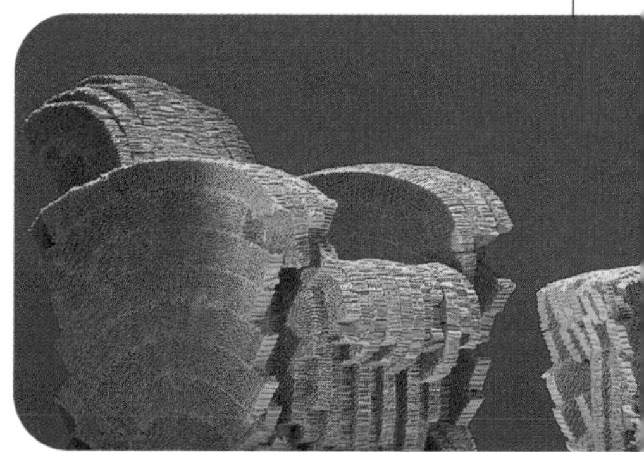

Stül, SE 68, 1998

An economical 1950s design, which originally used plywood seating and back rest, has been reproduced using multicoloured plastic sheeting originating from waste packaging. Where renewable materials are in short supply or costly, recycled plastic offers a viable alternative.

Designer	*Professor E Eiermann, Germany*	
Manufacturer	*Wilde & Spieth GmbH, Germany*	326
Materials	*HDPE sheeting, steel*	295, 341
Eco-design	• *Recycled and recyclable materials*	327

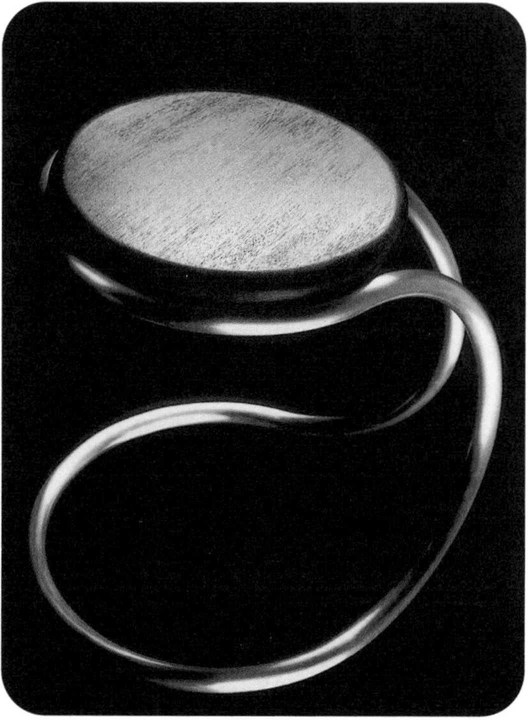

Stool

Simplicity is the key driver in this design, resulting in economical use of materials and low-energy input during fabrication. Durable materials ensure robustness and a long life. Mahogany can be salvaged, obtained from a sustainably managed forest (as certified by the FSC) or substituted by a sustainable temperate hardwood.

Designer	*ijs designers (Bridget Reading and Monique van den Hurk), UK and Netherlands*	307
Manufacturer	*Limited batch production*	
Materials	*Stainless steel, mahogany*	295, 339
Eco-design	• *Economy of materials usage* • *Low-energy manufacturing*	327, 328

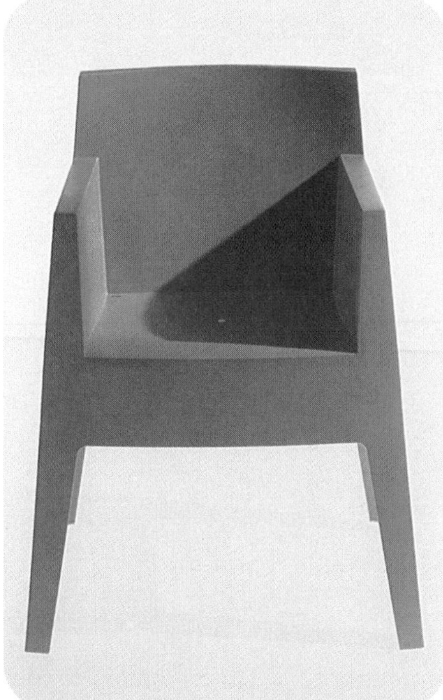

Toy Chair

Tough, durable and colourful, polypropylene has been a favoured material with designers for nearly half a century. Toy Chair is a wonderful celebration of technological progress in single-piece injection moulding, with its hollow arms and 'angle-iron' legs. Starck brings his usual wit and economy of line to this chair, which is equally happy in a garden, an urban loft or a café. As it is fabricated entirely from PP with a small, easily removable, stainless-steel plug around the drainage hole in the seat, it easy to recycle the materials at the end of the item's life. By 2030 manufacturers may even be requesting that their products be returned by the current custodian for dismantling and recycling of components and materials. The material content of the Toy Chair will then be valued as much as the comfort and pleasure given through its lifetime.

✎	*Philippe Starck, France*	310
⚙	*Driade SpA, Italy*	315
▮	*Polypropylene*	341
♻	• *Recyclable single material* • *Economy of materials usage in manufacturing*	327

Thinking Man's Chair

Tubular and flat steel are combined in a deliberately 'engineered' look, further enhanced by the red oxide-type finish complete with written dimensions. A durable design for indoor or outdoor use, which, being made from a single material, is easily recycled.

✎	*Jasper Morrison, UK*	309
⚙	*Cappellini SpA, Italy*	314
▮	*Steel*	295
♻	• *Recyclable single material*	327

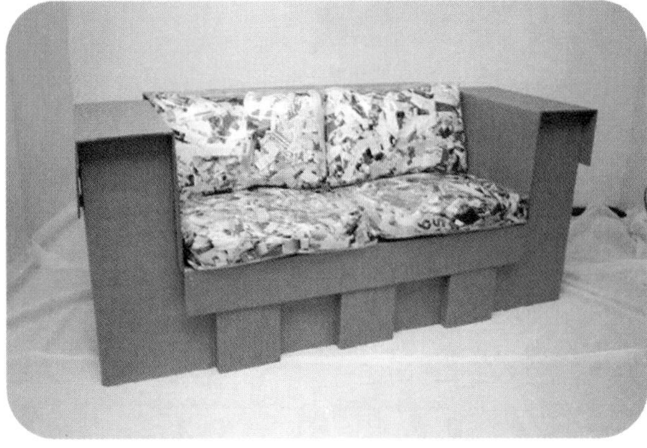

✎	*Ronaldo Edson da Silva, Brazil*	305
⚙	*Papa-Papel, Brazil*	322
▰	*Paper, cardboard, plastic*	283, 288-9
♻	• *Materials from local sources* • *Recycled materials* • *Low-energy manufacturing*	327, 328
✪	*First prize, Post-Consumption category, 1997 Brazilian eco-design awards*	

Zorg

All the raw materials to manufacture this two-seat sofa originate from the Manaus free-trade zone, Amazonia. Cardboard finished in natural sealants forms the main frame supporting four transparent plastic-bag cushions filled with shredded magazines. The manufacturing technique, which involves simple cutting, folding and gluing, precludes the need for special tools or an assembly plant. This is an excellent example of the application of industrial ecology in a manufacturing locality.

The Draught

Wicker is imaginatively combined with steel for this exciting range of chairs. Traditional weaving of wicker is abandoned in favour of methods in which the withies are held tightly together with steel or inserted into solid beech. The results bring nature, with all its innate variability, into the living space.

✎	*Pawel Grunert, Poland*	307
⚙	*Limited batch production*	
▰	*Steel, wicker*	281, 295
♻	• *Renewable and compostable materials* • *Recyclable materials*	327

XL1 kit chair

This lightweight chair, weighing just 2.2 kg (4.7 lb), won the 1999 Jerwood Applied Arts Prize coordinated by the Crafts Council, UK. Marriott combines materials and ready-made components, which are readily available from local builders' merchants and DIY stockists, into an honest, economical, multipurpose chair. In the UK, DIY interior decoration, building and gardening are obsessions, so it is refreshing to see a designer encouraging such enthusiasts to apply themselves to designing furniture.

✎	*Michael Marriott, UK*	308
⚙	*Self-assembly chair design*	
▬	*Beech, birch plywood, zinc-plated mild steel*	295, 339
♻	*• Renewable and recyclable materials* *• Economy of materials usage* *• Use of ready-made components*	327

Chair

Dolphin-Wilding preserves the quirks of nature's patterns in her unique wooden chairs, letting the natural forms dictate the structure of her hand-crafted reincarnations. In doing so she takes us back to days before 'craft' work became a highly skilled profession or before 'industrial design' produced technologically refined furniture.

✎	*Julienne Dolphin-Wilding*	306
⚙	*One-off/small batch production*	
▬	*Timber*	339
♻	*• Renewable materials* *• Low-energy fabrication*	327, 328

Wiggle series

Originally designed in 1972 as economical furniture and manufactured by Jack Brocan in the USA, the Wiggle side chair has been reproduced by Vitra from 1992. Each layer of corrugated cardboard is placed at an angle to the next layer to provide significantly increased durability compared with the folding cardboard chairs by the likes of Peter Raacke and Peter Murdoch in the 1960s.

✎	*Frank O Gehry, USA*	306
⚙	*Vitra AG, Germany*	326
▬	*Cardboard, glues*	287-8, 299
♻	*• Renewable materials* *• Low-energy manufacturing*	327, 328

Flower pot table

Clay flower pots are given a fresh, sophisticated image in this simple but well-executed design for a durable, functional occasional or side table, which uses raw materials that are readily available worldwide.

Designer	*Jasper Morrison, UK*	309
Manufacturer	*Cappellini SpA, Italy*	314
Materials	*Clay, glass*	295
Eco	• *Abundant materials from the lithosphere* • *Economy of materials usage*	327, 340

Ash round table

Combining excellent rigidity and ample leg-room, the simplicity of this design relies on the strength of the solid ash, which comes from local English woodlands. A range of table sizes to seat three to ten people is manufactured to the same basic design. Trannon Furniture successfully blends traditional furniture-making techniques with a modern aesthetic to produce durable, quality seating, tables and shelving.

Designer	*David Colwell and Roy Tam, UK*	305
Manufacturer	*Trannon Furniture Ltd, UK*	325
Materials	*Solid ash wood*	339
Eco	• *Renewable materials with stewardship sourcing* • *Low-energy construction techniques*	327, 328

Mooving Image/Sony flat-screen coffee table

Old TVs never die, they just find a new home. Jam's TVs don't work but they still grab the attention. Electronics manufacturers are being forced to realign their entire business strategies in accordance with EU legislation (such as the WEEE Directive), which encourages them to take back their products. Fabricating furniture from TV tubes isn't really dealing with the problem of disposal (of heavy metals, gases, glass) but it provides an interim solution while suitable disposal methods are sought.

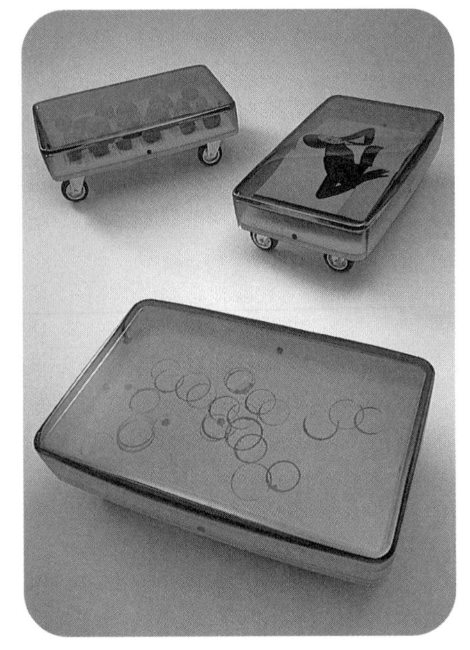

✎	*Jam Design & Communications, UK*	307
⚙	*Jam Design & Communications, UK*	307
▮	*TV tubes, steel, castors*	341
♲	• *Reuse of end-of-life components*	330

Concrete table

Concrete has a similar embodied energy to timber, or lower, so its use in creating robust, durable yet customizable furniture is welcome.

✎	*Pamela Hatton, UK*	307
⚙	*One-offs*	
▮	*Concrete, glazed ceramic tiles*	295
♲	• *Low-embodied energy* • *Durability*	328, 340

Plaky

Sophisticated extrusion and moulding of the ABS-polycarbonate blend of plastic recyclate adds value to this waste stream by turning it into a desirable item of furniture. The anodized aluminium pedestal stem completes the 'up-market' effect.

✎	*Christopher Connell, Australia*	305
⚙	*Wharington International Pty Ltd for MAP (Merchants of Australia), Australia*	320, 326
▰	*Recycled ABS-polycarbonate, aluminium*	341
♺	*• Recycled and recyclable materials*	327

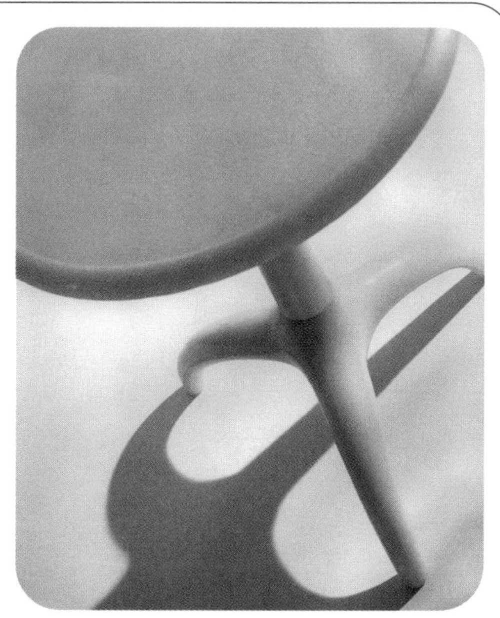

✎	*Setsu Ito, Japan*	307
⚙	*Front Corporation, Japan*	317
▰	*Steel*	295
♺	*• Single material for easy recycling* *• Extremely durable material*	327

Saita

Almost 90 per cent of the steel in circulation has been recycled at some time, so it is refreshing to see steel being used with great sculptural panache in this table design. Long the preserve of architectural and structural engineers, steel offers fresh perspectives for furniture designers.

Schraag

This table-cum-desk minimizes on materials by using three legs, not the traditional four, for each lightweight aluminium trestle. A range of standard 2 x 0.9-metre (6ft 7in x 3ft) tops can be chosen from laminated bamboo, glass or red multiplex. Simplicity and ease of assembly bring the old-fashioned trestle table into the modern world.

✎	*Martin van Severen, Belgium*	311
⚙	*Bulo, Belgium*	313
▬	*Aluminium with bamboo, glass or multiplex*	281, 295
♻	*• Renewable material option • Recyclable materials • Design for disassembly*	327, 328

Ledge

The density and strength of ABS, even in recycled form, contributes to lightness in design, in Christopher Connell's vision.

✎	*Christopher Connell, Australia*	305
⚙	*Prototype, MAP, Australia*	320
▬	*Recycled ABS*	341
♻	*• Recycled material*	327

✎	*Paul Nijland, graduate, Design Academy Eindhoven, Netherlands*	309
⚙	*Prototype*	
▬	*Wood, metal*	295, 339
♻	*• Economy of materials usage • Low-energy manufacturing, distribution and assembly*	327, 328

Table 0.85 x 1.20m

Table design is stripped down to the bare essentials – a wooden worktop, four tubular metal legs, the whole easily disassembled. No fuss, minimal production costs, easy flat pack and low-energy production input.

Table

Hertz reveals the workability of Syndecrete® in his individualistic, sculptural tables.

✎	*David Hertz, USA*	307
⚙	*Syndesis, Inc., USA*	324
▮	*Syndecrete®, glass*	295
♻	*• Recycled materials*	327

Side table

Syndecrete® is a lightweight composite concrete utilizing mixed industrial and post-consumer waste, pulverized fly ash and PP fibre waste. The material is well suited to detailed moulding and can be polished to reveal a terrazzo-like surface.

✎	*David Hertz, USA*	307
⚙	*Syndesis, Inc., USA*	324
▮	*Syndecrete®*	295
♻	*• Recycled materials*	327

Folding table

Easily mass-produced, with low energy input, this simple folding table combines low cost with transportability and the use of Environ and Ranger MDF particleboards.

✎	*Ann Girand and Brian Champian, USA*	307
⚙	*One-off*	
▮	*Environ, Ranger MDF*	278
♻	*• Recycled and renewable materials*	327
✪	*IDRA award, 1995*	332

Table

Gridcore, a recycled paper honeycomb core sandwiched between layers of fibre sheeting and veneer, provides sufficient rigidity to support a glass table top.

✎	*Dan Cramer, USA*	305
⚙	*One-off*	
▬	*Gridcore, glass*	295
♲	*• Recycled and recyclable materials*	327
✪	*IDRA award, 1998*	332

Table Op-Lá

Morrison's economy of design is exemplified in his ability to make the connection between the usually separate roles of displaying and serving food and drinks. This dual-function tray-cum-table uses the bare minimum of materials.

✎	*Jasper Morrison, UK*	309
⚙	*Cappellini SpA, Italy*	314
▬	*ABS, stainless steel*	295, 341
♲	*• Dual-function object*	329

Nested tables

Jurinec sees cardboard as a noble material with great worth in its unrefined naturalness, low cost and transient durability. Cardboard encourages minimalism in design and is non-materialistic. It is also easily returned to the recycling loop.

✎	*Ksenkja Jurinec, Croatia*	307
⚙	*One-offs*	
▬	*Recycled cardboard*	288-9
♲	*• Recycled materials*	327
✪	*IDRA award, 1997*	332

Bookcase

This concertina-like bookcase has an interesting juxtaposition of natural materials. The craft aesthetic has always embraced experimentation with nature's primary materials but further possibilities are emerging to create a new 'industrial craft' production.

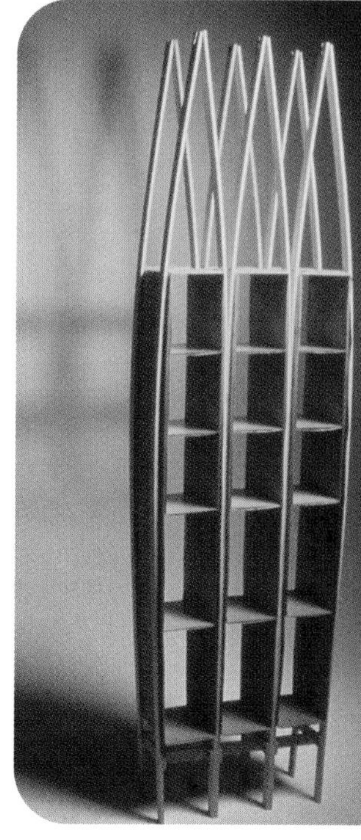

✎	*Jan Konings and Jurgen Bey, Droog Design, Netherlands*	308
⚙	*DMD/Droog Design, Netherlands*	307, 315
▮	*Maplewood, paper, linen*	288-91, 339
♻	*• Innovative use of natural, renewable materials*	327

Chest of drawers

An assortment of salvaged drawers is reincarnated as a new chest of drawers in Remy's functional yet quirky design. The drawers looks as if they could have been strapped on to the back of a pick-up truck and indeed the designer encourages this metaphor by binding the drawers together with the webbing and steel ratchet used by truckers. Chest of Drawers is an object suspended in time, neither permanent nor transient, and demonstrates the recycling of dozens of original (drawer) designs that fashion had consigned to the junk shop.

✎	*Tejo Remy, Droog Design, Netherlands*	309
⚙	*One-off/small batch production, Droog Design, Netherlands*	307
▮	*Old drawers, webbing, steel*	341
♻	*• Reused and ready-made components • Cold, low-energy construction*	327, 328

I Just Moved In

The layers of meaning are as numerous as the shelves in this intriguing design, which promotes individualism and juxtaposes the old, the new and the banal. The design raises a question about the attitudes of designers: should the construction details of Wiesendanger's bookshelf be published so that anyone can assemble a bookshelf on similar principles but using locally found materials? Or is the limited batch production an exclusive process that guarantees status to the purchasers?

✎	*Köbi Wiesendanger, Switzerland*	311
⚙	*Limited batch production, Avant de Dormir, Italy*	313
▮	*Pinewood, cups and saucers (used to prop up shelf units)*	339, 341
♻	*• Reuse of ready-made components* *• Renewable materials*	

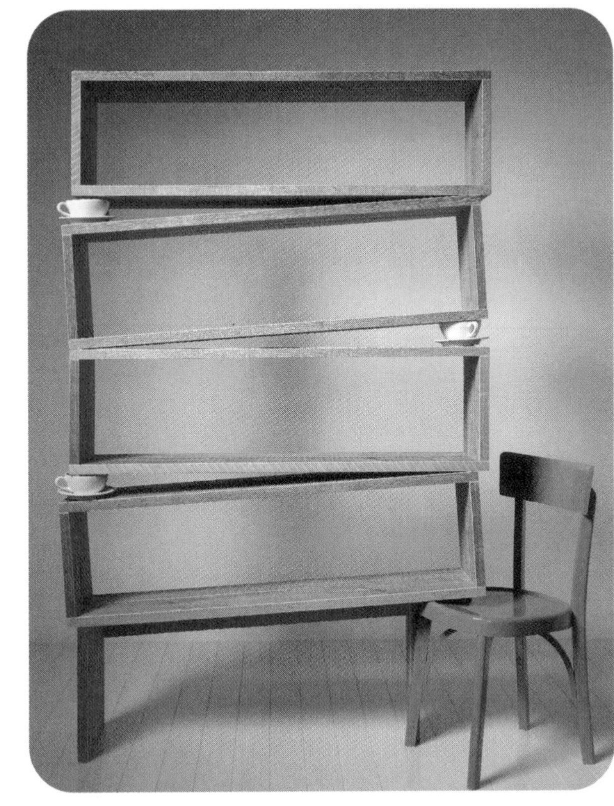

Boox

Plastics are the by-products of our desire to burn fossil fuels and are integral to our modern lives. Yet plastics are perceived as a major culprit in despoiling our environment, even though they have made possible resilient, functional and technologically advanced products for over half a century. Philippe Starck's 'Boox' shouts, 'look at me, I'm plastic, proud of it, cherish me, I'm a valuable resource.' This modular extruded and injection-moulded shelving system is well conceived and should persist for many decades before it is disassembled ready for a new lease of life as another recycled product. Boox gives plastic credibility and in doing so makes us re-evaluate the essential worth of the material.

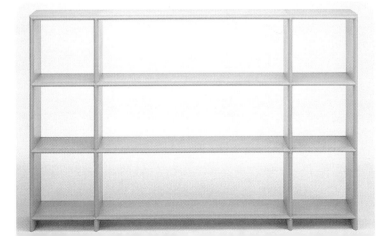

✎	*Philippe Starck, France*	310
⚙	*Kartell, Italy*	318
▮	*Thermoplastic polymer*	282
♻	*• Durable modular design* *• Recyclable materials*	327

Plug It

Boredom is a factor that consigns many an object to the auction house, second-hand dealer or, in the worst scenario, a landfill site. Roberto Feo's modular shelving system ensures that the user can rearrange and add new modules to refresh and restimulate the visual senses at the same time as extending the storage volume.

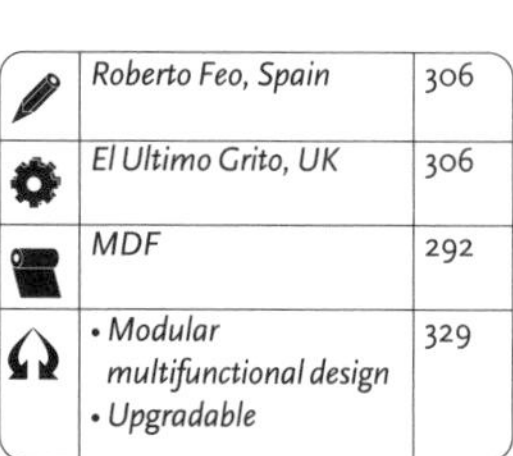

	Roberto Feo, Spain	306
	El Ultimo Grito, UK	306
	MDF	292
	• *Modular multifunctional design* • *Upgradable*	329

Modular bookshelf

This dual-function bookshelf and/or storage unit is pared down to an essential modular component of a box frame and removable box 'drawer'. It is a simple, versatile system that can be expanded to meet the user's needs. It offers excellent storage capacity in relation to its footprint and can also double as a screen to divide a room.

	Giulio Polvara, Italy	309
	Kartell, Italy	318
	ABS, lacquered polyurethane	341
	• *Modular storage system*	329

Robostacker and Hola Hoop

Traditionally manufacturers strive to serve specific markets and, where possible, increase their market share. Jam are a design group focused on developing symbiotic relationships with manufacturers to explore whether their ready-made components can be adapted to create fresh products for new markets. The 'Robostacker', produced in 1997 in collaboration with Italian white-goods manufacturers Whirlpool, converts three stainless-steel washing-machine drums into a storage unit. Developing the concept further, Jam created the Hola Hoop shelving using painted or stainless-steel-finished drums and glass sheets. Ready-made components can be obtained from pre-consumer (factory) or post-consumer (municipal or other waste-disposal centres) sources. Jam have liaised with other well-known manufacturers to produce flat-screen mobile coffee tables from components made by Sony. Reuse of manufactured components seems to offer endless possibilities but does not absolve the designer from examining the green credentials of the original components and manufacturers' environmental commitments.

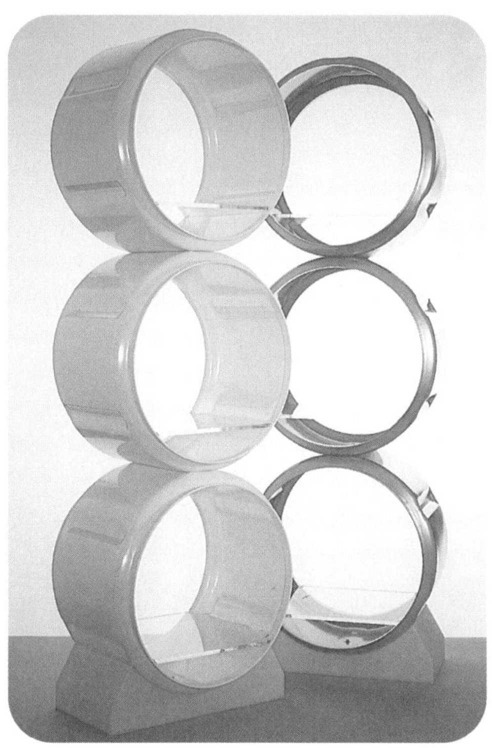

✎	*Jam Design & Communications Ltd, UK*	307
⚙	*Jam with Whirlpool, UK/Italy*	307
▮	*Stainless steel*	295
♻	*• Reuse or re-application of ready-made manufactured components*	327

Es

Nine beechwood rods are inserted into four plywood panels and locked into place using plastic rings. Grcic tests the boundaries of stability with a design that wobbles yet doesn't fall over. His design appears to fly in the face of man's desire to remove nature from the process of manufacturing, being deliberately made to look naïve and in a DIY style. The rods permit the shelving to double as a coat rack and clothes stand.

	Konstantin Grcic, Germany	307
	Moormann Möbel, Germany	320
	Beechwood, plywood, plastic	283, 339
	• Renewable materials, economically applied *• Ease of assembly/ disassembly*	327, 328

Sten

The Sten system of storage and shelving is a series of standard flat-pack components, which can be bolted together in a range of bespoke combinations. Shelving, uprights and storage-box panels are manufactured from untreated Scandinavian softwood from managed forests or IKEA's own woodlands. Coach screws and ties are used to fix the individual elements into a rigid structure and the assembled unit can be easily disassembled for reuse or recycling. The shelving is robust and capable of holding up to 500kg (1,100lb).

Designer	*IKEA, Sweden*	319
Manufacturer	*IKEA, Sweden*	319
Materials	*Wood, steel*	295, 339
Sustainability	• *Renewable and recyclable materials* • *Low-energy manufacturing and assembly* • *Customizable furniture*	327-9

Shell

Moulded aircraft-grade plywood, just 3mm (about ⅛ inch) thick, is fixed with 3-D metal corner fixings to create a basic shell that can be fitted out internally as required with shelving and a clothes rail. A longitudinal hinge permits much better access to the contents than conventional wardrobes.

Designer	*Ubald Klug, France*	308
Manufacturer	*Rothlisberger, Switzerland*	323
Materials	*Plywood, metal*	295, 339
Sustainability	• *Economy of materials usage* • *Low-energy manufacturing*	327, 328

Hoover

This lightweight wardrobe features stretchable side panels, which provide extra capacity for those awkwardly shaped objects. N2's minimalist philosophy excludes extraneous detail and incorporates a reductionist approach to the use of materials.

	Jörg Boner, N2, Switzerland	305
	sdb industries, Netherlands	323
	Various	
	• Economical use of materials *• Greater capacity than traditional designs*	327, 328

Eco table/sideboard

Joinery skills are applied to this table/sideboard, which is made of 95 per cent Environ, a biocomposite, and 5 per cent Durawood, an HDPE plastic lumber recyclate. These materials complement the simplicity of the design elements and echo the style of classic Shaker furniture made from American hardwoods.

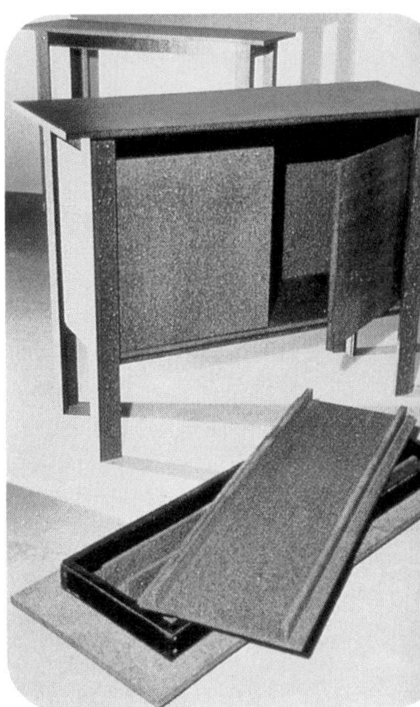

	George Ettenheim, Ettenheim Design, USA	306
	Ettehneim Design, USA	306
	Environ, Durawood	278, 293
	• Recycled materials	327
	IDRA award, 1995	332

Italic

There are just two components in this beautifully simple shelving system: bent steel rods whose ends are dipped in natural liquid gum to provide a good grip, and wooden shelves. Users could add extra components to expand their existing shelving.

	Lorenz Wiegand, Germany	311
	Prototype	
	Steel, liquid gum, wood	287, 295
	• *Economy of materials usage* • *Low-energy production*	327, 328

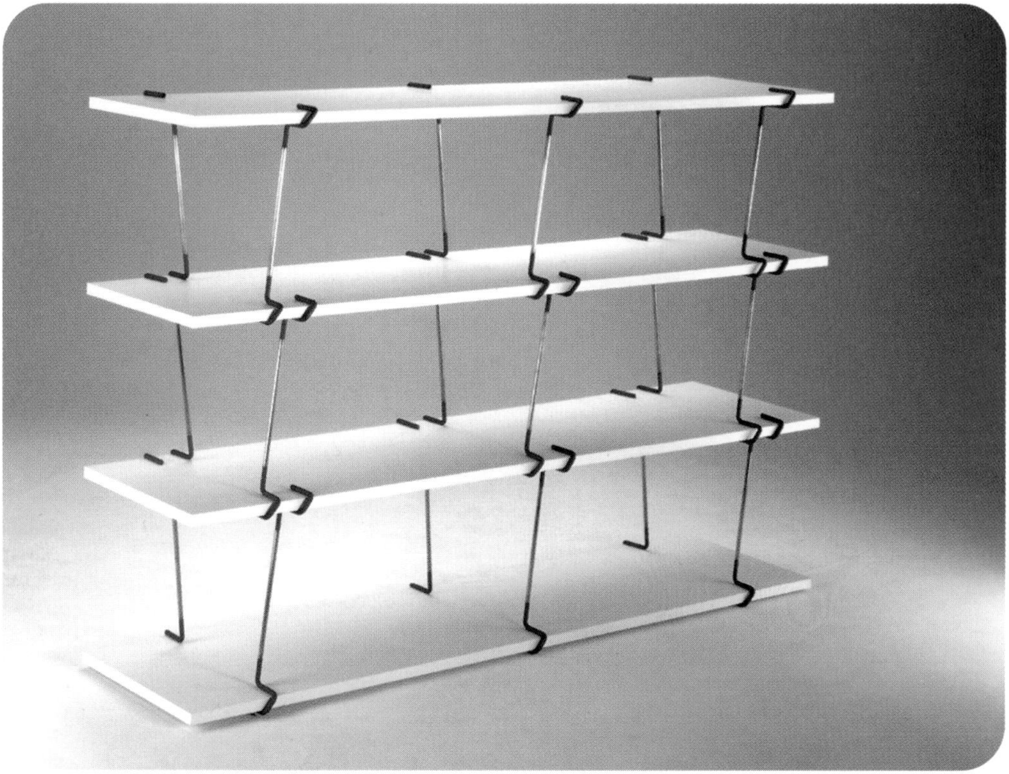

Console and shelving system

Bär + Knell demonstrate the versatility of recycled HDPE plastic board with this eclectic range of furniture. The message is unequivocal: waste is valuable and recycled waste extends the palette of materials for the designer.

✎	*Bär + Knell, Germany*	304
⚙	*One-offs, Bär + Knell, Germany*	304
	Recycled plastic	327
	• Recycled content	327

Turris

Components include shelving and side panels of Fiberbond Wallboard made from recycled newspaper and gypsum and rolled steel angles using 60 per cent-recycled steel. The wheels that allow the shelves to be moved are made from used rubber conveyor-belts.

✎	*Sheri Shumacher, USA*	310
⚙	*Small batch production*	
▮	*Recycled steel, Fiberbond Wallboard, reused rubber*	283, 295
♲	• *Recycled and reused materials* • *Easy assembly/ disassembly*	327, 328
✪	*IDRA award, 1996*	332

Shelf system

Lightweight materials commonly used for packaging can provide a viable alternative to 'traditional' shelving materials such as steel, aluminium and wood. These shelves are constructed using techniques similar to those used to manufacture moulded packaging for eggs and electronic goods. Part of the challenge to designers is to reappraise conventional practices and test the suitability of materials, especially biocomposites, for new applications.

✎	*Jasper Startup, Startup Design, UK*	310
⚙	*Small batch production*	
▮	*Recycled newspapers, reused fruit trays*	341
♲	• *Recycled materials* • *Reused components* • *Compostable*	327
✪	*IDRA award, 1995*	332

A Collection of Mammoth Pillows

Anthropometrics fixes the scale of human objects in the home, but if you break the rules refreshing new concepts can emerge. The humble pillow scaled up to 'mammoth' size becomes a foldable sofa, an armchair for a corner between walls, a mattress or a comfortable zone on which to relax.

✎	*Judith Kant, graduate student 2000, Design Academy Eindhoven, Netherlands*	307
⚙	*Prototype*	
▬	*Furnishing fabric, filler*	285
⟲	*• Multifunctional furniture*	329

Table-into-chest-of-drawers

With a simple action this sparse chest of drawers cantilevers gracefully out to form an occasional table. For the Azumis this design reflects Japanese cultural needs where rooms are often multifunctional and futons and tables are removed or reconfigured as required.

✎	*Shin and Tomoko Azumi*	304
⚙	*Small batch production, Shin and Tomoko Azumi*	304
▤	*Wood, metal*	295, 339
♻	*• Dual-function design*	329

Communications furniture

The time is right for a design revolution in the computer industry. Although the iMac revitalized the styling of computers, they still remain working machines designed, primarily, for the formality of the office environment. Sander de Klerk's characterful stool, reminiscent of a Barbara Hepworth sculpture, is a fun, portable, wireless computer with a touch screen linked by an umbilical cord to the stool. The user can take this charming object with him/her to the bathroom, kitchen or garden. In the twenty-first century we should expect to see less of the grey personalities of existing PCs and more machines that are really useful even if they aren't even switched on! Here's a step in the right direction.

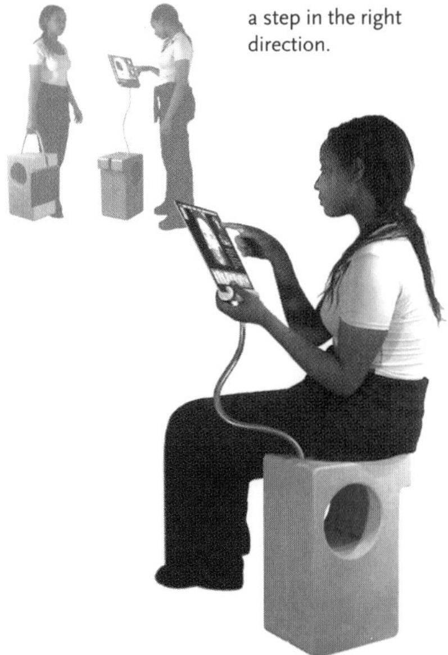

✎	*Sander de Klerk, graduate student 2000, Design Academy Eindhoven, Netherlands*	305
⚙	*Prototype*	
▤	*Various*	
♻	*• Improved functionality for computer hardware • Design for need*	328, 329

Dia

Adaptability and durability are the two primary prerequisites for furniture that is intended to survive the elements and robust use in the garden. This range offers a high degree of flexibility – the chair has an upright and a low position, the table height is adjustable and the sunbed has eight possible profile permutations. Polished stainless steel and strong fabric, impregnated with waterproofing and UV-stabilized, ensure a long life. Thanks to these high-quality materials, this range of furniture is also suitable for indoor use and thus offers flexibility and dual-functionality.

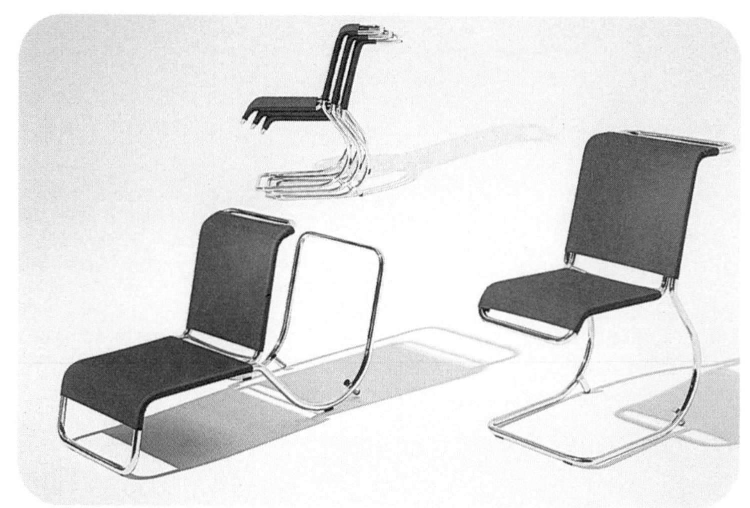

	Gioia Meller Marcovicz, UK	308
	ClassiCon, Germany	314
	Stainless steel, waterproofed/UV-stabilized fabric	290-1, 295
	• Durability, multifunctionality	329

Flexipal

These identical interlocking plastic modules can be articulated and held in fixed positions by tightening the adjusting screws to configure a range of furniture from tables to chairs, beds and platforms as desired. This encourages the owner to experiment with his or her own concepts and offers flexible functionality.

Designer	*J R Miles, UK*	308
Manufacturer	*Retail Place Ltd, UK*	323
Material	*Plastic*	283, 295
Eco	• *Multifunctionality, ease of upgrading* • *Single material to facilitate recycling*	327, 329

Kaststoel

The joined halves of this interesting seat/shelf/magazine rack amply demonstrate the multiplicity of uses to which a merged object can be put.

Designer	*Paulo Nervo, graduate student 2000, Design Academy Eindhoven, Netherlands*	309
Manufacturer	*Prototype*	
Material	*Polymer*	282, 296-7
Eco	• *Multifunctional furniture*	329

Kokon

Old wooden furniture is revived by covering it with a PVC-based coating. The opportunities to create quirky new custom furniture are legion but the technique needs further refinement to find a substitute for PVC, whose environmental track record is poor. How to isolate the timber of the reclaimed furniture from intimate contact with the PVC and what to do with the items at the end of their lives are unanswered questions.

✎	*Jurgen Bey, Droog Design, Netherlands*	304
⚙	*Limited batch production, Droog Design, Netherlands*	306
▤	*Reclaimed furniture, PVC coating*	341
♻	*• Reuse of ready-made components*	327

Nature Technology Symbiosis

As civil engineers use plants to reinforce geotechnical structures (bioengineering), designers can use plants to strengthen their designs. Edwin Wannet believes that the symbiosis of technological and living elements in this 'living cabinet' raises questions about the types of products that could be developed, product-life expectations and emotional responses.

✎	*Edwin Wannet, graduate student, Design Academy Eindhoven, Netherlands*	311
⚙	*Prototype*	
▤	*Wood, glass, living plants*	295, 339
♻	*• Multifunctionality* *• Living, respiring object*	329

Low Living

Reviving maritime techniques and skills, such as spool knitting, creates strong, rhythmic textures in this multifunctional range of Low Living products suitable as blankets, wraps or cushions. Turn down the heating and retreat to your cocoon!

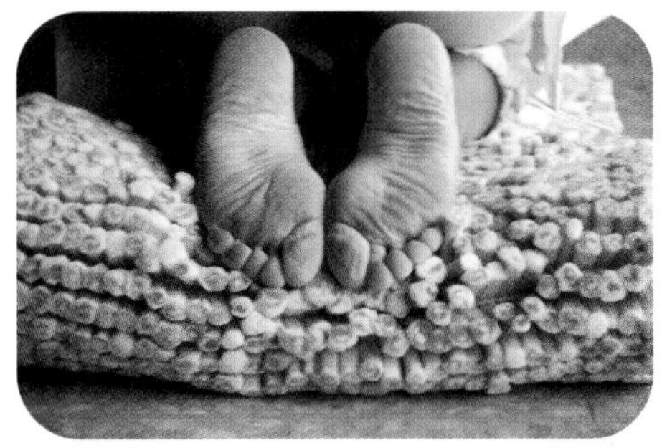

✎	*Gonnie Constansia, graduate student 2000, Design Academy Eindhoven, Netherlands*	305
⚙	*Prototypes*	
	Wool	290-1
	• Renewable materials	327

Pouffe

A temporary bed, suitable for day-time lounging or use by an overnight guest, unfurls out of a pouffe, the exterior upholstery doubling as a blanket.

✎	*Erik Bakker, graduate student, Design Academy Eindhoven, Netherlands*	304
⚙	*Prototype*	
	Various textiles	290-1, 300-1
	• Multifunctionality	329

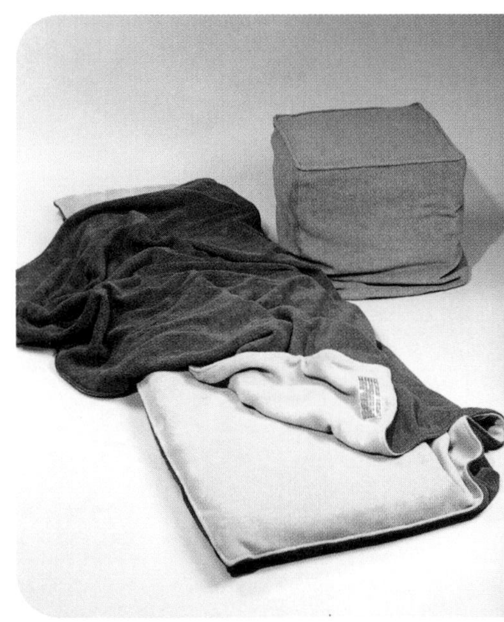

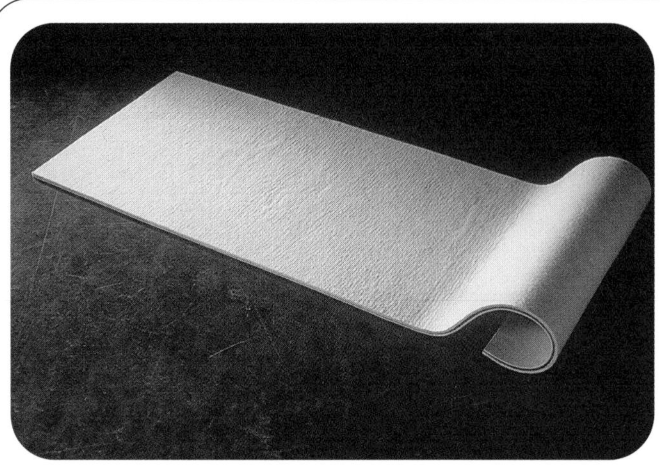

Wave

Two layers of felt sandwich a layer of polyurethane to create a flexible matting, which is curved and stiffened at one end by changing the mix of elastomers in the PU. When not in use the mat can be wound around the formed end. The result is a unique object that can be used as a mat, a recliner or a chaise longue.

✎	*Martin Hoogendijk, Netherlands*	307
⚙	*DMD/Droog Design, Netherlands*	306, 315
▬	*Felt, polyurethane*	290-1 341
⟲	*• Multifunctional object*	329

Hide-away

This intriguing design invites the user to take out a book from the shelf, crank the handle to raise the day-bed and settle down for a good read.

✎	*N2, Switzerland*	309
⚙	*Prototype, sdb industries, Netherlands*	323
▬	*Aluminium, birch plywood, polypropylene*	295, 341
⟲	*• Multifunctional furniture*	329

Table lamp and table chair

Dual-function design is pared down to its ultimate simplicity in Richard Hutten's witty yet practical furniture. He demonstrates the same thoughtful economy, bordering on the austere, in the Table Lamp and Table Chair, pragmatic and lovable designs which will be cherished.

✎	*Richard Hutten, Netherlands*	307
⚙	*Limited batch production, REEEL, Netherlands*	323
▮	*Beechwood, MDF, metal*	295, 339
↻	• *Dual-function designs* • *Economy of materials usage*	327, 329

Mind the Gap

For those who like to relax with a coffee and a magazine, 'Mind the Gap' is the only accessory required. It combines efficient dual functionality with economical use of materials and imbues the combination with a cheeky persona. There's really no need to buy a table and a magazine rack ever again.

✎	*El Ultimo Grito, Spain*	306
⚙	*EL Ultimo Grito, UK*	306
▮	*Rubber, steel/alloy*	283, 295
↻	• *Multifunctionality* • *Economy of materials usage*	327, 329

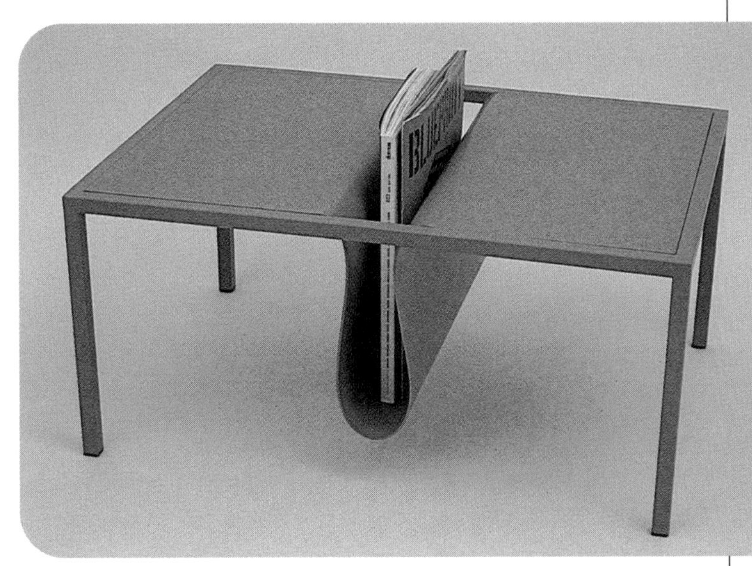

Nomad

For those who like nothing better than to lounge around on a deep pile carpet here's the ideal solution that avoids the use of all those unwanted big cushions while giving your back a rest. Wanders has metaphorically and literally elevated the status of the humble carpet well above the tacky examples of shag-pile of the 1970s.

✎	*Marcel Wanders, Netherlands*	311
⚙	*Cappellini SpA, Italy*	314
	Wool, metal	290-1, 295
	• Multifunctional object	329

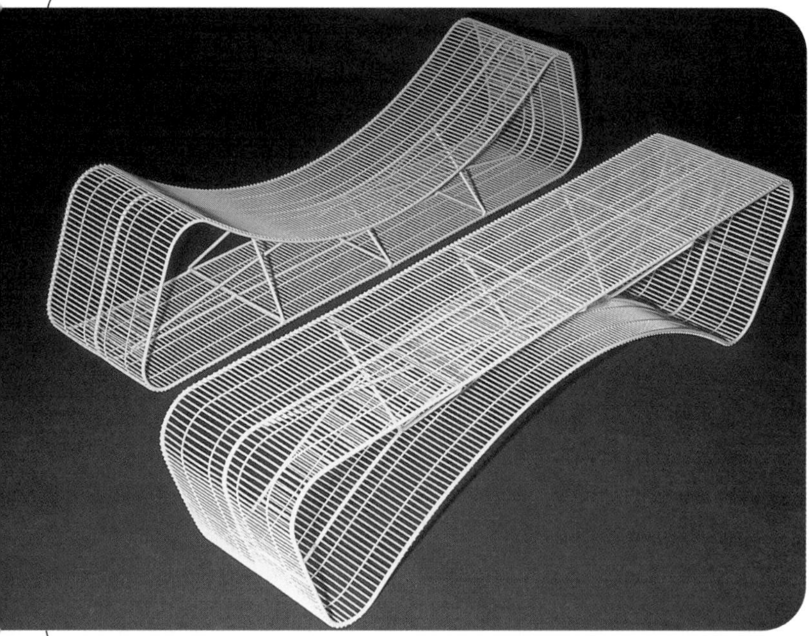

Wire-frame reversible bench

Inspired by the technological achievements of supermarket shopping baskets and 3D computer modelling, the Azumis were able to create this lightweight bench, which can be reversed to make a chaise longue or stacked with other benches to provide shelving.

✎	*Shin and Tomoko Azumi, UK*	304
⚙	*Small batch production, Shin and Tomoko Azumi, UK*	304
	Nickel-plated or powder-coated steel	295
	• Multifunctional design	329

Anna Chaise

Ratchets on the alloy frame permit the sides of this armchair to be lowered to suit the occupant and convert the armchair to a chaise longue or day-bed. An excellent example of practical, multifunctional furniture.

Gioia Meller Marcovicz, UK	308
Habitat, UK	317
Alloy, padding, fabric	290-1, 295
• Multifunctionality • Inexpensive materials	329

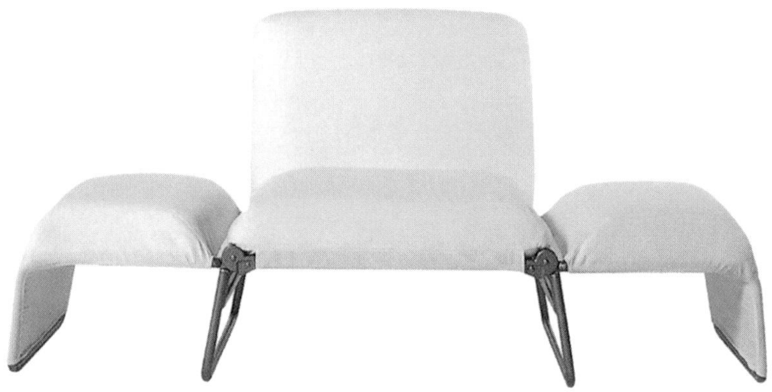

Three and One-Half Minutes

This lightweight screen encapsulates fragments of time in old processed film stock bound in an aluminium frame. Although the aluminium is easily recycled at the end of the product's life, a question mark hangs over the film stock impregnated with silver halides and other chemicals. Will future processes be devised to dissolve and separate the constituents? In the meantime the screen represents an ingenious way of storing the non-recyclable component.

✎	*Jam Design & Communications, UK*	307
⚙	*Jam Design & Communications, UK*	307
▰	*Aluminium, old film stock*	295, 341
♻	*• Recycled materials*	327

Carta

Shigeru Ban creates structures with cardboard and succeeds in elevating this humble material to a new aesthetic level. His use of cardboard tubes in projects as diverse as furniture, temporary housing for refugees and buildings for communities reveals superb understanding of the capabilities of the material.

Carta is a range of furniture that makes minimal use of low-embodied-energy materials.

✎	*Shigeru Ban, Japan*	304
⚙	*Cappellini SpA, Italy*	314
▰	*Cardboard*	288-9
♻	*• Renewable materials • Economy of materials usage • Recyclable*	327

Fasal corner joint

Fasal is a new material consisting of wood fibres, cornmeal and natural resins, which can be readily moulded or sprayed. It provides an alternative to non-renewable materials such as plastic polymers. Jacqueline Andringa has

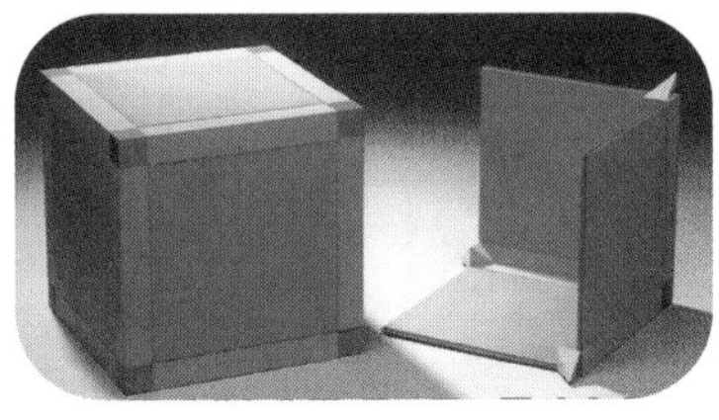

extended its usefulness by creating a universal corner joint that locks any two or more equal-sized components, opening up opportunities in furniture and product manufacturing and timber-frame construction.

✎	*Jacqueline Andringa, graduate student, Design Academy Eindhoven, Netherlands*	304
⚙	*Prototype*	
▬	*Fasal*	278
♻	• *Renewable and compostable material* • *Universal jointing system*	327, 329

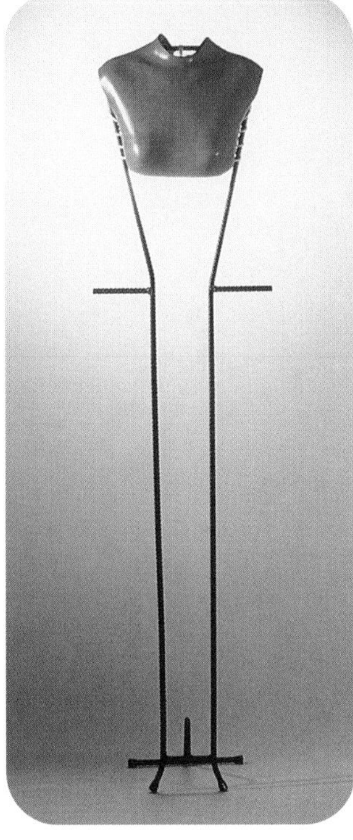

Herz

Steel reinforcing rods, similar to those used in construction with concrete, are welded and bolted into a simple frame to which a moulded leather breastplate is attached, providing a functional, minimalist coat stand. The materials used are easily recycled and the design is both aesthetically pleasing and durable.

✎	*Anthologie Quartett, Germany*	304
⚙	*Robert A Wettstein, Germany*	326
▬	*Leather, steel*	285, 295
♻	• *Recyclable and compostable materials* • *Economy of materials usage* • *Low-energy manufacturing*	327-9

Frontal

Transparent plastic cushions are stuffed with discarded sweet and food wrappings, offering a graphic reminder that 'We are what we eat'!

✎	*Bär + Knell, Germany*	304
⚙	*One-off*	
▬	*Plastics, plastic-coated papers*	283, 295
♻	• *Encourages recycling* • *Low-energy manufacturing via 'self-assembly' using locally sourced materials*	327, 329

Hülsta 'Muvado' range

Germany is undoubtedly one of the 'greenest' consumer markets in the European Union and Hülsta is a significant manufacturer of domestic and office furniture with a proven commitment to environmental performance. It was one of the first companies to register to the quality assurance standard, ISO 9001, and its entire production is certified under the Blue Angel eco-label scheme. In collaboration with Danzer, a leading veneer company, Hülsta initiated the 'veneer passport' guaranteeing that it does not originate from a tropical rainforest. Only four of their current ranges of furniture use solid wood, again not sourced from rainforests. Particleboard or MDF is the primary material. In-house designers apply lifecycle analysis to extend the projected lifespan of products, of which most are already expected to last between thirty and forty years.

✎	*Hülsta, Germany*	318
⚙	*Hülsta, Germany*	318
▮	*Veneers, solid wood, particleboard*	278-80
♻	*• Renewable materials • Blue Angel eco-label • Corporate environmental vision and policy*	327

Spiga

Mimicking an ear of corn, this lightweight coat rack, made of seven thin, wave-shaped, plywood cutouts attached to a metal-rod frame, is an ideal resting place for coats, hats, umbrellas, bags, newspapers and more throughout its entire length.

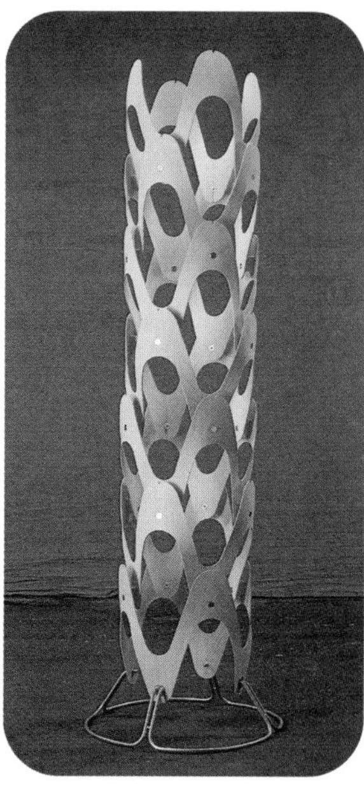

✎	*Ubald Klug, France*	308
⚙	*Rothlisberger, Switzerland*	323
▮	*Plywood, metal*	295, 339
♻	*• Economy of materials usage • Multifunctional*	327, 329

Good Morning Miss Moneypenny

Not all waste newspapers and magazines need to be manhandled down to the nearest local authority recycling point. Save those special editions and insert them into a specially cut polypropylene tube to create an eclectic, customized hat and coat stand. El Ultimo Grito wittily create a valid green design by combining recycled and recyclable materials with self-assembly. They revitalize the 'Heath Robinson' approach to invention and elevate recycling to a new art form. Tired with the current look? Simply exchange the old papers with fresh, up-to-date material.

✎	*El Ultimo Grito, Spain*	306
⚙	*El Ultimo Grito, UK*	306
▬	*Newsprint*	341
♺	*• Reuse of domestic waste* *• Low-energy construction and self-assembly*	327, 328

Hut Ab

Aluminium fixings allow simple machined pieces of ash wood to articulate around a pivot to provide a multifunctional clothes and hat stand, drying rack or structure for suspending house plants. Low-energy requirements during production make this an efficient design at low cost.

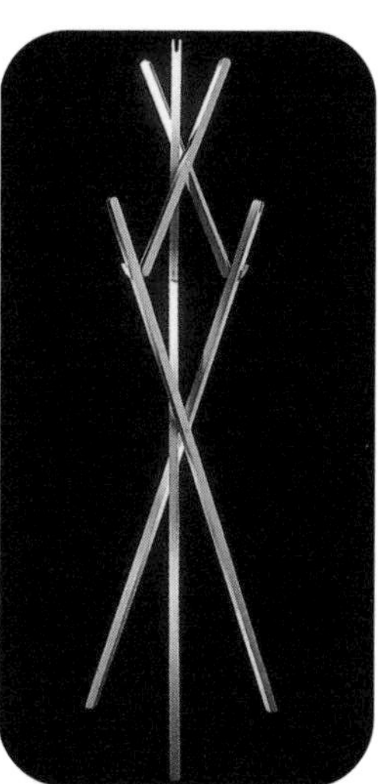

✎	*Konstantin Grcic, Germany*	307
⚙	*Nils Holger Moormann, Germany*	321
▬	*Ash wood, aluminium*	295, 339
♺	*• Multifunctional design* *• Renewable and recyclable materials* *• Low-energy manufacturing*	327, 329

Screen

A slender metal frame supports a web of interwoven plastic string. This lightweight screen can be fabricated from virgin or recycled materials, doesn't require specialist machinery to construct and is easily dismantled at the end of its life, when the materials can be salvaged. Fabrication can easily be adapted to suit locally available materials.

Fernando and Humberto Campana, Brazil	305
One-off limited batch production	
Metal, plastic string	283, 295
• Economy of materials usage	327

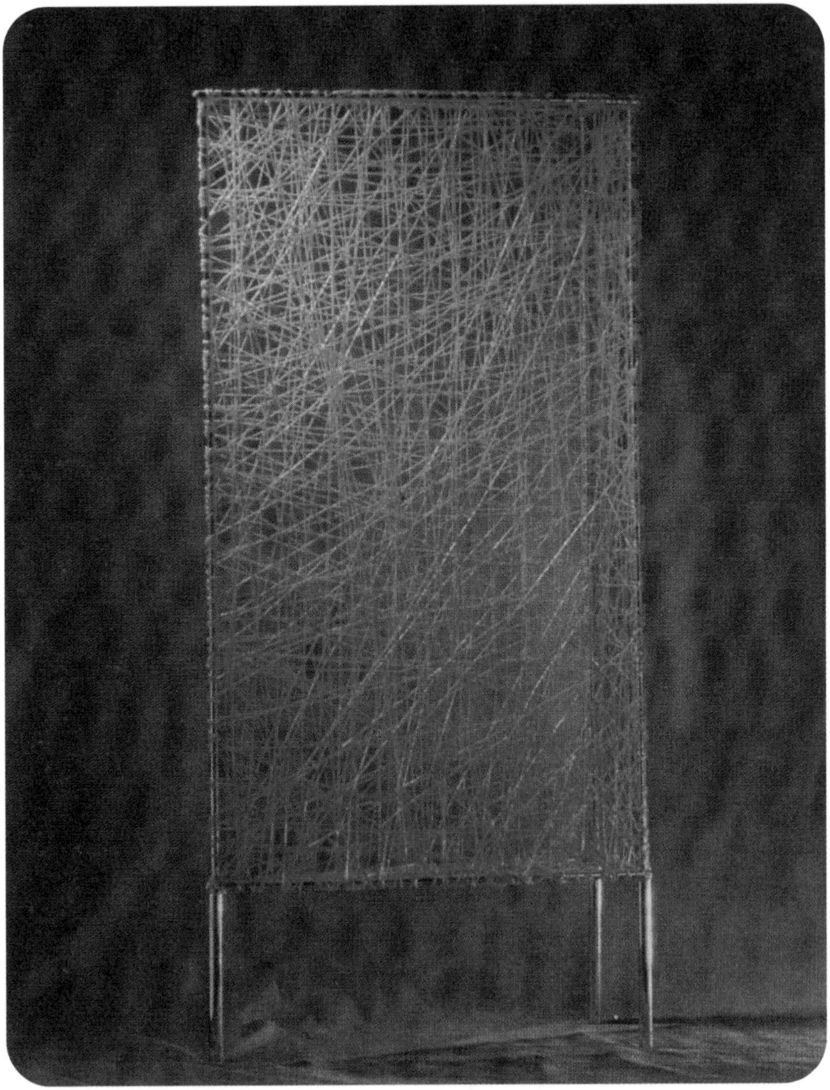

Screens, various furniture

Designer-maker Jason Griffith goes by the venerable title of 'underwoodsman'. The ancient craft of the underwoodsman can be traced back five thousand years in Europe. Using a wide variety of timber taken from native or naturalized coppiced trees (those deliberately cut to cause multistems), he fashions everything from hazel hurdles or screens to tables, benches and chairs. The output of the underwoodsman is sustainable thanks to low-energy production techniques based on manual labour and locally sourced wood as well as encouragement of the system of coppicing, which helps maintain biodiversity.

✎	*Jason Griffiths, UK*	307
⚙	*One-offs and small batch production*	
▬	*Coppiced wood of oak, ash, yew, sycamore, lime, alder, hazel, birch, willow, sweet chestnut*	339, 341
♻	• *Renewable resources* • *Encourages conservation and biodiversity* • *Low-energy production*	327, 328, 330

Portable double bed

Anyone who has moved house knows that the most cumbersome item is the double bed. Not so for this superb example, an entire double bed that can be neatly carried in its own suitcase. Bucking the trend for self-assembly furniture to be flat, stylistically drab and infuriatingly difficult to assemble, Steinmann and Schmid have devised a construction system that is not only rapid to assemble but also visually appealing.

✎	*Peter Steinmann and Herbert Schmid, Switzerland*	310
⚙	*Atelier Alinea, Switzerland*	312
▬	*Beechwood, plywood, steel, rubber*	283, 339
♻	• *Portable, self-assembly furniture* • *Economy of materials usage*	327, 328

Bernini

Fabricated from Tyvek, a HDPE fabric containing 25 per cent-recycled content, this flouncy chandelier illustrates the drapability of plastic fabrics. Water-based adhesives and the use of a single material facilitate later recycling.

Designer	*Ruth McDermott and Rina Bernabei, Australia*	304, 308
Manufacturer	*One-off*	
Material	*Tyvek*	301
Eco	*• Part recyclate fabric • Recyclable*	327
Award	*IDRA award, 1996*	332

Coral, Polyp, Spores

Moerel demonstrates the flexibility and hence the beauty of her raw material in this series of designs, which are inspired by the same basic module, a ceramic sphere. Coral and Polyp are two variants for unusual pendant lights, while Spores are individual candleholders. Economy of scale is possible if large-scale production can utilize different modular spheres to make a range of products.

Designer	*Marre Moerel, Netherlands/USA*	308
Manufacturer	*Small batch production*	
Material	*Clay*	295
Eco	*• Use of abundant materials from the geosphere • Durable*	329, 340

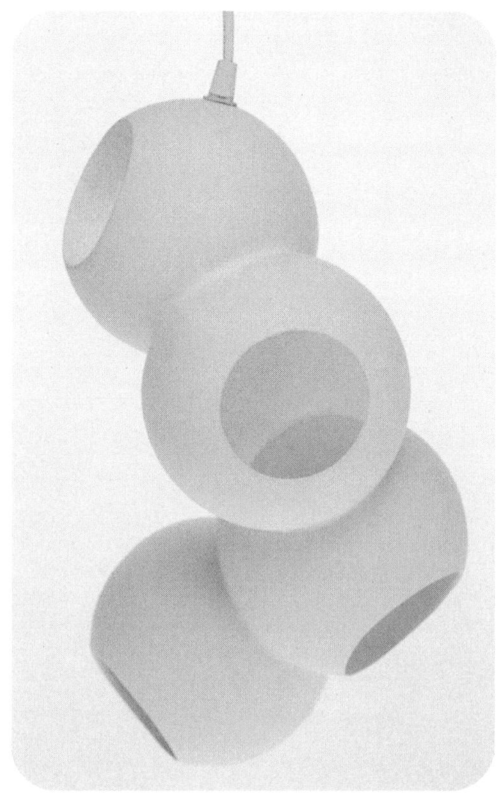

Quentin

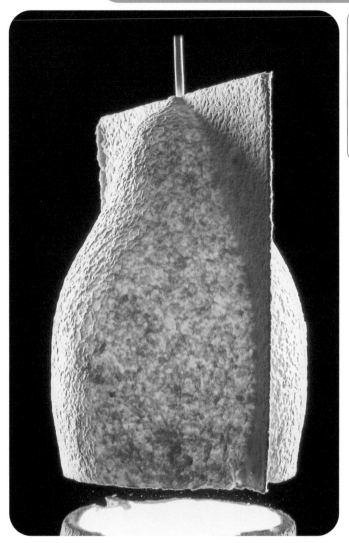

The designers were inspired by the complex forms of folded cardboard packaging and utilitarian products such as egg boxes. Working in collaboration with a local Glaswegian manufacturer, they sought to create a product utilizing pulp from recycled newsprint and paper-mill waste. An individual shade comprises two identical but mirror-image halves, which are formed in a mould where the pulp is vacuum-drawn. These innovative lampshades are semi-opaque, giving a unique light output. The shades can be deployed individually or in groups to form customized arrangements. At the end of its useful life the lampshade can be repulped ready for its next reincarnation. Potentially this product can sit within a closed recycling loop, ensuring maximum reuse of paper fibre and minimizing the energy required to remanufacture the product.

	Ian Cardnuff and Hamid van Koten, VK & C Partnership, UK	311
	Universal Pulp Packaging, UK	325
	Newsprint, paper waste	341
	• *Recycled and recyclable materials* • *Low-energy manufacturing*	327, 328

Fish-lamp

Drilling holes in a standard pendant lamp fitting enables the brass suspension arms to support the frosted glass pane, which acts as a diffuser for the down-lighting spotlight.

	Mikala Naur, Denmark	309
	Limited batch production	
	Brass, glass	295
	• Recyclable materials • Economy of materials usage	327

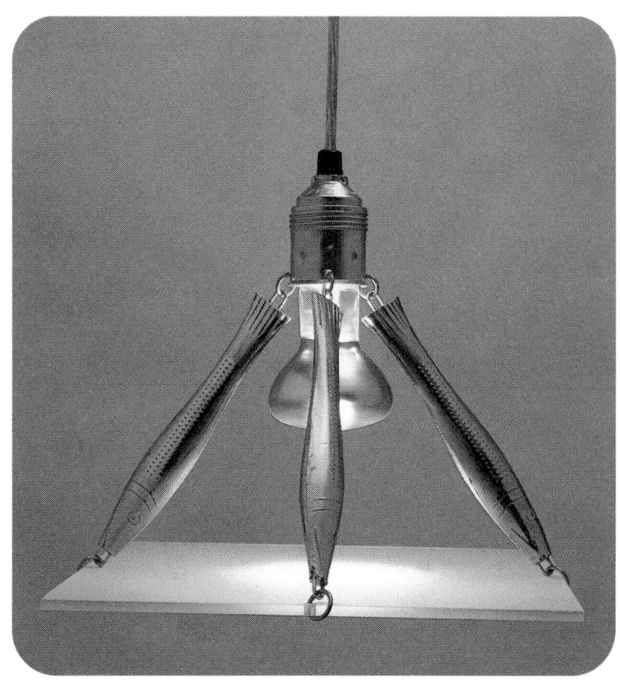

Flirt

Flirt is a redesigned object using a plastic float made for commercial fishing nets to create a dramatic lampshade with two different lighting zones – a diffuse zone from the body and a white cone from beneath the shade. An aluminium 'hat' is the only specially made part.

	Sergio Macchioni, Italy	308
	Prototype	
	Fishing floats, aluminium	295, 341
	• Use of ready-mades • Low-energy manufacturing	327, 328

Lampshade

Interlocking moulded forms of corn-starch biopolymer fit together to make this organic shaped lampshade. This prototype avoids the use of adhesives, is recyclable and/or compostable and demonstrates the potential of biopolymers to replace non-renewable plastics.

✎	*Brian Dougherty, USA*	306
⚙	*Prototype*	
	Corn-starch biopolymer	282
	• *Renewable, compostable biopolymer*	330
	IDRA award, 1998	332

Lampshade

This reversible shade permits a choice of two strong lighting directions depending upon whether the reflector is uppermost (for down-lighting) or on the underside (for up-lighting). This eloquent design embodies principles of minimalism and dual-functionality, both of which are very relevant to designs with reduced environmental loads.

✎	*Sebastian Bergne, UK*	304
⚙	*Radius GmbH, Germany*	322
	Steel	295
	• *Dual-function design* • *Economy of materials usage*	327, 328

Miss Ceiling light

Efficient use of a single natural material creates a lampshade with sculptural characteristics, permitting shafts of light and a warm glow to penetrate the semi-opaque natural plywood and creating a dramatic light source.

✎	*Jasper Startup, Startup Design, UK*	310
⚙	*Startup Design, UK*	310
▦	*Plywood*	339
♻	• *Renewable single material* • *Economy of materials usage* • *Low-energy manufacturing*	327, 328

Milk-bottle light

Since the early 1990s designers have responded to the challenge to consider their ethical responsibilities to the environment. In the Netherlands Tejo Remy explored the issue using discarded plastic milk bottles and in the UK Jane Atfield did the same with her RCP2 chairs using recycled plastic sheeting. As a consequence the message – that modern design must use recycled materials – is eloquently delivered.

✎	*Tejo Remy, Droog Design, Netherlands*	306, 309
⚙	*Droog Design/DMD, Netherlands*	306, 315
▦	*Discarded bottles*	341
♻	• *Reuse of waste ready-mades*	327

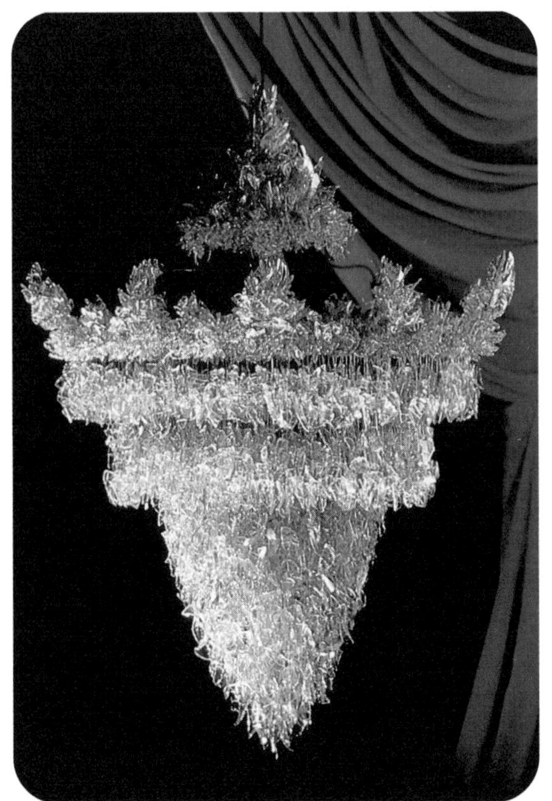

Northern Fleet chandelier

Shards of broken glass are painstakingly assembled into a cascade of light in this unique chandelier. The jagged edges of the glass make an exciting contrast with the sheer beauty of the final form and the design gently mocks at the cut-glass chandeliers of grand houses and public buildings. Quality, one-off designs may enjoy long lives, since they may attract greater custodial care than run-of-the-mill, mass-produced objects.

✎	*Deborah Thomas, UK*	310
⚙	*One-off*	
▮	*Glass, wire*	295
♺	*• Recycled materials*	327

Loop

Distributed as a flat-pack pendant shade or floor light, the Loop, made of polypropylene, simply snaps together.

✎	*Roy Sant, UK*	310
⚙	*Roy Sant, UK*	310
▮	*Polypropylene*	341
♺	*• Lightweight, recyclable single material*	329

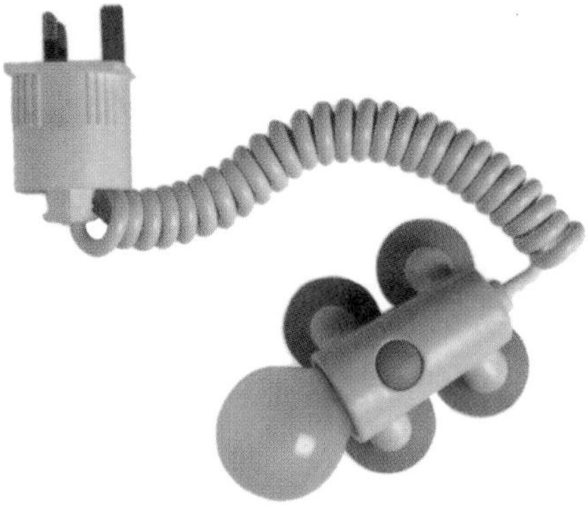

Bogdan light

Wherever there is a power point let there be light! With the 'sucker' feet on the housing of this minimalist portable light you can attach it to any smooth surface. Except for the bulb holder, all other parts are readily available from existing manufacturers.

✎	*Erik Espmark, Sweden*	306
⚙	*Prototype*	
▬	*Plastics, copper wire, brass*	283, 295
♻	*• Multifunctionality*	329

Cape light

The lightweight polypropylene structure is assembled by pushing together the steel studs. A swivelling head permits direct down-lighting for home-office working and up-lighting for those romantic domestic encounters.

✎	*Stephen Philips, UK*	309
⚙	*Stephen Philips Design, UK*	309
▬	*Polypropylene, steel*	295, 341
♻	*• Dual-functional lamp • Lightweight materials • Low-embodied energy of transport*	328, 329

'ComeBack' series

Plastic packaging waste is reincarnated as a beautiful series of shades for table, standard and pendant lamps. The diversity of colour of the original waste source is reflected in the random, mosaic-like arrangement in the manufactured sheeting that is the base material for the shades.

	Bär + Knell, Germany	304
	Bopp Leuchten GmbH, Germany	313
	HDPE waste	341
	• Recycled material	327

Clips

A simple stainless-steel frame clips over a discarded drinks can and supports a polypropylene shade. As your favourite brand of drink changes you can dispose of the old one (at a can bank) and insert a can that held the flavour of the month.

✎	*Bernard Vuarnesson, France*	311
⚙	*Sculptures-Jeux, France*	323
▬	*Polypropylene, stainless steel*	295, 341
♻	• *Encourages reuse of ready-mades* • *Reduction in materials usage*	327

Flamp

This wooden-based table lamp is dipped in phosphorescent coating so that it absorbs the energy from sunlight and reradiates it for up to twenty minutes. An ideal 'emergency' light after sunset.

✎	*Martí Guixé, Spain*	307
⚙	*Small batch production*	
▬	*Phosphorescent paint, wood*	286-7, 298
♻	• *Solar-powered non-electric light*	329

Corkscrew/lamp

Complex messages originate from this seemly simple design by Carl Clerkin. The candle set in the wine bottle is given a sophisticated turn as ready-made components are clipped together, giving us a new look at the phenomenon of electricity. This design can encompass the whole social spectrum, from wine buffs keen to impress with their empty vintage bottles to cash-poor students.

✎	*Carl Clerkin, UK*	305
⚙	*Small batch production*	
▬	*Reused wine bottle, corkscrew, electrical components*	341
♻	• *Reused and ready-made components* • *Easily disassembled*	327, 328

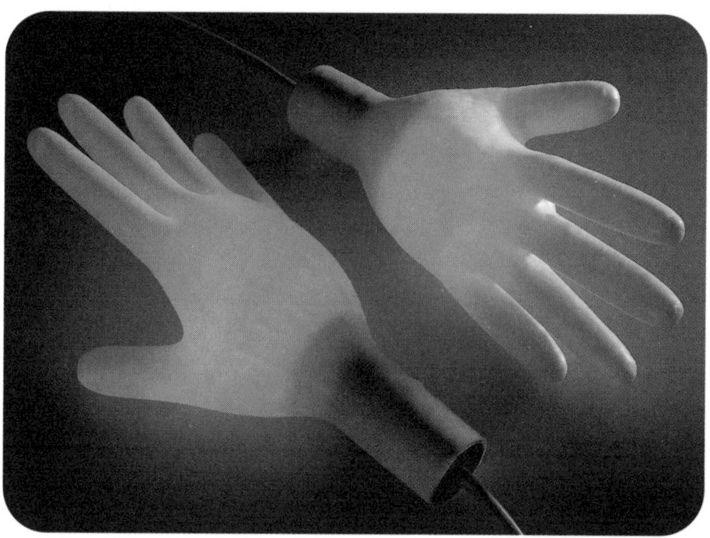

Hand (to Hold)

This lamp generates surreal mood lighting by combining a familiar ready-made, a rubber glove, with a 4W lamp unit.

✎	*Anette Hermann, Denmark*	307
⚙	*Frandsen Lyskilde, Denmark*	317
▬	*Latex, lamp*	283, 341
♻	*• Ready-made component • Renewable material*	327

Table/floor lights

Recycled cardboard may carry a print message from its previous incarnation as packaging. Reuse of cardboard in a new context, in this case a lamp, extends the life of this otherwise transient raw material, which is just waiting to be recycled. In short, this lamp is the temporary custodian of the cardboard, which has its own life to be lived over and over again.

✎	*Ksenkja Jurinec, Grupa Dizajnera, Croatia*	307
⚙	*Prototype*	
▬	*Recycled cardboard*	341
♻	*• Recycled materials*	327
✪	*IDRA award, 1997*	332

Light Wall 2

A room divider made up of plastic floppy-disk cases on a low-voltage (12V) wiring loom provides a unique display for a range of semi-transparent pictures and casts a pattern of shadows and light.

Designer	*Janne Øhre, Denmark*	309
Manufacturer	*MDD, Denmark*	320
Materials	*Plastic disk cases, aluminium profiles, wires, bulbs*	341
Eco-design	*• Low-voltage lighting • Ready-made components*	327, 329

Lumalight lamp

This family of free-standing lights, made of recycled paper, reveals that the use of recycled materials does not inhibit creativity. In the hands of the right designer, the fact that the materials are obviously recycled is lost in the beauty of the overall design.

Designer	*Roland Simmons, USA*	310
Manufacturer	*Interfold, USA*	318
Materials	*Recycled paper*	341
Eco-design	*• Recycled materials*	327
Award	*IDRA award, 1995*	332

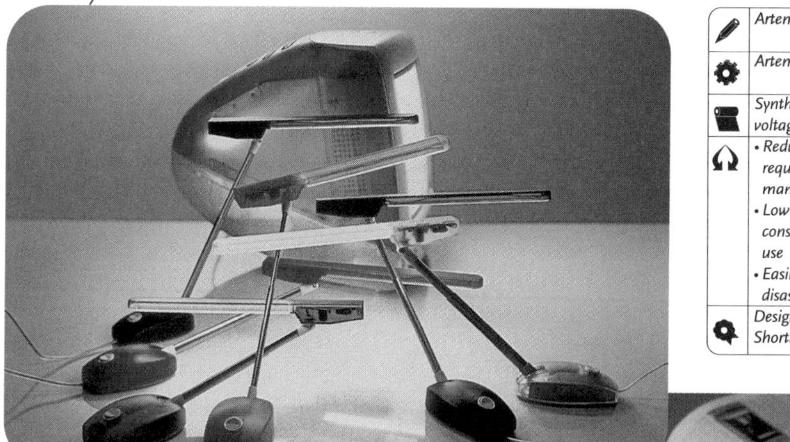

✎	Artemide SpA, Italy	312
⚙	Artemide SpA, Italy	312
▮	Synthetic polymers, low-voltage lamp	296-7, 341
♻	• Reduction in materials required in manufacturing • Low energy consumption during use • Easily repaired and disassembled	327, 328
✪	Design Sense awards, Shortlist, 1999	332

e-light

The e-light integrates a number of technological improvements over conventional desk lamps. The lifetime of the lighting filament is twenty times greater than that of an incandescent bulb and two to three times that of a fluorescent bulb and uses one-fifteenth as much mercury as the latter. Creating a light spectrum similar to daylight, it is five times brighter than a tungsten bulb. As the e-light produces negligible thermal emissions, the need for heat-resistant materials is significantly reduced. Components can be easily separated, facilitating recycling and reuse. Reversible joints and compact design provide flexible lighting configurations and a small footprint.

Obinjo

Candles and paraffin lamps were the portable light sources usurped by the invention of electricity and the tungsten bulb. Yet electricity tethered lamps to a fixed circuit and output sockets. So it is refreshing to see that Frits Vink has reintroduced us to the benefits of portable lamps. Obinjo recharges itself on a base connected to the mains supply and is therefore completely portable. With this we can wander from room to room without having to switch on any fixed lights.

✎	*Frits Vink, Netherlands*	311
⚙	*Prototype*	
▮	*Various*	
♲	*• Portable, rechargeable, multifunctional lighting*	329

Mini desk lamp

Good ideas are often recycled, but the Mini Desk Lamp actually goes one step further by reusing part of an iconic design of the late 1950s, British Leyland's Austin Mini car designed by Alec Issigonis. Original Austin Mini parts for the distinctive sidelights are rehoused in a plastic body, fitted with an automatic on/off tilt switch and painted in the original body paintwork colours. The rebirth of a mini Mini classic?

✎	*Paul Topen, Designed to a 't', UK*	306, 311
⚙	*Designed to a 't', UK*	306
▮	*Steel, plastic, electrical wiring*	341
♲	*• Reuse of ready-made components*	327

Tube

The familiar fluorescent light gets the minimalist treatment from Christian Deuber. A slender synthetic tube protects the light with steel- and rubber-footed closures, allowing the light to be placed wherever it is required. The use of fluorescent bulbs, in this case 58W, which are much more efficient users of energy than incandescent sources, adds to the versatility of this product.

✎	*Christian Deuber, N2, Switzerland*	306, 309
⚙	*Palluco, Italy*	321
▮	*Fluorescent light, steel, rubber*	283, 341
♲	*• Multifunctional light • Economy of materials usage • Low energy consumption*	327, 328

PO98 10/10C, 11/11C, 12/12C

In a clever extrapolation of scale, the table lamp becomes a floor or standard lamp. These lightweight constructions combine visual stimulation and humour in an economical design.

Designer	*Marcel Wanders, Netherlands*	311
Manufacturer	*Cappellini SpA, Italy*	314
Materials	*Wire, polymer*	296-7
Eco	*• Economy of materials usage*	327

Pharos floor lamp

The designer has succeeded in transforming a garden cane with a cylindrical papyrus shade into an elegant, minimalist standard lamp. Natural variability within the papyrus paper creates a range of unique textures and light patterns, mimicking the spun-fibre shades of the 1950s.

Designer	*Jasper Startup, Startup Design, UK*	310
Manufacturer	*Startup Design, UK*	310
Materials	*Bamboo, papyrus paper*	281
Eco	*• Renewable materials* *• Low-energy manufacturing*	327, 328

PO/9902C-D

Framing the bulb not only focuses the viewer on the light source but also provides a protective package during distribution and retailing.

✎	*Jeffrey Bernett, UK*	304
⚙	*Cappellini SpA, Italy*	314
	Cardboard, lampholder	288-9, 341
	• Economy of materials usage	327

Soft Box

Special clays are fashioned into durable lighting units. Ceramics are traditionally used for bases for table lamps but here the material forms the base and the shade.

✎	*Marre Moerel, Netherlands*	308
⚙	*Prototype*	
	Earthenware, porcelain	295
	• Abundant, inorganic materials	327

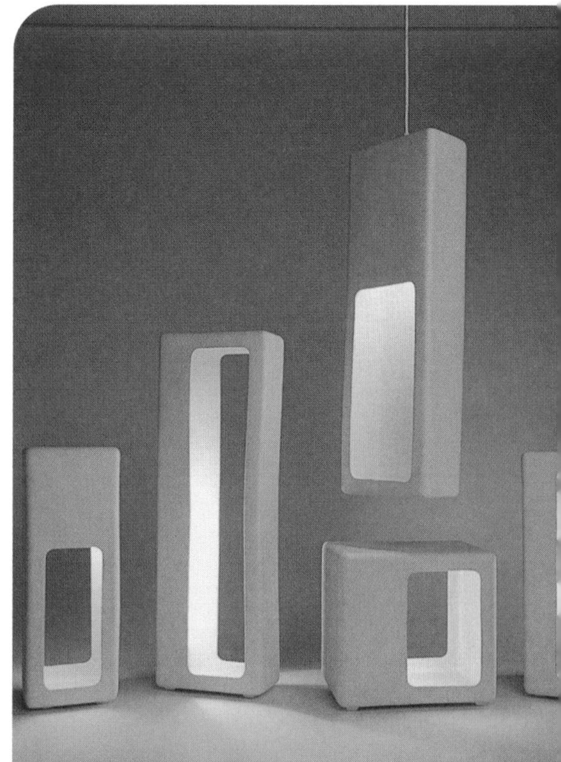

Post It lamp

A strong cardboard tube with plastic end caps arrives through the post, the contents are extracted and within minutes it is assembled into a compact but functional table light. While not particularly robust, the Post It Lamp minimizes transport emissions and costs, as the packaging is used to form the lamp base. This is a neat idea that can be extended to other design applications.

✎	*2pm Limited, UK*	312
⚙	*2pm Limited, UK*	312
▬	*Cardboard, plastic, paper, electrical components*	341
♻	• *Economy of materials usage* • *Reduction in energy of transport and assembly*	327, 328

Table lamps

Inexpensive extruded tubes of 100 per cent-recycled HDPE are cleverly juxtaposed with another extruded component to produce an easily assembled and attractive floor lamp. This is proof that the use of recyclates does not limit or stifle design. Indeed, it can be argued that the constraint of using only recyclates can generate creativity.

✎	*Wojtek Stachowicz, USA*	310
⚙	*One-offs, small batch production*	
▬	*Recycled HDPE*	341
♻	• *Recycled materials*	327
✪	*IDRA award, 1995*	332

Sailbuoy Canvas

Four coloured filters can be fitted to the polypropylene-paper laminate shade to alter lighting mood. A wooden base is fitted with a lampholder for a 10-watt compact fluorescent lamp (CFL), ensuring low energy consumption and heat output.

✎	*Neil Wilson, UK*	311
⚙	*Lampholder 2000 plc, UK*	319
▬	*Polypropylene, paper, wood*	341
♻	*Multifunctional task or mood lighting*	329

The Eye of the Peacock

Plastic bottles are shredded and reconstituted to form a fascinating melange of colour and texture, the original bottle tops and sealing rings further enhancing the texture and variety of this wall panel. Illuminated from behind with fluorescent lighting, this wall panel illustrates the capacity of new materials to create a visual stimulus.

✎	*Bär + Knell, Germany*	30
⚙	*One-off*	
▮	*HDPE and LDPE bottles*	34
♲	*• Recycled materials*	32

Table/floor lights

Precision laser-cut Trupan MDF is combined with paper and steel rods with birch ball feet to create an intriguing form, which exposes all the unfinished raw materials. Economical use of natural coloured materials illustrates the ability of such products to compete with more established lighting designs.

✎	*Burges Zbryk, E + Z Design, USA*	306, 311
⚙	*E+ Z Design, USA*	306
▮	*MDF, paper, steel, birchwood*	295, 339
♲	*• Renewable and recyclable materials*	327
✪	*IDRA award, 1997*	332

Table lamp

This little lamp recontextualizes banal, everyday objects such as cutlery into a new, revitalized, sculptural form. Examining the potential uses of existing products has its rewards.

Stichting Art Depot, Netherlands	310
Small batch production	
Reused cutlery	341
• *Reused objects* • *Reduced energy of manufacturing*	327, 328
IDRA award, 1997	332

Light columns

Plastic packaging waste offers a wonderful palette of colours and graphical shapes when recycled and reconstituted into thin, semi-opaque sheeting. Suitable for one-off, small-batch and high-volume production, these long cylinders of plastic recyclate illuminated with fluorescent lamps create an eclectic range of decorative lights.

Bär + Knell, Germany	304
One-off	
Discarded plastic packaging	341
• *Recycled materials*	327

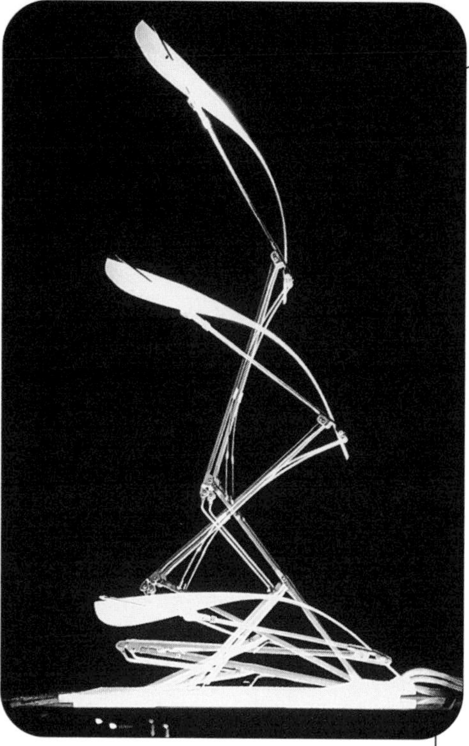

Valvestem candlestick

This product is the culmination of researching local sources of suitable salvaged manufactured components available in sufficient quantities for large-scale production. The original design was driven by the availability of a stock of valve stems from diesel engines. Other components were tested to see if they would fulfil the required functions of holding the candle and collecting wax. Valve lifter springs proved particularly effective as candleholders and are easily cleaned of excess wax by bending the spring.

✎	*R+r Sustainable Design, USA*	309
⚙	*R+r Sustainable Design, USA*	309
▮	*Reused valve stems and lifter springs*	341
♻	*• Reuse of redundant manufactured components*	327
✪	*IDRA award, 1997*	332

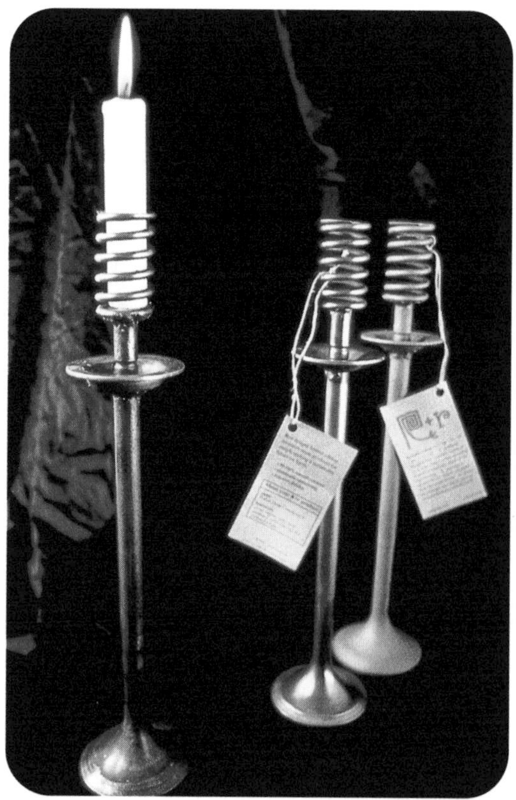

Viva

Borrowing from the Italian tradition of using ready-mades espoused by Achille Castiglioni and others, the designers took an existing folding umbrella, called Knirps, and converted it into a quirky, amusing, folding light. Many other products await a similar process of reincarnation.

✎	*Manuel Ribeiro Bandeira de Vianna, Brazil, and Francisco Gomez Paz, Argentina, Domus Academy, Italy*	306
⚙	*Prototype*	
▮	*Reused umbrella*	341
♻	*• Reuse of existing product*	327

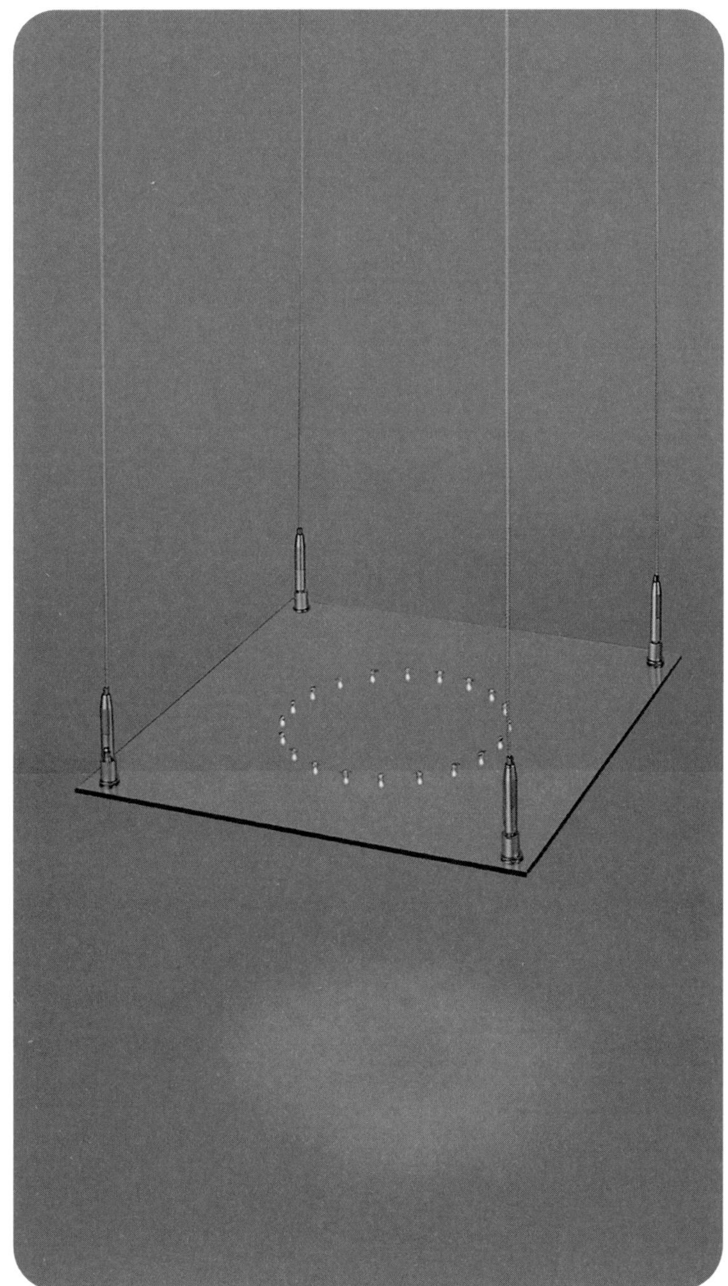

Powerglass®

A sandwich of conductive material, which is completely transparent, is embedded between layers of ordinary glass. Single or multilaminate conductive glass affords different power-carrying capacities, so this patented technology can be used a range of applications for lighting, switches, electronic displays and so on, especially for low-voltage applications.

✎	*Glas Platz, Germany*	317
⚙	*Glas Platz, Germany*	317
▬	*Transparent conductive material, glass*	295
♺	*• Transparent electrical conductor*	329

Delight

This decorative wall panel doubles up as a wall lamp. The seductive ambience of the light is provided by the coloured shade of silicon. Individual units can be paired to create distinctive floor lamps.

✎	*Adrien Gardère, France*	306
⚙	*Ligne Roset, France*	319
▬	*Silicon, electronics, lamp*	341
♻	*• Multifunctionality*	329

Wall bracket

Stripped down to its bare essentials, this wall bracket represents an economical design. The electronic ballast and compact fluorescent lamp (CFL) holder sit on a simple pressed-metal bracket to which a curved sheet of polypropylene is attached.

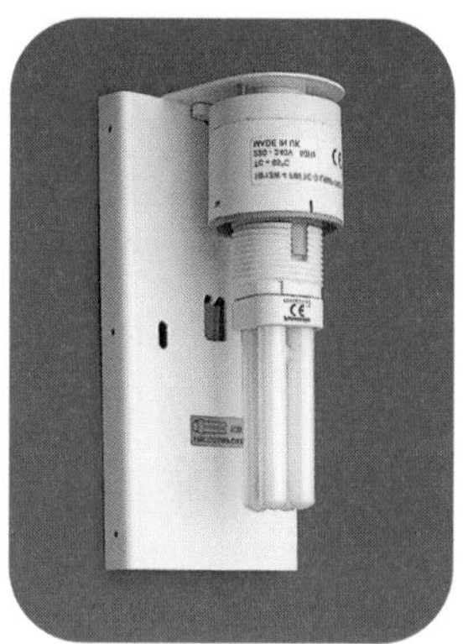

✎	*Lampholder 2000 plc, UK*	319
⚙	*Lampholder 2000 plc, UK*	319
▬	*Metal, polypropylene*	295, 341
♻	*• Economy of materials usage* *• Low-energy lighting*	327, 329

Helmut

This tough, colourful outdoor lamp reveals its origins from the different coloured fractions of HDPE recycled plastics that are reconstituted in this interesting design, which shows off their innate characteristics to maximum effect.

✎	*Bär + Knell, Germany*	304
⚙	*Bopp Leuchten GmbH, Germany*	313
▬	*Recycled plastic*	283, 295
♻	*• Recycled content*	327

Moonlight MFL

A robust, weatherproof, semi-translucent, polyethylene material is moulded in four sizes and fitted with different sockets to enable the low-wattage lamps (5-23 watts) to be fixed into the earth or used on hard surfaces. Feel a mood swing coming on? Simply change the coloured bulb filter, choosing from up to 250 colours. Moonlight MFL is a versatile, low-energy, 'mood and colour', indoor/outdoor lighting system.

✎	*Moonlight Aussenleuchten, Germany*	320
⚙	*Moonlight Aussenleuchten, Germany*	320
▬	*Polyethylene*	341
♻	*• Multifunctional lighting* *• Low energy consumption*	329

Pod Lens

Most lighting is static, irredeemably rooted to the electric cabling built into the fabric of the building. Pod Lens is a modular system of a polycarbonate pod unit with bulb and flex and a series of bases for standard or floor lighting. For indoor or outdoor use, the pods provide for flexible and decorative lighting at the whim of the user.

	Ross Lovegrove, UK	308
	Luceplan, Italy	320
	Polycarbonates, electrical components	296-7
	• *Multifunctional lighting system* • *Upgradability and repairability*	329

Outdoor light

Plastic recyclate feedstock was worked by rotational moulding to create a tough, translucent, granite-like textured shade. Special fittings were developed to take advantage of the energy savings of compact fluorescent light bulbs.

	Meta Morf, Inc., USA	320
	Meta Morf, Inc., USA	320
	Recycled plastic, aluminium scrap, regard steel	341
	• *Recycled materials* • *Low-energy lighting system*	327, 329
	IDRA award, 1997	332

Solar Bud

A photovoltaic panel generates energy from sunlight, stores it in a battery and releases it to three low-voltage, red LEDs, all in a self-contained unit, which is placed in the desired position by pushing it into the soil or other suitable medium. Ideal for garden decorative or safety lighting, the Solar Bud would also be at home in the window box of an urban bedsitter.

	Ross Lovegrove, UK	3[illegible]
	Luceplan, Italy	32[illegible]
	Metals, photovoltaics and light emitting diodes (LEDs)	29[illegible]
	• *Solar-powered lighting* • *Very low-energy LED bulbs*	32[illegible]

Tsola

Most outdoor, solar-powered lights are above-ground installations, which makes them vulnerable to the elements, accidental damage and vandalism. Tsola is designed to be installed flush with the ground and can be walked or driven upon without damage. This low-maintenance light is equipped with a timer that automatically switches the light off in extended hours of darkness to conserve the stored energy in the battery.

✎	*Sutton Vane Associates, UK*	324
⚙	*Sutton Vane Associates, UK*	324
▬	*Photovoltaics, heavy-duty glass, stainless steel, battery*	295
♻	*• Solar power*	329

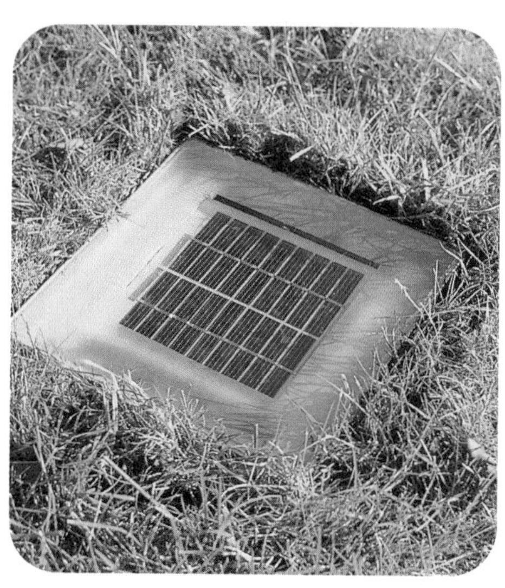

Outdoor light

Proving that form and function are not compromised by using recyclates, this outdoor light fitting is made from 60 per cent-recycled glass blasting beads. Its curvaceous form reveals an inner glow suitable for security and decorative outdoor lighting.

✎	*John M Staton, USA*	310
⚙	*One-off*	
▬	*Recycled glass*	295
♻	*• Recycled materials*	327
✪	*IDRA award, 1995*	332

✎	Iain Sinclair Design, UK	318
⚙	Iain Sinclair Design, UK	318
▣	Stainless steel	295
♻	• Economy of materials usage and energy consumption	327
✪	iF Design Award, 2000	332

EON
Applications with LED lighting technology encourage economical use of materials, none more so than this credit card-sized torch made of stainless steel in a recyclable casing.

Freeplay flashlight

Manufacturers of the renowned Freeplay wind-up radios have extended their product range with this hand-powered torch.
The design represents a significant improvement on the inexpensive but fairly useless small torches produced since the 1970s, in which squeezing a lever by hand generates a feeble and rather wobbly light. Now a few minutes' cranking produces a steady, reliable light source without the need to consume lots of toxic batteries.

✎	Freeplay Energy Europe, UK	317
⚙	Freeplay Energy Europe, UK	317
▣	Plastics, rechargeable battery, electronic components	296-7
♻	• Human-powered light • Avoidance of hazardous consumables	329

Aladdin Power

Generating electricity by using a hand-wound generator is not a new idea. The Russian army has supplied its conscripts with a robust, hand-powered torch since the 1940s and plastic-bodied, hand-cranked torches have been available since the 1970s. But Nisso Engineering's design uses lighter, modern materials to improve the efficiency of the design and possibly make this an attractive option for powering other hand-held electronics such as mobile phones. However, these hand-cranked torches do not permit any energy storage in a battery or in a wind-up mechanism as featured in Freeplay Energy's products.

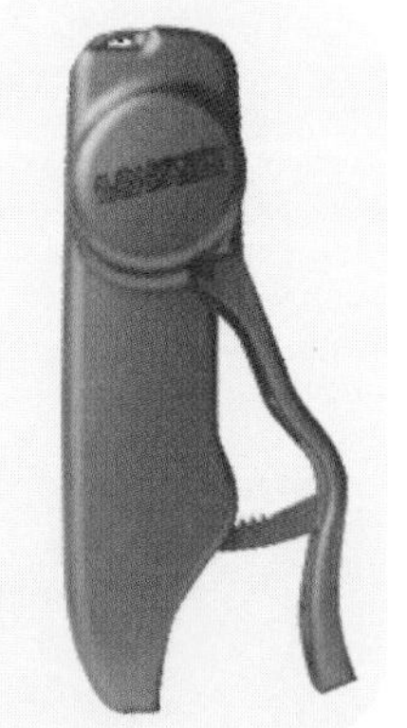

✎	Nisso Engineering, Japan	321
⚙	Nisso Engineering, Japan	321
▣	Polymers, electronic components, dynamo	296-7
♻	• Renewable energy source • Reduces waste (battery) production	327, 328

Hedda Besse, IDEO Product Development for BP Solar International, UK	304, 307
BP Solar International, UK	313
Photovoltaic cells, polycarbonate, stainless steel	341
• *Solar power*	329

L48 Solar lantern

A photovoltaic panel charges the battery, which can provide up to four hours' light from one charge. The lamp is robust and portable and operates in extreme temperatures.

SL-Torch

An 80 per cent reduction in materials usage is achieved by making the battery into the handle in this neat torch design. Insert the battery into a housing, which holds the bulb, and twist to turn on the torch.

Antoine Cahen, Les Ateliers du Nord, Switzerland	305
Leclanché, Switzerland	319
Battery, bulb, plastic	341
• *Reduction in materials usage*	328

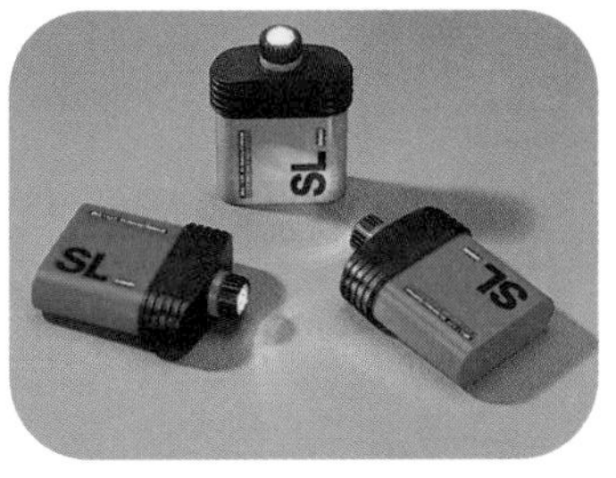

Solaris™ lantern

Two hours of sun provide one hour of light for this lantern, which is capable of functioning at -30°C (-20°F) and altitudes in excess of 7,000 metres (23,000 feet). Fully charged, the NiMH battery, which is free of mercury, cadmium and lead, will provide light for six hours, but if the battery discharges 90 per cent of its capacity a low-voltage disconnect is automatically triggered. This saves battery life and ensures it will last for up to a thousand recharges.

Light Corporation, USA	319
Light Corporation, USA	319
Photovoltaics, plastics, NiMH battery	341
• *Renewable power source* • *Avoidance of hazardous substances in the battery*	329

Ecotone Ambiance Slimline

As the process of shrinking the compact fluorescent lamp (CFL) continues, Philips have developed a matt-glass, candle-shaped bulb with an E-14 thread. This encourages use of CFLs in a wider range of light fittings and so can help save energy. Available in 6W, 9W and 11W, the lamps are manufactured with a minimal amount of mercury and lead and have a projected lifespan of six years or so.

Designer	*Philips Lighting BV, Netherlands*	309
Manufacturer	*Philips Lighting BV, Netherlands*	309
Materials	*Glass, metals including mercury and lead*	295
Eco	*• Encouraging energy conservation*	329
Award	*iF Ecology Design Award, 2000*	332

Mini-Lynx Ambience

Although this CFL looks like a conventional incandescent bulb and is of the same size, it uses 80 per cent less energy. Making CFLs this size has been a considerable challenge, since the electronic ballast and convoluted fluorescent tubes produce bulbs that often protrude beyond conventional light fittings. Sylvania have extended the market reach by shrinking a standard CFL into the recognizable shape of an incandescent bulb and offering the bulb in white and, unusually, apricot and rose.

Designer	*Sylvania Design Team, UK*	310
Manufacturer	*SLI Lighting, UK*	324
Materials	*Glass, electronic ballast, plastic*	295
Eco	*• Low energy consumption*	329

Lampholder 2000

Compact fluorescent lamps (CFLs) with standard bayonet fixings include their own electronic ballast to 'kick-start' the light. Lampholder 2000 is a light fitting (in pendant, batten-holder, flush-mounted or down-light formats) with an integral electronic ballast suitable for direct usage of four-pin-connector CFLs. After three changes of a four-pin CFL it is more cost-effective than the standard bayonet CFL and reduces materials usage in production.

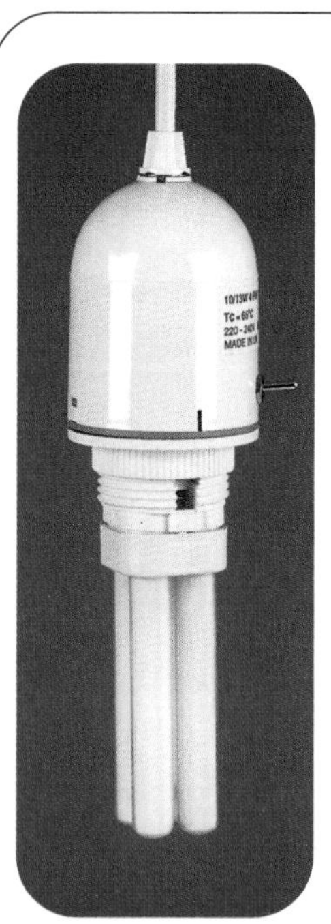

Designer	*Lampholder 2000 plc, UK*	319
Manufacturer	*Lampholder 2000 plc, UK*	319
Materials	*Various*	
Eco	*• Energy conservation • Reduction of materials usage*	329

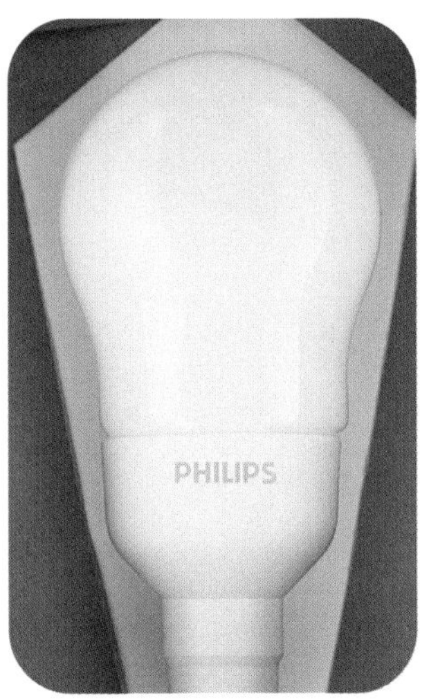

Philips Ecotone Ambiance

Although compact fluorescent lamps consume up to 80 per cent less energy than incandescent tungsten bulbs, the early CFL designs included a U-shaped tube, which often protruded when used in conventional fittings. Philips have created a satisfying compromise by reshaping the CFL to conventional lines and size, while still accommodating the electronic ballast in the base. Bulbs to 5W, 9W or 11W output are to the same basic design. The only downside of this energy-efficient story is that small amounts of mercury are required to manufacture each lamp.

✎	*Fons Baohm and Patrick van de Voorde, Philips Lighting BV, Netherlands*	309, 311
⚙	*Philips Lighting BV, Netherlands*	309
	Glass, plastics, electronics, mercury	283, 295
	•Low energy consumption •More universal shape for standard fittings •Long life	329

LED® DecorLED

Light emitting diodes (LEDs) operate on low voltages and are very efficient. Ledtronics offers a range of standard Edison base-fitting AC light bulbs in pear, globular and spot shapes. A bulb fitted with 17 LEDs provides full-spectrum white light equivalent to the illumination provided by a 25-watt conventional tungsten bulb but consumes only 1.7 watts. Typically these LED bulbs generate very little heat, 3.4BTUs/hr, compared with 85BTUs/hr for an equivalent tungsten bulb. Aside from offering huge energy savings, LEDs last up to ten times longer than CFLs and 133 times longer than tungsten bulbs.

✎	*Ledtronics, USA*	319
⚙	*Ledtronics, USA*	319
	LEDs, metal, glass	295
	• Reduction in energy consumption • Extended lifespan	329

iChef

Induction technology uses magnetic fields to transfer heat from a wire coil, generated by electrical energy, into the contents of a cooking vessel. Almost 95 per cent of the electrical energy is converted into heat, which is claimed to be five times more efficient than a gas ring and significantly faster than a conventional electric hotplate. Glass is used to separate the wire coil from the cooking pan or kettle but, as all the heat is transferred to the vessel, the glass top remains cool, providing a safety advantage over conventional cookers. Precise temperatures can be selected by using a digital display.

✎	*Induced Energy, UK*	318
⚙	*Induced Energy, UK*	318
▬	*Metal, glass*	295
♻	• *Improved energy efficiency and safety*	329

Aga

Aga-Rayburn cookers are a symbol of durable, classic design with over half a million units supplied to the UK and exported worldwide. 'Agas', as they are fondly known, have been made near the iron-making town of Telford, Shropshire, since the beginning of the Industrial Revolution. Indeed, the Coalbrookdale foundry, which supplies castings for the cooker, made sections of the world's first iron bridge in 1779 at Ironbridge. Scrap and pig iron are the raw ingredients to create the handmade cast iron sections that form the basic components of the cooker. Poor-quality castings are simply recycled. Originally a solid-fuel cooker, the Aga-Rayburn has been improved over the years to accept oil, natural or propane gas or off-peak electricity, and since the 1940s also can provide domestic hot water and central heating needs. Agas are a coveted status symbol in any domestic kitchen, representing 'good middle-class taste'. There may be more energy-efficient designs on the market but few can match the lifespan of an Aga, which, of course, can be refurbished and/or recast in the future.

✎	*Dr Gustaf Dalen, Swedish physicist, 1920s*	
⚙	*Aga-Rayburn, UK*	312
▬	*Cast iron*	295
♻	• *Recycled and recyclable materials* • *Durability*	327, 329

Solar cooker

Cardboard coated with a special reflective surface focuses the sun's energy on to a dark-coloured cooking pot. In subtropical and tropical regions it is possible to save the equivalent of 30 per cent of the annual firewood consumption of a typical household using this cooker. This device provides people in the developing world who face fuel wood shortages with the means to sterilize water and have hot food.

✎	*Bernard Kerr and Pejack Campbell, USA*	304
⚙	*Solar Cookers International, USA*	324
	Cardboard, reflective foil	341
	• Passive solar power	329

Café Duo HD 1740/42, Cucina Duo

This slimline one- or two-cup coffee maker combines aesthetic flair with Philips's high eco-standards. In-line drip filters are easily removed from the top, the product in stand-by mode does not consume any electricity and all parts are marked for recycling.

✎	*Philips Design, Netherlands*	309
⚙	*Philips Electronics BV, Netherlands*	322
	Metal, thermoplastic, electrical components	341
	• Energy efficient • Design for disassembly and recycling	328, 329
	iF Design Award, 2000	332

Glass kettle, glass toaster, microclimate

Stefano Mazzano, director of design at Philips Electronics, coordinated a project whose task was to consider the issue of 'anonymity in design'. In the ultra-competitive marketplace for electronic products, often it is only the brand name that identifies the product, although companies such as Apple Computers have consistently demonstrated that eye-catching aesthetics with product performance will always capture market attention. Consumer surveys conducted by Philips indicated that functionality is not the only criterion on which purchases are made. Products are purchased because they reflect something of the consumer's personality. This fact was well established in the mid-1990s and is catered for by the Philips-Alessi range of products dating from that time on. The challenge is still to re-engage consumers and encourage them to re-examine kitchen appliances. Philips see a vital combination of enhanced functionality, greater application of digital technology and inclusion of more 'personality' into future appliances. The Glass Kettle, Glass Toaster and Microclimate are conceptual prototypes that strive to reflect this new approach. The challenge is still to re-engage consumers and encourage them to re-examine kitchen appliances.

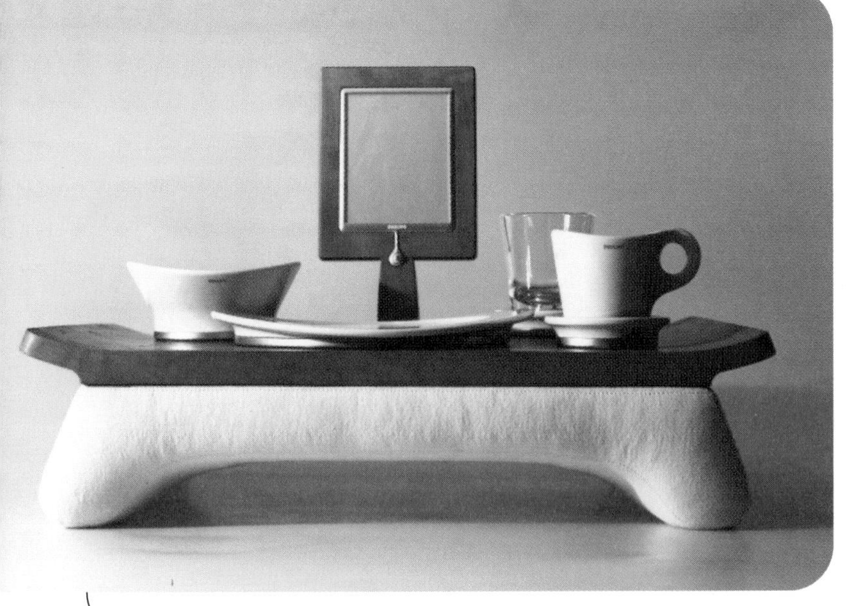

✎	*Philips Electronics BV, Netherlands*	322
⚙	*Conceptual prototypes*	
▮	*Glass, plastics, electronics*	295
♺	*• Improved energy performance and user functionality* *• Potential increase in longevity*	329

Rondo

All components of this hand-held sprayer can be separated for repair and recycling. This facility also means that customers can choose the colour and finish of the central 0.75-litre-capacity (1.3-pint) ball. An adjustable nozzle and pump pressures up to 3 bar make this a functional cleaning tool.

✎	*BEST, Büro für Produktgestaltung, Germany*	304
⚙	*Gloria-Werke, H. Schulte-Frankenfeld, Germany*	317
▬	*Various polymers and metals*	295-7
♻	*• Recyclable components*	327

POLTI Ecologico AS810

For those who suffer from asthma this vacuum cleaner is a boon. Its water-based filtration system removes 99.99 per cent of dust up to 0.3 microns including pollen, dust-mite faeces and cigarette smoke. Paper bags are replaced with a removable water filter, which is emptied after use and has an approximate lifetime of six months.

✎	*Polti, Italy*	322
⚙	*Polti, Italy*	322
▬	*Various plastics, metals*	295-7
♻	*• Reduction in use of consumables* *• Improved health environment*	328, 329

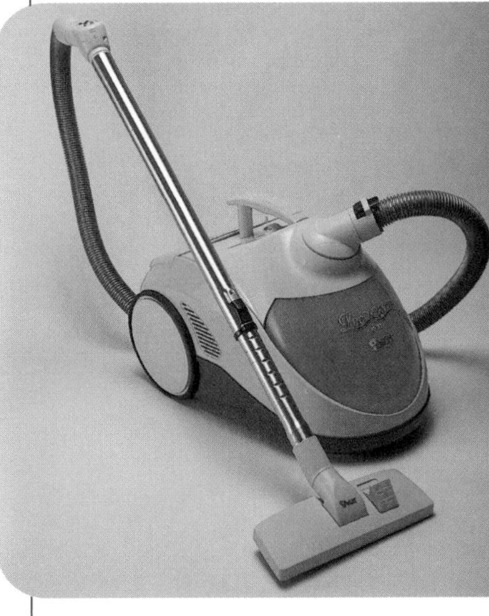

Kärcher 670 M

This product incorporates many design features that will become standard practice for manufacturers who have a responsible attitude to the environment. Metal and plastic components are discrete and easily separated, the latter being mainly ABS and PA, which are recyclable. The manufacturer guarantees to take back the product when its useful life is over. The original cardboard packaging is kept to a minimum, the manual is printed on recycled paper and the machine is virtually maintenance-free.

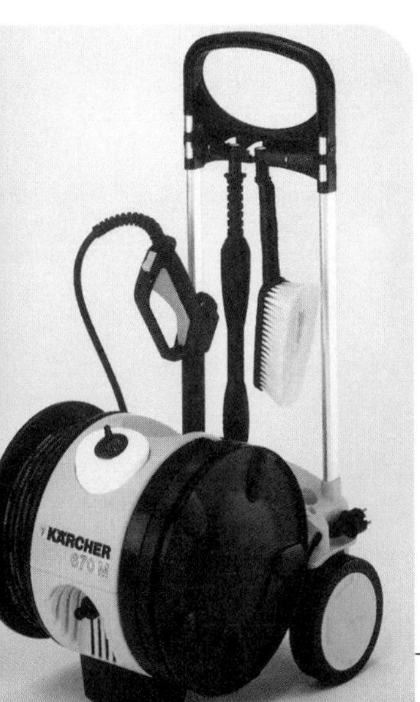

✎	*Teams Design, Germany*	310
⚙	*Alfred Kärcher GmbH, Germany*	312
▬	*recyclable plastics, metals*	295-7
♻	*• Design for disassembly, maintenance-free* *• Manufacturer takes back product at end of its life* *• Minimal-packaging efficiency*	327, 328, 330

Dyson Dual Cyclone range

Hoover and other major manufacturers of vacuum cleaners watched their global market share decrease as James Dyson's bagless version, using two ultra-fast spinning centrifugal chambers, grabbed a significant market share in the 1990s. Unlike conventional cleaners, in which suction decreases as filters and bags become full, the cyclone system maintains 100 per cent suction and the troublesome task of removing a full bag is replaced with emptying the contents of the main chamber. The original Dyson Dual Cyclone was introduced to the UK in 1986 but didn't find commercial success until 1993, when the DC02 became the best-selling upright cleaner. Dyson Appliances now produce a range of upright and horizontal vacuum cleaners and the cyclone system has been established worldwide as other manufacturers introduced similar machines to their existing ranges. Today the principle of centrifugal vacuum design is well established, eliminating the wastage of vast quantities of paper bags.

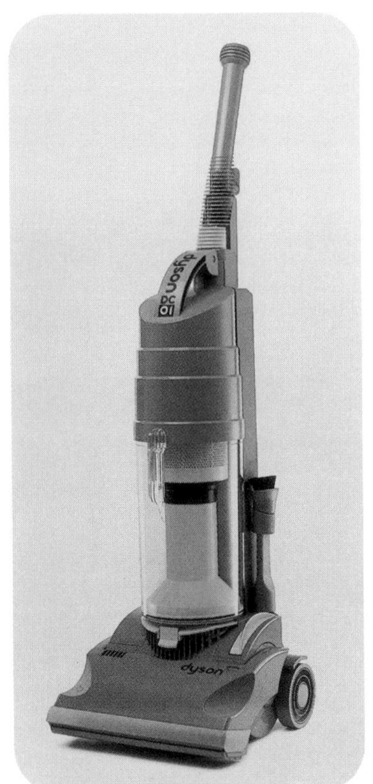

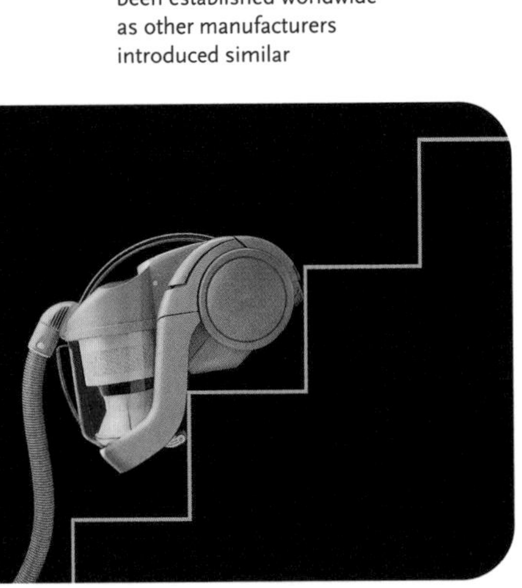

✎	*James Dyson and Dyson Appliances, UK*	306
⚙	*Dyson Appliances, UK*	315
▮	*Plastics, motor, electrics*	283, 295
♻	*• Avoids use of consumables (paper bags)* *• Improved efficiency with greater cleanliness and health* *• Design for easy maintenance*	327

POLTI Vaporetto 2400

Super-heated steam is an effective agent in cleaning and sterilizing carpets, mattresses and upholstery, which obviates the need to use strong and/or toxic chemical cleaners. Steam is also a safer method than insecticides of killing dust mites and other insects. Tap water is heated in a pressurized steel container and dispersed via the outlet hose, which can be fitted with a range of brushes and hose-ends.

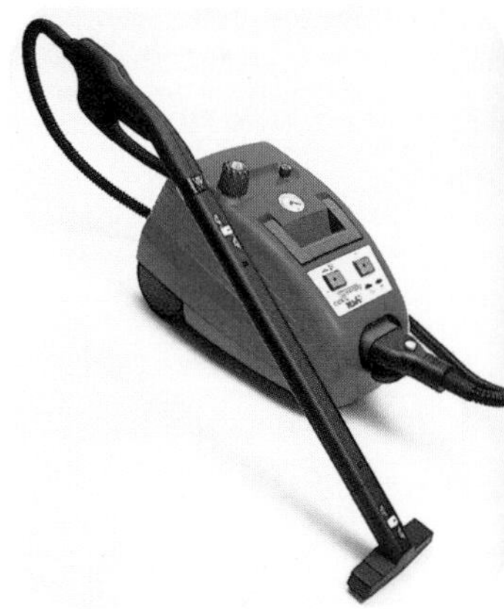

✎	*Polti, Italy*	322
⚙	*Polti, Italy*	322
▮	*Various plastics, stainless steel*	283, 295
♻	*• Reduction in use of consumables* *• Improved health environment*	327

Öko-Lavamat 86720**

Combine advanced rinse technology (ART) with Fuzzy-Logic microprocessors in an Öko-Lavamat body and one is close to defining one of the world's most efficient washing machines. Five kg (11 lb) of dirty cotton laundry washed at a 60°C (140°F) cycle require only 39 litres (8 gals) of water and 0.89 kWh of electricity, placing model 86720 in the EU's Energy Label highest-efficiency 'A' class and well within the EU Eco-label thresholds. Water quantity, wash temperature and cycle time are controlled by the microprocessor, which can be upgraded as new detergents and other washing aids are developed.

✎	*AEG, Germany*	312
⚙	*AEG, Germany*	312
▬	*Steel, metals, rubber, electronics, motor and pump*	283, 295
♻	• *Energy and water conservation*	329, 330

Titan

Ever thought of putting your laundry basket inside your washing machine? This is the solution developed by Monotub Industries, which designed a laundry tub that is inserted at an angle into the machine. Water is delivered from stainless-steel jets embedded into the walls of the tub, whose load capacity is 40 per cent higher than average machines. With its wide-opening door and push-button control panel using familiar symbols and icons, the Titan meets EU 'A' ratings for wash performance and energy efficiency.

✎	*Monotub Industries with TKO Design and Cock & Hen, UK*	320
⚙	*Monotub Industries, UK*	320
▬	*Polypropylene, steel, electronics*	295, 341
♻	• *High energy and water efficiency* • *Combined laundry storage and washing system*	329, 330

Hoover Quattro Whisper Easy Logic model AE230

In 1993 Hoover became the first manufacturer of washing machines to be awarded the EU Eco-label, which sets threshold values of 0.23kWh/kg for energy usage and 15 litres of water per kilogram (1.5gals/lb) of laundry, with its New Wave range of machines. The company has steadily built on its reputation for efficient machines 'A' rated under the EU Energy Label. The current range includes the Quattro Whisper Easy Logic system, which uses sound-absorbing panels and improved suspension to reduce operational noise. A Powerjet spray system and larger than average drum facilitate wash movement, ensuring that a 5kg (11lb) load takes only 49 litres (10.8gals) of water.

✎	*Hoover Group, UK*	318
⚙	*steel, plastics, electric pump and motor*	283, 295
▬	*Various*	
♻	*Low energy and water consumption*	329, 330

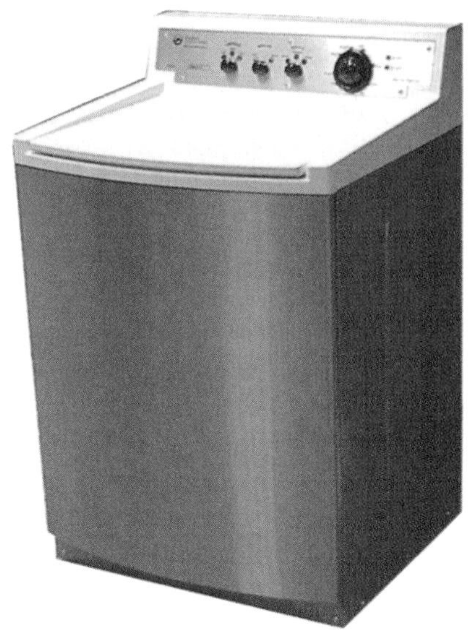

Staber System 2000

Bucking the trend for horizontal-axis-driven front-loading washing machines, the Staber System 2000 offers a top-loaded machine into which the stainless-steel basket of laundry is introduced. Energy-saving features include the use of a variable-speed motor. Easy access to the internal components can be gained by lifting the front panel and fitting a self-cleaning filter, thus facilitating maintenance. The manufacturers claim reduced energy, water and detergent consumption.

✎	*Staber Industries, USA*	324
⚙	*Staber Industries, USA*	324
▬	*Stainless steel, steel, resin and various other materials*	284, 295
♻	*• Energy and water conservation • Energy efficient to Energy Star guidelines*	330

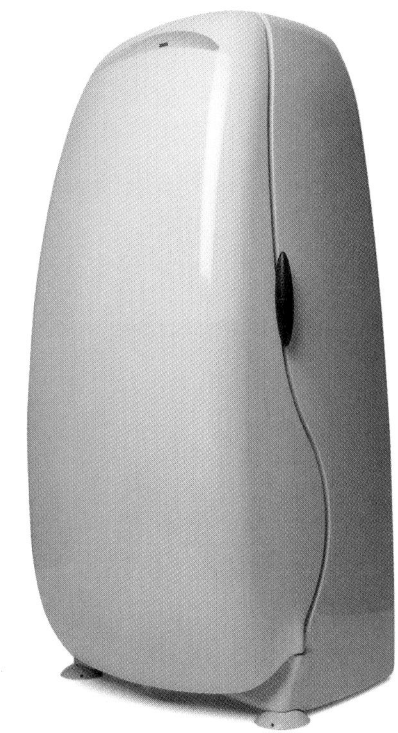

OZ23

Curvy lines and a 'rollerball' foot to the door give better access than conventional fridge-freezers to the cold storage and freezer spaces, which here have a capacity of 211 litres (46 gallons). Attention to detail is evident in the use of 'CFC-free' isobutane R600A coolant and cyclopentane insulation, which reduce the impact of harmful aerial emissions; in the EU Energy Label 'A' rating for appliances; and in the low noise level of the compressor motor, which hums along at a quiet 38dbA. Whether this model has greater longevity than other current models and is easy to maintain and repair remain to be seen but an appliance with such personality might just receive a bit more care and attention from the owner. The end-of-life scenario is also important – will Electrolux Zanussi be taking these back?

	Roberto Pezzetta, Luciano Pesavento, Zanussi Industrial Design Centre, Italy	309
	Electrolux Zanussi, Italy	315
	Various	
	• Improved functionality *• Energy efficient*	329

Planet DC

This DC refrigerator/freezer of 0.33cu m (11.6cu ft) capacity, operates from 12V or 24V and can be sustained with any small, domestic, renewable-energy system using deep-cycle batteries, for example, a photovoltaic module capable of generating 150W.

	Planet, USA	322
	Planet, USA	322
	Various	
	• Low-voltage device for domestic renewable-energy systems	329

Supercool™

Traditional refrigerant manufacturing involves the use of chlorofluorocarbons (CFCs, HCFCs) as coolants but Supercool AB have exploited the Peltier effect of a doped bismuth telluride thermocouple, which avoids using any of the ozone-depleting gases. A thermoelectric panel operated on a low-voltage system (12V, 24V) consumes a modest 10W to provide sufficient cooling for a small hotel minibar. A further advantage is that the mechanism operates silently, unlike the familiar hum of conventional coolant systems.

Supercool AB, Sweden	324
Supercool AB, Sweden	324
Thermoelectric module, bismuth telluride, plastic	341
• *Reduction in energy consumption* • *Non-toxic refrigeration system free of CFCs or HCFCs*	329, 340

Supercool™ box

A panel of thermocouples of doped bismuth telluride is capable of pumping heat and provides the cooling for this transportable refrigeration box suitable for commercial or domestic use at 12V or 24V.

Supercool AB, Sweden	324
Supercool AB, Sweden	324
Thermoelectric module, bismuth telluride, plastic	341
• *Reduction in energy consumption* • *Non-toxic refrigeration system free of CFCs or HCFCs*	329, 340

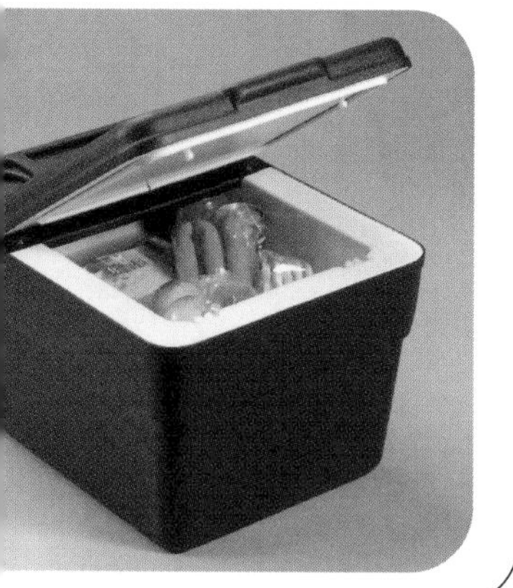

Vestfrost BK350

Vestfrost is one of the world's largest manufacturers of refrigerators and freezers and took an early lead in showing environmental responsibility by removing all CFCs and HFCs from its model range in 1993.

Using the alterrnative 'Greenfreeze' refrigerants, Vestfrost remains the only manufacturer in Europe holding the EU Eco-label for this category of appliances.

David Lewis, UK	308
Vestfrost, Denmark	325
Metal, plastics, rubber, electric motor and compressor	341
• *Low energy consumption* • *Clean production*	327, 329

Sycamore fan

Inspiration for the form of this mono-blade fan came from the humble winged seeds of the sycamore tree. This organic design uses recycled PET to create a lightweight blade that is energy efficient and quiet.

✎	*Danny Gasser, Michael Hort, Ben Sheperd and Quisinh Tran, Australia*	306
⚙	*Limited batch production*	
▮	*Recycled PET*	341
♲	• *Recycled materials* • *Reduction in energy consumption*	327, 329
✿	*IDRA award, 1997*	332

Soft fan

Resembling a wilted flower, the stationary fan comes to life as the electric motor builds up speed and centrifugal forces unfurl the fabric 'blades'. Once fully taut, the blades produce a whorl of colour and generate a wide-angle breeze. Unlike conventional metal- or plastic-bladed fans, the Soft Fan requires no guard.

✎	*Paul Priestman in collaboration with the Aeronautics Department, Imperial College, London, UK*	309
⚙	*Prototype*	
▮	*Fabric, plastic, electric motor*	283, 290-1
♲	• *Reduction in materials usage over conventional designs*	327

Wind

In the Industrial Revolution iron and steel usurped natural materials, so it is refreshing to see the process cleverly reversed in the housing of this electric fan, in which woven rattan replaces the conventional pressed sheet steel or plastic. At the same time the fan is transformed from an object of cold functionalism to one of playful character. Most of the materials can be recycled or composted.

✎	*Jasper Startup, Startup Design, UK*	310
⚙	*Gervasoni SpA, Italy*	317
▮	*Rattan, steel, electrics*	281, 295
♲	• *Recyclable and compostable materials*	327, 330

Felt 12 x 12

Be your own fashion designer using Fortunecookies's felt squares backed with Velcro: assemble a jacket, trousers, wedding dress or any other garment in your own personalized style. Bored with the look? Deconstruct your design and start again. Fashion is placed back in the hands of the consumer.

	Fortunecookies, Denmark	306
	One-off, Fortunecookies, Denmark	306
	Felt, Velcro	301
	• *Modular system for reuse of components* • *Renewable material (felt)*	327

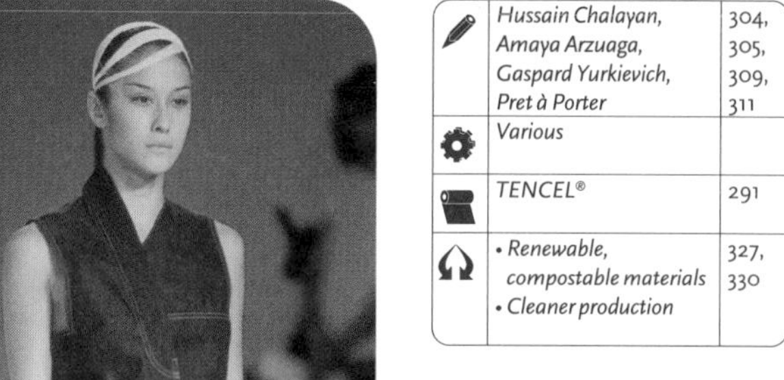

	Hussain Chalayan, Amaya Arzuaga, Gaspard Yurkievich, Pret à Porter	304, 305, 309, 311
	Various	
	TENCEL®	291
	• Renewable, compostable materials *• Cleaner production*	327, 330

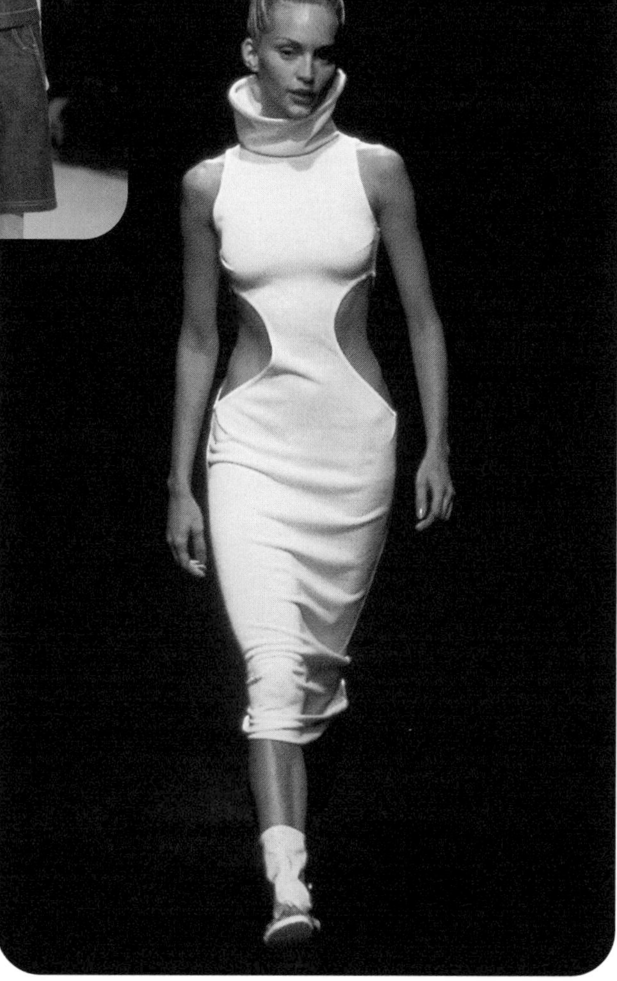

TENCEL® fashion garments

Three internationally renowned designers reveal the versatility of a manmade fibre using natural cellulose derived from managed forests. TENCEL® is from renewable resources and is manufactured in a closed-loop clean production process. With good drapability and a wide choice of surface finishes and weaves, TENCEL® fabrics offer the convenience and feel of modern synthetics and have a reduced impact on the environment. All this is proof that today's levels of comfort and style can be maintained without sacrificing the environment. TENCEL® is one of the modern success stories of the global textile industry.

10939 wedding dress

Hess Naturtextilien examined how the eco-efficiency of a typical wedding dress could be improved, bearing in mind the extravagance of using such a dress for a single day only. Their solution is to make a dress using 40 per cent woven hemp with 60 per cent silk with an organic cotton undergarment and lace. Manufacturing processes dramatically reduce chemical treatments and water consumption. For the first year of its life the dress is lent to a series of happy brides, thereafter it is made available for purchase. Hydrocarbon dry-cleaning replaces the traditional cocktail of volatile chemicals in between loans. And with luck the dress will be further reused by the bride's friends and relatives before being recycled via textile reclaimers.

Designer	*Hess Naturtextilien GmbH, Germany*	318
Manufacturer	*Hess Naturtextilien GmbH, Germany*	318
Materials	*Hemp, silk, cotton*	291
Eco-strategies	*• Hire rather than ownership* *• Renewable materials* *• Clean production*	327, 328
Awards	*Design Sense awards, Shortlist, 1999*	332

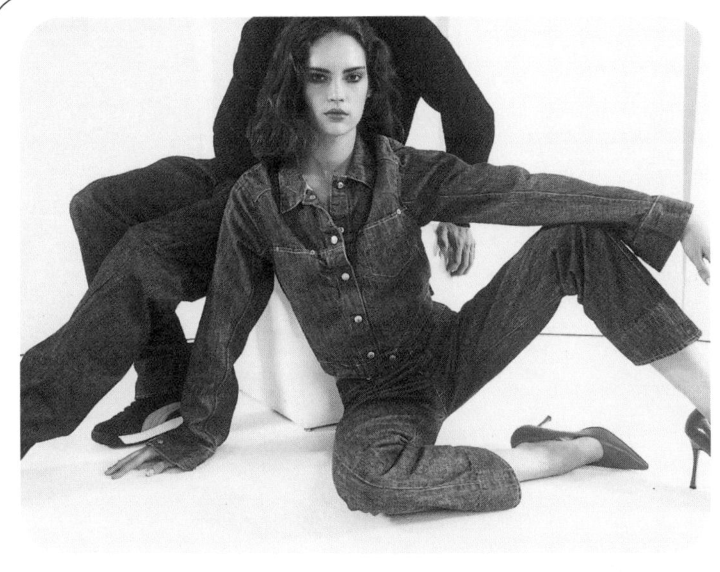

Levis Engineered Jeans

Jeans are firmly rooted in popular culture and have been the workwear garment of choice for millions over the last century. Cotton fibre has been the favoured raw material for all jeans manufacturers but cotton fabrics carry a significant raft of environmental burdens from pesticide applications and other toxic agents used in the textile production process. Today Levi Strauss, one of the world's largest clothing manufacturers, uses a special natural cellulose-based, low-environmental-impact fibre called TENCEL® for its new line of Levis Engineered Jeans.

✎	*Levi Strauss, Inc., USA*	319
⚙	*Levi Strauss, Inc., USA*	319
▬	*TENCEL®*	291
♲	*• Renewable, compostable materials* *• Clean production*	327

New Nomads

Out of the Vision for the Future project originated by Philips in 1997 emerged a collection of seventy prototypes including a range of New Nomads wearable clothing and objects for the IT age. Central to the concept of being able to wander around like a nomad while remaining connected to the information superhighway was the need to recharge equipment. Hence a multipocketed waistcoat becomes a recharging station for hand-held electronic equipment, as an attached solar panel stores energy in slim, lightweight batteries.

✎	*Philips Design, Netherlands*	309
⚙	*Prototypes, Philips Design, Netherlands*	309
▬	*Various textiles, electronics*	291
♲	*• Solar-powered wearable generator* *• Reduction in battery consumption*	329

Sensor sportswear

Today's fascinations with fashion and electronic technology find a meeting point in these prototype garments by Philips Design/Philips Research. Street-cred denim is embedded with an audio system in Audio Streetwear and in-flight communications are integrated into the stretch wool Imaginair-Airline Workwear outfits for cabin crew. Sensor Sportswear includes electronics to monitor bodily functions, while snowboarders intent on going off-piste can do so in the knowledge that the in-built global positioning satellite will stop them from getting lost. Water and electronics don't generally mix, so presumably the electronic elements can be detached before the clothing is consigned to the laundry bin.

	Philips Design/Philips Research, Netherlands	309
	Prototype	
	Textiles, electronics	291
	• Improved functionality	329

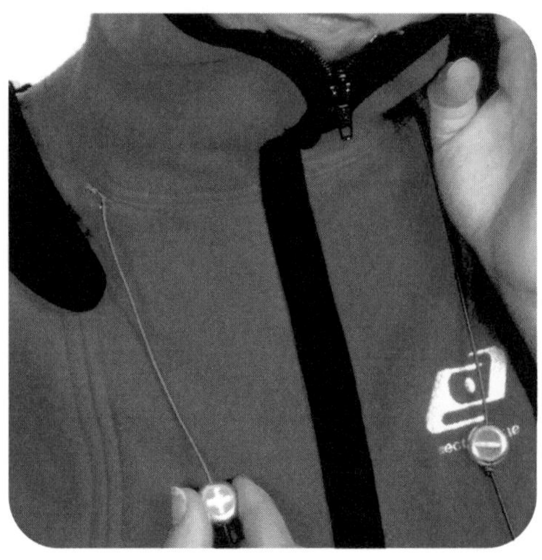

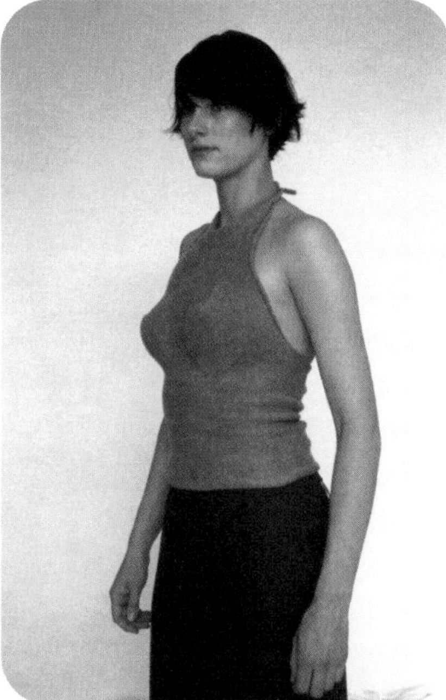

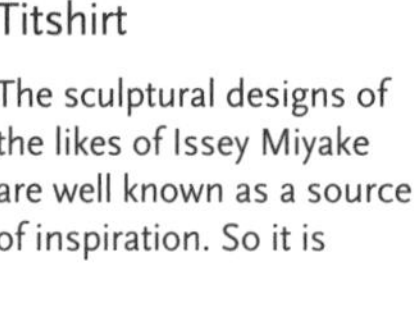

Titshirt

The sculptural designs of the likes of Issey Miyake are well known as a source of inspiration. So it is refreshing to see new talent examining the potential of 3-D techniques such as knitting to create garments that literally embrace the female form. Perhaps the days of the Wonderbra are numbered.

	Marije Vogelzang, graduate student 2000, Design Academy Eindhoven, Netherlands	311
	Prototype	
	Yarn	290-1
	• Exploring more comfortable clothing	329

Euro comfort...with an edge!™

Deep E® is a manufacturer of casual footwear with a policy of using environmentally and socially responsible materials. Part of the Brazilia collection, Euro comfort...with an edge!™ are durable slip-on casuals made from Sustana® leather and Nativa Rubber. Sustana® leather is from the organically raised cattle of the Coleman ranch, Colorado, and is tanned in Wisconsin with low-toxicity, trivalent chromium, chorine-free, water-based dyes and finishes and with maximum recycling and minimum effluent. Nativa Rubber is produced from latex harvested from wild trees in the Amazon, thereby helping to sustain the forest and local economy. Components are fixed with water-based rather than solvent-based glues. Deep E® is an excellent example of a business whose existence is based on the fundamental principle of sustainability.

✎	*Deep E®, USA*	315
⚙	*Deep E®, USA*	315
▤	*Leather, rubber*	283, 285
♻	• *Materials from renewable resources* • *Supply-chain management*	327

Wool felt slippers

A single piece of thick, 100 per cent-wool felt is wrapped around the foot and fastened with Velcro tape to form a comfortable slipper.

✎	*Daniel Ohlsson, Sweden*	309
⚙	*Small batch production*	
▤	*Felt, Velcro*	301
♻	• *Cold fabrication* • *Renewable material* • *Economy of materials usage*	327, 328

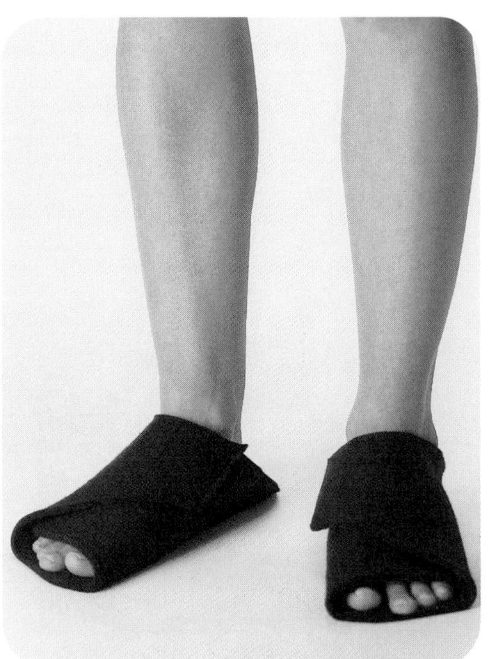

The Body Shop range

Since its formation in the 1970s the ethos of The Body Shop has been to provide a holistic, natural approach to body care and hygiene, with due consideration to the environmental, ethical and social responsibilities of the business. That approach still drives what has now become the role model for an ethical international business. Encouraging recycling of packaging materials, such as the HDPE bottles used for many formulations, is an integral part of the day-to-day business. Having used up the product, the user is encouraged to take the bottle back either for a refill or for recycling. Product information is generally printed directly on to the bottles to eliminate the need for stick-on labels and facilitate recycling.

	The Body Shop, UK	313
	The Body Shop, UK	313
	Natural oils, conditioners, soaps and recyclable HDPE	341
	• *Reusable and recyclable containers* • *High natural-content ingredients*	327, 330

DOMINO 4

Leather offcuts from hides processed using natural vegetable tannins are cleverly cut and stitched into new bags, the smooth surface of the leather contrasting with the texture of the cowhide. Fashion emerges from the production waste stream in a modern makeover of a classic 1970s design.

	BREE Collection GmbH KG, Germany	313
	BREE Collection GmbH KG, Germany	313
	Leather, cowhide	285
	• *Renewable materials* • *Reduction of production waste*	327, 328
	iF Design Award, 2000	332

La Vie Prolongée

There are two sides to the fashion coin: the mass-produced high-street brands and the unique one-offs or limited editions. Trachsel's work exemplifies the craft-based techniques. She takes old magazine pages, impregnates them with sunflower oil and encloses them in delicate organza fabric. These handbags exhibit a light touch in all senses of the word.

✎	*Sonja Trachsel, Switzerland*	310
⚙	*Small batch production, Sonja Trachsel, Switzerland*	310
▮	*Recycled magazines, sunflower oil, organza*	341
♻	*• Economy of usage of recycled and natural materials*	327

The Inner Tube

In the UK over 70 per cent of all inner tubes are incinerated or dumped in landfill sites. McDonagh transforms this waste into an eclectic fashion statement. Evironmental concern meets clubbers in the twilight zone. This design received a UK Millennium Product award.

✎	*Julie McDonagh, UK*	308
⚙	*The Inner Tube, UK*	318
▮	*Rubber from consumer uses*	283
♻	*• Reuse of waste materials*	327

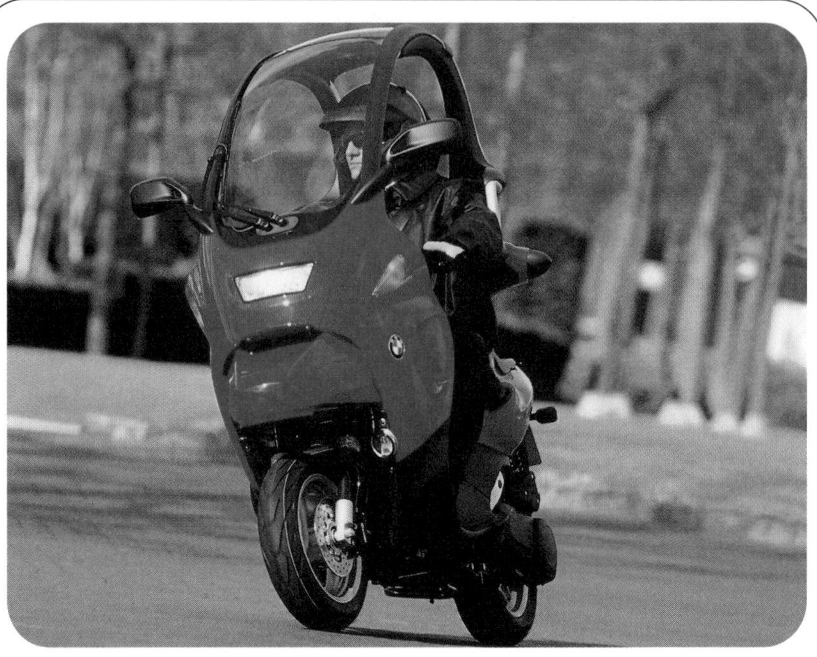

Citymobil C1

In May 1998, at the annual BMW Day of Technology, the Citymobil C1 was announced as a new-concept vehicle specially designed to offer individual mobility in cities and metropolitan areas. Single-occupancy cars account for almost 80 per cent of urban journeys. The C1, launched in April 2000, provides an alternative for urban car drivers who are frustrated with congested roads. Conscious of some of the drawbacks of two-wheeled transport, BMW have striven to improve safety standards and comfort. Crash bars and fairings and a stiff frame, resistant to twisting, provide front-end collision protection similar to that of a small car. An ABS option ensures skid-free braking and a unique curved windshield arches over the driver, providing better weather protection than conventional motorscooters. Fuel consumption is a respectable 2.9l/100km (about 97mpg) and emissions are reduced by a three-way catalytic converter. Can the C1 capture a new audience with its lower road tax and operating costs, reduced fuel consumption and lower emissions? The big question is whether the city suits and trendsetters will be lured out of the comfort of their existing vehicles.

	BMW, Germany	313
	BMW, Germany	313
	Alloy frame, rubber wheels, various plastics – some recyclable, recycled	285, 341
	• Reduction in fuel consumption and emissions *• Alternative mode of transport to single-occupancy cars*	329
	Design Sense awards, 2000	332

Ecobasic

If any European manufacturing company understands the requirements of the low-cost, small-car market it is Fiat. From the Topolino and the Fiat 500 series in the late 1940s and early 1950s to the Panda and Cinquecento in the 1980s and 1990s, Fiat has always kept true to its vision of economical products to ensure that the 'freedom of the road' really reaches a mass market. Ecobasic is the prototype for a production model capable of yielding about 35km/litre (100mpg) at a price of £3,300. This minimalist design incorporates a steel frame to which coloured plastic panels and a one-piece polycarbonate tailgate are fixed. A 1.2-litre, sixteen-valve, four-cylinder Fiat JTD turbodiesel engine is coupled with a five-speed manual gearbox. Selection of the 'econ' transmission mode automatically cuts the engine if the car is stationary for more than four seconds but the engine restarts as soon as the accelerator is pressed. Fixed rear side panels can be exchanged for doors if a four-door version is required.

✎	*Fiat Auto, Italy*	316
⚙	*Prototype, Fiat Auto, Italy*	316
▮	*Steel, thermoplastics, various other materials*	295, 341
♲	*• Reduction of fuel consumption* *• Lightweight, modular construction*	329

EV1

Launched in December 1996, the EV1 was General Motors's first production vehicle for non-commercial use to be entirely powered by an electric engine. It was an attempt to deal with the effects of state legislation to reduce vehicle emissions, such as the 1985 Californian law that set a 2 per cent sales volume of zero-emission cars by 1998. Capable of achieving 100km/h (62.5mph) in 9 seconds from a standing start and with a top speed of 129km/h (82mph), the EV1 was no slouch, but its performance was constrained by the 533kg (1,172lb) of batteries needed to move the vehicle's mass of 817kg (1,797lb). Fortunately developments in battery technology have ensured that such power-to-weight ratios are now a thing of the past.

✎	*General Motors, USA*	317
⚙	*General Motors, USA*	317
▮	*Various*	
♻	*• Zero emissions (assuming it is recharged from a renewable energy supply)*	329

Insight

Claimed to be the world's most efficient petrol-powered car, the Insight is actually a hybrid petrol/electric car featuring Honda's Integrated Motor Assist (IMA™). The IMA combines a high-efficiency 995cc petrol engine with a 10kW ultra-thin, in-line, brushless DC electric motor to achieve about 30km/litre (83mpg) and 80gm/km (4.5oz/mile) CO_2 emissions (less than half the EU2000 limit). Connecting directly to the crankshaft, the electric motor draws power from a 20kg, 144V nickel metal-hydride battery via an electronic Power Control Unit (PCU) when the car is accelerating, to provide 'Motor Assist'. This improves power output and low-speed torque. During deceleration the batteries are recharged, so the car is independent of external electricity sources. Reduction in kerb weight, which is just 835kg (1,837lb), is achieved by a lightweight aluminium body (borrowing design principles from the Honda NSX sports car).

✎	*Honda, Japan*	318
⚙	*Honda, Japan*	318
▮	*Various*	
♻	*• Fuel economy • Lightweight construction*	329

Daimler Chrysler CCV (Composite Concept Vehicle)

Borrowing heavily from the remarkable low-cost design of the Citroën 2CV (originally designed in 1949), the CCV project of 1997 focused on the need to produce an economical car for the markets in developing countries where rough roads and excessive loading regularly make unusual demands of passenger vehicles. An injection-moulded composite body is made of two halves attached with four bolts and adhesives to a steel frame and requires no painting. Production times are thus reduced to one-third or less of those for conventional cars, which are typically twenty hours per car. Costs of the PET are between 10 and 20 per cent of conventional material costs and reduce body weight to 545kg (1,200lb) and permit reasonable fuel economy, about 18km/litre (50mpg), for the small two-cylinder engine.

Designer	*Daimler Chrysler, USA*	314
Manufacturer	*Daimler Chrysler, USA (working prototype)*	314
Materials	*Main body panels: recyclable polyethylene terephthalate (PET)*	341
Eco-features	*• Recyclable plastic body panels • Reduction in use of materials and energy during production • Reduction in use of fossil fuels • Easily dismantled at end of life*	328, 329, 330

G90

Innovative weight-saving and excellent aerodynamics give fuel economy, which is further improved by the three-cylinder ECOTEC engine developed for the Corsa by Vauxhall Motors Ltd in the UK.

Designer	*General Motors, USA, with Vauxhall Motors Ltd, UK*	317, 325
Manufacturer	*General Motors, USA, with Vauxhall Motors Ltd, UK*	317, 325
Materials	*Various*	
Eco-features	*• Improved fuel efficiency*	329

ICVS (Intelligent Community Vehicle System)

The realization that transport systems need an urgent rethink has prompted industry, government and academia to examine so-called intelligent transport systems (ITS). One of the more advanced concepts is Honda's ICVS (Intelligent Community Vehicle System), whose working components are three electric vehicles and an electric/manual bicycle, which operate within a defined geographical area and under shared community usage. The City Pal four-five-seater compact electric car is a multi-user option and the other versions are for a single user. Two personal electric vehicles, the 'Stepdeck' and the 'Monopal', offer short-distance mobility suitable for inner-city business users, commuters and shoppers. Finally, the electric-assisted bicycle, 'Racoon', is an all-purpose, utilitarian mode of transport. In the ICVS cars and bicycles function as complementary tools in an urban ecosystem.

✎	*Honda, Japan*	318
⚙	*Prototypes*	
▬	*Various*	340
♲	• *Community rather than individual ownership* • *Reduction in air emissions from vehicles* • *Possibility of powering from renewable energy sources*	328, 329

Multipla and Multipla Hybrid Power

The Multipla is capable of carrying six passengers, in an upright steel space frame. Power unit options include a dual-fuel, 1.6-litre, sixteen-valve, four-cylinder engine capable of using petrol or methane. Methane is a clean fuel free from benzene and particles and gives a reduction of 25 per cent in carbon dioxide in the exhaust emissions. Further reductions are achieved in the Multipla Hybrid by combining a petrol engine with electric motor system. In hybrid operating mode 6.8 litres (1.5gals) of fuel plus 3kWh are consumed per 100km and in electric mode power consumption is about 30kWh per 100km (62 miles). The car produces about half the emissions of a conventional petrol-engined version.

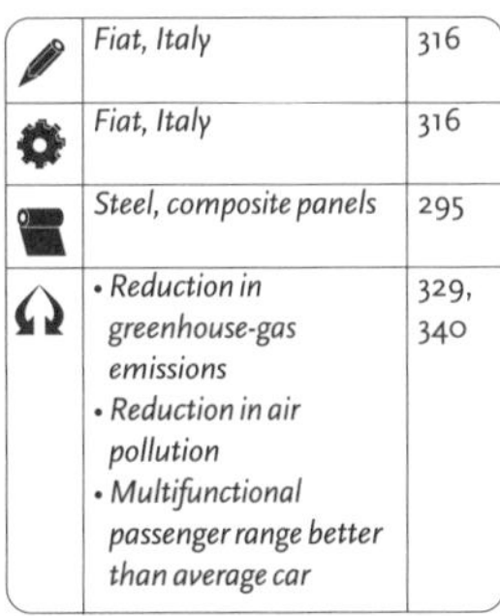

	Fiat, Italy	316
	Fiat, Italy	316
	Steel, composite panels	295
	• *Reduction in greenhouse-gas emissions* • *Reduction in air pollution* • *Multifunctional passenger range better than average car*	329, 340

P2000 HFC Prodigy

Ford unveiled the fuel-cell technology for the hybrid hydrogen-fuelled electric Prodigy family sedan at the Geneva Motor Show in 1999. In a joint programme with Ballard Power Systems and Daimler Chrysler AG, Ford has developed an advanced power unit that is capable of delivering 75kW (100PS) from four hundred hydrogen cells in a three-stack Proton Exchange Membrane (PEM) weighing 172kg (378lb). An additional 91kg (200lb) is added by the electric induction motor, which delivers 120PS. An on-board capacity of 1.4kg (3lb) of hydrogen gives a range of around 160km (99.3 miles) with a combined Urban/Highway EPA-cycle fuel economy equivalent to 28.5km/litre (80mpg) of petrol. With a total kerb-weight of 1,514kg (3,330lb), acceleration is about 14 seconds from 0 to 100km/h (62mph) with a top speed of 145km/h (91mph). These HFC cars are now being tested in a three-year programme in California. Other variants of the P2000 range include a lightweight version being developed at the Ford Forschungszentrum Aachen (FFA) in Germany. Weighing just 900kg (1,980lb) and powered by an experimental 1.2-litre DiATA compression-ignition, direct-injection engine, fuel consumption is 26.2km/litre (74mpg).

	Ford Motor Company, USA	316
	Ford Motor Company, USA	316
	Various	
	• *Zero hydrocarbon emissions from fuel cells* • *Fuel economy*	329

Prius

In October 1997 Toyota became the first major global car manufacturer to launch a mass-produced hybrid power system permitting continuous variable combination of a petrol internal-combustion engine and 43-kilowatt electric motor. Toyota's commitment to cleaner technologies and environmentally improved products was outlined in a twenty-page supplement that appeared in the November 1997 issue of *Time* magazine. So, has Toyota lived up to expectations? To date over ten thousand units have been sold in Japan and the vehicle is now being sold in North America and Europe. Toyota opted for a parallel hybrid system (THS or Toyota Hybrid System), alternating between petrol and electric power, as opposed to a series hybrid system in which the drive is provided by an electric motor and the (petrol) engine is used only to generate electricity. THS provides the most efficient combination of the two power sources according to the drive pattern. If the car starts out at low speed the electric motor operates, but during normal driving the petrol engine predominates. On acceleration the motor and engine work together and on braking or deceleration the kinetic energy is used to produce electricity, which is stored in high-performance NiMH batteries. THS provides a fuel efficiency of 28km/litre (90mpg; Japanese 10-15 Test Mode), which is double that of a Toyota Carina with automatic transmission. Emissions of CO_2 are cut by 50 per cent and CO, HC and NOx are reduced to 14, 8 and 12 per cent respectively. The heart of these environmental gains is the Atkinson-cycle engine coupled with a permanent-magnet motor and generator. Combustion efficiency is improved with Variable Valve Timing-Intelligent (VVT-I) technology and a high expansion ratio to improve power conversion from expansion to the drive train. Recycled and recyclable materials, especially the easily recycled Toyota Super Olefin Polymer (TSOP), are used for bumpers, dashboard, pillar and other interior trim. Overall body weight has been reduced, window glass reduces incoming UV wavelengths and cuts down solar heating and end-of-life dismantling has been facilitated wherever possible.

✎	*Toyota, Japan*	325
⚙	*Toyota, Japan*	325
▮	*Various*	
♻	• *Reduction of fuel consumption* • *Improved use of recycled materials and disassembly*	327, 329

Sparrow

Those who recall the infamous C5 electric car designed by Sir Clive Sinclair in the early 1980s in the UK, regarded by many as a liability in fast-moving traffic, might just consider this new one-seater electric car. With body styling reminiscent of the 'bubble' cars of the 1960s, the Sparrow can achieve speeds of up to 112km/h (70mph) from the thirteen batteries that store the electrical energy. A full charge gives a range of 96 kilometres (60 miles) at a cost of about 50 pence, making it extremely economical. With side-door access and full weather protection, the Sparrow might tempt people who are unwilling to venture out on a motor scooter or motorcycle. When it is being charged up, however, it has to be remembered that the vehicle is only as green as the mains electricity supply to which it is connected.

	Corbin Motors, USA	314
	Corbin Motors, USA	314
	Various	
	• *Zero emissions when using renewable energy supplies* • *Weatherproof, one-person commuter transport*	329

Smart Car

In October 1998 the Smart Car, jointly developed by the German manufacturer Daimler-Benz and Swatch, the renowned manufacturer of colourful modern watches, passed prolonged safety tests and was launched in the European market. This super-compact car looks as though it has been driven straight out of the pages of a comic strip. Measuring a mere 2.5m (8ft 2in), it is half the length of a standard car (reducing materials consumption) and uses one-third less petrol (on average 21km/litre, or 60 mpg) than its market rivals, the Ford Ka and Volkswagen Polo. Although the car is designed as an urban runabout, the turbo-charged petrol engine provides rapid acceleration (60km/h, or 37.5mph, in six to seven seconds) and a top speed of 130 km/h (82mph) to meet the high expectations of today's motorists. The occupants are protected by a strong monocoque steel frame and there is a range of modular panels and interior elements allowing personal customization, catering for changing fashions and facilitating repair. This could herald an important development in the car industry in which interchangeable components contribute to extending the lifespan of a vehicle.

	Daimler Chrysler, Germany	314
	Daimler Chrysler, Germany	314
	Various	
	• *Reduction in fuel consumption* • *Improvements in upgradability and repairability*	329

TH!NK City

Almost twenty-five years elapsed between the time this low-environmental-impact car was conceived and the time when a production model emerged. Stimulated by the energy crisis in 1973, Lars Ringdal and Bakelittfabrikken of Norway examined the possibility of building a lightweight car with plastic panels. For nearly two decades the idea languished before it was revived by PIVCO (Personal Independent Vehicle Company) in 1990. The first prototype, which successfully joined an aluminium frame with a thermoplastic body, emerged in 1992. By 1998 a model complying with all EU safety standards rolled off the production line at PIVCO Industries AS. The following year the Ford Motor Company obtained a majority shareholding of the company and it was renamed TH!NK Nordic AS. Production capacity now stands at five thousand vehicles per annum. Designed for urban users, the TH!NK City is powered by a three-phase electric motor with an output of 27kW or 45bhp. Rapid acceleration takes the car from 0 to 50km/h (31mph) in seven seconds and gives it a top speed of 90km/h (56mph). Nineteen nickel cadmium batteries provide a range of 85 kilometres (53 miles) when fully recharged over eight hours from a 220V supply. Energy is regenerated from braking and when the car is going downhill. Manufacturing practices differ from the usual assembly line. There are ten production centres, and plastic panels clip and clamp together with the aluminium passenger shell, which sits on the high-strength steel frame. The net result is a car that requires only 425 parts compared with the thousands typical of conventional cars. This facilitates end-of-life disassembly and recycling. In short, the TH!NK City embraces the benefits of integrating lifecycle assessment into the design and manufacturing process and perhaps sets a blueprint for small-car manufacturers. As the recently approved End of Vehicle Life (EVL) Directive comes into force in the EU in 2005, requiring 90 per cent of a car's components to be recycled, TH!NK Nordic AS is moving in the right direction.

✎	*TH!NK Nordic AS/Ford, Norway*	325
⚙	*TH!NK Nordic AS/Ford, Norway*	325
▬	*Polyethylene, aluminium, steel*	295, 341
♻	• *Zero emissions (if electricity is obtained from renewable energy)* • *Lower-than-average energy consumption during manufacturing* • *High recyclability of components and batteries*	327-9

Triax

Three propulsion options are available for this third-generation electric vehicle: all-wheel-drive electric, all-wheel-drive hybrid electric and two-wheel drive internal combustion.

✎	*General Motors, USA*	317
⚙	*General Motors, USA*	317
▮	*Various*	
♺	• *Improved fuel efficiency* • *Zero emissions option*	329

VW Lupo 3L TDI

In Berlin on 16 May 2000 a Volkswagen Lupo 3L TDI commenced a journey to circumnavigate the world. It was fitted with a three-cylinder, 1.2-litre (1/4-gal)Turbo Direct Injection (TDI) engine and the objective was to break existing records by making this the most fuel-efficient car to undertake this challenge. A total of 53,333km (33,333 miles) was travelled in eighty days across five continents at an average speed of 85.6km/h (53.5mph) at a remarkably economical fuel consumption of 2.38 litres per 100 kilometres (0.84 gallons per 100 miles). Production models of the Lupo achieve 2.99 litres per 100 kilometres (1.05 gallons per 100 miles) under MVEG cycle tests. The designation '3L', for 'three-litre', here refers to its fuel economy rather than to the more traditional indication of engine size.

This economy translates into a thousand-kilometre (625-mile) journey on one full tank of fuel and carbon-dioxide emission levels below 90g per kilometre (5.1oz per mile). An efficient engine is complemented with lightweight construction materials, especially aluminium, in body, chassis and running gear components. An automated five-speed, direct-shift gearbox and automatic stop-start system assist in maximizing fuel economy. The big question is: why can't all manufacturers produce such fuel-efficient compact cars?

✎	*Volkswagen AG, Germany*	326
⚙	*Volkswagen AG, Germany*	326
▮	*Various*	
♺	• *Significant reduction in fuel use*	329

NECAR 4

NECAR 4 (New Electric Car) is based on a Mercedes Benz A-class compact car fitted with a hydrogen-gas fuel cell power unit that generates electricity for a 75hp (55kW) motor and produces water vapour as the only emission. This zero-emissions vehicle has a range of 450km (280 miles) on a full tank of gas, is capable of a top speed of 144km/h (90mph) and can take up to five passengers. Improvements in fuel cell efficiency by dbb Fuel Cell Engines GmbH (a joint subsidiary of Daimler Chrysler, Ballard Power Systems and Ford Motor Company) generate 30 per cent more energy than the same-sized system used in the NECAR 2 and yield an increase of 15 per cent energy density (amount of energy generated per unit of weight) for the NECAR 4. This is another step towards Daimler Chrysler's target of marketing fuel cell vehicles by 2004.

✎	*Daimler Chrysler AG with dbb Fuel Cell Engines GmbH, Germany*	314
⚙	*Daimler Chrysler AG, Germany*	314
	Various	
	Zero emissions	329

Independence™ 3000 iBOT™

Conventional wheelchairs, whose design has largely remained static for several centuries, offer only limited mobility. IBOT enables disabled people to navigate rough, uneven surfaces, to 'stand' up and to climb/descend stairs. This is achieved by gyroscopic articulations of the frame and three sets of wheels.

✎	*DEKA Research and Development and Independence Technology, USA*	307, 315
⚙	*Prototype*	
	Various	
	• *Improved functionality and mobility for disabled people*	329

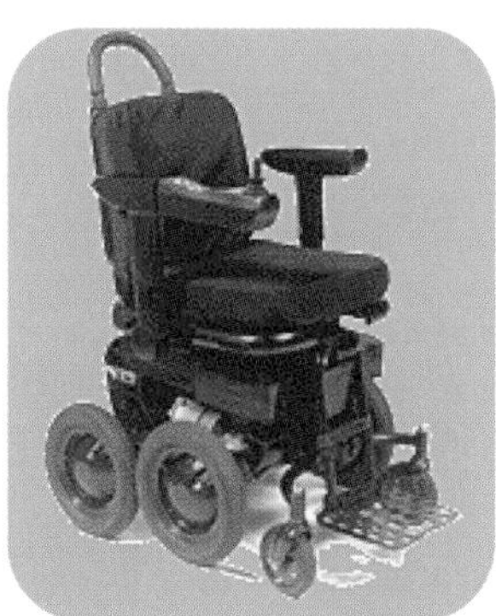

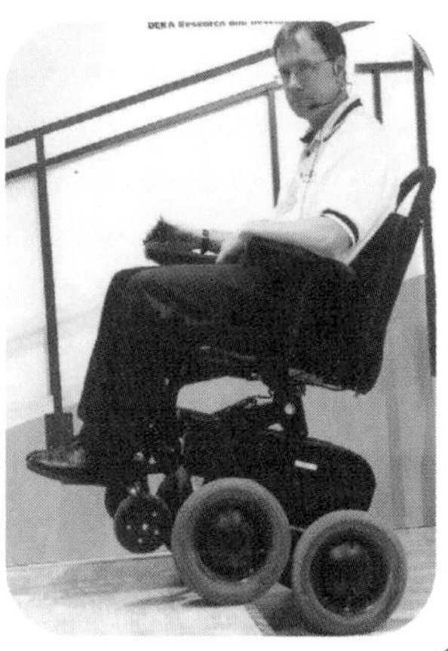

The Bamboo Bicycle

Bamboo is hand-worked, strengthened with wood and interlocked with carbon-fibre joints to form the frame of the bicycle. Block-dyed black chrome is also used for parts of the frame and the front forks. Wheel rims are crafted from beechwood, the seat is leather and handlebar grips are of cork. The proportion of organic, renewable, biodegradable materials is significantly higher than in a conventionally manufactured bicycle but obtaining consistently high-quality bamboo supplies does pose quality-assurance issues.

✏	*Antoine Fritsch, France*	306
⚙	*Prototype for Hermès, France*	318
▬	*Bamboo, beechwood, cork, leather, block-dyed black chrome and steel*	281, 285, 295
♻	• *Increased usage of renewable materials* • *Reduction in embodied energy of construction*	327, 328

Hybrid bike

Prestigious car manufacturers are entering the fray in the electric-assist bicycle market. This offer from Mercedes Benz provides about 30km (18.75 miles) of assisted travel on a full battery charge, which takes five and a half hours. Build quality matches the brand name, so we can expect this bicycle to be durable.

✏	*DaimlerChrysler Japan Holding, Japan*	314
⚙	*DaimlerChrysler Japan Holding, Japan*	314
▬	*Various*	
♻	• *Electric and human power* • *Zero emissions if recharged from renewable power sources*	329

Delite

A standard frame fitted with a range of modular components can suit either touring or racing bicycles or a hybrid. Suspension is provided by front fork dampers and a damped rear sub-frame assembly.

✎	*riese und müller GmbH, Germany*	323
⚙	*riese und müller GmbH, Germany*	323
	Various	
	• Modular design	329

Electrical bike

This is a unique folding bike with an integral battery and motor in the middle of the frame adjacent to the pedal crank and shaft drive. Multiple seat and handlebar adjustments permit the most comfortable personal fit.

✎	*Christophe Moinat, Ecole cantonale d'art de Lausanne, Switzerland*	308
⚙	*Prototype*	
	Various	
	• Hybrid human- and electrically powered vehicle	329

Nexus cycle

Reinvention of the bicycle as 'the mountain bike' in the late 1980s in California led to a global resurgence of interest in recreational cycling. Can the hi-tech aerodynamic bicycle do the same for those seeking an alternative urban transport solution to the car? Building on the technology developed for speed cycling in the velodrome, the Nexus combines striking looks with low drag coefficients. The cyclist has to adopt a new body posture to make the best use of this vehicle.

✎	*Seymour Powell Ltd, UK*	310
⚙	*Prototype*	
	Various	
	• Human-powered personal transport	329

Strida 2

Unfolding the Strida 2 takes ten seconds and immediately reveals its radical triangular frame, a departure from the typical arrangements in other folding bicycles. It weighs in at just 10kg (22lb), the tubes being of aluminium and the wheels and other components made from glass-reinforced polyamide, a strong, durable, lightweight polymer. A conventional chain is replaced by a belt drive over low-friction polymer cogs, making for an oil-free and low-maintenance bicycle. Tyre and belt repairs are facilitated by the offset frame-wheel arrangement. Apparently it takes time to master the ride as the frame is not as tortionally stiff as other folding bikes, but thereafter the rider is guaranteed an intrigued audience as s/he sails by car-bound commuters.

✎	*Mark Sanders, Roland Plastics, UK*	310
⚙	*Roland Plastics, UK*	323
▰	*Glass-reinforced polyamide, aluminium, rubber, stainless steel*	341
♻	• *Economy of materials usage* • *Ease of maintenance*	327

Windcheetah

A cruciform frame enables the rider to adopt a low centre of gravity, which, when coupled with carbon-fibre fairing, provides very efficient aerodynamics. Pinpoint accuracy of steering is achieved by means of a unique joystick system that gives good stability in cornering. Lightweight materials and precision engineering make this the Rolls Royce of recumbents. The efficiency of the design has attracted interest from courier and local delivery companies who wish to develop zero-emissions transport policies for urban areas.

✎	*Advanced Vehicle Design, UK*	312
⚙	*Advanced Vehicle Design, UK*	312
▰	*Metal alloys, rubber, carbon fibre, Kevlar*	341
♻	• *Human-powered transport*	329

Rattan bicycle

Rattan is a vigorous thorny briar found in tropical rainforests. Its long stems are stripped to reveal an inner core that, once dried, forms an extremely durable cane, which can be woven and shaped. Non-load-bearing components of this bicycle, such as the fenders, chain cover, basket and handlebar grips, are 100 per cent rattan. Other components combine steel and rattan. So the main frame is steel covered by rattan, the saddle is of woven rattan and the forks, handlebars, luggage carriers and fender stays are also wound with rattan. Although the bicycle still relies on the steel for a rigid frame, the proportion of organic cyclic materials has been significantly increased.

	Unknown	
	Prototype	
	Rattan, steel, rubber	281, 283
	• *Renewable material components*	327

Brompton

Folding bicycles are not a new invention but Brompton has manufactured durable products over the last three decades and is probably one of the most popular brands in the UK. The robust 'full-size' steel frame can be folded within twenty seconds to make a compact package that weighs less than 12kg (27 lb) and measures only slightly bigger than the 40-cm (16-inch) wheels. Currently the range includes two three-speed (L3, T3) models, one four-speed (L5) and one five-speed (T5), all with rear carrier and dynamo. The T types are supplied with lights too. Optional extras allow customization but the design remains fundamentally little changed since its inception, making it less prone to the whims of fashion. Owning a folding bicycle significantly increases mobility options for work and pleasure. Overall journey times can be cut by combining cycling with public or other private transport and a folding bike is easier to take on a train, bus or aeroplane than a conventional bike. Folding bicycles make a viable contribution towards a more integrated and sustainable transport system.

	Brompton Bicycle Ltd, UK	313
	Brompton Bicycle Ltd, UK	313
	Rubber, steel, plastic	283, 295
	• *Multifunctionality* • *Durability*	329

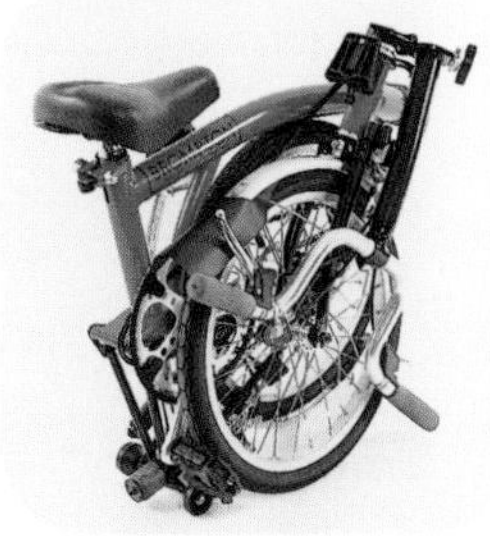

✎	*Students, professors and alumni, Massachusetts Institute of Technology, USA*	320
⚙	*Students, professors and alumni, Massachusetts Institute of Technology, USA*	320
▮	*Photovoltaics, lightweight metals and composites*	341
♻	*• Renewable energy* *• Zero emissions*	329

Daedalus 88

Weighing just 31.4kg (69lb), the Daedalus 88 aircraft set a new endurance distance record for a human-powered aircraft of 199km (129 miles) over 3 hours 54 minutes, from Crete to the island of Santorini, Greece. The feasibility of man-powered flight is beyond doubt but translating the technological advances into everyday transport provides a significantly greater challenge.

Gossamer Albatross

Powered flight was made a reality by the Wright Brothers but it was Paul McCrady of AeroVironment who pioneered human-powered flight with the Gossamer Albatross aircraft that made the crossing of the English Channel in 1979. Made of lightweight synthetic materials, this strange craft collates expertise in materials technology with advanced aerodynamics. This was a welcome invention but it has proved difficult to design larger human-/solar-powered passenger-carrying aircraft.

✎	*Paul McCrady, AeroVironment, USA*	304, 308
⚙	*Prototype, AeroVironment, USA*	304
▮	*Carbon-fibre and graphite resins, Kevlar*	284
♻	*• Zero emissions*	329

The Pickup

City-centre traffic in many countries crawls along at speeds similar to or slower than cyclists. Motorized vehicles are subject to entry and parking restrictions. So it is timely that Robert Dixon gave the familiar trishaw/rickshaw, so familiar in South-east Asia, a thorough redesign for use in the developed world. The Pickup is packed with features to ensure it is comfortable for its human power source and adaptable as a load carrier. A composite fairing protects the semi-recumbent rider on the articulated four-wheeled chassis. Seven-speed hub gearing coupled with a lightweight differential ensures that the drive train and steering are optimal for urban conditions. Speeds of up to 22km/h (14mph) can be maintained and there is an electric-assist facility for hills. The rear of the carrier can be adapted as a people-carrying taxi or a flatbed to carry a standard Euro-palette giving a capacity of 1.8 cubic metres (63.6cu ft). There is also a covered-van configuration. Versatile and affordable, The Pickup is even being considered by the US Mail service and TNT for courier deliveries.

	Robert Dixon, Advanced Vehicle Design, UK	306
	Advanced Vehicle Design, UK	312
	Various	
	• *Zero emissions* • *Human-powered*	329

Ciro Magic

This strong, compact, folding scooter is a convenient portable vehicle for short urban journeys or for sports and recreation. Faster than walking, more portable than the smallest folding bicycle, the scooter can offer an intermediate solution to personal mobility. Polyurethane wheels cushion the rider from the road or pavement, a robust brake is activated by standing on the flexible rear bar and steering is achieved by shifting weight.

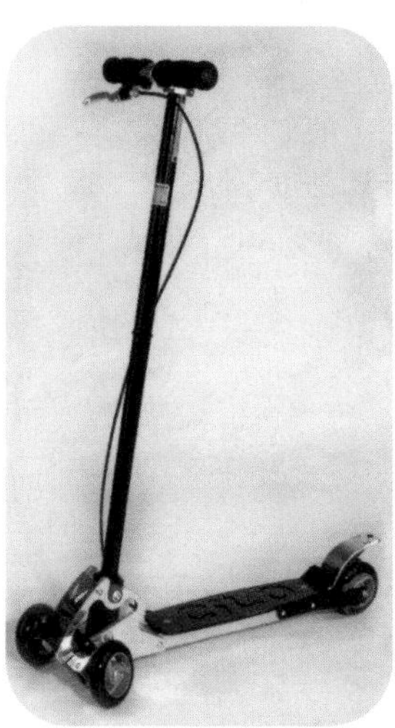

	sTRAKa sPORTs Giromachines GmbH, Germany	324
	sTRAKa sPORTs Giromachines GmbH, Germany	324
	Polyurethane, metals	283, 295
	• Human-powered transport	329

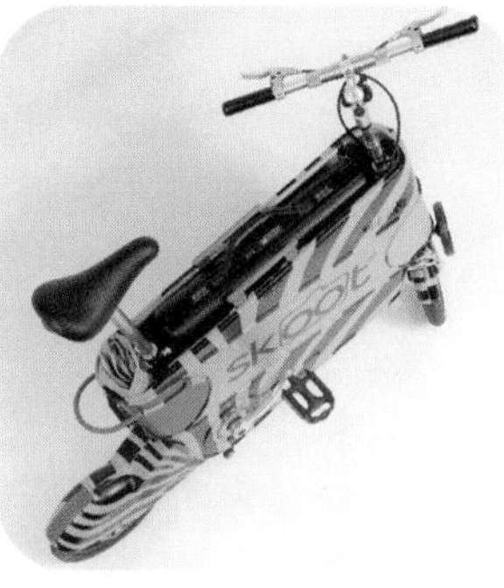

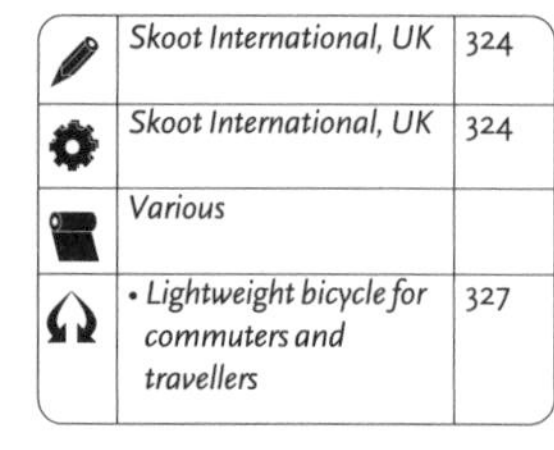

	Skoot International, UK	324
	Skoot International, UK	324
	Various	
	• Lightweight bicycle for commuters and travellers	327

Skoot

Is it a suitcase? No, it's a bicycle that unfolds in twenty seconds and weighs just 15kg (33lb). The Skoot might require some interesting handling in strong cross winds but it is guaranteed to keep the rider free of oil and grease and so may appeal to city slickers.

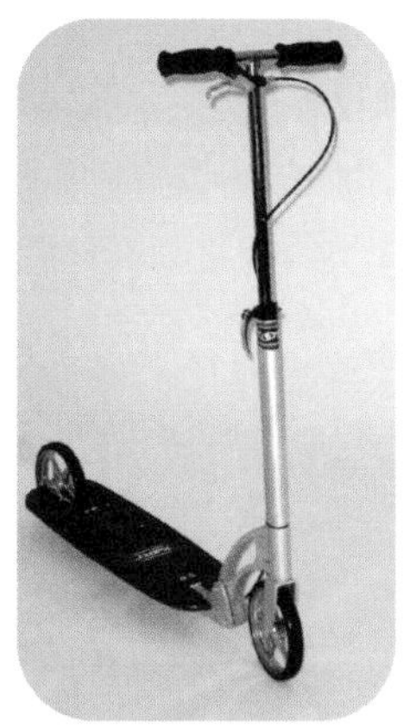

	Nova Cruz Products, USA	321
	Nova Cruz Products, USA	321
	Birchwood, aluminium, polyurethane	283, 295
	• Human-powered transport	329

Xootr Cruz

Skateboard culture meets the bicycle in this resurrection of the old push scooter. Lightweight aluminium frame, cast wheels and a low-slung laminated birchwood deck ensure manoeuvrability and stability. This vehicle is very portable, weighing just 4.5kg (10lb) and folding to a package less than 800mm (31in) long.

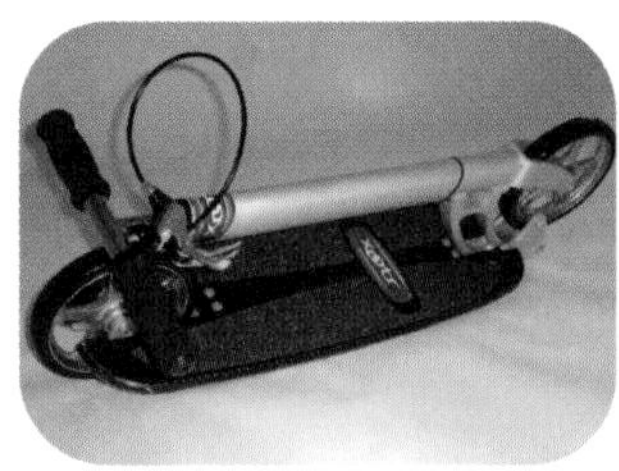

Tricycle, Euro, Classic, Mountain, Folding

Powabyke is a range of electric-assist bicycles to suit young and old, urban commuters and recreational users. The range without pedal assist varies from 21 to 48km (13–30+ miles) according to the exact model. Batteries are 14-amp, 36V, sealed lead acid, which reach full charge over eight hours and drive a 150W or 200W front- or rear-hub-drive DC motor. A folding version offers commuters an easy, less energetic start to the day.

✎	*Powabyke Ltd, UK*	322
⚙	*Powabyke Ltd, UK*	322
	Various	
	• *Encouraging hybrid human-/electric-powered transport*	329

Plumber's cart

Tradespeople with a local catchment area may find it a considerable advantage to be able to choose between a car and an alternative form of transport. Michel Zillig's bicycle trailer holds all the necessary equipment and tools a plumber needs. It is easily unhitched from its towing vehicle and, aided by the rotating triple wheel, can be readily pulled up kerbs and stairs. Here is the trailer as mobile workshop.

Designer	*Michel Zillig, graduate student, Design Academy Eindhoven, Netherlands*	311
Manufacturer	*Prototype*	
Materials	*Synthetic polymers and rubbers*	296-7
Eco	*• Encourages use of human-powered transport • Multifunctionality*	329

SRAM 9.0 sl

SRAM manufactures brakes, gears and gear shifts to high standards of aesthetics and functionality, using between 30 and 50 per cent-recycled content for many of the sub-components, which can be disassembled for pure-grade recycling in the future.

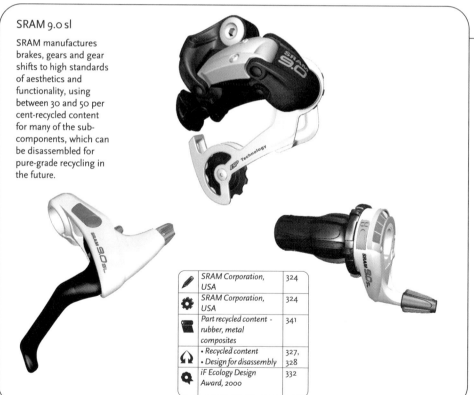

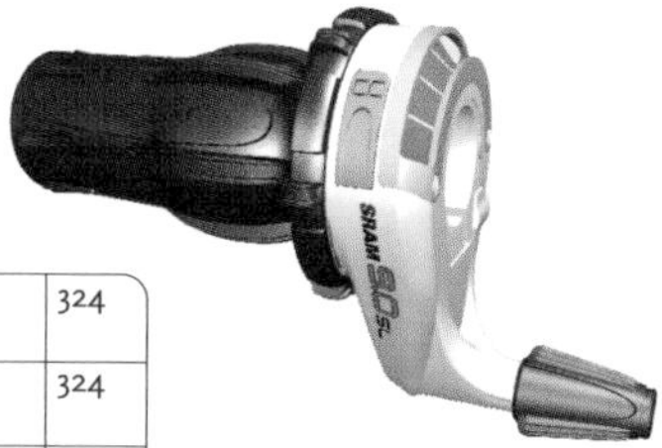

Designer	*SRAM Corporation, USA*	324
Manufacturer	*SRAM Corporation, USA*	324
Materials	*Part recycled content - rubber, metal composites*	341
Eco	*• Recycled content • Design for disassembly*	327, 328
Award	*iF Ecology Design Award, 2000*	332

Airsaddle

Improving comfort for cyclists in intimate contact with their saddles has been the object of designers for over 125 years. Here lateral thinking has provided a solution - an inflatable rubber saddle that provides air cushioning. The 'Airsaddle' incorporates a conventional air valve and can be infinitely adjusted, employing the same pump used to inflate the tyres, to suit the needs of the individuals and the terrain being traversed.

Ian Thorp and Steve Morris, Slough Rubber Company, UK	310, 324
Slough Rubber Company, UK	324
Rubber, steel	283, 295
• Reduction in materials usage compared to conventional saddles • Improved ergonomics	327, 329

Leggero Twist

Safety features of this bicycle trailer for children include a low centre of gravity, seat belts, a protective plastic shell and a warning flag. All-weather protection allows flexibility of use and ensures that the children have a good view and can feel the breeze.

Christophe Apotheloz, Switzerland	304
Bruggli Produktion & Dienstleistung, Switzerland	313
Various	
• Encourages human-powered transport for the family	329

Wissel horse saddle

This flexible, lightweight plastic saddle, with a new girth strap fitted with an easy-to-use ratchet-strap, sits gently on the horse and provides comfort for the rider. The mounting stirrup has a clip-free adjustment and the covers over the plastic saddle are changeable, so improving hygiene and offering opportunities for customization using covers of different colours.

✎	*Marit de Haas, graduate student 2000, Design Academy Eindhoven, Netherlands*	305
⚙	*Prototype*	
▮	*Lightweight plastic, metal*	283, 295
♺	• *Animal-friendly product* • *Improved user comfort*	329, 330

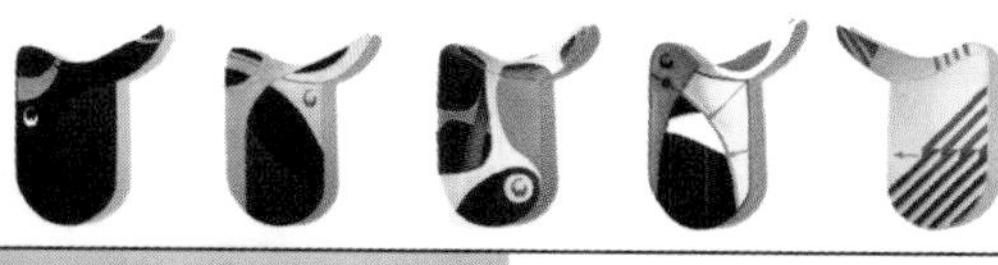

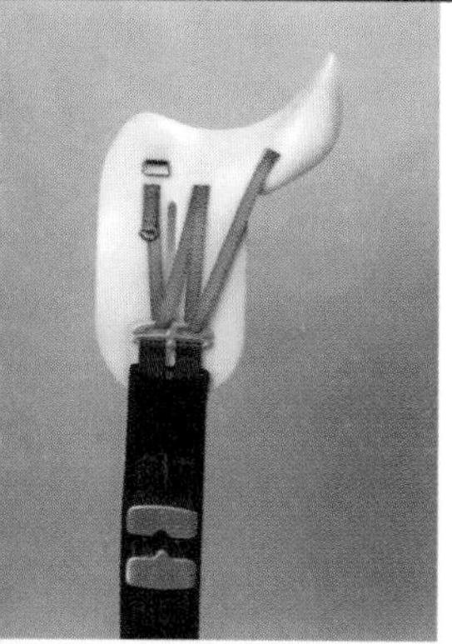

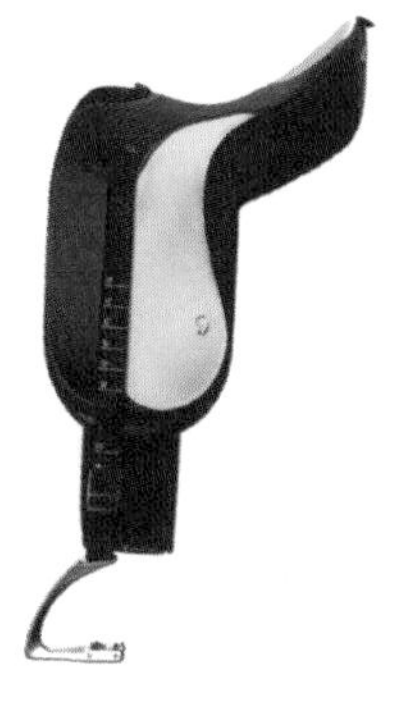

Synchilla® Snap T®

In 1991 the outdoor clothing manufacturer Patagonia declared in their catalogue that 'Everything we make pollutes'. This was the beginning of the company's process of reducing its environmental impacts by switching to organically grown cotton and by manufacturing fleeces derived from recycled plastic bottles. Post-consumer recycled (PCR) Synchilla® fleece was developed with Wellman, Inc., in 1993. Each garment saves twenty-five two-litre PET bottles from landfills.

✎	*Patagonia, USA*	322
⚙	*Patagonia, USA*	322
▮	*Synchilla® Fleece, Supplex® nylon*	300-1
♺	• *Recycled materials* • *Reduced emissions (compared with virgin PET fibre)*	327, 329

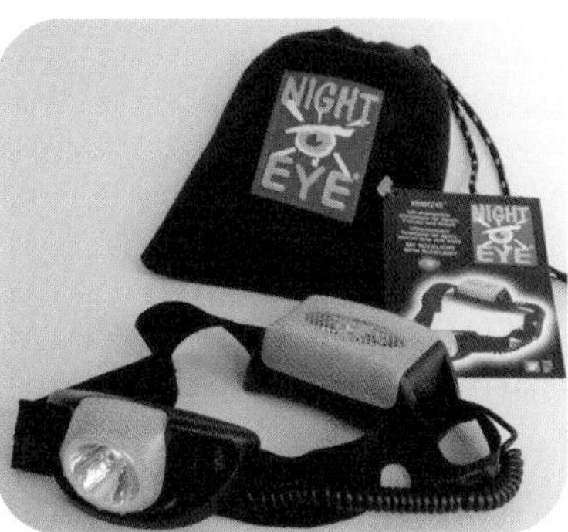

NIGHTEYE®

This lightweight headlamp is fitted with the patented Ultralight using a low-energy Xenon bulb with a special reflector to provide a quality light source. A rear red LED personal safety light fits to the back of the headband. All components, including the polycarbonate casings, clip together and so can be separated for recycling.

✎	*PROFORM Design, Germany*	309
⚙	*Nighteye GmbH, Germany*	321
▬	*Polycarbonate, elastic, LEDs, Xenon bulb*	341
♻	*• Low energy consumption*	329
✪	*iF Design Award, 2000*	332

Pod floating lounger

This clever product embodies several guiding principles of good green design. It is made entirely of recycled soda bottles, Partek recycled plastic lumber and other material and components, is easily assembled and disassembled allowing easy repair (and further recycling at end of life) and it is economical in its use of materials. John Amato sees this product as part of a continuous cyclic process. All such objects are ephemeral in the long view.

✎	*John Amato, Meta Morf, Inc., USA*	304, 320
⚙	*Meta Morf, Inc., USA*	320
▬	*Soda bottles, plastic lumber*	294, 341
♻	*• Recycled materials and components • Design for disassembly and ease of repair • Low materials usage*	327, 328
✪	*IDRA award, 1995*	332

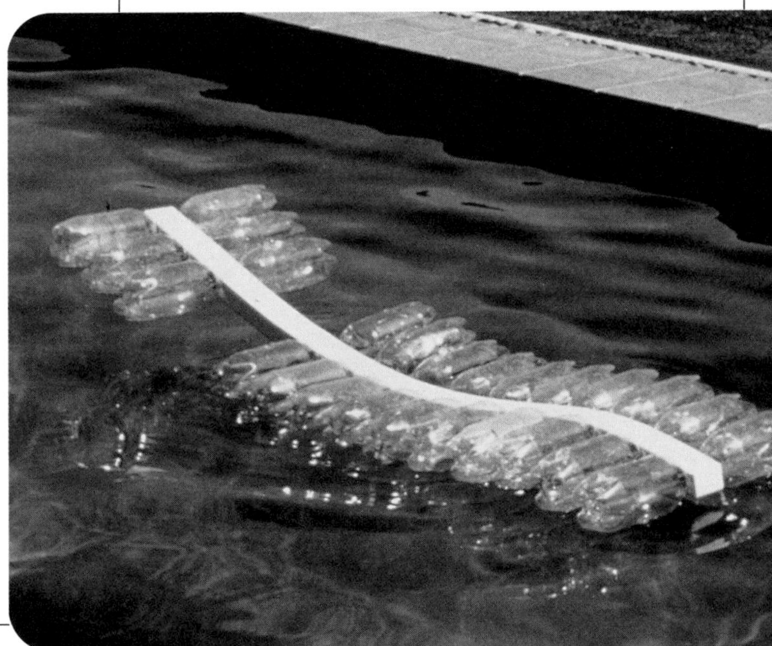

Veloland

Veloland is an information provider and service company responsible for a network of over 6,300km (4,000 miles) of national and regional cycling trails in Switzerland. Maps, guides and a website provide wide access to information nationally and beyond. Trails have been linked with public-transport networks and bicycle rental at SBB railway stations and the whole system is covered with consistent, standardized signage.

	Veloland Schweiz, Switzerland	311
	Various	
	Various	
	• *Encouraging integration of recreational cycling with public transport*	329

Kayak

Old kayaks don't die, they just get recycled and face the white water again. Ocean Kayak encourage customers to cut defunct kayaks and send them as collect freight to their factory, where the polyethlene is ground up for reconstituting in a new mould.

	Tim Niemeir, USA	309
	Ocean Kayak, USA	321
	Recycled polyethylene	341
	• *Continuous recycling of materials* • *Product take-back*	327, 329

Skystreme 729 model

This inflatable kite, weighing 43 grammes (1lb 8oz) and not much bigger than a credit card, fits easily into your pocket

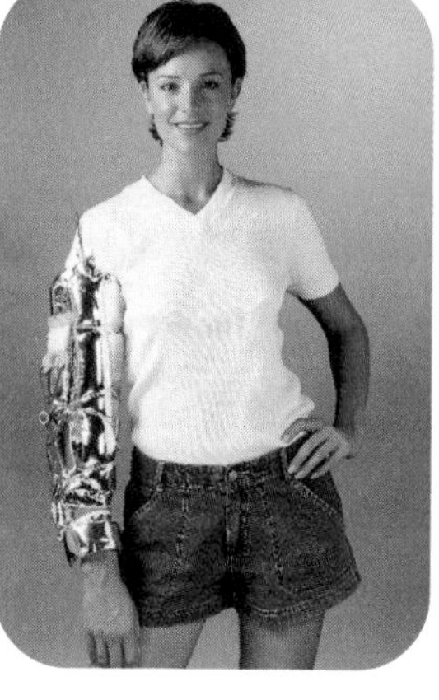

ready to assist you in an emergency. Once inflated, the kite soars high, thanks to a unique aerofoil system, making a rescue beacon easily detected by sight or by radar. The Skystreme provides protection against hypothermia and can be inflated to use as a splint for a broken limb.

	Skystreme UK Ltd, UK	324
	Skystreme UK Ltd, UK	324
	Lightweight, highly reflective plastic	283, 295
	• *Economical use of materials* • *Multifunctional* • *Improved health and safety*	327, 329

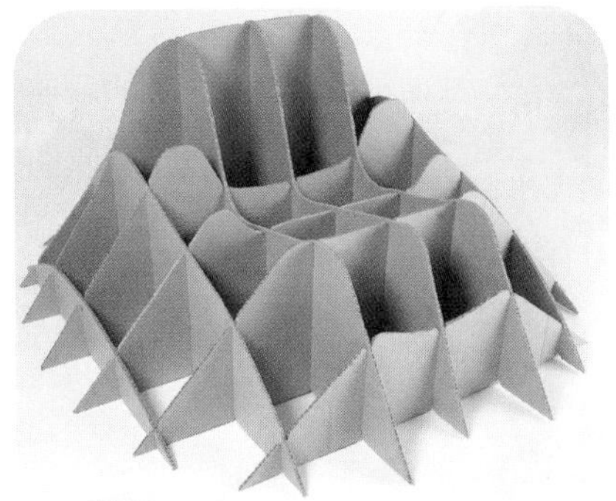

✎	*N Fornitore, Italy*	321
⚙	*N Fornitore, Italy*	321
▬	*Corrugated cardboard, grass seed, soil*	292
♻	*• Renewable, compostable and locally sourced materials*	327, 330

Terra Grass Armchair

A subtle merging of man and nature is embodied in this witty outdoor seat reminiscent of some mini Bronze Age burial mound. The stuctural framework is provided by corrugated cardboard to which locally sourced soil is added and grass seed applied. Just a few weeks later succulent grass covers your very own green throne for the garden.

E-tech

The E-tech two-stroke motor for chainsaws and strimmers combines efficient power production with a new catalytic converter, ensuring that these motors meet the world's strictest standard for emissions for motorized hand-held garden and forestry equipment, the 1995 California Air Resources Board (CARB) standard. Electrolux, the world's largest manufacturer of chainsaws, has also forged partnerships with petroleum companies to develop fuels that reduce emissions. For example, the Finnish company Raision offers a vegetable chain oil for chainsaws through Husqvarna.

✎	*Husqvarna/The Electrolux Group, Sweden*	315
⚙	*Husqvarna/The Electrolux Group, Sweden*	315
▬	*Metals, plastics*	283, 295
♻	*• Reduction in emissions and consumables*	329

Can-O-Worms

A compact self-assembly series of nested circular trays, made from 100 per cent post-consumer recycled plastic, is supplied with a coir fibre block. This block is moistened and broken up, then placed in the bottom tray to provide 'bedding' for a colony of native composting worms. As a tray is filled with household or garden waste, another is added to build up the stack. The worms migrate up and down the stack through the mesh in the bottom of each tray, digesting waste and turning it into compost.

✎	*Reln, Australia*	323
⚙	*Reln, Australia, with Wiggly Wigglers, UK*	323, 326
▮	*Plastics, live worms*	283, 295
♻	• *Encourages local biodegradation of waste* • *Recycled and renewable materials*	327, 330

Compost converter

Manufactured from 95 per cent-recycled plastic, the 220-litre (48-gal) capacity Compost Converter is a strong, rigid bin with a wide top aperture, which facilitates disposal of biodegradable domestic and garden waste and its conversion into compost. A wide hatch at the bottom permits removal of the mature compost. Blackwall make a range of compost bins from 200 litres up to 708 litres (44–156gals) capacity for domestic use, from injection-moulded, flat-pack, wood-grain-effect, recycled thermoplastic bins to blow-moulded, cylindrical bins mounted on a tubular galvanized-steel frame, permitting aeration of the compost by regular inversion or tumbling. Bins are guaranteed for at least ten years.

✎	*Blackwall Ltd, UK*	313
⚙	*Blackwall Ltd, UK*	313
▮	*Plastics, tubular galvanized steel*	283, 295
♻	• *Encourages local composting* • *Recycled materials*	327, 330

Nature's Choice trellis range

A versatile trellis system, offering gardeners many different permutations of plant support, uses a material made of 80 per cent-recycled and 20 per cent-virgin polystyrene, which is available in four permanent UV-stable colours. It looks and feels like wood, yet this recycled material is water- and rot-resistant and does not need any toxic preservatives as required by conventional timber trellis.

✎	*Metpost, UK*	320
⚙	*Metpost, UK*	320
▮	*Polystyrene*	341
♻	• *Recycled materials* • *Reduction in toxic consumables*	327, 329

MicroBore

Porous piping placed in or on the soil surface provides a means for the precise delivery of water direct to the plant root zone. The flexible, rubber-based hose made from shredded, recycled tyres is perforated with holes, allowing water to trickle into the soil. Pipe diameters vary from 4mm or 7mm(1/6–1/4 inch) for the MicroBore, which is ideal for watering window boxes and office plant displays, to 13mm,16mm or 22mm (1/2, 1/3 or 9/10 inch) for the HortiBore and ProBore, which are for commercial horticulture and landscaping. System accessories allow you to customize the irrigation system and permit the use of stored rainwater with in-line filters, taps, tee-junctions and end-stops.

✎	*Porous Pipe, UK*	322
⚙	*Porous Pipe, UK*	322
▬	*Recycled tyres*	283
Ω	*• Water conservation • Recycled materials*	327, 330

Pedal Lawnmower

Traditional 'push-mowers' are fine for a pocket-handkerchief lawn but even these have been usurped by electric 'flymos' and petrol-driven, two-stroke-engined mowers. Pedal power in this four-wheeled mower ensures exercise for the driver, easy coverage of medium to large lawns and zero emissions.

✎	*Remko Killaars, graduate student, Design Academy Eindhoven, Netherlands*	308
⚙	*Prototype*	
▬	*Metals, rubber, plastics*	283, 295
Ω	*• Zero emissions • Ease of maintenance and repair*	329

Solar mower

In 1997 Husqvarna combined robotic technology with solar power to create a unique lawnmower capable of autonomously maintaining an area of up to 1,200 square metres (1,440sq yds). By 1998 the Auto Mower offered another robotics-driven option able to recharge itself from a mains electricity supply.

✎	*Husqvarna/The Electrolux Group, Sweden*	315
⚙	*Husqvarna/The Electrolux Group, Sweden*	315
▬	*Photovoltaics, plastics, metals, motor, battery*	283, 295
Ω	*• Solar-powered • Zero emissions*	329

Glass Sound

Chunky speaker cabinets are redundant in this ultimate minimalist sound system. Suspended from stainless-steel wires, which carry the signal, a thin glass diaphragm emits sound waves. This system uses NXT technology to deliver the sound.

✎	*Christopher Höser, Designteam, Glas Platz, Germany*	306, 317
⚙	*Glas Platz, Germany*	317
▮	*Glass, stainless steel*	295
♻	*• Minimal usage of materials*	327
✪	*iF Ecology Design Award, 2000*	332

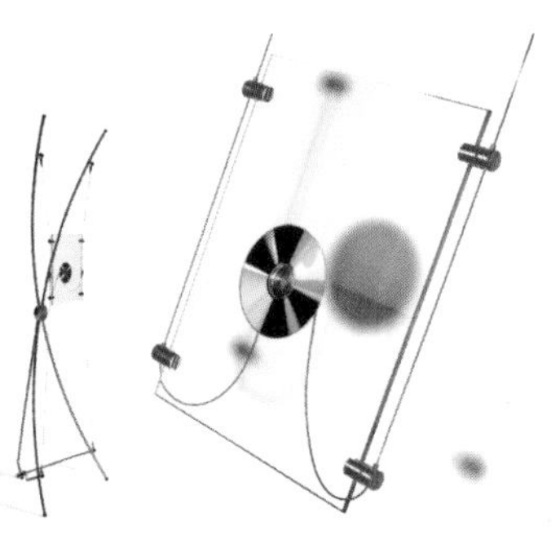

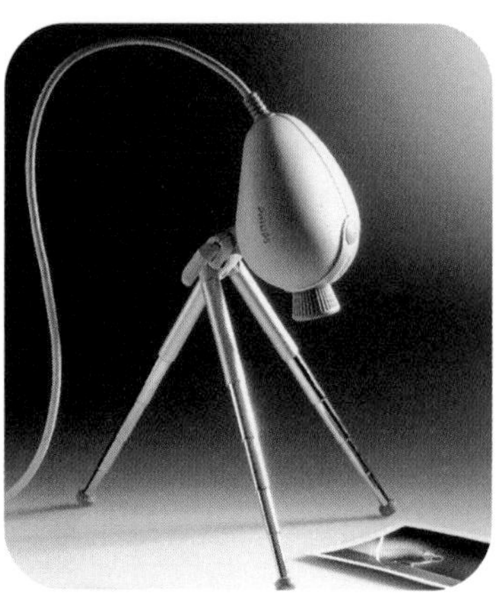

V-Mail camera

An adjustable tripod and variable focal-length lens permit digitization of any flat-copy graphical or photographic original and 3-D scene. Linking directly with a PC permits instant downloading of image files via a user-friendly interface. This award-winning camera embodies Philips's design ethos by using recyclable materials.

✎	*Philips Design, Netherlands*	309
⚙	*Philips Electronics, Netherlands*	322
▮	*Recyclable plastics and metals*	283, 295
♻	*• Recyclable materials* *• Dematerialization of photographic process*	327
✪	*Winner, Gold Industrial Design Excellence Award, 1999, Industrial Society of America*	

Canon IXUS

A new film format, Advanced Photo System (APS), was introduced worldwide by the photographic industry in the mid-1990s. APS encouraged new camera designs since the film area is 24 per cent smaller than standard 35mm film, resulting in much smaller cameras than conventional SLRs. Other advantages include multiformat-frame option (normal, intermediate or panoramic), automatic mid-film rewind/reuse and a strip on the edge of the film that records exposure details to improve printing results. In short, APS offers significant reductions in the consumption of raw materials, film and prints in the consumer market. Launched in 1996, the IXUS camera quickly became the compact camera to carry in your pocket and was probably responsible for converting many newcomers to APS, with its James Bond looks and sharp prints. The current model is the IXUS -M1.

✎	*Yasushi Shiotani, Canon, Inc., Japan*	310, 314
⚙	*Canon, Inc., Japan*	314
▬	*Stainless steel, polycarbonate, ABS*	341
♲	*• Reduction in materials and consumables usage*	327

Digital Mavica FD73H

Digital cameras dematerialize the process of photography by replacing silver halide film with a light-sensitive digital recorder. From the mid-1990s onwards a steady trickle of digital cameras emerged for the consumer market from the world's leading photographic-equipment manufacturers. By 1998 there were over fifty models with a mesmerizing range of different PC cards (CompactFlash, Smart-Media and PCMCIA), providing transfer media in which to store images prior to downloading to the computer. Sony, streetwise as ever, avoided the battle raging between the different storage formats and launched the Digital Mavica FD7, which stored images on the ubiquitous 3.5-inch floppy disk. No need for special PC card readers or camera-to-computer cabling, simply pop in the floppy and instantly view your images. Sony's design is innovative and is inherently less demanding of the environment since consumers don't need to buy new computer peripherals.

✎	*Shin Miyashita, Sony Corporation, Japan*	309, 324
⚙	*Sony Corporation, Japan*	324
▬	*Plastics, metals, electronics, CCD chip, floppy disk*	341
♲	*• Encourages dematerialization (of photographic film) • Universal storage medium*	327

Freeplay FPR2 and Global Shortwave radios

Inventor Trevor Bayliss was struck by the difficulties of trying to inform and educate the societies of developing countries using the media of television and radio. The absence of mains electricity and high cost of batteries mean that millions do not have access to media that the developing world takes for granted. His solution was to design a radio that could work by human power. Just sixty manual turns of the original BayGen on-board generator provided thirty minutes of playing time. Provision of AM, FM and SW band width was necessary for gaining access to a wide range of frequencies for maximum local penetration of programmes, be they news, cultural items, natural disaster and health warnings, or distance learning and literacy initiatives. An ABS casing was selected because it was durable, water-resistant, attractive and easy to manufacture. The radio was originally manufactured in South Africa, where the factory employed a high proportion of 'special needs' adults, giving them much-needed work experience and therapy. The radio has been endorsed internationally by aid agencies and United Nations programmes. More recent models developed by Freeplay Energy Europe for the international market include contemporary transparent plastic casings, a solar panel for power generation and a mains electricity adaptor. If the mains electricity is purchased from a renewable source these new models retain their original environmental sensibilities. However, if everyone simply plugs the radios into a mains socket using electricity from a coal-burning power station, then Freeplay may have drifted off-target. Are we really too lazy to crank a handle to hear our favourite radio station?

✎	*Freeplay Energy Europe, UK*	317
⚙	*Freeplay Energy Europe, UK*	317
▬	*Various*	
♺	*• Human- and/or solar-powered*	329

Freeplay s360

The original BayGen Freeplay wind-up radio was designed for use by remote communities in Africa. Demand from retailers in developed countries soon led to the development of new models for the consumer market. First came a triple-power option – wind-up, solar, mains – but it retained the bulk and weight of the original design. Next came this lightweight, compact version with a solar panel, wind-up generator and energy-storage unit providing up to fifteen hours of radio listening.

✎	*Freeplay Energy Europe, UK*	317
⚙	*Freeplay Energy Europe, UK*	317
▬	*Various*	
♺	*• Renewable solar or human energy* *• Most components recyclable*	329

Radio

The designer of this radio rejected the current obsession with miniaturizing everything and could therefore explore the use of non-plastic materials, in this case wood from old machine boxes. MDF was used for inner panels and dyed fabrics from old flour bags for the front and back panels. Consumers can choose the colour of the fabric dye and there's a special button for the user to select his/her favourite radio station. Use of natural materials and hand-finished production potentially create an object that will resist the tide of fashion. It can be made in small workshops, thereby creating new rural employment and so avoiding centralization of production in urban areas.

This design harks back to the early aspirations of the leading Arts and Crafts designers in late nineteenth-century Britain but updates the process with a modern aesthetic and a rechargeable battery. The wooden case will develop a patina with old age and it is interesting to speculate whether this will endear it to its owner. Plastic tends not to age with grace.

	Singh S Kartono, Indonesia	308
	Small batch production	
	Reused wood, MDF, fabric, rechargeable battery	341
	• Renewable and reused materials *• Rechargeable energy source* *• Anti-fashion and anti-obsolescence*	327, 329

AE1000 Free-power Radio

Philips have taken the concept of the original BayGen wind-up radios and shrunk them to create a pocket-sized version. Thanks to the built-in high-efficiency power generator, one minute's winding of the handle provides enough electricity for thirty minutes' listening time to AM/FM programmes. A LED display lights up when the charge rate reaches optimal speed. No more batteries, no more searching for the mains adaptor, because this handy radio needs only muscle power.

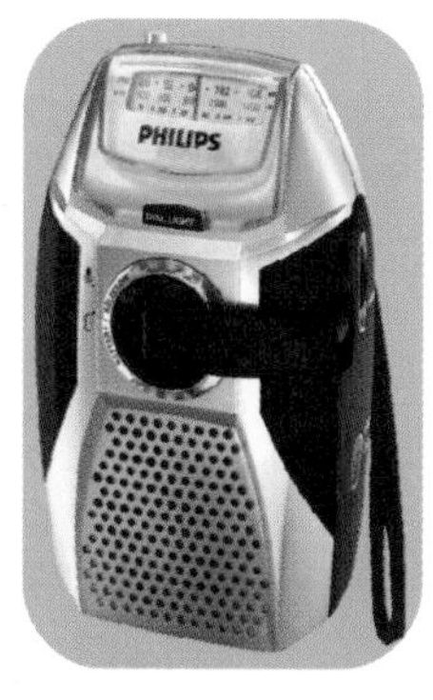

	Mike Jerome, Philips Electronics, Netherlands	307
	Philips Electronics, Netherlands	322
	Various	
	• Renewable energy	329

Tykho

Tough thermoplastics predominate in casings for electronic goods but Marc Berthier demonstrates that bucking convention produces a new sexy look for his VHF radio. Rubber also confers benefits over plastics by offering some shock resistance and weatherproofing.

	Marc Berthier, France	304
	Lexon Deisgn Concepts, France	319
	Rubber, electric components	283
	• Renewable and/or synthetic material	327

Grundig 15" Colour TV

This TV operates on 12V or 24V DC supply and on 90V-260V AC supply at 50/60Hz, making it suitable for use in recreational vehicles and boats or for low-voltage domestic renewable-energy systems. An internal satellite receiver and tuning system guarantee good reception.

✎	*Grundig, Germany*	317
⚙	*Grundig, Germany*	317
▬	*Various*	
♻	*• Low-voltage television set*	329

FL5 range

This model range, dating from 1997, is an example of long-term thinking, which assumes that manufacturers will in future normally take back electronic products after the end of their serviceable lives. The outer casing is made from a single material, which facilitates recycling of the material when the product reaches the end of its life. Water-based paints reduce environmental load.

✎	*Philips Corporate Design, Netherlands*	309
⚙	*Philips Electronics, Netherlands*	322
▬	*Single-material, water-based suede paints*	286-7
♻	*• Design for disassembly and recycling of materials*	327, 328

SmartWood Les Paul

Gibson Guitars are renowned for the quality and sound of their acoustic and electric guitars. This model uses hard maple, Honduras mahogany and chechen woods certified under the SmartWood and FSC schemes and supplied by EcoTimber, Inc. There's good evidence that 'Gibson' guitars are cherished by their owners and accordingly have an in-built longevity. Use of certified woods for high-value products seems doubly to reinforce the message about designing for longevity using materials from sustainable sources.

✎	*Gibson Guitars, USA*	317
⚙	*Gibson Guitars, USA*	317
▬	*Various woods, metal, electronics*	295, 339
♺	• *Renewable materials* • *Certified SmartWood, FSC timber*	333

The Basic Bass

Modular construction using standardized parts gives this instrument considerable flexibility. It can be used in guitar or standing pose and can be configured for left- or right-handed people. Microphones and electronics can be easily removed for repair or upgrading. Here is an object stripped down to its bare essentials, minimalist yet functional.

✎	*Jean-Remi Conti, graduate student 2000, Design Academy Eindhoven, Netherlands*	305
⚙	*Prototype*	
▬	*Various*	
♺	• *Reduction in materials usage* • *Upgradability* • *Universal design*	327

Savvy

This feature-packed mobile phone provides a 'joystick' central control to access menu options, which include a calculator, clock with stopwatch and games. Customers can choose from a range of coloured plastic components to

customize the look of their phone. This same feature ensures parts are easily disassembled to update as fashion dictates or repair or recycle. With low power consumption and a 30 per cent reduction in the number of components, Philips are striving to give today's modern icon of communication a green conscience.

✎	*Philips Design, Netherlands*	309
⚙	*Philips Electronics, Netherlands*	322
▬	*Recyclable plastics*	283, 295
♻	*• Design for disassembly and recycling* *• Low energy consumption*	328, 329

Xenium™ 939 Dual Band

Philips Electronics are continuously developing their policy of designing products with reduced environmental impact, as is evident in their latest mobile phone. With a casing of punched metal, a 35 per cent reduction in components, reduction in energy consumption and use of smaller recharge batteries, this phone has a smaller ecologcial footprint than previous models. At the end of its life it is easily disassembled into pure-grade materials or material groups. And it blends functionality with simple good looks.

✎	*Philips Design, Netherlands*	309
⚙	*Philips Electronics, Netherlands*	322
▬	*metal, electronics*	295
♻	*• Reduction in energy consumption and consumables*	329
✪	*iF Design Award, 2000*	332

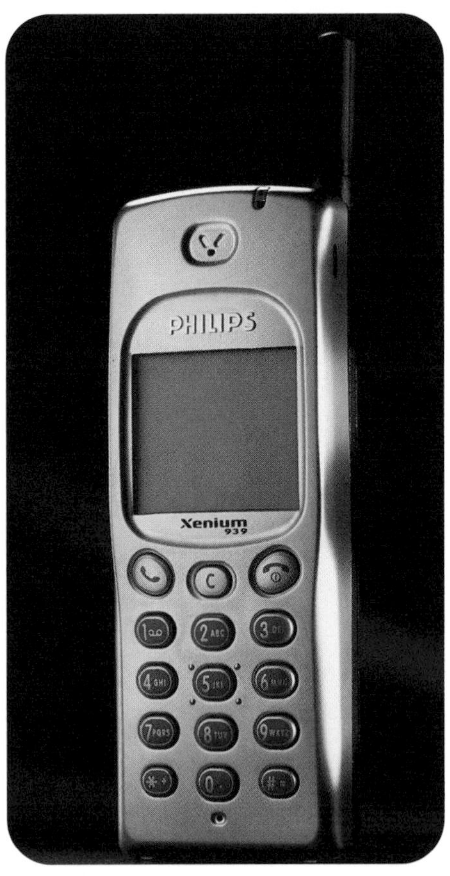

ROCKET eBOOK

In a supreme irony, Amazon.com, one of the most successful American Internet companies, sells old-fashioned, paper-based books through the electronic medium of the Internet. However, it may not be long before Amazon are poised to delivered electronic books via the Internet for consumers to read on a device such as the ROCKET eBOOK, saving vast forests in the process. Although many prototype electronic books were stillborn in the 1990s, the current generation of e-books appears to be making the grade. Maybe the book will also revive the concept of the 'DailyMe' newspaper.

	Ralf Gröne and Dallas Grove, Palo Alto Products International, USA	307, 309
	NuvoMedia, USA	321
	ABS plastic, electronics	341
	• *Potential huge reduction in consumption of paper, printing inks, packaging and transport energy*	327, 328

Morphy One project

Open-source software, in which developers have complete access to the source code in order to innovate with new applications, received a major boost recently when Linus Torvals launched the Linux operating system. Unlike the proprietary systems of Microsoft, Apple and other leading IT companies, Linux is available free for all to use. Yet until the advent of the Morphy One project, an open-source hardware system, to complement the open-source software, was not available. Morphy One grew out of a dedicated Nifty Hewlett Packard user forum where users of the HP 200LX palmtop chatted online. When production of the HP 200LX ceased in October 1999 the group asked the question 'what next?'. One group member, a Mr Toyozo (his electronic pseudonym), began developing new hardware circuitry, published his results to the user group and received a fantastic response. The outcome is Morphy One, a palmtop PC capable of running MS-DOS and Linux operating systems. Other hardware developers have access to the design data and source code. Morphy One provides a tiny lifeline to those wishing to maintain a philanthropic influence on the development of the Information Age and ensure that the global IT multinationals don't dictate the whole process.

	Mr Toyozo and the Nifty Hewlett Packard PC user forum, Japan and worldwide	309
	Various prototypes	
	Various	
	• *Open-access design or design with philanthropy!*	327

Bob

This cold-construction concrete vase challenges the dominance of ceramics and searches for new expressions of that most modern of materials, concrete. Only a detailed lifecycle analysis will reveal whether ceramics, with their high-energy requirement to fire the clay, are more or less benign than concrete, which also requires energy and results in emissions to the air during the manufacture of the cement.

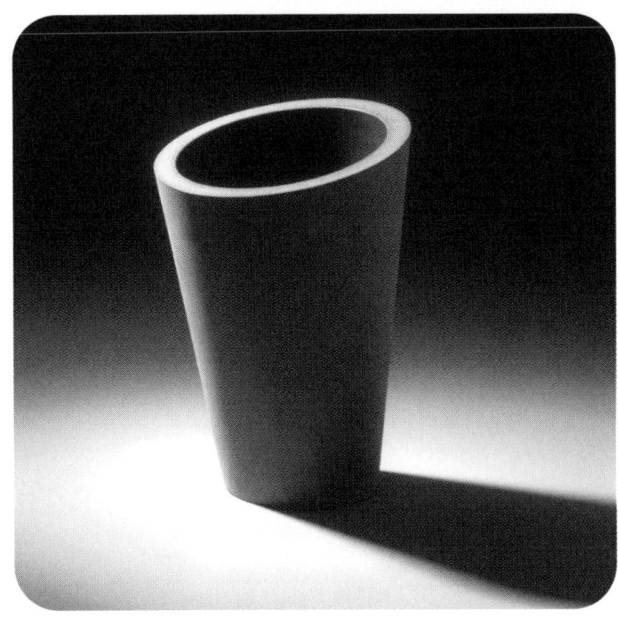

Goods, Netherlands	317
Goods, Netherlands	317
Concrete	295
• *Use of naturally abundant geosphere materials*	327, 340

Ecolo

A booklet conceived and written by Enzo Mari and published by the renowned Italian manufacturer Alessi inspires the reader to transform the effluent of consumer culture into delicate, beautiful objects. A shampoo bottle is transformed, like a butterfly emerging from its pupa, from useless spent object to graceful flower vase. Design is taken out of the hands of the specialists and returned to the masses.

Enzo Mari, Italy	308
Alessi, Italy	312
Post-consumer containers	341
• *Reuse of waste objects* • *Democratization of design*	328

Malvinas

Steel is one of the most efficiently recycled metals in the world but is rarely found in a decorative context outside hand-forged iron furniture and similar accessories. Here this humble material is elevated to an elegant centrepiece, suitable for a table, sideboard or window sill.

✎	*Alfredo Häberli and Christophe Marchand, Italy*	307
⚙	*Danese srl, Italy*	315
▬	*Steel*	295
♻	*• Recyclable mono-material*	327

Fruit holders

Take a selection of redundant cutlery, insert into a special mixture of concrete, allow to set, then kiln-fire to produce unique devices for holding fruit. These whimsical designs allow the fruit to take centre stage. Probably more suited to manufacturing in small batches, the design principle can be easily adapted to provide a variety of functional objects.

✎	*Pamela Hatton, UK*	307
⚙	*One-offs*	
▬	*Concrete, reused kitchen utensils*	295, 341
♻	*• Reuse of existing products* *• Materials with low embodied energy*	340

Wagga-Wagga

This piece balances harmony and tension using readily available materials. The principle can be extended to a wide range of materials using cold construction and/or heat deformation.

✎	*Camille Jacobs, Australia*	307
⚙	*Limited batch production*	
▬	*Float glass, bamboo*	281, 295
♻	*• Economy of materials usage* *• Recyclable materials*	327

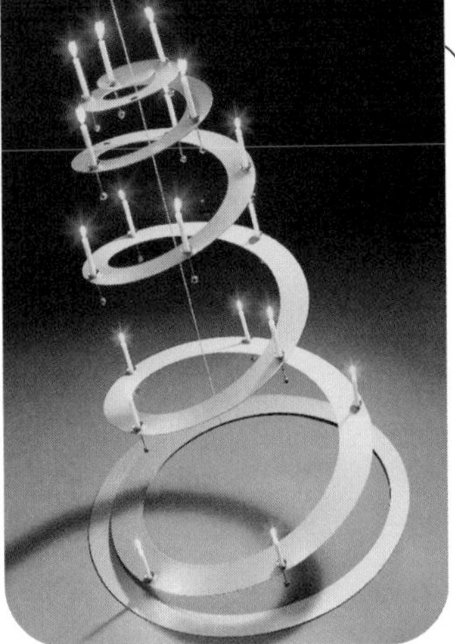

Spiralbaum

This flat-pack, laser-cut, plywood square unfolds as a helix when suspended. It is the ultimate in minimalist Christmas trees, is easily stored away for the next festive season and saves another Sitka spruce from being consigned to the landfill site each New Year.

✎	*Feldmann & Schultchen, Germany*	316
⚙	*Prototype for Werth Forsttechnik, Germany*	326
Material	*Plywood, steel*	295, 339
♻	• *Reusable product*	331

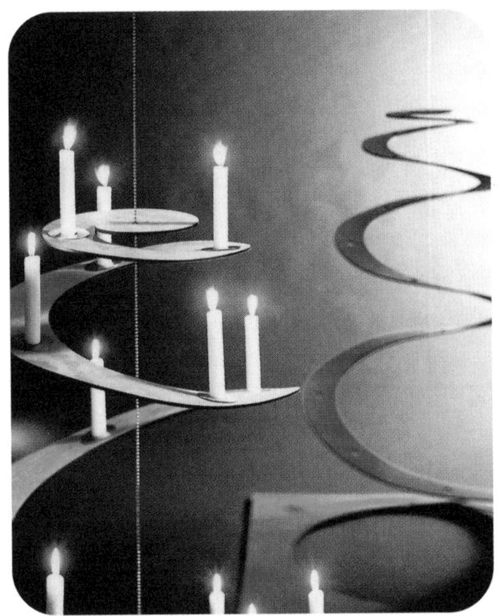

Sponge vase

Marcel Wanders commandeers nature's own manufacturing, adds his own porcelain tube and sets vase design on a new course. Designers should actively seek opportunities for 'harvesting' nature's products, which, with minimal energy input or modification, can be re-manufactured into new objects. Can we look forward to specialist 'product farms' where sponges are 'bio-manufactured' in neat rows, bamboos grow to EU regulation size in specially built moulds and bio-plastics spontaneously grow to predetermined forms?

✎	*Marcel Wanders, Droog Design, Netherlands*	306, 311
⚙	*Wanders Wonders, Netherlands*	326
Material	*Natural sponge, porcelain*	295
♻	• *Renewable material*	328

Tableware

This range of plates and serving platters is made from textured glass diffusers removed from fluorescent light fittings in a US government building that was undergoing a refit.

✎	*Maria Ruano, USA*	310
⚙	*Bedrock Industries, USA*	313
▬	*Recycled glass*	295
♻	*• Recycled materials*	327
✿	*IDRA award, 1998*	332

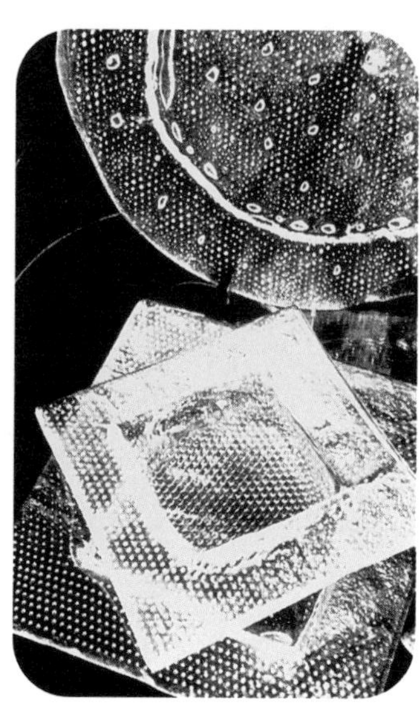

The Soft Vase

Challenging our perceptions about polymers and the way we use them, Hella Jongerius experimented with flexible rubberized polyurethane to create a traditionally styled vase. It provokes us to question how we value plastics. Objects made from plastics can be highly valued in the case of 'designer' objects or regarded as a throwaway item in the case of the ubiquitous plastic bag. Instead of using hard durable ceramics or tough shiny ABS, the traditional materials for a vase, Jongerius has chosen soft flexible polyurethane, thus encouraging the user to experiment with altering the shape of the vase.

✎	*Hella Jongerius, JongeriusLab, Netherlands*	307
⚙	*Droog Design, Netherlands*	306
▬	*Polyurethane, elastomers*	283, 295
♻	*• Improved user-friendliness* *• Durable* *• Recyclable*	329

Ceramic bowls

Ceramic waste from post-consumer and industrial sources is ground and mixed with fresh clay to produce these 'naturally' coloured bowls. Coloration depends upon the waste stream.

✎	*Annelies de Leede, Netherlands*	305
⚙	*Oak Product Design, Netherlands*	309
▬	*Ceramic waste, clay*	295
♻	*• Recycled materials*	327

Attila

Consumers' voracious appetite for convenience drinks will ensure that the humble steel or aluminium drinks can will be a feature of the twenty-first-century landscape. While recycling of these cans improved significantly during the 1980s, any device that actively encourages people to recycle more is a good thing. Attila is a durable crusher that is a pleasure to use: simply place your can in the bottom of the translucent column and enjoy that satisfying crumpling noise as the 'anvil' crushes the can with the downward push of the arms.

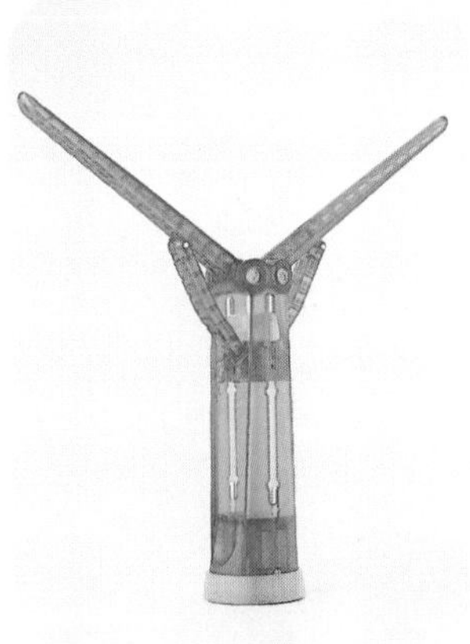

✎	*Julian Brown, Studio Brown, UK*	305
⚙	*Rexite SpA, Italy*	323
▬	*Injection-moulded ABS, polycarbonate, Santoprene*	297, 340
♻	*• Encourages waste recycling*	328

Cricket

Consumption of bottled water and soft drinks contained in PET plastic bottles has risen dramatically in the last decade, so any device that facilitates recycling is to be welcomed. This witty bottle crusher makes recycling fun and improves storage capacity of containers for collecting waste bottles.

✎	*Julian Brown, Studio Brown, UK*	305
⚙	*Rexite SpA, Italy*	323
▬	*Steel, plastic*	283, 295
♻	*• Encourages waste recycling*	328

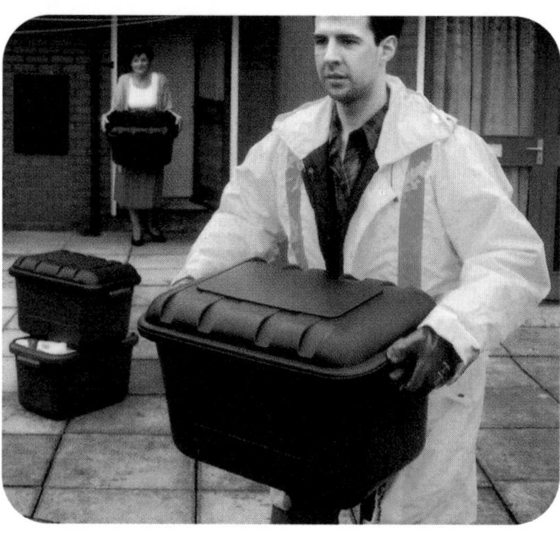

LINPAC environmental kerbside collection box

Since the introduction of the LINPAC Environmental kerbside collection box in 1996 to the city of Sheffield, UK, over twenty million plastic bottles have been diverted from landfill sites to recycling plants where the plastic is reused to create yet more boxes. This robust box, with high-impact and -deformation characteristics, encourages greater recycling by local authorities and private contractors.

✎	*LINPAC Environmental, UK*	319
⚙	*LINPAC Environmental, UK*	319
	Used HDPE bottles	341
	• Recycled materials *• Encourages recycling*	327, 328

Zago™

Recycling domestic waste has an image problem, so anything that can elevate this activity into fun is welcome. Three Zago™ triangular rubbish bins made from flat-pack, recycled cardboard neatly sit together to form a functional separator for different waste streams. The photographic exteriors clearly indicate each particular waste stream and reinforce the message that waste is a valuable resource.

✎	*Benza, Inc., USA*	313
⚙	*Benza, Inc., USA*	313
	Recycled cardboard	341
	• Recycled materials *• Encourages recycling*	327, 328

Bottle stopper and opener

Oxo have a reputation for excellent attention to detail and ergonomics for their hand tools. This easy-to-use device combines two functions and thus improves on conventional products.

Designer	*Human Factors in co-development with Oxo International, USA*	307, 321
Manufacturer	*Oxo International, USA*	321
Materials	*Hardened rubber*	283
Sustainability	*Dual-function device*	329

Cutlery

One design fits all in this elegant example of a fork made from bamboo, beech or steel. Manufacturing to this design with locally available rather than imported materials reduces transport energy.

Designer	*Patrick Laing, UK*	308
Manufacturer	*Prototypes*	
Materials	*Bamboo, beech, steel*	281, 295
Sustainability	• *Universal design suitable for locally available materials*	327

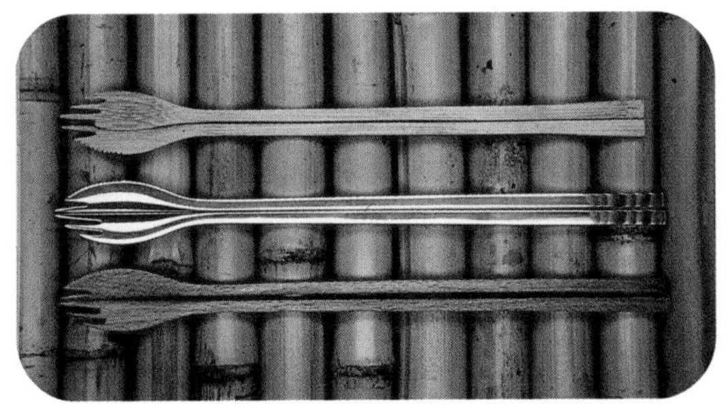

Cutlery tool

This could be the prototype for a 'universal' cutlery design as it cleverly combines the functions of knife, fork, spoon and teaspoon all in one piece.

Designer	*Nina Tolstrup, Denmark*	310
Manufacturer	*Prototype*	
Materials	*Plastic*	283, 295
Sustainability	• *Multifunctional* • *Economy of materials usage*	327, 329

Fold

Minimal waste is generated from the cutting and stamping of this basic range of cutlery, which is also witty and lightweight.

Designer	*William Warren, UK*	311
Manufacturer	*Small batch production, ww.modcons, UK*	326
Materials	*Stainless steel*	295
Sustainability	• *Economy of materials usage* • *Reduction in production waste*	327, 328

Double-cup

Espresso or cappuccino? The choice is yours in this neat tableware, in which the two parts are joined at the hip.

✎	*Erik-Jan Kwakkel, Netherlands*	308
⚙	*REEEL, Netherlands*	323
▰	*Porcelain*	295
♻	• *Dual-function design* • *Economy of materials usage*	327, 329

Disposable cutlery and bowl

Poplars are some of the fastest growing trees in Europe whose biomass can be harnessed to provide compostable, disposable cutlery.

✎	*Marcel Wanders, Droog Design, Netherlands*	306, 311
⚙	*Prototype for Oranienbaum project*	
▰	*Poplar wood*	339
♻	• *Renewable and compostable material*	327

Drinking glass

Clever cutting of two PET bottles enables two sections to be rejoined; an original screw top is used as the clamp to form a new glass. It remains unclear whether the offcuts are recycled or can be used to generate other products such as napkin rings.

✎	*Aki Kotkas, Finland*	308
⚙	*Limited batch production*	
▰	*PET bottles*	341
♻	• *Reused materials*	328

Drinking vessel

Boontje lovingly cuts, smooths and blasts old wine bottles, giving them a minimalist makeover and a new lease of life. As pitcher and drinking glass they serve to remind us of the beauty of the material and the unjustifiable waste of one-trip packaging, as embodied in the original product.

	Tord Boontje, Netherlands	305
	Small batch production	
	Post-consumer glass bottles	328, 341
	• *Recycled materials* • *Low-energy manufacturing*	327, 328

Wine rack

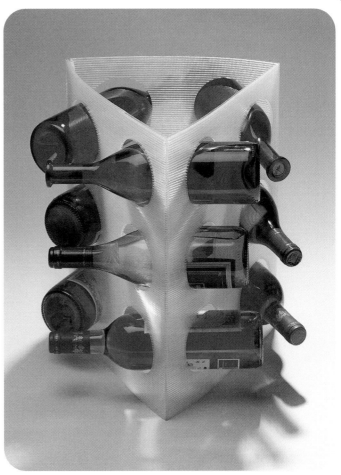

This flat-pack, triangular, fluted polypropylene wine rack generates no waste in its production as the cutouts are supplied as coasters in the mail order package.

	Stuart Bristow, UK	305
	Designed to a 't' Ltd, UK	306
	Polypropylene	283, 295
	• *Zero production waste* • *Recyclable*	327, 328

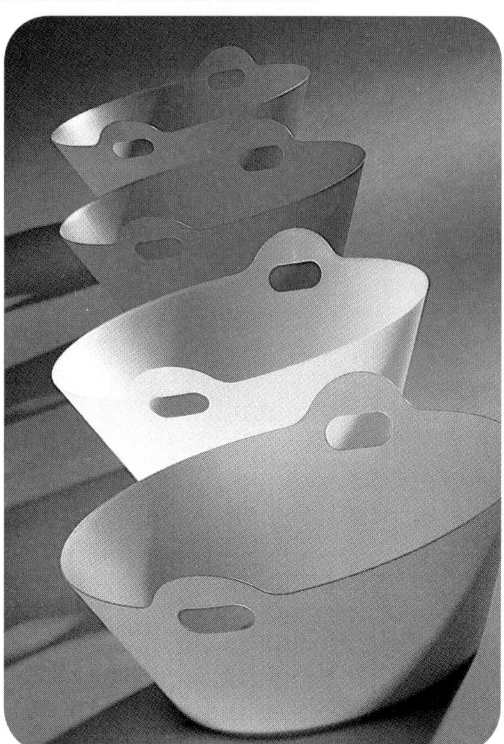

Basket 2 Hands

With their range of colourful, robust, yet elegant household objects, Authentics have succeeded in elevating the status of plastic in the home. Grcic's minimalist approach, understanding of the raw material and tongue-in-cheek reference to traditional basket design encourage respect from the user.

✎	*Konstantin Grcic, Germany*	307
⚙	*Authentics artipresent, Germany*	313
▰	*Recyclable polypropylene*	283, 295
♻	*• Recyclable material*	327

Barnacle

In the 1990s Droog Design encouraged a rethink for the humble 2-D tile. Moerel expands the theme with these organic-shaped, earthenware ceramic tiles, which offer visual relief for all those boring bathroom walls and provide a useful place to hang towels and clothes.

✎	*Marre Moerel, Netherlands/USA*	308
⚙	*Small batch production*	
▰	*Clay*	295
♻	*• Use of abundant materials from the geosphere • Durable • Multifunctional*	329, 340

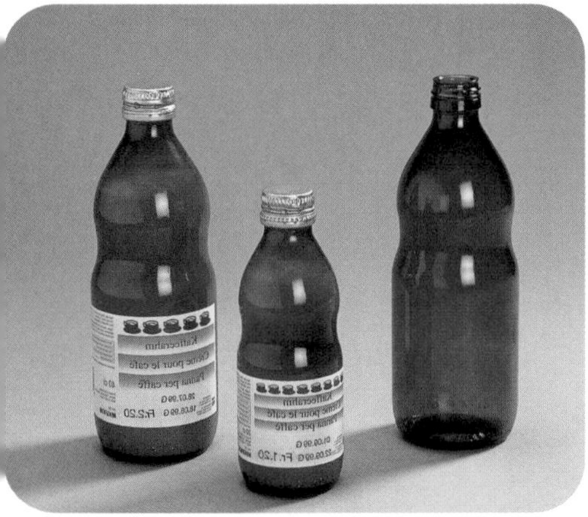

Coffee cream bottle

Attention to detail provides environmental benefits for this family of bottles designed for the central dairy in Aargau. A sharp internal radius and inwardly curved rim at the bottle's mouth ensure that milk doesn't migrate around the screw thread. This facilitates sterilization on reuse of the bottles, which in turn saves energy. Savings are also made on transport energy, since the new bottle shape can be packed more densely.

	Thomas Liebe, Ad Rem Design, Switzerland	304
	Vetropack, Switzerland	326
	Glass, metal	295
	• *Reduction of energy consumption during manufacturing and distribution*	327, 328

Elster

Inexpensive renewable materials are combined to create a funnel-shaped oblong waste paper basket made by hand. Brown packaging paper is stretched taut and glued over a softwood frame.

This simple technology has been applied by Wettstein to other furniture items such as armchairs, footstools and chaises longues.

	Robert A Wettstein, Switzerland	311
	One-off/small batch production, Robert A Wettstein	311
	Paper, wood	288-9, 339
	• *Renewable materials* • *Low-energy manufacturing*	327, 328

Durex Avanti

Natural or synthetic latex has long been the preferred material for manufacturing condoms but the material still suffers from an image problem. Latex produces its own distinctive odour and, owing to the thickness of material required to ensure full protection during intercourse, can result in a lack of sensitivity to the wearer. It also produces an allergic reaction in some people. After considerable research a version of polyurethane proved itself in tests. It is as strong as latex but 40 per cent thinner, is odourless and almost transparent. Add a little flavouring – do you fancy tangerine, strawberry, spearmint? – and here is a little self-help device guaranteed to assist in population control and the fight against the spread of sexually transmitted diseases including AIDS.

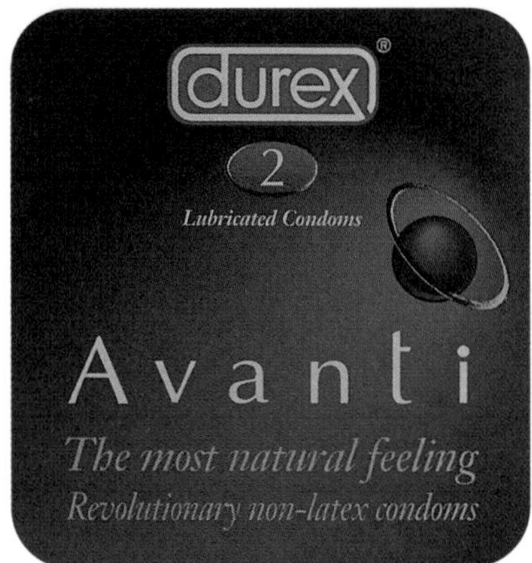

Designer	*Durex, UK*	315
Manufacturer	*LRC Products, UK*	319
Material	*Polyurethane*	341
Eco	*• An aid to reduce population growth and improve human health*	328

Earthsleeper™

Made entirely of Sundeala board from recycled newsprint with wood corner joints, and wood nuts and bolts, these coffins are highly biodegradable and make less environmental impact than conventional wooden coffins. Coffins are available ready-assembled or as flat-pack, self-assembly units.

Designer	*Vaccari Ltd, UK*	325
Manufacturer	*Vaccari Ltd, UK*	325
Material	*Sundeala board*	292
Eco	*• Recycled materials* *• Compostable*	327, 328

eco-ball™

Those sensitive to today's chemically based washing powders have an alternative method available in the form of the eco-ball™. This is a plastic ball, which contains ionic powder that releases ionized oxygen into the water and so facilitates penetration of water molecules into fabrics to release the dirt. A little washing soda helps deal with very dirty washing but it is claimed that a set of three balls will help clean the equivalent of 750 washes before losing their activity.

✎	*eco-ball*	315
⚙	*eco-ball*	315
▰	*Plastic, ionic powder*	283, 295
♺	• *Reduction of usage of washing powders*	328

Ecover®

The name of Ecover, like The Body Shop, needs little introduction to those who became green consumers in the 1980s. Established in 1979, Ecover has always espoused a business policy that recognizes that economics must be in harmony with ecology. This policy extends to product development, the green architecture of its main factory in Belgium and the international distribution network through twelve thousand small health food shops, still accounting for 45 per cent of turnover, as well as the supermarket giants. Company policy dictates that products must originate from a natural source with a low level of toxicity to minimize their burden on the environment and they must be equally efficient as conventional, more polluting products. Ecover products are not permitted to include petrochemical detergents/perfumes/ solvents/acids, polycar-boxylates, phosphonates, animal soaps, perborates, sulphates, colourings, phosphates, EDTA/NTA, optical brighteners and chlorine-based bleaches. Animal testing is also banned. Ecover also have an integrated packaging policy and encourage consumers to refill 1-litre ($1\frac{3}{4}$-gal) containers of washing-up liquid at shops stocking 25-litre (44-gal) bulk containers, which are themselves refilled at the factory. These polyethylene bottles (with polypropylene tops) have extra-wide necks, a level indicator, plastic labels (also recyclable) and a life expectancy of twenty refills before recycling, saving on waste and landfill space. Ecover's product range includes washing powder, bleach, water softener, liquid wool wash and fabric conditioner.

✎	*Ecover Products, Belgium*	315
⚙	*Ecover Products, Belgium*	315
▰	*Various cleaning agents, plastic containers*	341
♺	• *Reduction of water-borne toxins and pollutants* • *Reuse and recycling of containers* • *Retailing system geared to small and large outlets*	328

Fingermax

These finger brushes offer creative opportunities to those who find holding a conventional paint brush difficult. Universal fitting is achieved by moulding a thermoplastic resin polymer in a spiral shape with an elliptical cross-section.

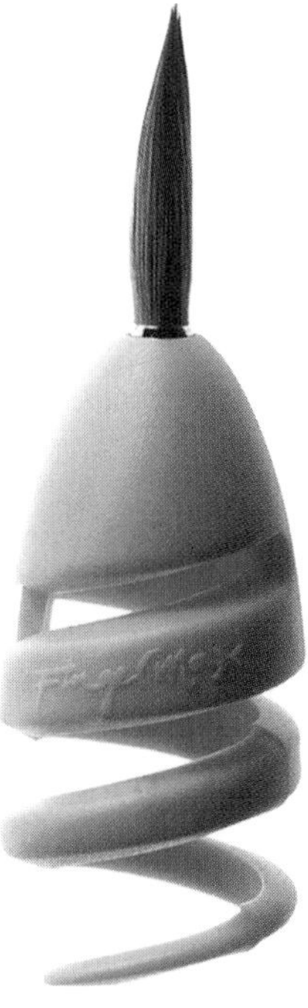

✎	*Büro für Form, Germany*	305
⚙	*Fingermax Gbr, Germany*	316
▮	*Polymer*	296-7
♻	*• Universal design* *• Design for need*	327, 328
✪	*iF Design Award, 2000*	332

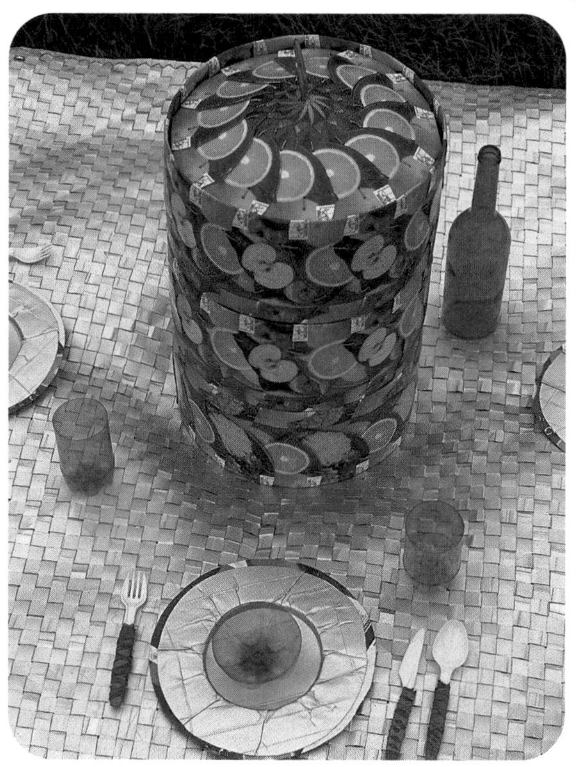

Juice cartons

In 1996 at an exhibition entitled 'Recycling: Forms for the Next Century – Austerity for Posterity', staged by the Crafts Council in the UK, craftspeople showed their skill in reusing post-consumer waste to breathe life into new products. The consummate skill with which these cartons are woven and stitched together and the final design reveal the satisfying outcomes that can be achieved with materials given the generic label of 'waste'. Similar materials and weaving techniques were applied to a picnic box whose tableware was all fashioned from reused or recycled materials.

✎	*Lois Walpole, UK*	311
⚙	*One-off*	
▮	*Post-consumer juice cartons*	341
♻	*• Reused and recycled materials*	327, 328

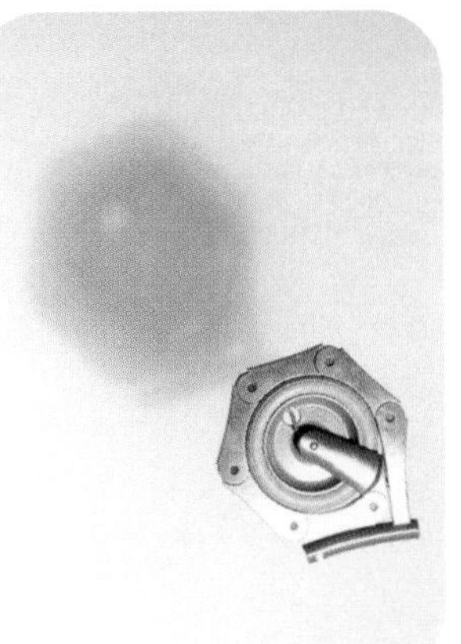

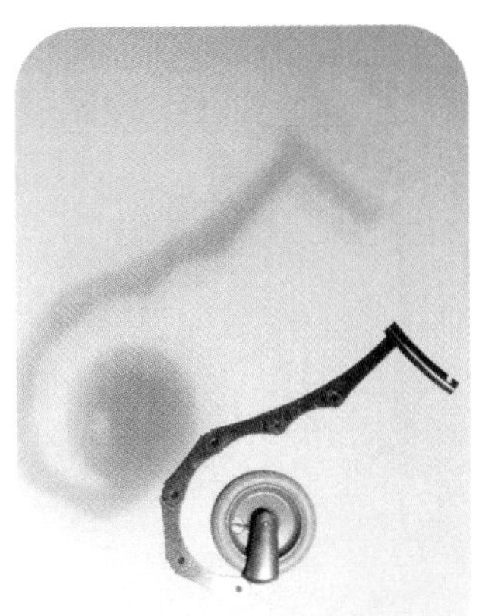

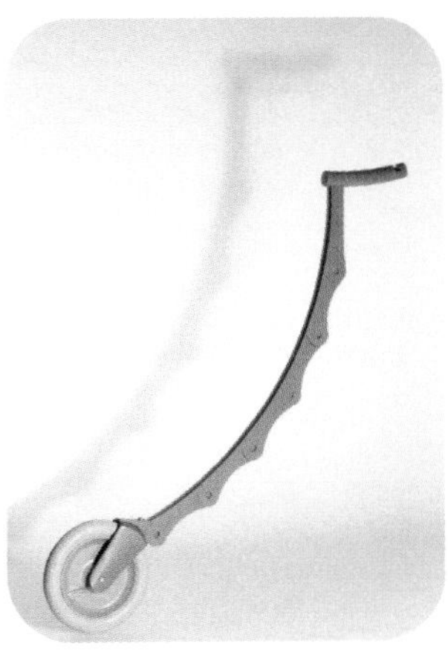

Kango

Here's a means of cutting down on the number of car journeys to local supermarkets. This mono-wheel trolley is capable of carrying a week's worth of groceries, is easily manoeuvred and, after use, is folded up into a handy package. Ideal for regular or casual use, for leisure or travel purposes, the Kango leaves all those ugly, two-wheel, tartan leatherette trolleys in the dark.

✎	*Feldmann + Schultchen, Germany*	316
⚙	*Patented prototype – Feldmann + Schultchen, Germany*	316
▭	*Cordura fabric, rubber, fibre-reinforced plastic*	283
♺	*• Encourages energy-efficient shopping*	329

Muscle Power toothbrush

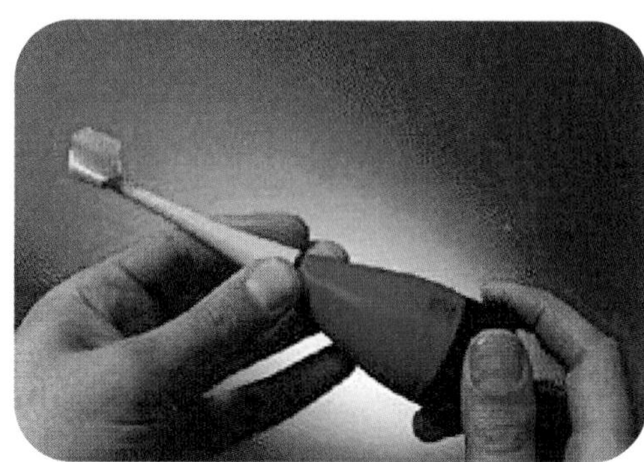

Muscle Power products raise consumer awareness at the point of purchase by posing the question, 'Do I really need to buy a battery-powered tooth brush?' The consumer is confronted with a choice of energy sources for the simple preventative health-care task of brushing his/her teeth. The solution is provided by designing a wind-up toothbrush, which can be used in static mode, like a conventional toothbrush, or can deliver a rigorous massage. Schreuder found that thirty seconds is the average time people spend cleaning their teeth, but that up to two minutes is really required for effective action of fluorides. Fully wind up the mechanism and exactly two minutes of power are delivered. A daily drudge becomes less taxing, especially for children, in whom habit-forming hygiene needs to be induced.

✎	*Hans Schreuder, Netherlands*	310
⚙	*Muscle Power, MOY, Netherlands*	320
▬	*Plastics*	283, 295
♻	*• Encourages improved health* *• Human-powered*	329

Magazine rack

Pared down to the bare minimum, the aluminium one-piece legs interlocking with the bent and cut ply, this magazine rack is a rational design with minimum usage of materials.

✎	*Mark Rogers, UK*	310
⚙	*Small batch production, BUT, UK*	313
▬	*Birch ply, aluminium*	295, 339
♻	*• Economy of materials usage*	328

Mega Solar

This solar clock is the modern equivalent of the sundial, that ancient device for telling the time using the shadows cast by the sun. Today the energy from the sun is harnessed by fitting a photovoltaic panel coupled to a battery. Even in northerly latitudes with cloudy days, sufficient energy is stored to power the low-voltage digital display that gives an accurate read-out of time and date.

✎	*FrogDesign, Germany*	306
⚙	*Junghans Uhren GmbH, Germany*	318
▬	*Photovoltaics, electronic components, battery*	341
♻	*• Reduced energy consumption*	329

Pin Up clock

Reviewing default uses of materials for specific products encourages experimentation. Rigid materials are the norm for clock face applications but Benza has been inspired to use wool fleece pinned to the wall.

✎	*Giovanni Pellone and Bridget Means, Benza, USA*	309
⚙	*Benza, Inc., USA*	313
▬	*Wool fleece, pins, clock mechanism*	341
♻	*• Renewable material*	328

Mega 1

There are two main methods of providing energy to operate a wristwatch without the need to wind it up mechanically daily or to use consumable batteries. The first is kinetic energy, in which movement of the wearer generates a small electric current to power the watch. The second, illustrated here, is to capture the power of the sun with a small photovoltaic panel linked to a storage battery. Solar watches are not new but this minimalist yet robust design sets a new benchmark.

✎	*FrogDesign, Germany*	306
⚙	*Junghans Uhren GmbH, Germany*	318
▬	*Photovoltaics, electronic components, battery*	341
♻	*• Reduced energy consumption*	329

Phoenix Thermos

Off-cuts of waste cloth sourced from a manufacturer of yacht sails are fabricated into a draw-top, double-layer bag filled with insulation wadding, to provide a thermal blanket to keep drinks cool or hot. Breaking with the convention of a rigid thermos flask, the Phoenix Thermos is easily kept in a pocket or handbag, ready to be used at any time. In one sense this design has a down side, since it appears to endorse the culture of drinking ready bottled water and soft drinks contained in the ubiquitous PET bottles. However, it will work just as well for a drink made at home.

✎	*SMAC, Sergio Macchioni, Italy*	308
⚙	*Small batch production, SMAC, Sergio Macchioni, Italy*	308
▬	*Sailcloth, rope, metal*	290-1, 300-1
♻	*• Recycled materials*	327

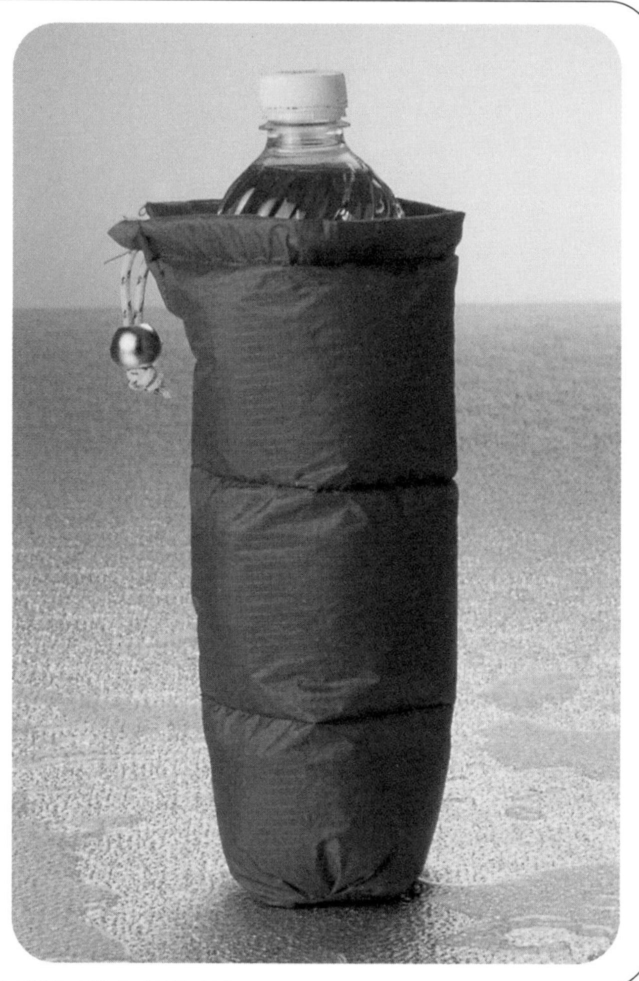

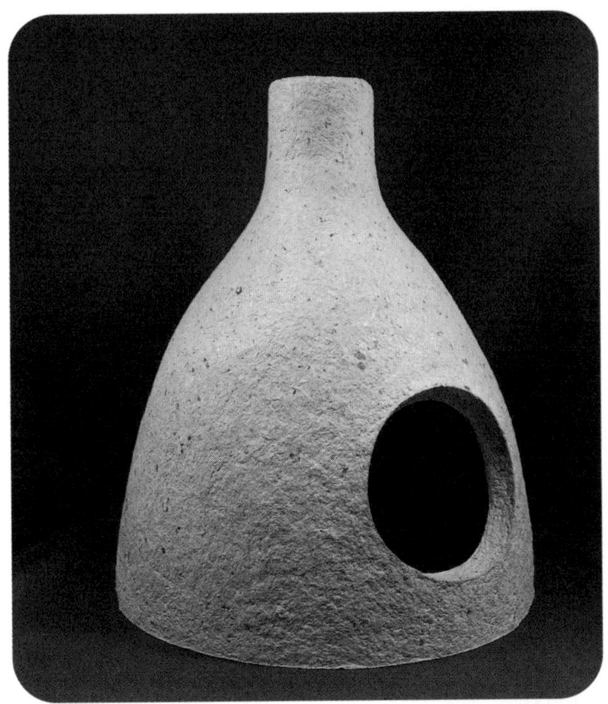

Pet Pod™

This quirky design makes a comfortable shelter and living space for a cat or small dog. The papier mâché gives insulation, so the Pet Pod is the ideal solution for pets housed in unheated buildings.

✎	*Vaccari Ltd, UK*	325
⚙	*Vaccari Ltd, UK*	325
▮	*Papier mâché*	288-9
♺	*• Recycled materials* *• Compostable*	327, 330

Rollerbag

This unique, one-wheeled trolley doubles as a shopping bag or suitcase, taking the strain and coping with smooth or rough surfaces.

✎	*Feldmann + Schultchen Design, Germany*	316
⚙	*Traveller, Germany*	325
▮	*Various*	
♺	*• Dual-function object*	329

Stationery goods

Reject circuit boards from electronics manufacturers are reused as stiff protective covers for key rings, ring binders, photo albums and clipboards. As legislation forces electronics manufacturers to be more accountable for disposal of waste and end-of-life disposal of products, this type of waste may no longer be available for recycling. One wonders also what happens to the reused circuit boards when they are discarded by the consumer. Does this form of recycling disperse potential metal pollutants through municipal landfills? Cutouts also manufacture stationery products from plastic sheeting made from recycled HDPE and LDPE.

✎	*Cutouts, UK*	314
⚙	*Cutouts, UK*	314
	Recycled circuit boards, plastics	341
	• *Reused and recycled materials*	327

U-Box

This multipurpose polypropylene box offers several compartments and permits boxes to be stacked. It provides a versatile storage unit for home, workshop or office.

✎	*Hansjerg Maier-Aichen, Authentics artipresent, Germany*	308, 313
⚙	*Authentics artipresent, Germany*	313
▬	*Recyclable polypropylene*	341
♻	• *Recyclable materials* • *Multifunctional*	327, 329

Waste paper bin

The printing industry generates vast quantities of material that is never actually used for the purpose intended. Excess print runs, abandoned promotional literature, pulped magazines and books – the volume of waste generated is high. Forty-eight-sheet advertising posters are extremely difficult to recycle because of high concentrations of coloured inks and special waterproofed papers. These latter characteristics are ideal for certain new products, as Goods demonstrate with their eye-catching waste paper bins made out of the very same advertising posters. Creative ideas from a brainstorming session often end up in the bin; now even the best ideas, with a wonderful ironic twist, become the bin!

✎	*Goods, Netherlands*	317
⚙	*Goods, Netherlands*	317
▬	*Unused billboard advertisements*	341
♻	• *Reuse of waste* • *Low-energy manufacturing*	327, 328

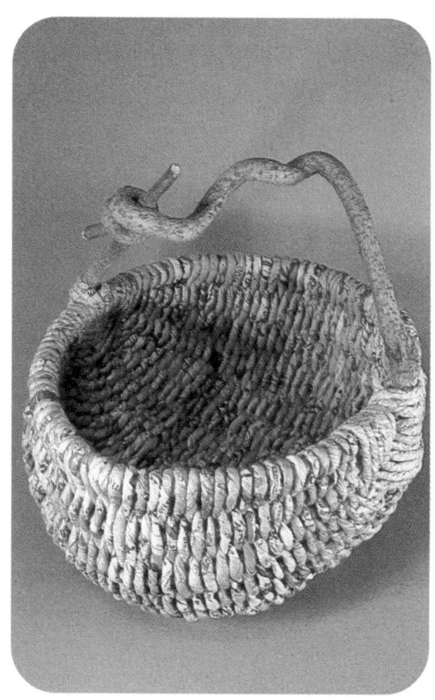

Basket

Newspaper twisted into a yarn is woven with tough vines to create durable baskets with a unique look.

✎	*Brian Dougan, USA*	306
⚙	*One-offs*	
▮	*Reused newspaper, woody vines*	281, 341
↻	*• Reused and renewable materials*	327, 328
✪	*IDRA award, 1998*	332

Litter bin

Waste metal strapping from shipping containers is woven and riveted into a robust bin suitable for use in a private garden or public space.

✎	*Arunas Oslapas, USA*	309
⚙	*One-off*	
▮	*Metal*	295
↻	*• Reused materials*	328
✪	*IDRA award, 1998*	332

Clock

Post-modernism, with an Indian flavour, is invested in this mantel or table clock made from wood harvested from sustainable sources and finished in coloured lacquers.

✎	*Abhijit Bansod, India*	304
⚙	*Titan Design Studio, India*	304
	Wood, lacquer, clock mechanism	341
	• Renewable and sustainable materials	327
	IDRA award, 1998	332

Talking alarm clock

This touch-sensitive alarm clock made of 70 per cent-recycled HDPE demonstrates imaginative use of materials and takes clock design into the twenty-first century. A clock with personality may, over time, encourage greater custodial care!

✎	*Pedro Carrasco, Portugal*	305
⚙	*Prototype*	
	Recycled HDPE, clock mechanism	341
	• Recycled materials	327
	IDRA award, 1995	332

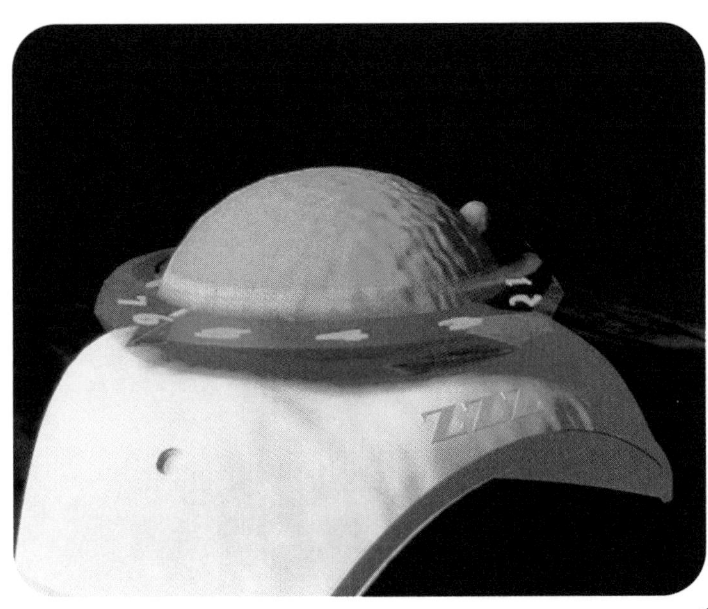

2.0 Objects for Working

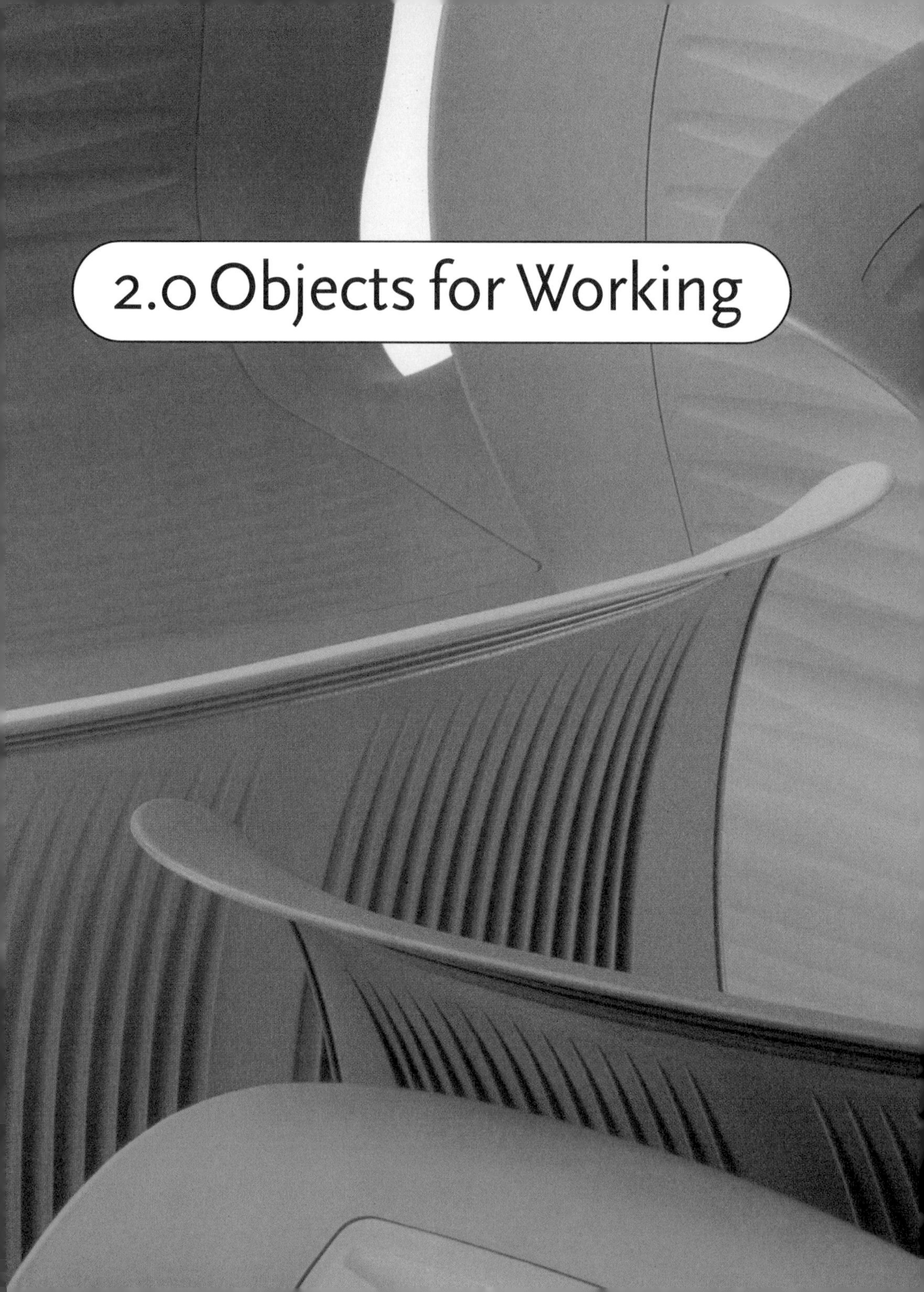

Work: An Evolving Concept

Although there is a tendency to think of the world as one huge post-industrial society, the reality is that it is a myriad of societies, some still firmly rooted in feudal agrarian systems, others heavily industrialized and still others dominated by service industries. It is therefore untrue, and possibly dangerously misleading, to think that everyone perceives problems of sustainability and work in the same way.

In the developed world 'information' is just as much a raw material as timber, iron, steel and chemicals are in an industrialized society. The main difference is in their environmental impacts. In the information society the worker needs access to a workstation, which may be in the office, at home or (in the case of a laptop computer) somewhere in between. Mobile phone and wireless technology means that workstations no longer have to be connected to physical local area networks (LANs) or fixed telecommunications points. The worker may not need to travel personally to a physical place of work and thus less transport energy is used. In an industrialized society, however, the worker has to travel to the factory where other workers and physical materials are gathered for the purpose of fabricating a product. But both the information and industrial workers consume finite resources and energy and produce waste, toxins and hazardous chemicals. All societies must therefore design products, materials and services that reduce their environmental impacts.

Work continues beyond the workplace. Domestic products that have become essential to a way of life, such as washing machines and toilets, need improvements to increase their efficiency of energy and water use. Other appliances such as kettles and cookers must also become more efficient during their lives as such and be capable of disassembly for recycling of the materials at the end of their lives.

Transporting people and distributing goods

Work involves transporting people, distributing goods or both. While electronic networks can reduce the need to move people physically, most work involves some travel. More efficient transport systems are therefore critical. Fuel efficiency needs to be improved for modes of transport that run on internal combustion engines. At the same time, lower-impact fuels and transport products powered with renewable energy need to be developed. Above all, public transport systems have to be coordinated to provide people with the flexibility and freedom.

The average super-market, furniture store or trade outlet, especially in the developed northern hemisphere, will have products from all over the world. Transported over great distances, expending vast quantities of energy, a product's transport energy can sometimes exceed the energy used to make it. Reduction in packaging weight and volume is a perennial challenge to distributors. Even the smallest saving in packaging for each product can represent huge savings in transport energy and waste production for the retailer or middle-man in the distribution chain. One-way-trip packaging can often be replaced by lightweight, reusable packaging systems, and a emphasis on local products sold in local markets could also result in large savings.

Working lightly: a sustainable day

At the office and factory more efficient working practices are aided by well-designed, durable, easily maintained products. It is now possible to have one office machine to serve a network and provide facilities to fax, photocopy, print and scan. Digital files can be shared on local and international networks. The paperless office is a partial reality. Offices can be equipped with durable, modular furniture systems and carpets can be replaced under a lease-maintenance contract. Office consumables can use recycled content and reused components.

In industrial production facilities designers, in coordination with environmental managers, can reduce inputs of energy and materials and increase efficiencies in production and distribution. Waste streams provide another source of raw material and closed-loop recycling of process chemicals and materials ensures improved eco-efficiency, better profits and improved worker health. Design can help deliver a 'triple bottom line' of reduced impacts on the environment, improved social benefits and profitability.

Work tasks in the home vary from washing the dishes, the clothes or the car to keeping the house in good repair. Future activities might include maintenance to check the efficacy of renewable power appliances or water-conservation systems or removing compost from the waterless toilet.

A sustainable working day in 2025 might involve some of the products that follow on these pages.

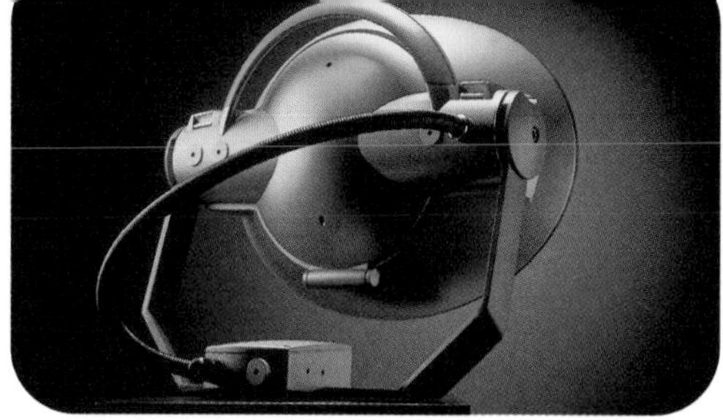

Arena Vision 401

This oval-shaped unit is suitable for exterior and interior lighting of sports facilities. Light output has been improved by 10-15 per cent for the same power input. Disassembly allows separation of the component materials and most parts can be recycled.

✎	*Philips Design, Netherlands*	309
⚙	*Philips Electronics, Netherlands*	322
▮	*Die-cast aluminium, glass*	295
♲	*• Improved energy efficiency* *• Design for disassembly*	328, 329

XK series

Exit signs fitted with incandescent lamps can now be fitted with energy-efficient LED lamps with potential energy savings of up to 90 per cent. A retrofitting kit includes the appropriate screw bases and sockets.

✎	*Lumatech Corporation, USA*	320
⚙	*Lumatech Corporation, USA*	320
▮	*LEDs*	
♲	*• Improved energy efficiency*	329

Virtual Daylight™ systems

Many office workers suffer from fatigue and illness as a direct result of the poor lighting in their work environment. Virtual Daylight™ Systems use a combination of polarization, high frequency and full-spectrum technology to reproduce daylight-quality illumination. The systems are designed to use less energy than conventional office lighting and offer a significant boost to those prone to Seasonal Affective Disorder (SAD).

✎	*Clearvision Lighting, UK*	314
⚙	*Clearvision Lighting, UK*	314
▮	*Various*	
♲	*• Simulated daylight for healthier work environment*	328

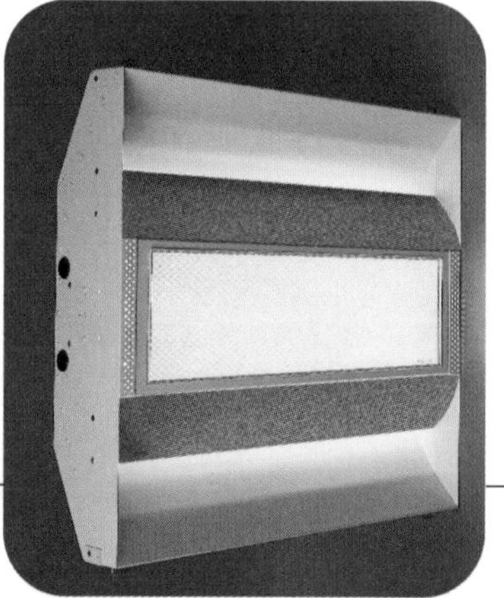

LED 100-TE

The LED 100-TE system offers a range of customized diffusers and reflectors for down-lighting, which can be fitted into two basic housings. There are nine 'Architectural', four 'Deco' and six 'Eco' diffuser/reflector options. Each housing incorporates a tilting light holder for low-energy bulbs and is fitted with electronic control gear, saving 30 per cent over conventional ballasts.

✎	*Concord Lighting, UK*	314
⚙	*Concord Lighting, UK*	314
▮	*Die-cast aluminium and polycarbonate*	
♲	*• Energy-saving, customizable lighting system*	329

Biomorph multidesk

Correct posture while working at a computer is essential for good health. This desk permits adjustment of the height of the platforms holding the computer monitor and the keyboard and features safe, rounded edges to all components.

✎	*Stephen Barlow-Lawson, USA*	304
⚙	*Ground Support Equipment (US) Ltd, USA*	317
▮	*Painted fibreboard, steel*	339
♺	• *Fully adjustable desk offers health advantages*	329

Aeron

The Aeron chair represents a step change in the way office chairs are designed. It is manufactured in three sizes to accommodate diversity of the human form and weight, making it suitable for users up to 136kg (200lb) in weight and from the first percentile female to the ninety-ninth percentile male. It has very advanced ergonomics. Pneumatic height adjustment, a sophisticated Kinemat tilt system and the Pellicle, a synthetic, breathable, membrane, are components of the seat pan, which adjusts to individual body shapes. The manufacturing process uses less energy than conventional foam construction and the use of discrete components of synthetic and recycled materials facilitates disassembly and ease of repair for worn components (which are subsequently recycled). Such design improves the longevity of the product. Components are made of one material rather than a mixture of materials to facilitate future reuse and recycling.

✎	*Bill Stumpf and Don Chadwick, Herman Miller*	305
⚙	*Herman Miller, Inc, USA, 1991 to present*	318
▮	*Plastic (PET, ABS, nylon and glass-filled nylons), steel, aluminium and foam/fabric*	341
♺	• *Improved ergonomics* • *Design for disassembly, recycling and remanufacturing* • *Single-material components*	328, 329

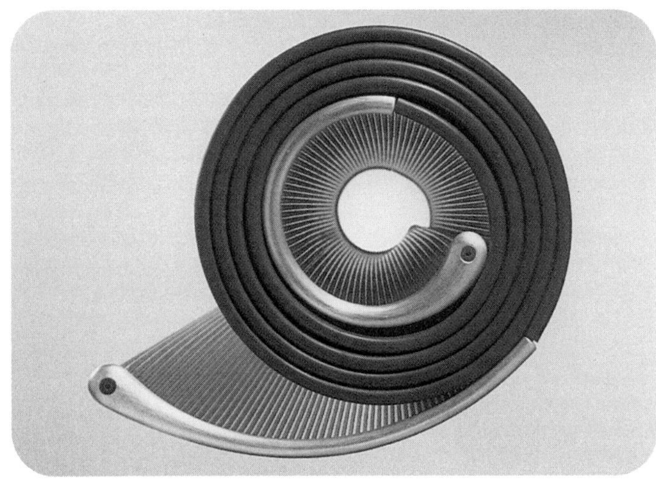

Cartoons

Cartoons is a flexible, free-standing screen suitable for partitioning in domestic and office spaces. Corrugated paper-board extracted from pure cellulose is stiffened at the edges with a closure of cold-processed, CFC-free polyurethane and at the ends with die-cast aluminium. This configuration allows the screen to be positioned in a sinuous style to suit the user and to be rolled up when not in use.

✎	*Luigi Baroli, Italy*	304
⚙	*Baleri Italia SpA, Italy*	313
■	*Corrugated paper board, aluminium, CFC-free technopolymer*	339, 341
♻	*• Renewable and/or recyclable materials* *• Clean production*	327, 328

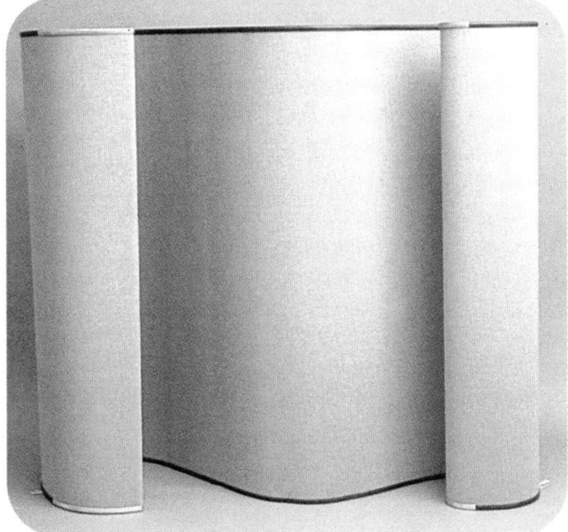

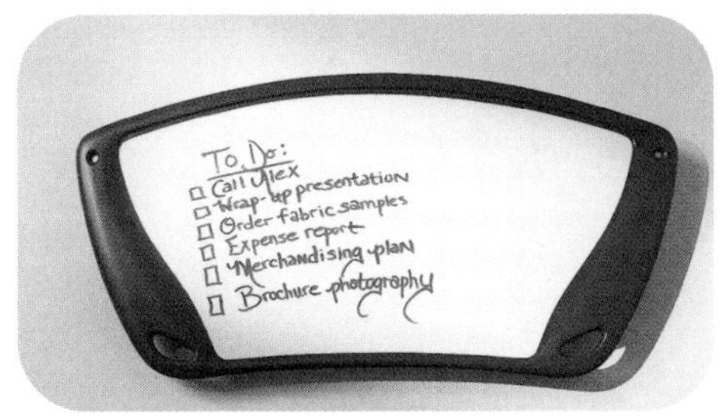

Lap desk

Office work practices, such as 'hot desking' and working remotely via intra- and extra-nets, are nowadays demanding more flexibility from equipment. Desk space has never been at such a premium, so Haworth have produced an accessory that improves efficiency in even the most overcrowded office - the Lap Desk, an extended area on which to rest your laptop computer and use as a white-board for that vital 'to do' list.

✎	*Haworth, Inc., USA*	317
⚙	*Haworth, Inc., USA*	317
■	*Various polymers*	
♻	*• Multifunctional office accessory*	329

Natura

In 1993 the company launched a new collection of office chairs, called 'Natura'. The basic premise of the design brief was to create a group of products that could be taken back by the company at the end of their active life and be easily refurbished or the components reused. Additional criteria were to improve durability, use environmentally benign materials and extend product life. Grammer had to introduce a new system to permit product return and worked closely with existing customers to make sure the scheme was accepted. This product range exemplifies producer responsibility and the adoption of the long view.

✎	*Grammer AG, Germany*	317
⚙	*Grammer AG, Germany*	317
▮	*Various polymers, metals including recycled content*	295-7
♻	*• Recyclable and reusable materials and components • Product take-back*	327, 328

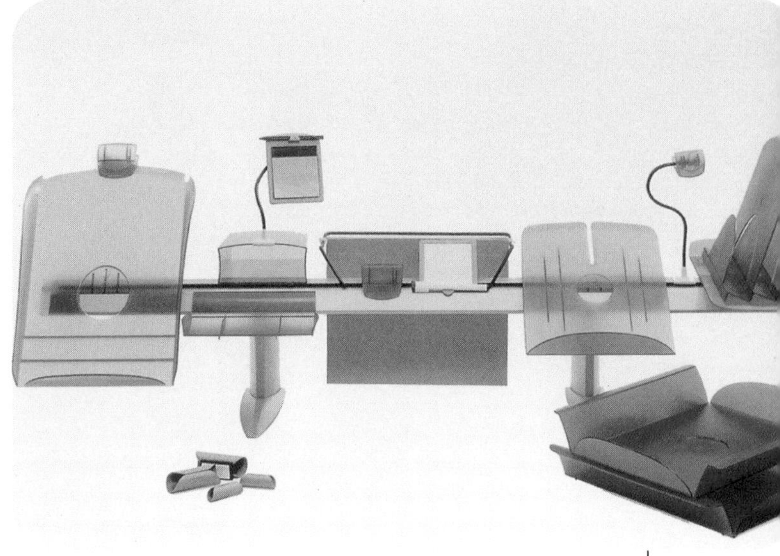

Jump Stuff, Jump Stuff II

Everybody customizes their domestic space, so why not the work space too? Through an extended series of projects and development of conceptual prototypes in the mid- to late 1990s, such as the Flo & Eddy workstation, Haworth examined the cognitive ergonomics of the desk area. The outcome is the Jump Stuff system, which allows individuals to select the components they require to maximize the functionality and comfort of their own desks. The spine of the system is a free-standing or panel-/wall-mounted rail to which the modular components can be attached. Whatever your regular tasks, you can attach and orient the appropriate accessory to the mounting rail. Different types of task lights can be attached to the rail and all the accessories can be easily adjusted for a 'hot desking' role. Although there are four basic variations to the system it is also possible to purchase each module independently so you can 'grow' the system to suit your needs.

✎	*Haworth, Inc., USA*	317
⚙	*Haworth, Inc., USA*	317
▮	*Various metals and polymers*	295-7
♻	*• Multifunctional modular system • Design for need*	328, 329

Ensemble B10

This injection-moulded seat is made of Stapron N, a blend of ABS and PA, which is manufactured with integral air pockets. It is soft and more pliable and provides improved comfort over polypropylene, which is often used for this type of chair. Stapron N is designed to be fully recyclable.

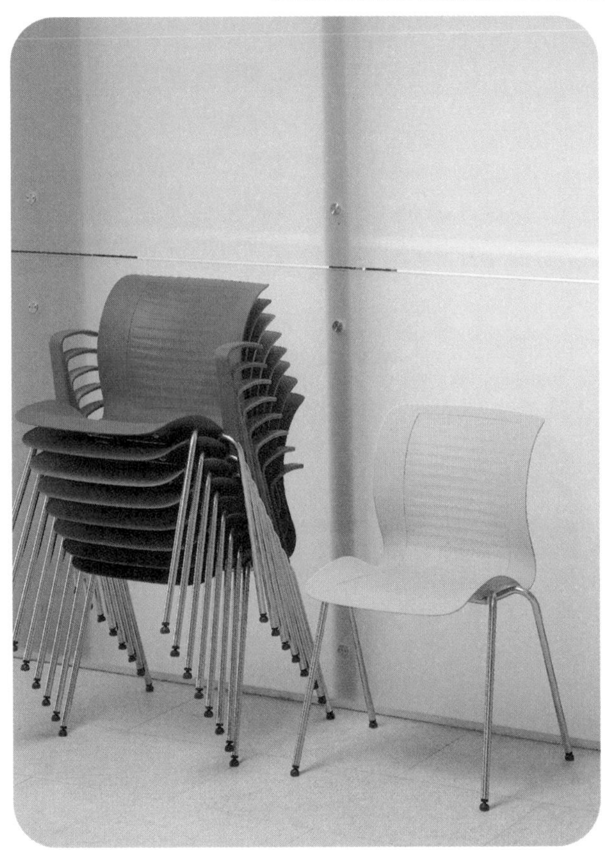

✎	*Alfred Hofmann, Denmark*	307
⚙	*Fritz Hansen, Denmark*	317
▣	*Stapron N, chrome-plated steel*	295
♲	*• A recyclable plastic*	327

Herman Miller Office Environment

Today's offices are often a conglomeration of products competing for space and visual attention and bound together by a matrix of unruly cables. Traditionally designers of office space treat flooring and furniture as distinct components. Not so Ross Lovegrove, who has considered office design literally from the floor up. The Herman Miller Office Environment exploits the full panoply of modern materials to achieve an integrated, modular but flexible system. A floor tile sits on a baseplate providing a cavernous space for ducting of service cables and pipes. Table supports fit into the tiles and lightweight table tops connect to the supports. This 3-D matrix offers a neutral, translucent, above-floor environment, which can be perfectly customized to suit clients' current and future needs. Precision-engineered components encourage easy maintenance, replacement of worn parts, expansion of existing facilities and ease of disassembly and reuse or recycling. As legislation for 'producer responsibility' gathers more momentum in the USA other manufacturers may be driven to rethink their existing designs. This system is one that shows the way.

✎	*Ross Lovegrove, UK*	308
⚙	*Conceptual prototype, Herman Miller, USA*	318
▣	*Technopolymers, high-impact polystyrene, aluminium, steel, gas-filled polymers*	295-7
♲	*• Customizable, modular system • Design for durability, maintenance and disassembly*	328, 329

Dr Oola

This fully adjustable footrest, designed for people who spend long hours at desks or workstations, is made from recycled plastic. Utilitarian objects, such as this footrest, are ideal candidates for specifying recyclates as opposed to virgin materials.

✎	*Philippe Starck, France*	310
⚙	*Vitra AG, Germany*	326
▮	*Recycled plastics*	341
♻	• *Recycled and recyclable materials* • *Single material to facilitate recycling*	327

Eddy workstation

Comfort and ergonomics at the average office workstation leave a lot to be desired. Haworth considered a number of concept designs in 1996–97 that embraced cognitive ergonomics, i.e. making the functionality of the space mirror the activity of the human brain. In this workstation, information, working notes and devices can be physically grouped on the most relevant area of the curvilinear fibreglass shelving.

✎	*Clarkson Thorpe and Steve Beukema, Haworth, USA*	310, 317
⚙	*Prototype, Haworth, USA*	317
▮	*Fibreglass, Plexiglass, leather, silicone, latex rubber, steel*	
♻	• *Improved working environment for greater productivity and comfort*	329

Leap™ seating

Building on the lessons learnt from the design of the Protégé Chair in 1991, Leap™ Seating is one of Steelcase's leading products with respect to recycling, waste reduction and low-impact manufacturing. The basic design is very durable but parts can be easily removed for repair or upgrading if required. At least 92 per cent of the chair's parts are recyclable and the cushioning used in the upholstery is made of 50 per cent-recycled PET. During manufacture adhesives and paints with no or limited Volatile Organic Compounds (VOCs) and water-based metal-plating processes considerably reduce aquatic and aerial emissions. Employee working conditions at the Grand Rapids, Michigan, factory have also been re-engineered to provide a more healthy environment. What will happen to the chair at the end of its life has not yet been defined, but leasing and take-back are options all responsible manufacturers will have to consider in the near future.

✎	*Steelcase, Inc., USA*	324
⚙	*Steelcase, Inc., USA*	324
▮	*Recycled PET, plated steel, polyester*	341
♻	*• Design for disassembly and ease of repair • Recycled and recyclable materials • Low-impact manufacturing*	327, 328

Model 4070

Germany is the only country in the world where used laminated beverage cartons are transformed into dense, strong sheeting suitable for furniture, displays and office accessories. This set of conference table and chairs uses Tectan® fixed to steel frames. Tectan® comprises about 75 per cent paper, 20 per cent polyethylene and 5 per cent aluminium, reflecting the original ratio of materials in the cartons produced by international manufacturers such as TetraPak. Waste is collected under the DSD (Duales System Deutschland AG), then sorted and shredded to create downcycled feedstock of 5mm (1/5 in) particles. The feedstock is fed into a mould where it is subjected to sufficient heat and pressure to bond the particles without adding new adhesives.

✎	*Tectan, Germany*	324
⚙	*Tectan, Germany*	324
▮	*Tectan®, steel*	292
♻	*• Recycled materials*	327

Armchair

Organic office furniture is the aim of Adam Berkowitz, who uses oak from sustainably managed forests, woven hemp webbing and organic citrus oils and paints for finishing.

✎	*Adam Berkowitz, USA*	304
⚙	*Arbor Vitae, USA*	312
▮	*Oakwood, hemp fabric, organic finishes*	290-1, 339
♻	*• Green procurement from certified sources • Renewable materials*	327

X-In Balance workplace screen

Economic use of materials is of direct benefit to the environment, yet achieving this aim is often a daunting task, in which lightness has to be balanced against the need to fulfil functional requirements. X-In Balance achieves this goal and more.

✎	*Gerald Wurz, Austria*	311
⚙	*Nova Form/Kautzky Mechanik, Austria*	319, 321
▮	*Balloon silk, steel*	290-1, 295
♻	• *Economy of materials usage* • *Lightweight recyclable materials* • *Low energy of manufacturing and transport*	327, 328

Picto, Kendo Stitz, FS range

Wilkhahn inititated a project in 1992 entitled 'Environmental Control' with the support of the Ministry for Environmental and Economic Affairs for the state of Lower Saxony. Following an audit of their corporate eco-balance of inputs and outputs, teams were set up to reduce environmental impacts in production and to select materials within an integrated IT framework. The Wilkhahn range of office seating is designed to minimize polluting processes during production. Chrome plating of metals is avoided and upholstery is made from durable, wear-resistant wool and polyester fabrics without gluing or welding.
All furniture is easily assembled/disassembled/maintained and individual components can be recovered for recycling upon disassembly.

✎	*Produkt Entwicklung Roericht, Germany*	309
⚙	*Wilkhahn + Hahne GmbH, Germany*	326
▮	*Pure-grade metals, thermoplastics*	295
♻	• *Clean production* • *Design for disassembly and recycling*	327, 328

Office furniture

This modular system of shelving, worktops and desks uses the composite materials Homosote and Medex with the natural look of cardboard in a minimalist design that emphasizes the simple virtues of the materials.

✎	*Erez Steinberg and Gia Giasullo, Studio eg, USA*	310
⚙	*Studio eg, USA*	324
▬	*Homasote, Medex, cardboard*	278
♻	*• Low-energy materials • Modular system*	328

Non-toxic workstation

This is essentially a modular, organic range of office furniture, which at the end of its useful life can be further recycled or composted, returning the constituents back to the biosphere. Attention to detail ensures a flexible working environment with a range of furniture configurations.

✎	*Erez Steinberg, Studio eg, USA*	310
⚙	*Bds/Studio eg, USA*	324
▬	*Organic materials, recycled and reused wood and paper*	341
♻	*• Renewable and recyclable materials • Low environmental impact*	327, 340

Sundeala medium board screen

The original Sundeala company began manufacturing fibreboard from waste cellulose in 1898 and for the last seventy years Sundeala boards have utilized recycled newsprint as the primary material. 'K' quality unbleached natural board is for interior use, while 'A' quality with natural binders and colouring to reduce moisture penetration is suitable for sheltered exterior use.

✎	*Celotex, UK*	314
⚙	*Celotex, UK*	314
▬	*recycled newsprint, natural binders*	341
♻	*• Reduced waste disposal • Recycled and recyclable material*	327, 328

Viper

Eliptical cross-section cardboard tubes made from recycled paper are connected to each other, top and bottom, by a specially moulded plastic capping. Extensive articulation between adjacent tubes permits the screen to be rolled up when not in use.

✎	*Hans Jakobsen, Denmark*	307
⚙	*Fritz Hansen, Denmark*	317
▬	*Cardboard, plastic*	283, 288-9
♻	*• Recycled material*	327

STEP

A combination of different-sized, lightweight, plywood veneered tabletops can be quickly assembled and linked together to form flexible arrangements as required. Legs and connecting plates are made of aluminium and all the various components can be stored on a purpose-built trolley.

✎	*Korb & Korb, Switzerland, and Dyes, Germany*	308, 315
⚙	*Dyes, Germany*	315
▬	*Aluminium, plywood*	295
♻	*• Lightweight, multifunctional furniture*	329

Supine workstation

This bespoke workstation was designed for a computer specialist who found it impossible to work at a conventional desk for any length of time because of three fused vertebrae in his lower back. The Center for Rehabilitation Technology developed a workstation that can be rolled towards the chair and locked in position. Once the user is seated the chair can be tilted backwards and the monitor and keyboard swung into position.

✎	*Julius T. Corkran and Alan Harp, USA*	305
⚙	*Center for Rehabilitation Technology, College of Architecture, Georgia Institute of Technology, USA*	305
▬	*Various*	
♻	*• Design for personalization providing extra comfort*	329

Curva

Reuse of existing materials or manufactured components requires very little or no energy input and is a quick way of reintroducing resources into the materials stream. De Denktank have come up with a stimulating example of reuse with their Curva flexible yet unbreakable ruler, made from discarded aluminium venetian-blind slats obtained from local recycling depots. Silkscreen printed graphics are printed on to the original coloured slats and 100 per cent-recycled packaging is used to protect the ruler during distribution and retailing. Simplicity is a key element of this design.

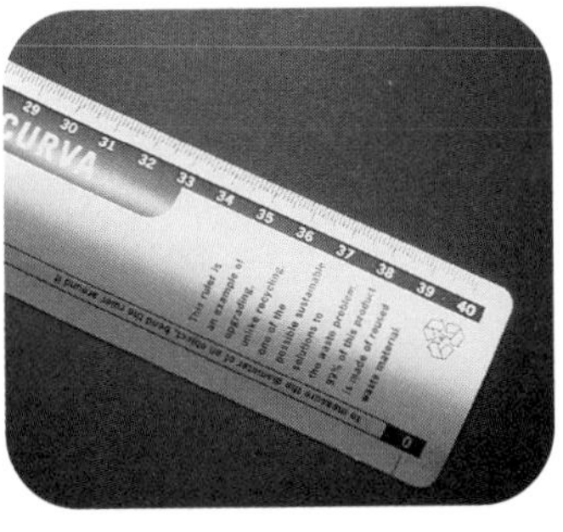

✎	*De Denktank, Netherlands*	305
⚙	*De Denktank, Netherlands*	305
▰	*Reused aluminium*	295
♻	• *Reuse of materials* • *Low-energy manufacturing*	328
✪	*Design Sense award, 1999*	332

Karisma

Sanford UK is part of the Sanford Corporation, which is the world's largest manufacturer of pencils based upon waste wood products, a mixture of wood flour and polymers. All wood-cased pencils manufactured by Sanford UK use wood from managed forests and, where possible, pencils are protected by water-based varnishes, which are hardened by ultraviolet light, rather than using solvent-based inks. Packaging and plastic waste are recycled at the production plant.

Episola

Using a pencil as the fulcrum, this exquisitely simple set of scales allows letters to be graded for correct stamping. It also serves as a letter opener and involves minimal use of materials and energy during manufacturing.

✎	*Teo Enlund, Sweden*	306
⚙	*Simplicitas, Sweden*	324
▰	*Metal*	295
♻	• *Economy of materials and low embodied energy*	327, 328, 340

✎	*Sanford UK Ltd, UK*	323
⚙	*Sanford UK Ltd, UK*	323
▰	*Wood, water-based varnishes*	298, 339
♻	• *Recycled materials* • *Clean production* • *Supply-chain management*	327, 328

Remarkable recycled pencil

Used polystyrene cups from vending machines are shredded and re-processed into a new 'plastic alloy', in which graphite and other materials are mixed with polystyrene and extruded in a special die to create a new type of pencil. It performs as well as traditional 'lead' pencils and helps reduce consumption of the timber that traditionally encases the lead.

(designer)	*Edward Douglas-Miller, Remarkable Pencils, UK*	307, 323
(manufacturer)	*Remarkable Pencils, UK*	323
(materials)	*Recycled polystyrene, graphite, additives*	341
(eco)	*• Reduces resource consumption • Reduces waste production • Recycling*	328

Save A Cup

Drinks vending machines daily consume vast quantities of standard 80mm polystyrene cups to satisfy the thirst of office workers and users of public spaces. All those spent cups - what a waste! Save A Cup has organized direct or third-party collection of used cups in all the major UK cities, using specially designed bins and machines to shred the cups. Companies registered with the UK's Environment Agency can obtain a Packaging Recovery Note (PRN) for the tonnage recycled to comply with the UK Packaging Waste Regulations. The feedstock

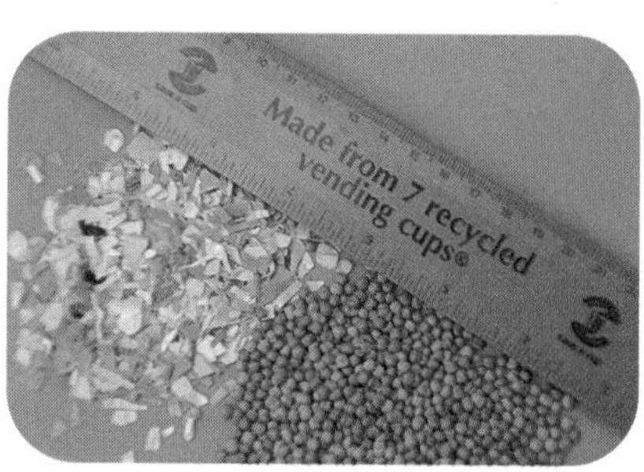

recyclate is suitable for low-grade use such as pens, rulers and key rings.

(designer)	*Save A Cup Recycling Company, UK*	323
(manufacturer)	*Save A Cup Recycling Company, UK*	323
(materials)	*Polystyrene*	341
(eco)	*• Recycled materials*	327

Sensa™ pen

Gripping a pen for an extended period can cause discomfort. A soft, non-toxic gel around the grip area moulds itself to fit the user's fingers as it warms up and consequently improves comfort. Once the gel cools it returns to its original shape.

(designer)	*Boyd Willat, USA*	327
(manufacturer)	*Willat Writing Instruments, USA*	327
(materials)	*Metal, gel*	295
(eco)	*• Design for comfort and customization*	329

GreenDisk

Ex-Microsoft program disks are recycled by deleting the data and triple-testing so as to guarantee that they are virus- and error-free. A new label is added and the disks are boxed in packs of ten or twenty-five using recycled brown cardboard.

(designer)	*GreenDisk, USA*	317
(manufacturer)	*GreenDisk , USA*	317
(materials)	*Recycled floppy disks*	341
(eco)	*• Reusing and recycling existing products*	327

EPSON Stylus Scan 2000

Convergence of digital technology has enabled Epson to combine three functions in one machine, with significant savings in materials resources. This small desktop machine permits printing, scanning and copying and embodies a design philosophy that is moving towards a Factor 4 reduction in resource usage. In recognition of the importance of aesthetics in the office, it has a range of coloured cover panels, allowing customers to choose one to complement their local decor.

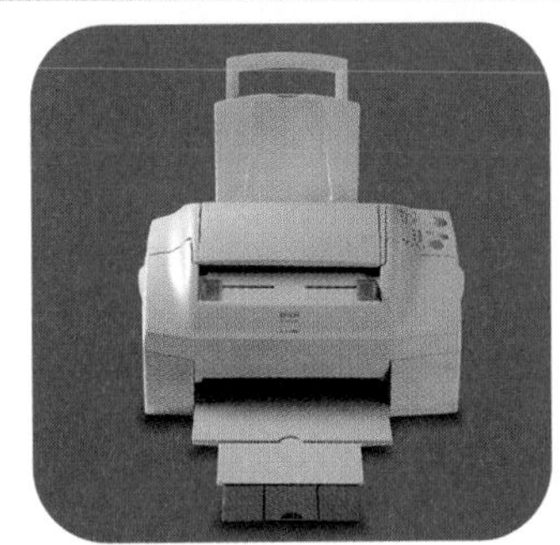

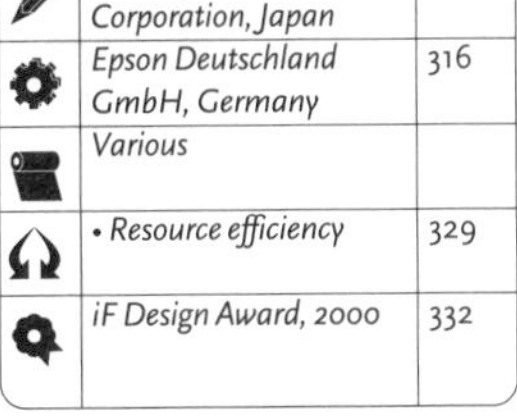

	Seiko Epson Corporation, Japan	310
	Epson Deutschland GmbH, Germany	316
	Various	
	• Resource efficiency	329
	iF Design Award, 2000	332

Single-handed keyboard

'Access for all' is the clarion cry of the proponents of the Information Age but conventional keyboard design denies access to individuals with disabilities. Maltron's single-handed head/mouth stick keyboards are tools to help them overcome this hurdle and to enjoy what others take for granted. The Etype keyboard is also a tool for those suffering from repetitive strain injury (RSI), that most modern of ailments. A curved keyboard and palm resting pads ensure less tiring movements.

	PCD Maltron Ltd, UK	322
	PCD Maltron Ltd, UK	322
	Various plastics, electronics	341
	• Improved user health *• Improved access to information for those with disabilities*	329

	Canon, Japan	314
	Canon, Japan	314
	Various	
	• Reduction in consumables and energy consumption	328, 329
	Environmental Choice EcoLogo M eco-label, Canada	

GP225 series

A photocopier, printer, fax machine and, more recently, a scanner have become the standard complement of desktop equipment for most businesses. Canon's Networked Office Systems, such as the GP225 Series, have avoided the unnecessary use of paper when using individual, mono-function machines by integrating the functions into one networked system. Productivity can be increased and use of consumables, such as toner and paper, is reduced.

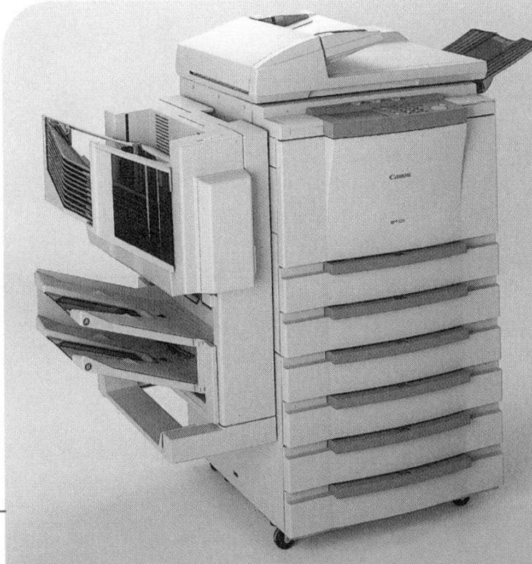

PagePro8

This compact desktop laser printer boasts a small footprint and low noise operation thanks to the absence of a ventilation fan. Low emissions, low energy consumption and a recyclable plastic casing combine to make the PagePro8 an excellent example of more environmentally conscious manufacturing.

	Yoshihiro Ichi, Industrial Design Division, Minolta, Japan	307
	Minolta, Japan	320
	Plastic casing, electronics	283, 295
	• *Low energy consumption* • *Low emission of harmful substances* • *Low noise* • *Recyclable materials*	328, 329
	iF Ecology Design Award, 1999	332

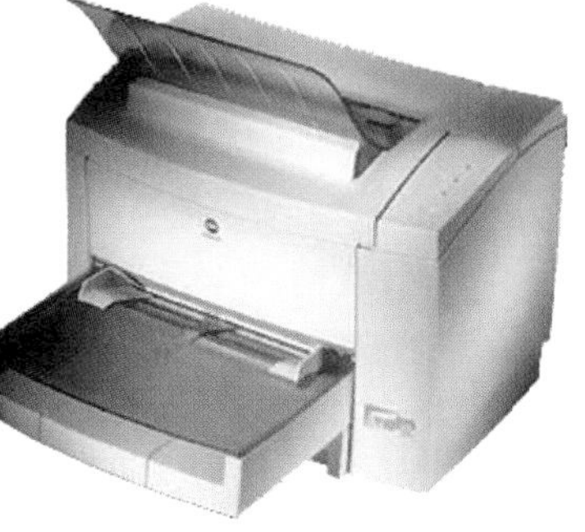

ECOSYS

The current range of nine ECOSYS laser printers manufactured by Kyocera constitutes a modular design system that permits upgrading from a simple desktop personal printer, the FS-680, capable of 8ppm, to the free-standing FS-9000, which has an output of up to 36ppm. These printers use specially developed long-life drum technology rather than cartridges, so only the toner has to be replenished. Consequently maintenance requirements and operating costs are low.

	F A Porsche with Kyocera, Japan	309
	Kyocera, Japan	319
	Various	
	• *Reduction in consumables* • *Modular upgrade path*	328

Xerox® Document Centre 470 and 460® series

The Xerox Corporation was an early adopter of greener manufacturing, environmental management systems and product take-back. This has meant designing standardized parts that are interchangeable across a range of products and are clearly identified to assist with reuse and recycling. Products are also designed for ease of disassembly to facilitate reuse, recycling or materials recovery. A reduction in the total number of parts in each machine is also central to the company's design philosophy. The Xerox® Document Centre 470 and 460® series are typical of networked, multifunctional machines capable of copying, printing, faxing and scanning. The series is Energy Star compliant, the sleep mode requiring just 65 watts, compared with 1,425 watts in operational and 260 watts in low power mode.

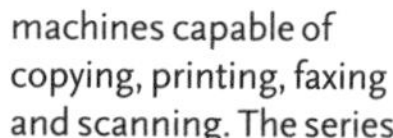

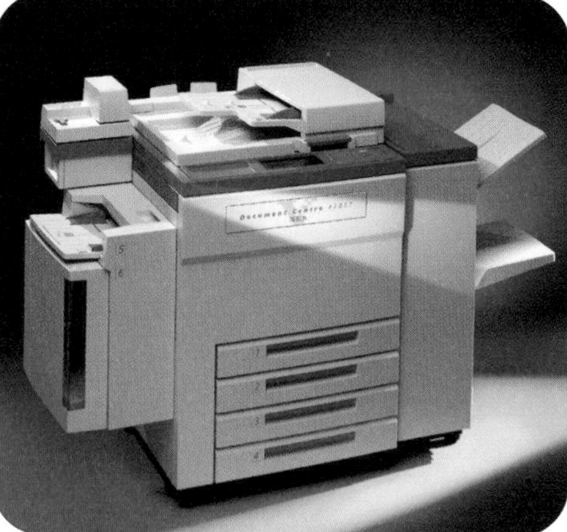

	Xerox Corporation, USA	326
	Xerox Corporation, USA	326
	Various	
	• *Multifunctionality* • *Design for disassembly* • *Reduction in materials usage in manufacturing* • *Product take-back*	327, 328, 329

Multisync® LT 140

This lightweight, compact data projector has a PCMIA-card drive, which permits the unit to be used without linking up to a PC. The total number of components has been kept to a minimum and upon disassembly materials are easily separated into pure-grades. A slot is provided to store the remote control and a peripheral mouse enables annotations to be made on the projected data.

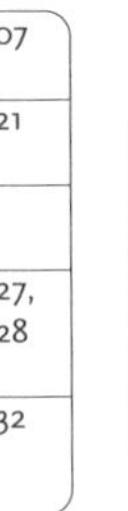

	IDEO Product Development, Japan	307
	NEC Deutschland GmbH, Germany	321
	Various	
	• Economy of materials usage *• Design for disassembly*	327, 328
	iF Ecology Design Award, 2000	332

IBM IntelliStation E Pro

This is the world's first PC to use 100 per cent-recycled plastics for the casings for the monitor, CPU and keyboard. These components are up to 20 per cent cheaper than those made from virgin materials. A small desktop footprint is matched to a high-specification workstation suitable for all types of professional uses from graphics to financial and business networks.

	IBM Personal Systems Group Design, IBM Corporation, USA	318
	IBM Corporation, USA	318
	Recycled plastics, electronics	283, 295
	• Recycled content	327
	iF Design Award, 2000	332

Air Box

Packaging materials are dead weight, which imposes a cost on the sender or recipient and consumes transport energy. Lightweight yet strong materials are the nirvana to which every packaging designer aspires. Air Box is an off-the-shelf range of inflatable, transparent nylon/PE bags with resealable valves, which add very little to gross parcel weight. Although the manufacturers advise additional external protection with cardboard to prevent puncture of the polymer mix, some users have discovered great publicity value in allowing the contents of their Air Boxes to be revealed. It is reported that IBM sent an invitation to a breakfast meeting with an egg enclosed.

✎	*Air Packaging Technologies, USA*	312
⚙	*Air Packaging Technologies, USA*	312
▮	*Nylon and polyethylene mixture*	296-7
♻	*• Lightweight, reusable packaging system*	328

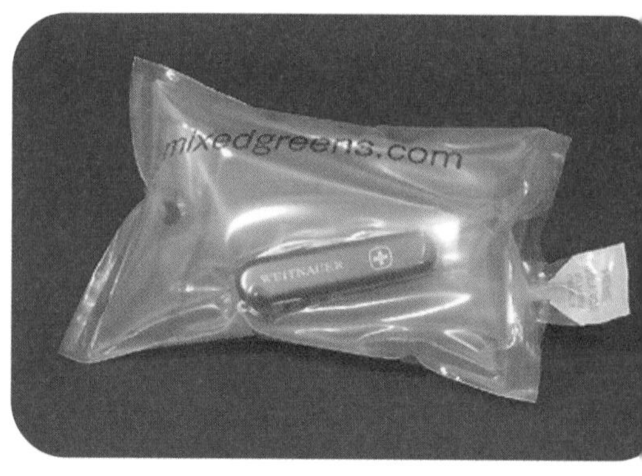

Akylux

Polypropylene sheeting is a resilient alternative to corrugated cardboard, especially when it can encourage multi-trip, reusable packaging. Kayserberg Packaging have designed numerous box systems with internal compartments, which can be reused for distribution of components and finished products. Being the only component in this product, the PP can easily be recycled when it reaches the end of its useful life.

✎	*Kayserberg Packaging, France*	319
⚙	*Kayserberg Packaging, France*	319
▮	*Polypropylene*	296-7
♻	*• Reusable and recyclable* *• Blue Angel eco-label*	328

Airfil

This lightweight packaging made of recyclable PE uses air as the shock-absorbing material to protect goods in transit. Airfil air bags are produced in standard and bespoke sizes, providing a viable, less expensive alternative to polystyrene 'chips' and 'bubble wrap'. The Airfil system significantly reduces storage space requirements and allows a reduction in the thickness of the outer packaging material. It is also reusable, clean and free of dust.

✎	*Amasec Airfil, UK*	312
⚙	*Amasec Airfil, UK*	312
▮	*Polyethylene*	296-7
♻	*• Reduction in materials usage* *• Use of a recyclable plastic*	327, 328

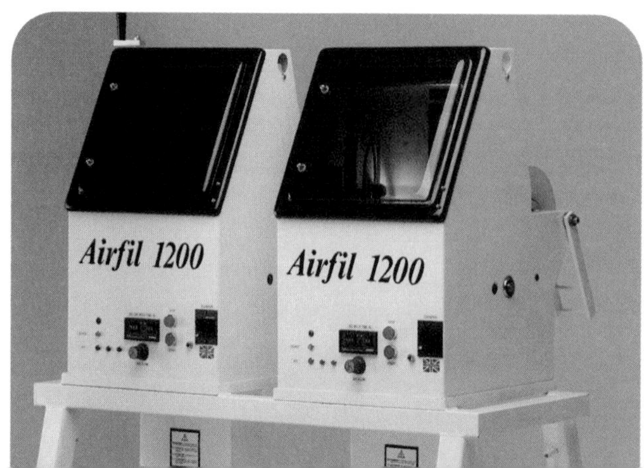

Compostable organic refuse bag

Disposal of municipal biodegradable waste, such as leaves, grass and weeds, is facilitated by using this sack made of a biodegradable thermoplastic, polylactide or PLA, derived from lactic acid. At landfill or compost sites the bags can be disposed of along with the waste. These bags offer a number of advantages over kraft paper bags, such as improved strength for wet contents and easier handling.

✎	*Cargill Dow Polymers, USA/Netherlands*	314
⚙	*Cargill Dow Polymers, USA/Netherlands*	314
▬	*PLA - EcoPLA®*	283
♺	• *Biodegradable plastic*	327

Natural gourd packaging

Harnessing nature to manufacture standardized goods has long been the preserve of the farmer, but now product designers may benefit too. Gourds, which are traditionally used in many tropical countries, can be encouraged to grow into specific shapes by surrounding them with a plywood mould, the final form being controlled by the intended usage.

✎	*A. J. Velthuizen, European Design Centre, and R. S. Wall, Rotterdam Academy of Architecture & Urban Planning, Netherlands*	311
⚙	*Prototype*	
▬	*Gourds*	339
♺	• *Renewable and compostable materials* • *Very low-energy 'bio-manufacturing'*	327, 328

Cull-Un Pack

This is a UN-certified packaging design for the transport of hazardous chemicals in glass containers. A strong moulded pulp base and top, made from used cardboard boxes, protects the containers, which are enclosed in a corrugated cardboard outer. It meets stringent safety tests, including a 1.9m (6ft) drop, which had previously been met only by using expanded polystyrene packaging. All the materials are from recycled sources and the packs can be delivered flat, saving valuable delivery space.

✎	*Robert Cullen & Sons, UK*	323
⚙	*Robert Cullen & Sons, UK*	323
▬	*100 per cent-recycled paper and board*	288-9
♺	• *Recycled, renewable materials*	327

IFCO returnable transit packaging

Eleven standard sizes of flat-pack, reusable plastic containers with ventilated sides are meant for transit packaging for all types of fresh produce. The IFCO system is used in over thirty countries and an estimated seventy million packaging units are in circulation. Compatible with loading on Euro and ISO pallets, the units are of constant tare, are easily cleaned and when folded reduce storage space requirements by 80 per cent. Unit weight-to-volume ratios are economical: tare weights vary from 0.65kg (1lb 7oz) to 1.75kg (3lb 14oz), giving respective storage volumes of between 0.01 square metres (0.11 square ft) and 0.05 square metres (0.54 square ft). At the end of their useful working lives the polypropylene is recycled. An ecobalance study by Ecobalance Applied Research GmbH revealed significantly less environmental impact from the IFCO system than from conventional one-way corrugated cardboard boxes.

International Food Container Organization GmbH, Germany	318
International Food Container Organization GmbH, Germany	318
Polypropylene	296-7
• Recyclable single material *• Closed loop system* *• Reductions in unit manufacturing and transport energy* *• Blue Angel eco-label*	328, 329

Pallecon 3 Autoflow

Made of sheet and solid steel, this container is suitable for transporting a wide range of industrial liquids from pharmaceutical products to foodstuffs. It is emptied via a sump through valves, which are recyclable, and is easily cleaned between consignments. It can be stored into one-third of its original size by folding the sides, thus saving valuable cargo space. Meeting EU standards and with an expected service life of ten years, the Pallecon 3 Autoflow can be entirely recycled at the end of its useful life.

LSK Industries Pty Ltd, Australia	319
LSK Industries Pty Ltd, Australia	319
Steel	295
• Single material to facilitate recycling *• Reusable and recyclable* *• Potential reduction of transport energy*	328, 329
iF Design Award, 2000	332

Presswood pallet

Unlike traditional timber pallets, the 'Inka' pallets don't need to be fixed with staples or nails since they are manufactured from recycled timber waste bonded with water-resistant synthetic resins. Other advantages over conventional pallets include more compact stacking and lower tare weight. Standard pallet sizes meet current European regulations and are recyclable. As of January 2000, wood is included within the EU Packaging Waste recovery and recycling regulations, so the reduced wood content of these pallets lowers the costs associated with these obligations.

✎	*Werzalit AG + Co., Germany*	326
⚙	*Werzalit AG + Co., Germany*	326
▬	*Waste timber, resins*	284, 339
♺	• *Recycled materials* • *Encourages reduction in transport-energy consumption*	327, 328

Rexpak™

This multi-trip cardboard box is being tested by the food-distribution industry in the UK. It is a collapsible box that is reconstructed when required by folding and using temporary Velcro® tape to keep its shape and strength. Each box is capable of up to ten trips before recycling, reducing materials consumption, labour and disposal costs.

✎	*Rexam, UK*	323
⚙	*Rexam, UK*	323
▬	*Corrugated cardboard*	288-9
♺	• *Reusable packaging*	328

VarioPac®

The struggle to extract CDs from their protective covers is consigned to the past thanks to this well-conceived and -manufactured product. Simply press the lever in the corner to eject the CD. An assessment by FH Lippe of the VarioPac Rover conventional cases revealed that the tactile, translucent and shatter-proof Metocene (metallocene polypropylene) requires 46 per cent less energy during manufacturing by injection moulding and reduces transport volume by 33 per cent – ample proof that this redesign reduces environmental impacts.

✎	*VarioPac Disc Systems GmbH, Germany*	311
⚙	*Ehlebracht AG, Germany*	315
▬	*Metocene X 50081*	296-7
♺	• *Reduction of materials usage* • *Reduction of embodied and transport energy*	327, 328
✪	*iF Ecology Design Award, 2000*	332

Sylvania

An important part of the turnover of Sylvania Lighting International is directly to electrical equipment wholesalers. While retaining the strong corporate identity with minimal graphics (the light beam and polar curve), the clear technical information printed on plain brown cardboard assists wholesalers in product identification while still providing adequate protection of the lamps. This philosophy is extended to other promotional and display material such as catalogues, retail displays and so on.

✎	*Premsela and Vonk, Netherlands*	309
⚙	*Sylvania Lighting International, Switzerland and USA*	310
▬	*Cardboard, paper, printing inks*	288-9
♻	• *Reduction in consumption of printing inks*	330

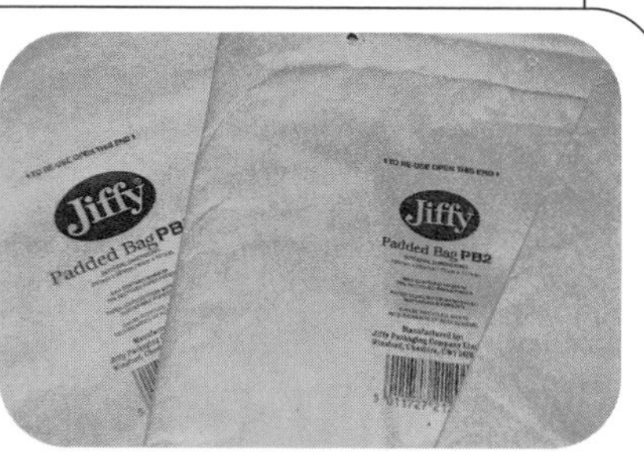

Jiffy®

Jiffy produce a range of bags to protect goods transported via postal and courier systems. The padding is made of 72–75 per cent-recycled, shredded newsprint and the exterior is a tough brown paper, which permits the bags to be reused.

✎	*Jiffy Packaging Company Ltd, UK*	318
⚙	*Jiffy Packaging Company Ltd, UK*	318
▬	*Recycled newsprint*	341
♻	• *Recycled materials* • *Reusable product*	327, 328

Schäfer Eco Keg

Die-cast, injection-moulded, thermoplastic base and top clip on to the stainless-steel body of this beverage container, avoiding the need to glue in place rubber or polyurethane sealing rings. All parts can be disassembled for repair, replacement and pure-grade recycling. The container is suitable for all automated KEG plants and can be stacked more easily than conventional containers, making for space savings and improved transport efficiency.

✎	*Schäfer Werke GmbH, Germany*	323
⚙	*Schäfer Werke GmbH, Germany*	323
▬	*Stainless steel, thermoplastic*	295
♻	• *Design for durability, disassembly and recyclability* • *Reduction in transport energy*	328, 329
✪	*iF Ecology Design Award, 2000*	332

Biopac

This biodegradable packaging is suitable for pharmaceutical and confectionery products. Biopac is composed of edible starch substances.

✎	*Haasa, Austria*	317
⚙	*Haasa, Austria*	317
▮	*Edible starch*	339
♻	*• Biodegradable, compostable*	327

3M™ 8000

Contamination of recycled plastic feedstock with unknown types of plastic can render recyclate unusable and damage production plant. It is not always possible to create labels by embossing the information on components or products, so 3M have produced a stick-on label that can be used when recycling ABS

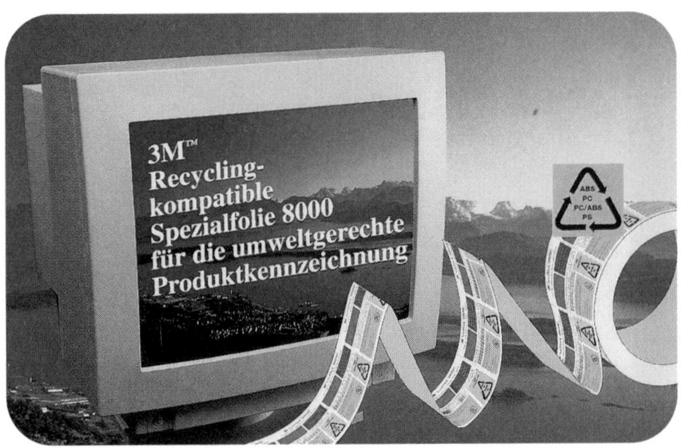

and polycarbonate, ABS/polycarbonate mixes and polystyrene. Such plastics are common in the electronics industry where identification of materials at disassembly will become more critical as the EU WEEE Directive on recycling of electronic equipment is applied over the next few years.

✎	*Hiep Nguyen, Gerald Schniedermeier, Yolanda Grievenow, Den Suoss, 3M Deutschland, Germany*	312
⚙	*3M Deutschland, Germany*	312
▮	*Plastics*	283, 295
♻	*• Facilitates plastics identification and recycling*	330
✪	*iF Ecology Design Award, 1999*	332

Top Box

The Top Box is a versatile storage container made of a collapsible, flat-pack, cardboard carcass with a hinged plastic lid incorporating a tamper-proof catch and carrying handles. It is square in section and stackable and so can be efficiently stored or transported without occupying excessive space.

✎	*Sams Design and Reed Corrugated Cases, UK*	310
⚙	*Reed Corrugated Cases, UK*	310
▮	*Cardboard, plastic*	288-9
♻	*• Reusable, multifunctional storage container • Potential reduction in transport energy*	328, 329

Allison bus

An improvement in fuel economy of 50 per cent over conventional powered units is achieved by using the Allison Electric Drives hybrid system developed Allison Transmission, a subsidiary of General Motors. The system also gives a significant reduction in emissions of carbon monoxide, hydrocarbons, particulate matter and nitrous oxide. The Allison Bus represents an opportunity to create cleaner public transport systems. A well-peopled bus equipped with such clean technology is patently more sustainable than lots of single-occupancy cars.

✎	*General Motors, USA*	317
⚙	*General Motors, USA*	317
▆	*Various*	
♲	• *Improved fuel efficiency* • *Reduction in emissions*	329

Metropolitan express train

In contrast to most modern trains, the interior of this new train system is made of entirely natural or recyclable materials. With moulded laminated wood shells and leather upholstery, this design makes significant reference to the original 1956 Herman Miller Model No. 670 and 671 lounge chairs designed by Charles and Ray Eames. For those who travel regularly by rail the little touches, such as a padded head pillow, will be much appreciated.

✎	*gmp - Architekten, Germany*	307
⚙	*Deutsche Bahn AG and Metropolitan Express Train GmbH, Germany*	315
▆	*Leather, plywood, stainless steel*	395
♲	• *Renewable and recyclable materials*	327
✪	*iF Design Award, 2000*	332

Checkpoint and Checktag

Loose wheel nuts can lead to accidents, with loss of life and possible spillage of pollutants and toxins into the environment. Checkpoint and Checktag are two types of plastic cap that are pushed over a nut once it has been tightened to the correct torque. The arrows on each cap should be aligned unless the nuts have worked themselves loose. A quick visual check is all that is needed to identify a rogue nut.

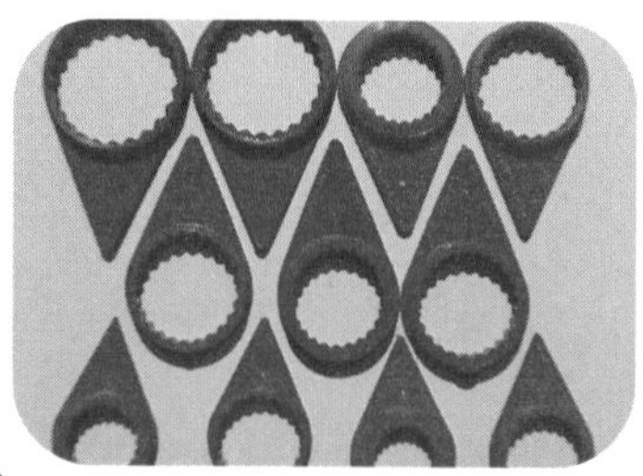

✎	*Mike Marczynski, UK*	308
⚙	*Business Lines, UK*	313
▆	*Plastic*	283, 295
♲	• *Improvement in road safety* • *Reduction in pollution*	328, 329

Cold Feather

With a maximum gross weight of 40 tonnes for all European road haulage vehicles, any reduction in the tare weight of an empty vehicle means potentially more cargo capacity. The design team were able to remove two longitudinal chassis girders because the lightweight trailer body made of dual layers of composites was sufficiently rigid. The deck layer comprises a mixture of aramid composite, glass fibre and balsa wood with a high compression strength, and the underneath layer consists of glass fibre and aluminium sheet with a PVC foam infill. Side panels are reinforced with carbon-reinforced resin beams and the outer skin is made of an aramid-epoxy resin. Aramid textiles are specially woven in layers with the fibres in adjacent layers orientated at 45 degrees to each other, giving them greater impact resistance and reducing flexing. Overall the design saves 3 tonnes tare weight over conventional designs.

✎	*Team of thirty designers, University of Technology, Delft, Netherlands*	311
⚙	*Conceptual prototype*	
▮	*Various composites, steel, aluminium*	395
♻	• *Reduction in fuel consumption*	330

EVEC

This device is fitted to the induction side of an internal combustion engine and can deliver up to 62 per cent reduction of carbon monoxide and 35 per cent of hydrocarbons in the exhaust gases. According to the manufacturers, lifecycle analysis shows a payback within 500 miles (800km) of the device's being fitted to a vehicle. EVEC can be retrofitted to old and new vehicles, unlike most catalytic converters, which work only on modern, lead-free fuel engines.

✎	*Hawtal Whiting Environmental, UK*	317
⚙	*Hawtal Whiting Environmental, UK*	317
▮	*Aluminium*	395
♻	• *Reduction of exhaust emissions*	329

Flexitec

Traffic-calming systems installed using conventional techniques require considerable manpower and cause disruption to traffic during installation. Flexitec, a hard-wearing modular system of kerbs, blocks and ramps, manufactured from recycled rubber, is installed by bolting each module to the existing road surface. It reduces road congestion during installation and can be used for permanent or temporary traffic calming.

✎	*BTM International Ltd, UK*	313
⚙	*BTM International Ltd, UK*	313
▮	*Recycled rubber*	283
♻	• *Recycled materials* • *Reusable system* • *Reduced energy of installation*	327, 328

Tank signal system

A radio transmitter monitors the fuel level in a storage tank and sends the information to a telemetry device called a Signalman fitted to the customer's telephone network point. This Signalman updates a PC at the fuel depot, so at any time the supplier can work out the best route and volume of fuel to deliver to his customers. This system can be used for domestic and industrial fuel supplies. It is estimated that it could save up to half of the road journeys by delivery vehicles.

✎	*Sensor Systems Watchman, UK*	323
⚙	*Sensor Systems Watchman, UK*	323
▮	*Radio transmitter, telemetry device, PC*	341
♻	• *Significant reduction in transport energy to deliver goods*	328

Electrically power-assisted steering (EPAS)

Most power steering systems involve installation of a hydraulic motor and associated piping. EPAS uses an electronically controlled direct-drive electronic motor and claims to achieve a 5 per cent improvement in fuel economy and easy, maintenance-fee installation. More importantly, it avoids the risk of contamination of the vehicle and environment with corrosive hydraulic fluid, which can prevent recycling. EPAS technology has already been sold to six car manufacturers for installation in their new models.

✎	*TRW Lucas Varity Electrical Steering, UK*	325
⚙	*TRW Lucas Varity Electrical Steering, UK*	325
▰	*Various*	
♲	• *Improved fuel consumption, avoids risk of escaping pollutants*	329

Continuously regenerating trap (CRT)

The CRT is a catalytic converter and particle filter for diesel-engined city trucks and buses operating on low sulphur-type fuels. The converter oxidizes the particulate matter at high temperatures using nitrous oxide rather than oxygen. As a result it is low-maintenance, requiring the filter to be turned in the housing every 160,000km (100,000 miles).

✎	*Johnson Matthey, UK*	318
⚙	*Johnson Matthey, UK*	318
▰	*Various*	
♲	• *Reduction of particulate emissions from diesel engines*	329

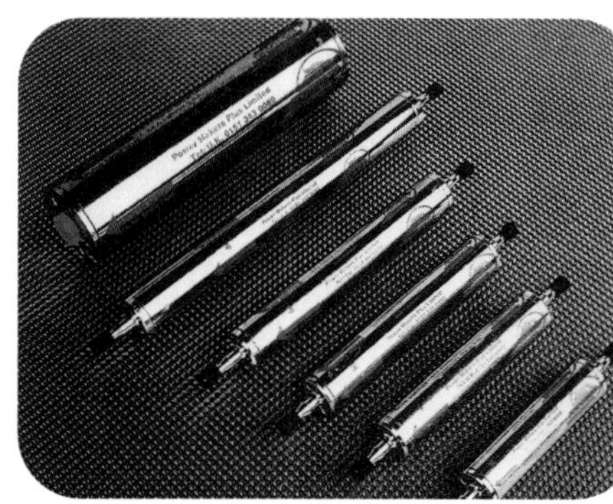

Wheel

Any technique that saves weight in road-vehicle wheels yields in-built savings in fuel consumption. Resin Transfer Moulding™ is a process of making lightweight, composite wheels. Textiles made of carbon-reinforced fibres are impregnated with catalyzed resin in a straightforward manufacturing process. Similar principles can be applied to other products traditionally made out of metal, such as safety helmets using aramide-fibre-reinforced textiles.

✎	*Prins Dokkum BV, Netherlands*	322
⚙	*Prins Dokkum BV, Netherlands*	322
▰	*Resin, carbon-fibre-reinforced textiles*	284, 300-1
♲	• *Reduction in fossil-fuel consumption* • *Conservation of metal reserves*	328

Fuel catalyst

Catalytic converters reduce the emissions from exhaust gases when retrofitted to internal combustion engines. Most use rare metals to 'treat' the gases. The Fuel Catalyst is a metallic alloy catalytic material made principally of tin-based materials, giving improved oxidation during combustion and therefore generating a cleaner exhaust stream and improving fuel efficiency. Each Fuel Catalyst is guaranteed to last 400,000km (250,000 miles). Users have reported reduction of exhaust emissions between 40 per cent and 70 per cent and fuel economy improved by 15 per cent.

✎	*PowerMakers Plus, UK*	322
⚙	*PowerMakers Plus, UK*	322
▰	*Tin and other metal alloys*	295
♲	• *Reduction of emissions, improved fuel economy*	328

Buses

Since the mid-1990s the German commercial vehicle manufacturers MAN Nutzfahrzeuge have been testing working prototypes using natural gas (CNG), liquefied petroleum gas (LPG), hydrogen fuel cells and a biofuel called rapeseed oil methylester (RME) as an alternative to diesel fuel. An articulated bus powered by CNG develops 310 bhp but, in combination with closed-loop catalytic converters, conforms to Euro 3 emissions levels proposed by Germany, which are less than or equal to 2 g/kWh carbon monoxide, 0.6 g/kWh hydrocarbons, 5 g/kWh nitrous oxides and 0.1 g/kWh of particulate matter (PM10s). These levels show a reduction factor of between 3 and 5 of the Euro 1, 1990, exhaust legislation. A further benefit is a reduction in noise to almost half the normal level of a diesel-powered bus. MAN's commitment to reducing environmental impacts is reflected in their accreditation to environmental management standards including EMAS and, at the Steyr factory, ISO 14001.

✎	*MAN Nutzfahrzeuge, Germany*	320
⚙	*MAN Nutzfahrzeuge, Germany*	320
▮	*Various*	
♺	*• Low emissions* *• Low noise pollution*	328, 329

Liquefied natural gas-powered vehicle

Chilled food is delivered daily to each store in the Marks & Spencer retail chain using articulated lorries with refrigeration units. Following a review of their distribution system with their lead contractor, BOC, the company examined ways of reducing vehicular emissions and noise pollution. This culminated in the development of a new fleet of natural-gas-powered vehicles equipped with quiet, non-polluting cryo-eutectic refrigeration units. Compared with the original diesel-engined vehicles, emissions from the natural-gas vehicles produce 89 per cent fewer particulates, 69 per cent fewer nitrous oxides and approximately 10 to 20 per cent less carbon dioxide.

✎	*Marks & Spencer in partnership with Varity Perkins, ERF, Gray and Adams and BOC Distribution Services, with support from the Energy Savings Trust, UK*	313
⚙	*Joint venture with BOC, UK*	313
▮	*Various*	
♺	*• Significant reduction in vehicle emissions and noise*	328, 329

Passenger information system

Saving up to 60 per cent of the energy consumption of other pulse technology displays, this modular aluminium-framed passenger information system uses hundreds of LEDs controlled with a patented system. With a legible display and clean lines, this system conveys information with maximum efficiency and minimum fuss. It is also easily maintained by one person.

Interform Design, Germany	307
LUMINO Licht Elektronik GmbH, Germany	320
Ceramic-coated dispersion glass, aluminium, LEDs	295
• *Reduction in energy consumption* • *Modular design with ease of maintenance*	328, 329
iF Ecology Design Award, 2000	332

Road transport containers

Many trailers of road haulage vehicles work at undercapacity since their 'flatbed' design means many types of cargo cannot easily be accommodated. For example, how do you transport a mixed load comprising gases, fluids, 'flowable' powers and solids? A conceptual solution is to store non-solids in strong bags that can be collapsed upon emptying. Potentially this could keep every vehicle operating nearer its gross carrying capacity and improve transport energy efficiency.

University of Technology, Delft, Netherlands	311
Conceptual prototype	
Various	341
• *Multifunctional use of distribution road vehicles* • *Reduced fossil-fuel consumption*	329

Partner Electric

Companies and local authorities that regularly deliver or work in their own localities would do well to examine the potential role of electric vehicles in their fleet. Not only can electric vehicles deliver high fuel-equivalent efficiency and low expenditure but there is no local pollution generated from emissions. And true zero emissions can be achieved if a renewable source of electricity is purchased. The Peugeot Partner Electric, which developed out of the Peugeot 106 Electric, is typical of the light electric vans available. It offers a payload of 500kg (1,100lb), 3 cubic metres (106cu ft) capacity and provides a range of up to 64km (40 miles) on an overnight charge. Twenty-seven 6V nickel cadmium batteries power the 28kW direct current motor, which permits a top speed of 96km/h (60mph). Already these vans form part of the fleet of postal and courier companies, including the Royal Mail in the UK.

Peugeot, France	322
Peugeot, France	322
Various	341
• *Reduced emissions (if electricity sourced from non-renewables)* • *Zero emissions (if electricity sourced from renewables)* • *Noise reduction*	329

Solar electric vehicle

An array of PV cells on the roof of the bus provides between one-third and one-fifth of the power, reducing fuel consumption of the conventional internal combustion engine. This design demonstrates the ability of solar power to reduce the output of combustion gases and so help reduce pollution, especially in congested urban areas.

✎	*Foster and Partners, UK*	306
⚙	*Prototype, 1992-94*	
▬	*Various, including photovoltaic panels*	341
♺	*• Solar power and reduction in use of fossil fuels*	329

Solo

Solo takes midi-bus design to new lows – that is, it provides a low-level platform to enable wheelchair users to mount from pavement to bus by an extendable automatic ramp. A low centre of gravity also produces less roll and a more comfortable ride for all.

And in the absence of any steps, buses can pick up and drop off passengers more quickly, enabling them to keep accurately to their specified timetables and reduce emissions while idling.

✎	*Optare, UK*	321
⚙	*Optare, UK*	321
▬	*Various*	341
♺	*• Equal access for all potential users to public transport* *• Improved efficiency of passenger loading/unloading*	328

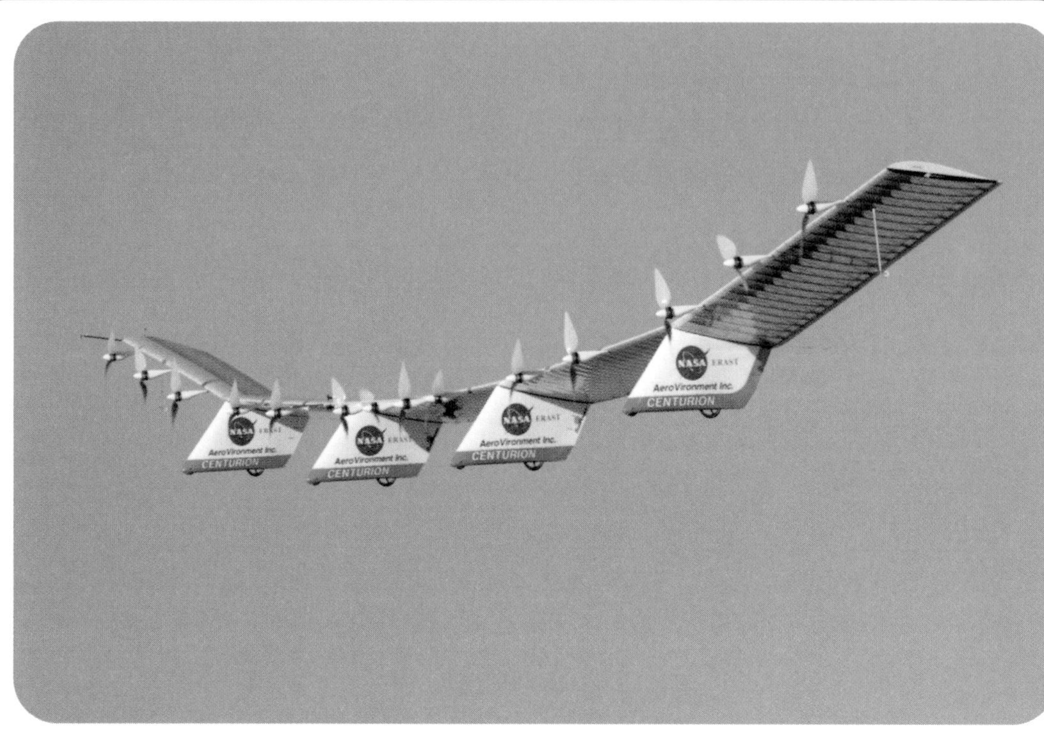

Centurion

Following an evolutionary trajectory started by NASA's early 1990s Pathfinder, the Centurion is currently the world's largest unmanned ultra-light wing capable of sustaining high-altitude flights. With an incredible wingspan of 61.8m (203ft) and a wing area of 153sq metres (1,647sq ft) almost entirely covered in photovoltaic panels, the 529kg (1,164lb) vehicle can carry a payload of up to 272kg (598lb) to 24,380 metres (80,000ft). Fourteen 1.5kW electric motors are powered by the photovoltaics for up to fourteen or fifteen hours in daylight plus two to three hours in darkness using on-board lithium batteries. The objective of the ERAST programme is to extend the performance of the craft to enable continuous flying even in extended periods of darkness. Capable of all sorts of monitoring activities from high altitude, the Centurion could provide intelligence for a variety of needs, including military, meteorological and biological, such as monitoring the health of growing crops and forests.

✎	*NASA's ERAST programme, AeroVironment, Inc., and Dryden Research Center, USA*	304, 306
⚙	*Prototype, 1999*	
▬	*Carbon-fibre and graphite epoxy resins, Kevlar, photovoltaics*	284, 341
♺	*• Solar-powered air transporter for scientific and multifunctional missions*	329

FanWing

High speed, noise and huge fuel bills are the hallmarks of today's fixed-wing aircraft. The FanWing, currently tested as a working model prototype, is an aircraft with near-vertical take-off capabilities that serves as a quiet, slow but fuel-efficient, load-carrying transporter. In an intriguing innovation, the designers have introduced a large rotor along the entire leading edge of the wing. The engine directly powers the rotor, which is capable of producing both lift and thrust as the cross-flow fan pulls air in at the front and accelerates it over the trailing edge of the wing. Wind-tunnel testing reveals 15kg (33lb) of lift per horsepower, equivalent to a payload capacity of 1 to 1.5 tonnes for a 100-horsepower power unit.

Moreover, it is simple and inexpensive to construct and therefore offers an economical air-transport system for everything from disaster relief work to fire-fighting and reconnaissance or traffic monitoring. Preliminary specifications for a three-passenger version show it weighing in at just 350kg (770lb) empty and having a top speed of 60km/h (37mph), a wingspan of 10 metres (33ft) and a flying time of ten hours.

✎	*FanWing, UK/Italy*	316
⚙	*Model prototype*	
▬	*Various*	341
♻	• *Improved fuel efficiency* • *Simple, low-cost construction*	328, 329

Helios

The Helios is an enlarged version of the Centurion 'flying wing'. It has a wingspan of 75 metres (247 feet), which is two and a half times that of the Pathfinder flying wing and longer than that of a Boeing 747 jet. AeroVironment's ambition is to enable Helios to fly at 30,500 metres (100,000ft) continuously for twenty-four hours and at 15,259 metres (50,000ft) for four days, all under solar power. This aircraft is known as an uninhabited aerial vehicle (UAV) and is suitable for remote sensing and reconnaissance with a multiplicity of applications for recording the weather, changes in vegetation cover and military operations.

✎	*NASA, Dryden Research Center, USA, with AeroVironment, Inc., USA*	304, 306
⚙	*NASA Dryden Flight Research Center, USA, with AeroVironment, Inc., USA*	304, 306
▬	*Photovoltaic modules, lightweight metals and composites*	341
♻	• *Zero emissions* • *Renewable energy*	329

Baby Stingray

Microlights and hang gliders are a familiar sight but the Baby Stingray makes a step change for small, lightweight, aeroplane travel. A single inflatable wing, spanning 13m (42ft 7in), provides an aerodynamic, muscle-like structure whose shape can be altered by inflating or deflating internal compartments within the wing to provide directional control. A larger version is currently being tested for potential passenger use. It is a hybrid design, a post-modern airship, which uses helium gas to provide extra lift to the 'wing' and has potentially high fuel efficiency.

✎	*Axel Thallemer, Festo Corporate Design, Germany*	316
⚙	*Prototype, Festo, Germany*	316
	Various	341
	• *Energy efficiency* • *Reduction in air pollution*	329

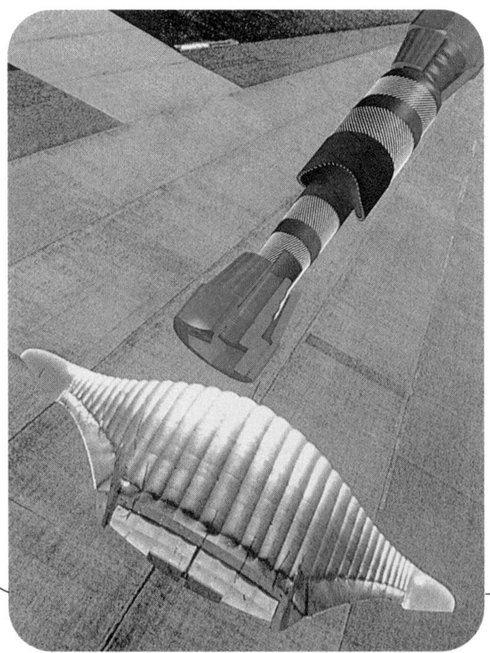

Trent 700

Rolls Royce, General Electric and Pratt and Whitney dominate engine manufacturing for aeroplanes. Rolls Royce have taken the lead in producing a fuel-efficient, lightweight and low-cost jet engine. Weight reduction was achieved with titanium fan blades comprising three sheets in close proximity, which were subjected to heat, causing flow of material and bridging between the layers to form a honeycomb structure. Other innovations include 'growing' metal by controlled cooling of the molten alloy in the mould to align all the molecules in one direction, forming an extremely strong single crystal. The turbine blades are made of this metal, which can operate at almost twice the melting point of normal crystalline metal. A three-shaft design is also more efficient and easier to maintain and upgrade. Aeroplanes with Trent engines, such as the Airbus A330, can carry more passengers for the same fuel consumption.

✎	*Rolls Royce, UK*	323
⚙	*Rolls Royce, UK*	323
	Various	341
	• *Reduction of fossil-fuel consumption* • *Reduction of air pollution*	328, 329

Solarshuttle 66 (Helio) and RA82

Kopf AG are pioneers in developing solar-powered ferries for inland waterways. The Solarshuttle 66, otherwise known as the Helio, is a scaled-up version of a ferry, which has operated between Gaienhofen, Germany, and Stoeckborn, Switzerland, since 1998. With a maximum speed of 24km/h (15mph), the Helio can operate for up to eight hours from the bank of 24 batteries without needing a recharge from the photovoltaic panels. The even larger RA82 has a capacity of 120 passengers and is in service in Hamburg and Hannover. Low operating costs and negligible environmental impacts could popularize this transport mode in urban areas served by waterways and in ecologically sensitive areas.

✎	*Dr Herbert Stark, Kopf AG, Germany*	310
⚙	*Kopf AG, Germany*	319
■	*Stainless steel, teakwood, photovoltaics, batteries*	340
↘	*• Zero emissions* *• Solar power*	329

RA

RA is a zero-emissions, solar-powered boat, which is ideal for freshwater transport where the pollution of conventional diesel or petrol motor boats is damaging to water quality. Built to a high specification using Burmese teak and stainless steel, it contains raw materials that are extremely durable, low-maintenance and 100 per cent recyclable. Greenpeace, the international NGO, assisted in obtaining the construction materials.

An added benefit of the solar generation and electric motor system is its quietness of operation, making it a more fitting companion for aquatic wildlife.

✎	*Kopf AG, Germany*	319
⚙	*Kopf AG, Germany*	319
	Stainless steel, teakwood, photovoltaics, batteries	340
	• *Solar power* • *Durability* • *Zero emissions*	329

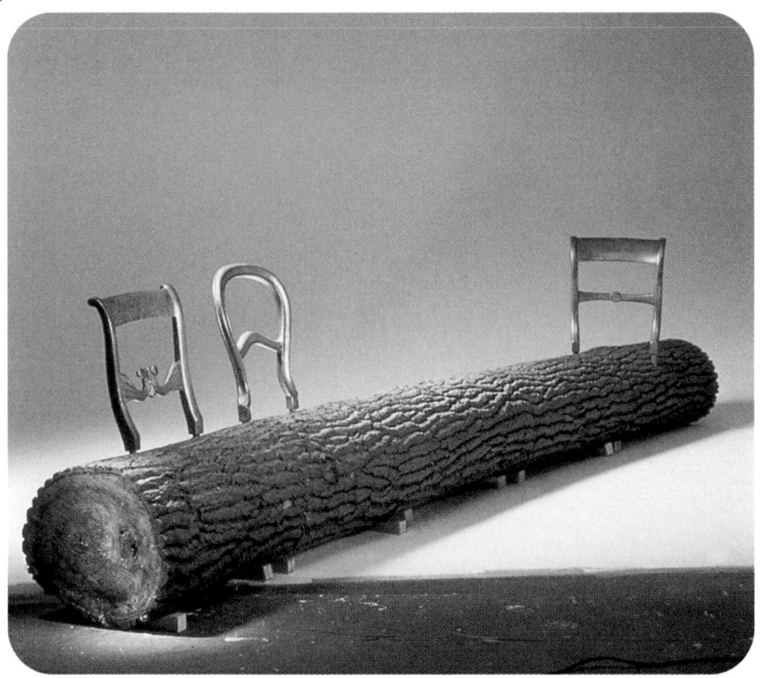

Treetrunk bench

Droog Design was commissioned by the Kulturstiftung Dessau Würlitz to create products for the seventeenth-century castle of Oranienbaum and its environs, in a depressed part of former East Germany. Bey brings a surrealist moment to woodland walkers with his witty bench fashioned from local cut timber and cast-bronze chair backs.

✎	*Jurgen Bey, Droog Design, Netherlands*	304, 306
⚙	*One-off, small batch production, Droog Design/DMD, Netherlands*	306, 315
	Wood, bronze	339
	• Renewable, local materials *• Low-energy fabrication*	327, 328

De Eurobank

Baccarne produce a range of outdoor/public seating exclusively from recycled plastics, a mix of polypropylene, polyvinyl chloride and polyethylene obtained from post-production waste streams such as window-frame manufacturing. Planks and sheeting provide basic yet tough functional furniture.

✎	*Baccarne Design, Belgium*	304
⚙	*Baccarne bvba, Belgium*	313
	Recycled polypropylene, polyvinyl chloride and polyethylene	295
	• Recycled materials	327

Navigator series

Ecologic produce a diverse range of indoor and outdoor furniture using a variety of recycled plastics or plastic composites. The Navigator picnic table series includes an extra-long slatted top of ECOlumber, which permits wheelchair access adjacent to the conventional fixed benches. Solid recycled plastic forms the resilient base for the top and benches. ECO+Plus indoor bedroom and living-room furniture mixes solid wood and Environ™, a biocomposite of recycled paper and soy flour.

✎	*Ecologic, USA*	315
⚙	*Ecologic, USA*	315
▮	*Recycled plastic*	295
♺	*• Recycled materials*	327

Sofanco

Stone is a most durable natural material. Oscar Tusquets Blanca has captured the strength of this material but rendered it in a fluid, organic form to create a design of great potential longevity, albeit requiring moderate energy input during manufacturing.

✎	*Oscar Tusquets Blanca*	305
⚙	*Escofet, Spain*	316
▮	*Stainless steel, reinforced cast stone*	295
♺	*• Natural, inorganic materials*	328

Street furniture

Small and medium-sized enterprises (SMEs) tend to be local employers and make an important contribution to the furniture manufacturing industry. People skilled in craft and industrial small-batch production typify these companies. Pendlewood is such a company operating in the north-west of England. All timber consumed is recycled, reclaimed or from sustainably managed forests and tends to come from local sources.

✎	*Pendlewood, UK*	322
⚙	*Pendlewood, UK*	322
▮	*Hardwoods*	339
♺	*• Recycled, reclaimed or sustainable sources of timber*	327

Public seating

Injection moulding is a process usually associated with single materials but in this case a bespoke biosynthetic composite material was used, comprising 60 per cent ALERT 'Moistureshield' LDPE and cedar pulp, 40 per cent polypropylene and wood flour. This design demonstrates the potential of mixing plant derivatives with plastics but does raise questions about recycling and/or disposal at the end of the product's life.

✎	*Danilea Blejer and Saskia Bostelmann, Mexico*	305
⚙	*Prototype*	
▬	*LDPE, cedar pulp, polypropylene, wood flour*	341
♺	*• Reduction in use of synthetic materials*	328

Photovoltaic umbrella

A tilting mechanism allows the umbrella to be angled to capture the maximum amount of energy as well as shading from sunlight on the photovoltaic panels. Batteries are housed in a planter that doubles as seating and contains lighting for night-time illumination.

✎	*Cinzia Abbate for the Italian Energy Authority*	304
⚙	*Prototype*	
▬	*Photovoltaics, batteries*	340
♺	*• Solar-powered, multifunctional public seating and shading*	329

SINE seat

Extruded plastic lumber provides the catalyst for this innovative public seating, which can be fabricated to bespoke lengths and curvatures depending on the client's requirements. Two styles of cast aluminium frame, one with a backrest, permit further customization. Achieving similar results in hardwood would prove more costly. Utilizing the recycled plastic also means that expensive resources are released for more valued activities.

✎	*V K & C Partnership, UK*	311
⚙	*V K & C Partnership, UK*	311
▬	*Recycled plastics, aluminium*	295
♺	*• Recycled and recyclable materials*	327

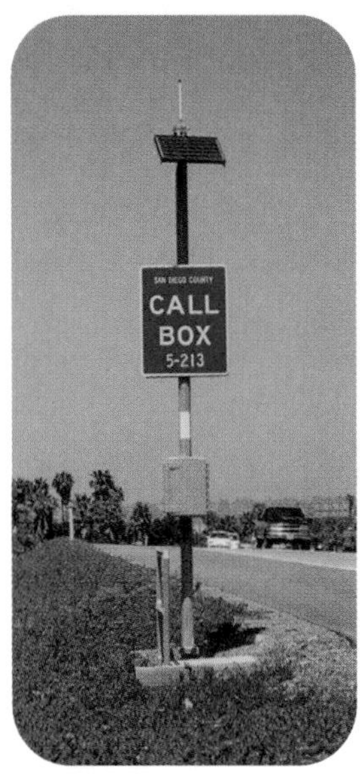

Solar call box

A cellular transceiver connects this communications point to a cellular-telephone network. The call box is powered by a 12V battery fed by a photovoltaic panel mounted on top of the metal pole. It is suitable for remote locations and for emergency services on highways.

✎	*Comarco Wireless Technologies, USA*	314
⚙	*Comarco Wireless Technologies, USA*	314
▮	*Polycarbonate, photovoltaics, steel, battery*	340
♺	*• Solar power*	329

ComPoint

Wall-mounted and open or covered free-standing communications units, equipped with telephone and information systems, are assembled from basic modules according to the services required. All components are designed for disassembly, repair and/or recycling. ComPoint is suitable for indoor and outdoor use and offers a wide range of customizable options.

✎	*Landmark Design for Public, Switzerland, for Swisscom AG*	308
⚙	*Landmark Design for Public, Switzerland*	308
▮	*Various*	341
♺	*• Modular design • Design for disassembly*	328

Epoch

Epoch is a durable, tough material made of 100 per cent-recycled HDPE and LDPE, offering similar properties to timber, metal and concrete. EPP manufacture a wide range of street furniture including benches, seating, picnic tables, planters, litter bins, fencing, signage and window boxes made with Epoch, which can be sawn and fixed just like wood but is impervious to most corrosive substances.

✎	*Environmental Polymers Group, UK*	316
⚙	*Environmental Polymers Group, UK*	316
▮	*Epoch recycled plastic*	293
♺	*• Recycled materials*	327

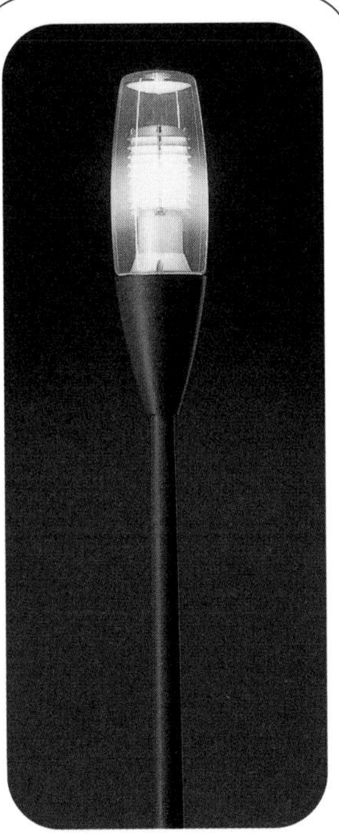

Metronomis

A new range of street lighting by Philips is specially designed for energy-saving lamps and low maintenance. Modular components are durable and vandal-proof and permit different design permutations according to customers' preferences.

✎	*Philips Design, Netherlands*	309
⚙	*Philips Electronics, Netherlands*	322
▭	*Metal, glass, lamp*	295
♻	*• Improved energy efficiency • Modular design • Design for disassembly*	328, 329

Nimbus

A tough acrylic housing contains a 12V/115Ah (amp hour) sealed, maintenance-free battery and a photovoltaic array of mono-crystalline silicon cells capable of generating 17.5volts/77 watts at an incoming radiation of 1,000W/sq m. An inverter, charge controller and automatic dusk switch and timer provide highly efficient use of stored power. Conventional low-pressure sodium lamps, low-energy fluorescent lamps or halogen bulbs can be fitted according to needs.

✎	*Solar Solutions (UK), UK*	324
⚙	*Solar Solutions (UK), UK*	324
▭	*Photovoltaic array, stainless and galvanized steel, acrylic*	295
♻	*• Solar power • Low maintenance*	329

Lumalux®

Designed for exterior lighting, the Lumalux® is the first high-pressure sodium lamp to eliminate all mercury and lead during construction to provide significantly cleaner production and reduce dispersal of toxic substances upon disposal. Osram Sylvania estimate this could save up to 150kg (330lb) of mercury and 14 tonnes of lead annually. The Lumalux® Plus lamp readily meets the Federal hazardous waste regulations as it contains 90 per cent less mercury than the standard Lumalux® and is constructed with a lead-free welded base.

✎	*Osram Sylvania, Germany and USA*	310, 321
⚙	*Osram Sylvania, Germany and USA*	310, 321
▭	*Various*	339
♻	*• Low mercury content • Cleaner production*	328, 329

Street Light F

Power generation using solar cells offers an opportunity to re-examine the design parameters for familiar objects. In this case the rectilinear shape of the 35-cell solar array was the prime component in configuring the polycarbonate diffuser to create the clean lines of this new generation of street lighting. Batteries in the base of the upright are capable of lighting the 18-watt fluorescent lamp for seven days without a recharge.

✎	*Roy Fleetwood, UK*	306
⚙	*YKK Architectural Products, Inc., Japan*	326
▮	*Aluminium polycarbonate, solar cells*	
♻	*• Solar power*	329

Tucan

Designers, challenged to use renewable energy sources to power street lighting, have eloquently met the challenge with this striking lamp by Ecke: Design. Tucan integrates the capacity to generate electricity from the sun with the need to radiate light. Here is an opportunity to rid ourselves of the banal visual language of traditional street lamp designs.

✎	*Ecke: Design, Germany*	306
⚙	*Uwe Braun GmbH, Germany*	325
▮	*Photovoltaic panel, glass, metal, batteries*	340
♻	*• Renewable power source*	329

Almere low-cost housing, Netherlands

Standard 12m (40ft) steel shipping containers form the basic structural framework, enabling rapid construction of low-cost housing. Reuse of an industrial component for distribution as a static component in the built environment is a large-scale attempt to extend the functionality of a manufactured product. Examination of the embodied energy of materials and the energy consumed during construction and running costs will reveal whether this is truly a useful housing concept with reduced environmental impacts.

✎	*Henk Tilder, architect, Netherlands*	310
⚙	*Various*	
▬	*Shipping containers*	340
♻	• *Reuse of existing containers*	328

BRE, New Environmental Office

Designed to use 30 per cent less energy than current 'best practice' in the UK, this building can accommodate over a hundred people. Cooling is achieved by natural automatic ventilation at night combined with ground water pumped through the concrete floors and ceilings, which has an efficiency of 1kWh output for pumping to an equivalent 12-16 kWh cooling energy input. Timber and steel are the primary materials for the structure and originate predominantly from recycled sources. Thanks to a combination of the thermal mass of the building, natural cooling and automated monitoring systems, the building regulates its own climate.

✎	*Feilden Clegg Architects, Buro Happold, and Max Fordham & Partners, UK*	306
⚙	*Various contractors*	
▬	*Various*	340
♻	• *Low energy consumption* • *Increased usage of materials from recycled sources*	328

Fred

Although the concept is not new, Fred is a portable building with some special features. The basic room unit is 3 x 3 x 3 metres (27 cubic metres, 953 cubic ft) but the floor area can be doubled to 18 square metres (194 square feet) by taking advantage of sliding wall/roof elements, which are electronically controlled. Each unit is equipped with a kitchen, toilet and shower and an area available for multi-purpose use, but the basic utility services have to be connected. A fully glazed wall provides excellent natural light and thick insulation in the walls and roof minimizes energy consumption.

✎	*KFN Kaufmann Produkt GmbH, Germany*	308
⚙	*Zimmerei Michael Kaufmann, Germany*	308
▬	*Timber, metal, glass*	295, 339
♻	*• Resource-efficient multi-use space* *• Low embodied energy of fabrication, transport and construction*	328, 329

Exhibition hall

Imagine a building of 3,600sq m (38,750sq ft) floor capacity made mainly of paper and cardboard. Impossible? Not in the hands of Shigeru Ban, the Japanese architect and designer with over two decades' experience of working with these materials to produce furniture and housing for disaster relief projects. The building premiered at EXPO 2000 in Hanover, where it became the first public building in the world to feature a 35m-span (115ft) paper/plastic textile roof supported with a latticework of tubular cardboard. The building is designed to be demountable and reused.

✎	*Shigeru Ban, Japan*	304
⚙	*Various contractors*	
▬	*Paper, cardboard, various*	288-9
♻	*• Renewable materials* *• A reusable building*	327, 330

Hope House

Hope House is a home, office, energy generator and leisure zone. Passive solar design combined with photovoltaic generation is sufficient to maintain an ambient internal climate and to run a Citroën electric car for up to 8,500km (5,300 miles) per year, resulting in a net saving of about 413 tonnes of carbon dioxide per year. Mains water usage is minimized by using a rainwater faucet for the toilets and laundry room. All greywater is reused to irrigate the garden after it has been passed through a sand filter. This project is a blueprint for a seventy-six-unit urban village with sun terraces planned for London by the Peabody Trust, a charitable organization that has, since Victorian times, been concerned with raising the social and environmental standards of British urban housing.

✎	*Bill Dunster Architects, Mark Lovell, and Oscar Faber, UK*	304
⚙	*Various*	
▬	*Various*	340
♻	*• Integrated energy-efficient home, workspace and domestic transport system* *• Water conservation system*	328, 330
✿	*Design Sense award, 1999*	332

Hooke Park Training Centre and Westminster Lodge

Untreated roundwood, of diameter 50mm to 250mm (about 1/5 to 1in) – the thinnings from forestry management – forms the basic construction material for unique organic forms of architecture that take advantage of the natural properties of the timber. The Hooke Park Training Centre is a large, free-span space housing workshops for The Parnham Trust, whose college provides training in furniture design with emphasis on using indigenous timber.

✎	*John Makepeace and others, Hooke Forest (Construction) Ltd, UK*	307
⚙	*Hooke Forest (Construction) Ltd, UK*	307
▬	*Roundwood timber*	339
♻	*• Use of timber from local sources for construction*	327

SU-SI

Many people associate mobile or trailer homes with holiday parks and dubious lifestyles. Not so this customizable twenty-first-century modular home system, which can be erected on site within a few hours and is easily disassembled and reused in another location. The factory-produced modules measure 12.5 x 3.5 x 3 metres (41 x 11ft 6in x 9ft 10in), each one interlocking with the next to create versatile domestic, office or exhibition spaces.

✎	*KFN Kaufmann Produkt GmbH, Germany*	308
⚙	*Zimmerei Michael Kaufmann, Germany*	308
▬	*Timber, metal, composites, glass*	295, 339
♻	*• Resource-efficient reusable homes • Low embodied energy of fabrication, transport and construction*	327, 328
✪	*iF Design Award, 2000*	332

The Seawater Greenhouse

Powered by the sun, cold deep-sea water and the wind, this house in Tenerife manufactures fresh water and cool air. This enables horticultural produce to be raised in the integral greenhouse. To meet the low-cost brief evaporators were made from corrugated cardboard. Over time these are naturally strengthened with deposits of calcium carbonate from the sea water. Condensers are of aluminium and the main frame of the building is from steel, both recyclable. Recyclable polythene covers the steel frame and helps modulate the greenhouse climate. Buildings are largely passive masses, their productivity being generated by the activity inside. By contrast, internal activity wouldn't happen in this house if the building were not working properly. Architecture reborn as manufacturing?

✎	*Charlie Paton, Light Works, UK*	309
⚙	*Various contractors*	
▮	*Various*	341
♻	*• Freshwater generator with renewable power* *• Low embodied energy and recyclable materials*	327, 328, 329
✪	*First prize, Design Sense award, 1999*	332

Solar Office, Duxford International Business Park

This office is designed to incorporate 900sq m (9,660sq ft) of photovoltaic cells into the south-facing glass facade inclined at 60 degrees. This array is capable of generating a peak output of 73kW equivalent to 55,000kWh per annum, meeting between one-third and one-quarter of the expected energy needs of the building. The solar-powered system is complemented by a natural stack ventilation system with sun-shading louvres, both systems being controlled and monitored by computer. Potential overall energy savings of two-thirds are anticipated compared with a conventional office building.

✎	*Akeler Developments plc, UK*	304
⚙	*Akeler Developments plc, UK*	304
▮	*Various including photovoltaic array, monitoring systems*	340
♻	*• Energy conservation and generation*	329

UNHCR shelter

In 1995 the United Nations High Commission for Refugees adopted Shigeru Ban's design for temporary shelters made from 110 waterproofed cardboard tubes. His easy-to-assemble structures were used in Rwanda and, with modifications to suit local needs, in the aftermath of the Kobe earthquake.

✎	*Shigeru Ban, Japan*	304
⚙	*Vitra AG, Switzerland*	326
	Cardboard, waterproofing agents	288-9
	• *Renewable materials* • *Low energy of manufacturing, transport and assembly* • *Reusable buildings*	327, 328

Weobley Schools Sustainable Development

Weobley Schools energy management system is a test-bed to extend the sustainable energy initiatives of a local authority in response to Local Agenda 21. A holistic approach led to a wood-fuel boiler, using locally harvested coppice roundwood, which was chosen on the grounds that it was the most sustainable system. The coppice suppliers are paid according to the heat output of the wood (supplied as chips) rather than the quantity, encouraging quality supplies. Insulation is to very high standards coupled with computerized monitoring of the under-floor heating and internal environment of the building work in tandem with passive design features including solar shading, daylighting and natural ventilation. The net effect is a very energy-efficient public building using local resources.

✎	*Hereford & Worcester County Council, UK*	307
⚙	*Various contractors*	
	Biomass fuel from coppice	339
	• *Energy conservation* • *Energy generation using biomass fuels*	328

Airtecture

Weighing just 6 tonnes and easily packed on to a road vehicle for transport, Festo's portable building comprises a protected floor space of over 357sq m (3,810sq ft). This is achieved by supporting an inflatable cross-beamed roof on two rows of inflatable, Y-shaped columns. Stiffness is given to thin cavity wall panels by tensioning them with pneumatic muscles, which contract to oppose the effect of the wind. Air is the main insulator to assist with internal climate control.

(design)	*Festo, Germany*	316
(manufacture)	*Festo, Germany*	316
(materials)	*Various*	339
(eco)	*• Reduction of resource consumption compared with conventionally constructed buildings of equal size • Reusable and portable building with multifunctional single space*	327, 329

Ecover factory, Oostmalle, Belgium Project

Growth of Ecover's business in the early 1990s required an expansion of the existing factory near Antwerp, Belgium. Using an ecological grading system, devised by the University of Eindhoven, building materials were selected for their minimal environmental impact. Structural timber was obtained from sustainably managed forests and bricks from a clay-based residue from the coal industry provided high-insulation material. A huge multi-ridged turf roof covers the 5,300sq m (57,050sq ft) building, providing excellent insulation, controlling storm-water runoff and helping integrate the factory into the local landscape. In line with the company's philosophy of balancing commerce with social and environmental concerns, the factory has been developed to enhance conditions for the workforce. Many roof-lights create natural lighting and there are solar-powered showers for the workforce.

(design)	*University of Eindhoven (Building Initiative Environmental Standards), Netherlands, with Ecover, Belgium*	311, 315
(manufacture)	*Various contractors*	
(materials)	*Various natural materials, turf roof, bricks from clay-residue*	339
(eco)	*• Turf roof for energy conservation and storm-water runoff control • Use of local materials from sustainable sources where possible • Natural lighting*	327, 329

BedZED Housing

BedZED is a pioneering mixed-use and mixed-tenure development of housing, work space and public areas, which is being constructed on an old sewage works, a 'brownfield' site, in Beddington, Sutton, south of London.
The whole scheme is designed to meet exacting environmental, social and financial requirements. Architect Bill Dunster and environmental consultants BioRegional have, in collaboration with the client, the Peabody Trust, adopted a holistic view of the local needs of the intended community, including a green transport system which was actually built into the planning permission and ratified by the local authority. BedZED hopes to cut total fossil fuel consumption to about half that of a conventional development by reducing the need to travel between living, work, health-care, shopping and recreational facilities. Reduced transport impacts are also encouraged by promoting good networking with existing train, bus and tram services and by providing decent bicycle storage facilities, attractive pedestrian links and on-site charging points for electric vehicles. There is a ten-year target to produce enough solar electricity on-site to power forty electric vehicles. Materials for the eighty-two flats and houses for sale and rent have been selected from natural, renewable or recycled sources, mainly near by. Each dwelling is an energy-efficient design using passive solar gain and a high insulation specification, including triple-glazed windows. A central combined heat and power-generation facility will utilize on-site tree waste to provide all the development's heat and electricity requirements. Further on-site generation from photovoltaics will make this the first large-scale 'carbon neutral' development in Europe. Water conservation will be encouraged by providing up to 18 per cent of on-site consumption from stored rainwater and recycled water and by installing water-efficient appliances.

	Bill Dunster and BioRegional	304
	Various contractors	
	Various, especially locally sourced	339
	• Zero-energy development • 'Carbon neutral' • Integrated transport plan • Socially mixed housing	328
	RIBA award, 'best example of sustainable construction', 2000	333

(designer)	*K-X Industries, USA*	319
(manufacturer)	*K-X Industries, USA*	319
(materials)	*Waste wood and fly ash, Portland cement*	339
(recycling)	*• Partially recycled and renewable content*	327

Faswall®

A post-and-beam structural grid is created by filling wall forms with reinforced concrete. Wall forms are manufactured using K-X® recycled wood waste chips. The entire wall structure, known as Faswall®, comprises up to 85 per cent K-X Aggregate (from waste wood) bound with Portland cement (containing up to 15 per cent fly ash content by volume). A finished Faswall shows good R-values (thermal insulation) of between 18 to 24 and it is an excellent sound barrier and substrate for drywall or direct finishes. Standard blockmaking equipment permits local manufacturing of Faswall® components.

Eco-shake®

Made of 100 per cent-recycled materials, reinforced vinyl and cellulose fibre, eco-shake® shingles are available in four colour shades designed to mimic weathered wooden shakes. The shakes qualify under strict fire-rating, wind and rain resistance and impact tests.

(designer)	*Re-New Wood, USA*	323
(manufacturer)	*Re-New Wood, USA*	323
(materials)	*Recycled wood, recycled plastics*	339
(recycling)	*• Recycled materials*	327

Criss Cross

Making a weclome change from the ubiquitous rectangular paving block, the Criss Cross paving system comprises four different forms that can be interlocked in regular or random patterns.

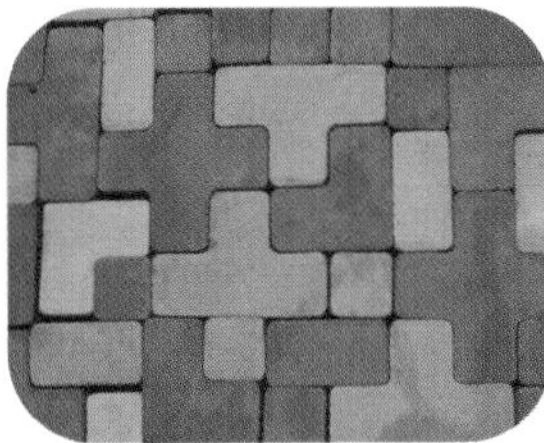

Glindower Ziegelei still fires these blocks in a kiln dating from 1870. Natural variation in the clay minerals yields a range of colours and textures.

✎	*Ecke: Design, Germany*	306
⚙	*Glindower Ziegelei GmbH, Germany*	317
▬	*Clay minerals*	295
♻	*• Abundant geosphere materials*	327
✪	*iF Design Award ,2000*	332

LockClad terracotta rainscreen

Combining the aesthetics and durability of fired clay tiles with ease of installation, this rainwater cladding on aluminium rails is a cost-effective method of protecting the exterior of a building from the elements. Each clay tile is locked in place on an extruded aluminium rail, LockRail, which meets all UK and Ireland wind loadings. This minimal-maintenance, lightweight cladding permits extra insulation materials to be applied to the outer skin of the building's structure, improving energy conservation. Natural ventilation behind the clay tiles and protection from the sun reduce temperature variations in the load-bearing structure.

✎	*Red Bank Manufacturing Company, UK*	323
⚙	*Red Bank Manufacturing Company, UK*	323
▬	*Clay, aluminium*	295
♻	*• Durable, recyclable materials • Improved energy conservation for buildings*	329

Ersgoldbacher Linea

These tiles are designed to interlock with a minor overlap to minimize quantity of materials per square metre, reduce laying time and provide greater security in high winds. Sinter tempering toughens the tile, making it very durable and suitable for commercial and domestic applications. It is rainproof at roof angles of up to 25 degrees.

✎	*Erlus Baustoffwerke AG, Germany*	316
⚙	*Erlus Baustoffwerke AG, Germany*	316
▬	*Sinter-tempered clay*	295
♻	*• Abundant geosphere material • Reduction in resource use and energy for transport*	327, 328
✪	*iF Ecology Design Award, 2000*	332

Majestic Slate

Guaranteed to last a minimum of fifty years, these lightweight slates, weighing just over 0.5kg (about 1lb) each, are made of 100 per cent-recycled rubber with added plastics to improve durability. These slates can be easily cut with a knife and are installed by nailing in the traditional manner and, being flexible, are not susceptible to damage.

✎	*Ecostar, USA*	315
⚙	*Ecostar, USA*	315
Material	*Recycled rubber, polymers*	283, 295
♻	*• Recycled materials*	327

Authentic Roof™

Moulded to mimic natural weathered slates, Authentic Roof™ tiles are made of 100 per cent-recycled rubber with polymers added to prolong the lifespan. Installation is similar to conventional materials.

✎	*Crowe Building Products, USA*	314
⚙	*Crowe Building Products, USA*	314
Material	*Recycled rubber, polymers*	283, 295
♻	*• Recycled materials*	327

SunPipe

Natural daylight provides a more relaxing spectrum of light for human vision than artificial light sources but, more importantly, reduces energy consumption in work spaces. SunPipe is a system of conveying natural sunlight from rooftops into buildings. Eight different versions are available in the SunPipe range but the components are similar – a transparent dome of UV-protected polycarbonate is held on the roof by an ABS/acrylic universal flashing. Below the dome is a tube made of Reflectalite 600, silverized coated aluminium sheeting with 96 per cent reflectance. Four standard-diameter tubes, 330mm up to 600mm (13-24in), and a range of elbow joints permit light to be directed into the required space(s).

A 200mm-diameter (8in) version is being developed for domestic spaces. A vertically orientated SunPipe of 330mm can deliver 890 Lux in full summer sun and 430 Lux in overcast conditions in the temperate British climate, which is sufficient to provide natural daylight to an area of approximately 14sq m (150sq ft). Doubling the diameter of the pipe roughly doubles the Lux delivered.

✎	*Terry Payne, Monodraught Ltd, UK*	320
⚙	*Monodraught Ltd, UK*	320
Material	*ABS/acrylic, polycarbonate, aluminium*	341
♻	*• Reduction in energy consumption for lighting*	329

Construcel

For millennia bricks for the construction of buildings have been designed around variations on a basic solid or hollow rectangular form. While it is possible to apply rectangular bricks to some spectacular architectural structures, vaulted ceilings being a classic example, the overriding tendency is to construct rectilinear structures. Marinho's triangular prism of polycarbonate, Construcel, offers an opportunity to reconsider the humble role of bricks in buildings. Each Construcel is an open-sided triangular box, which can be bolted to the next one and so on to create a variety of built forms. Rectilinear structures are easily constructed but this plastic brick is especially suited to large curved spans, such as those required for open-span buildings for sport, exhibitions and similar uses, as it does not require any supporting steelwork or concrete. It is quick to assemble and disassemble structures, so each Construcel is readily reusable and offers possibilities for temporary buildings for disaster relief work. Photovoltaics are easily incorporated in the external face of the 'brick'. Although further work is required to develop this innovation it appears to offer considerable potential.

✎	*Reginaldo Marinho, Brazil*	308
⚙	*Prototype*	
▬	*Polycarbonate*	295
♻	*• Reusable bricks* *• Reduction of materials required for supporting structures*	327, 328

Venetian blinds

Imagine an entire room composed of windows where the incoming flow and mood of light can be controlled using wooden Venetian blinds. Matteo Thun has created a 'Quiet Room' in which the wall and ceiling panels are fully adjustable, manually or automatically, using elliptical cross-section slats with a light and dark side. Light-coloured wood, such as basswood, is bonded to dark wood, such as black walnut, negating the need to introduce coloured surface finishes but relying on the natural reflectivity, absorption and colour range of the raw materials.

✎	*Matteo Thun, Italy*	310
⚙	*Prototype for Hi-wood project coordinated by the Domus Academy Research Centre, Italy, and the American Hardwoods Export Council, USA*	315
▬	*Hardwoods*	339
♻	*• Renewable materials* *• Solar light and warmth control*	327, 329

Parallam®, Timberstrand®, Microllam®

TJM produce a range of patented engineered timbers made by drying short or long veneer 'strands' or sheets, bonding them with adhesives or resins and subjecting them to high pressure and/or heat. TJM produce three 'timbers', Parallam® PSL, Timberstrand® LSL, Microllam® LVL and a special composite structural timber floor joist, the Silent Floor® Joist. TJM claim improved strength and avoidance of defects such as cracking and warping for all their timbers. Further, thanks to the raw veneer ingredients, they can use virtually the whole diameter of a sawn log and/or small-diameter second-growth trees. This results in a considerable saving on raw materials to produce the same amount of structural timber with sawn wood. For example, the Silent Floor® Joist system uses one tree to every two to three trees for a conventional sawn-wood joist/flooring system. Microllam® LVL uses 30 per cent more of the timber from each tree and, being stronger than solid timber, provides almost double the structural value per unit volume of raw material than sawn wood. However, quite a lot of energy is needed to make these composite timbers, so detailed examination of the embodied energy of TJM versus traditional sawn timber should be made on a case-by-case basis.

✎	*Trus Joist MacMillan (TJM), USA*	325
⚙	*Trus Joist MacMillan (TJM), USA*	325
■	*American softwoods and hardwoods, waterproof adhesives, polyurethane resin*	281, 339
♻	• *Efficient use of raw materials*	327

Ecoplan/ecoment

Freudenberg manufacture a diverse range of rubber flooring under the 'nora' range but 'ecoplan' and 'ecoment' are the only two made with up to 75 per cent factory and post-installation waste. Granite and marbled-effect patterns are available. All products are free of PVC, plasticizers, formaldehyde, asbestos, cadmium and CFCs and production facilities follow stringent waste-management procedures, minimal packaging and a zero-emissions environment for the workforce.

✎	*Freudenberg, UK*	317
⚙	*Freudenberg, UK*	317
▬	*Rubber, recycled rubber*	283
♻	• *Recycled and recyclable materials* • *Clean production process*	327, 328

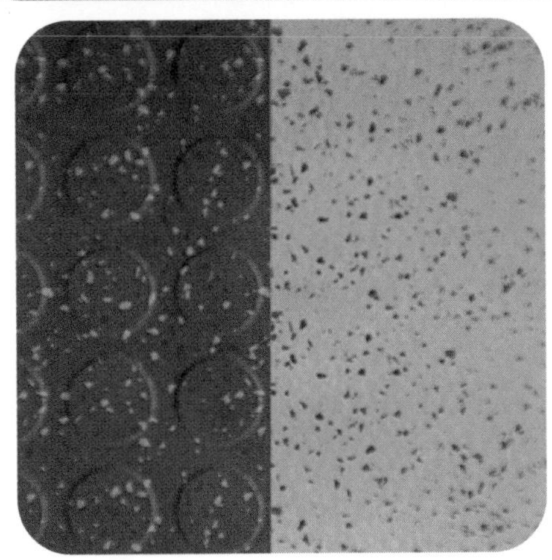

Modena

This velour carpeting range is available in seventy-five different colours, yet is made with a clean technology production in which all raw materials must be free of harmful substances and wastage is 80 per cent less than in previous technologies. Texback® forms an allergy-free backing fabric while the ecofix® Velcro enables carpets to be fitted without using adhesives.

✎	*Designteam, Hameln, Germany*	306
⚙	*Vorwerk & Co., Teppichwerke GmbH & Co. KG, Germany*	326
▬	*Velour, texback®, ecofix®*	290-1, 300-1
♻	• *Clean production process including waste reduction* • *Fitting without adhesives, facilitating reuse*	327, 328

Earth Square™

Milliken & Co. operate a closed-loop production system for their Earth Square™ carpet tiles. Tiles are replaced with new tiles or reconditioned as they become worn and the old materials are reintroduced into the recyclate:virgin fibre mixture used for the next generation of tiles. The Earth Square received the first Evergreen Award from the US General Services Administration, a government procurement agency.

	Milliken & Co., Carpet Division, USA	320
	Milliken & Co., Carpet Division, USA	320
	Various natural and synthetic materials	339
	• Clean production • Recycled content • Closed-loop production	327, 328

Dalsouple

Dalsouple manufacture standard and bespoke rubber flooring tiles in a huge variety of colours and surface textures which are 100 per cent recyclable. All Dalsouple rubber is free from PVC, CFCs, formaldehyde and plasticizers. Production waste is virtually all recycled within the manufacturing plant and emissions meet local statutory requirements. Service partners to Dalsouple include Uzin Adhesives, who offer water-based and solvent-free adhesives including polyurethane and epoxy resins.

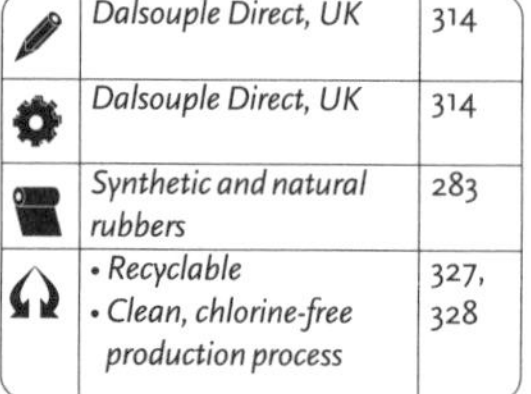

	Dalsouple Direct, UK	314
	Dalsouple Direct, UK	314
	Synthetic and natural rubbers	283
	• Recyclable • Clean, chlorine-free production process	327, 328

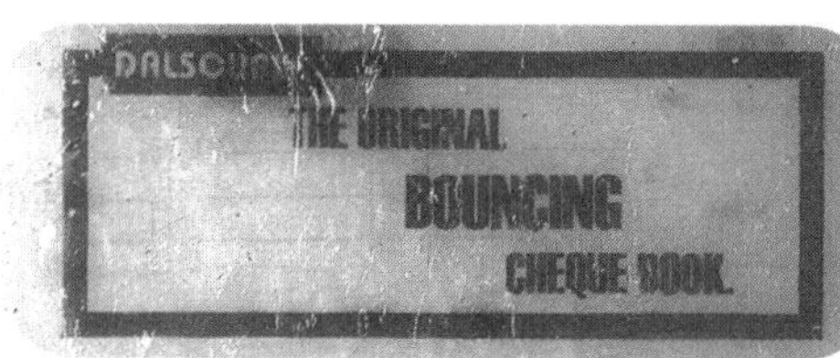

Evergreen

Interface were the first company worldwide to introduce a system of office carpeting in which, as manufacturers, they retained ownership of the product. When the product is worn or needs repairing, the company takes it back for repair and cleaning or for reshredding to use in manufacturing new carpet tiles.

	Interface, USA	318
	Interface, USA	318
	Various	339
	• Reuse, recycling • Leased product take-back	327, 330

Marmoleum® Real/Fresco

True linoleum is a heavy-duty, durable, non-allergenic floor covering containing at least 30 per cent linseed oil from flax or similar renewable oils from plants. Linoleums are predominantly constituted from natural raw materials such as linseed oil, rosin, wood flour and chalk, which are bonded under heat and pressure to a backing of jute (or occasionally polyester).

Forbo-Nairn is the largest linoleum manufacturer in Europe, supplying up to 25 million sq m (269 million sq ft) per annum. Marmoleum® linoleums have much lower emissions and lower acidification output than PVC floorings or carpeting. The Marmoleum® Real is available in thirty-six colourways and Marmoleum® Fresco in twelve marbled colourways.

✎	*Forbo-Nairn Ltd, UK*	316
⚙	*Forbo-Nairn Ltd, UK*	316
▬	*Linseed oil, pine resins, wood flour, cork, mineral fillers, jute*	339
♻	• *Renewable materials and abundant non-renewables* • *Reduction in emissions and toxins* • *Non-toxic*	327, 329

Papertex

A cotton-like yarn is produced from wood fibre forming the warp in the woven Papertex carpet. This tightly bound weave is hard-wearing and easy to clean and sits well with the modern Scandinavian aesthetic.

✎	*Ritva Puotila, Finland*	309
⚙	*Woodnotes Oy, Finland*	326
▬	*Wood (cellulose) fibre*	339
♻	• *Renewable and recyclable materials*	327

Madera®

Matrix Composites spent five years developing Lignasil®, the composite 'bio-alloy' from which Madera® solid flooring tiles are made. Lignasil® is a high-density thermal insulator, made from refined natural hardwood fibres, which are sintered in a patented manufacturing process. This material is easy to work but is tough, Class 1 Fire Rated, durable and easy to maintain. And it is completely recyclable.

✎	*Matrix Composites, Inc., USA*	320
⚙	*Matrix Composites, Inc., USA*	320
▬	*Lignasil®*	279
♻	• *Renewable materials* • *Recyclable*	327

Reykjavik

This domestic and office carpeting solution from Interface, the third largest carpet manufacturer in the world, uses a combination of renewable natural fibres mixed with a recycled synthetic component.

Designer	*Interface, Inc., USA*	318
Manufacturer	*Interface, Inc., USA/ Interface Europe - Asia Pacific, UK*	318
Materials	*Various*	339
Eco	*• Recycled and renewable components*	327

Papier Teppich 2000

This shiny black carpet is a sophisticated blend of natural materials creating a dense, durable wearing surface that is comfortable to bare or shod feet. Acid-free paper is reinforced with industrial hemp fibres and given a protective lustre finish with natural waxes. The philosophy of simple, natural design is extended to the sample boxes, which use overprinted recycled brown cardboard.

Designer	*Hugo Zumbuhl and Peter Birsfelder, Teppich-art-Team, Switzerland*	310
Manufacturer	*Anstalten Thorberg, Switzerland*	312
Materials	*Paper, hemp, natural wax*	288-9
Eco	*• Renewable, durable materials*	327

PLYBOO®

The basic component of all this company's products is strips of bamboo measuring 0.5 x 1.9 x 183cm (3/16 x 3/4 x 72in), which are extremely durable. These strips can be bent, woven and laminated as required for flooring, interior decoration/fittings and furniture. Four-, two- and one-ply laminates are available.

Designer	*Smith & Fong Company, USA*	324
Manufacturer	*Smith & Fong Company, USA*	324
Materials	*Bamboo, adhesives*	281, 287, 299
Eco	*• Renewable material*	327

Colorette, Linorette, Linodur, Marmorette, Uni Walton

This diverse range of linoleum products is fabricated from natural ingredients, such as linseed oil, with minerals including chalk bonded with heat and pressure to a jute or hemp backing.

✎	*Armstrong World Industries, Inc., USA*	312
⚙	*Armstrong World Industries, Inc., USA*	312
▮	*Linseed oil, flax, pine resins, wood flour, cork, mineral fillers*	339
♻	*• Renewable materials* *• Abundant geosphere materials*	327

Silencio 6

This is a special 6mm-thick (about 1/4in) fibreboard composed of 100 per cent-waste softwood fibre, which provides good attenuation against impact sound and insulation as an underlay for wooden and laminate floating floors.

✎	*Hunton Fiber (UK), UK*	318
⚙	*Hunton Fiber (UK), UK*	318
▮	*Recycled softwood fibre*	339
♻	*• Waste reduction* *• Recycled, recyclable materials*	327, 328

Stratica

Stratica is a laminated flooring product comprising a very tough, durable wear layer of chlorine-free, ionomer coating, DuPont Surlyn®, a printed layer, a backing layer to the print and a final bottom layer. Surlyn® is the finishing material on golf balls. Stratica is naturally flexible but doesn't use plasticizers and is free of Volatile Organic Compounds (VOCs). Over forty-five different 'natural' surfaces can be mimicked in the printing process, from stone to marbles, granites, terrazzos and woods, plus over twenty solid colours. Abrasion resistance is very high and maintenance costs are low. With certification to ISO 14001, recycling pre-consumer waste, preventing pollution and saving energy in production are high priorities.

✎	*The Amtico Company, UK*	312
⚙	*The Amtico Company, UK*	312
▮	*Dupont Surlyn®, mineral-filled ethylene copolymer*	295
♻	*• Clean production*	328

Underwood

Three-millimetre (1/8in) veneer is bonded to a thermoplastic shell, which is moulded to include ducts for underfloor services and a method of connecting each flooring 'block'. This system is more functional than standard hardwood or parquet flooring, is economical in its use of veneer and can be modified to suit bespoke requirements. Use of a thermoplastic recyclate would further boost the credentials of this system.

	Marc Sadler	310
	Prototype for Hi-wood project coordinated by the Domus Academy Research Centre, Italy, and the American Hardwoods Export Council, USA	306
	Hardwood veneer, thermoplastic	339
	• Modular system • Reduction in use of hardwood materials	327, 328

Super Duralay

Over 60,000 used car tyres are processed each week at a new Duralay plant to provide the raw material for a range of rubber crumb underlays suitable for carpets and wooden flooring. Super Duralay is rated for heavy domestic use but other grades are suitable for contract usage. Bacloc, a woven backing of paper and synthetic thread, gives extra strength to the underlay. Other grades use a mixed backing of jute and plastic.

	Duralay, UK	
	Duralay, UK	
	Recycled tyres, latex, Bacloc or polyjute	283
	• Recycled materials • Conservation of landfill space	327, 330

Smart Deck

This decking is a composite material using oak fibre and recycled polyethylene with foaming compounds and additives. Containing over 90 per cent-recycled materials by weight, it is very moisture-resistant and durable. It also weathers like conventional wood but without any associated rotting.

	SmartDeck Systems, USA	324
	SmartDeck Systems/US Plastic Lumber, USA	324, 325
	Composite wood	339
	• Recycled materials	327

CUADRO

Material inputs are significantly reduced in this aesthetically improved design, which combines the dual function of roofing component and solar collector. Traditionally solar collectors have been placed over existing roofing surfaces. The main casing is press-moulded using Cigelit®, which is a fully recyclable material.

✎	*AstroPower, USA*	312
⚙	*AstroPower, USA*	312
▮	*Recycled silicon, aluminium*	295
♻	• *Solar-power generator* • *Recycled materials*	327, 329

Aquair 100, Aquair U. W.

The Aquair 100 is a water turbine that can be towed behind a sailing vessel. The Aquair U. W. is designed to be stationary in a moving body of water. At 6 knots (3 metres or 10ft/second) the Aquair U.W. generates 6 amps at 12V whereas the Aquair 100 generates 5 amps continuous charge. Durable marine-grade materials are used with double 'O' seals and hydraulic fluid in the alternator body to provide maintenance-free turbines. An Aquair U.W. in a fast-running stream can generate up to 2.4kW per day.

✎	*Ampair Ltd, UK*	312
⚙	*Ampair Ltd, UK*	312
▮	*Marine-grade metals and plastics*	295
♻	• *Water-driven power generators*	329, 330

Rutland 913 Windcharger

Weighing just 13kg (28lb), this wind generator has a twenty-year pedigree and has been well proven in a wide variety of climates by yachtsmen and scientific researchers and for military and telecommunications operations. Continuous electrical generation starts at wind speeds of 5 knots (5.75 mph). Durable marine-grade materials are combined with quality engineering, units being manufactured to ISO 9001.

✎	*Marlec Engineering Company, UK*	320
⚙	*Marlec Engineering Company, UK*	320
▮	*Stainless steel/ aluminium, glass-reinforced polymer*	295
♻	• *Renewable wind power*	329

AstroPower

Single crystal solar cells are manufactured using silicon wafers obtained from recycled sources in the semiconductor industry. Such low-embodied-energy cells are very efficient energy converters and are mounted in aluminium frames, which fit industry-standard devices for tracking the movement of the sun.

✎	*AstroPower, USA*	312
⚙	*AstroPower, USA*	312
▤	*Recycled silicon, aluminium*	295
♻	• *Solar-power generator* • *Recycled materials*	327, 329

Furlmatic 1803

This three-phase alternator generates 340W at wind speeds of 10m/s (35km/h or 22mph) but is capable of generating electricity from wind speeds as low as 3 m/s. It provides sufficient output for off-grid domestic lighting and any remote site requiring power for lighting, pumping water or low-voltage equipment. An automatic system produces a furling point at 15 metres/second to protect the generator from damage by excessive winds. Other automatic features include an overcharge battery protection device, which stalls the turbine, and a 12V or 24V controller unit. This twin-blade turbine, diameter 1.87m (6ft), is mounted on a minimum 6.5m (21ft) tower. All components are manufactured at an ISO 9001-compliant factory.

✎	*Marlec Engineering Company, UK*	320
⚙	*Marlec Engineering Company, UK*	320
▤	*Stainless steel/aluminium, GRP*	295, 341
♻	• *Renewable wind power*	329

Farm 2000 'HT' boilers

A range of high temperature (HT) boilers has been designed to accommodate typical biomass fuels available on the farm, such as circular or 1-tonne rectangular straw bales, as well as woodchips, cardboard and other combustible wastes. Heat outputs vary from 20kW to 300kW depending on the boiler and the equivalent electricity costs per kWh are between 25 and 33 per cent of those of kerosene oil or natural gas. An upper refractory arch encourages complete burning of gases, improves the overall efficiency and minimizes atmospheric emissions. Annual or short-rotation crops for biomass fuels absorb carbon dioxide that is released on burning, so this cycle is neutral and makes no net contribution to the greenhouse effect.

✎	*Teisen Products, UK*	324
⚙	*Teisen Products, UK*	324
▤	*Steel*	295
♻	• *A carbon-dioxide neutral heating system* • *Biomass fuels obtainable locally*	328, 329

Filsol solar collector

Water heating in buildings in temperate climates can be readily supplemented by installation of a solar collector. Sunlight enters the acrylic collector, which transmits 89 per cent of incident light, and heats a 'Stamax' absorber plate made of specially coated stainless steel. Colourless oxides of chromium, nickel and iron provide an absorption of 0.93 of the incident energy, transferring it to an aqueous antifreeze mixture running in channels in the absorber plate. This hot aqueous mixture is pumped whenever its temperature is higher than the water in the hot-water tank, where further heat exchange ensues.

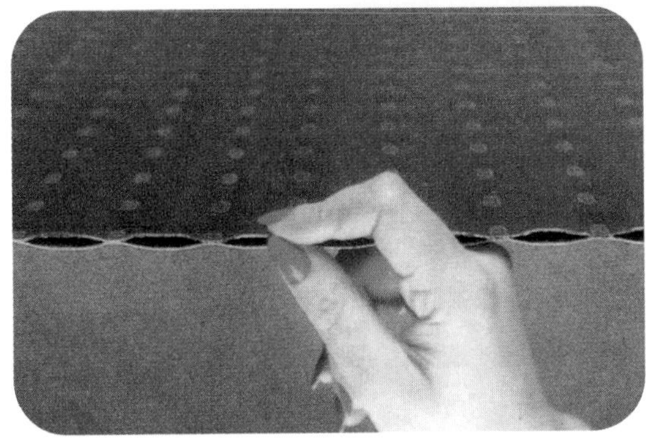

✎	*Filsol, UK*	316
⚙	*Filsol, UK*	316
▣	*Stainless steel, aluminium, alloys, acrylic, poly-isocyanurate foam*	295
♺	*• Reduction in energy requirement for water heating*	329

Enercon E-66

Windmills have entered a new era. Borrowing from aeronautical engineering, designers have introduced new features to the Enercon E-66 wind-powered generator. A tapered mast permits better load distribution on the 100-metre-high (330 feet) monster and the wing tips are bent to reduce turbulence and noise pollution. It will take twenty years to pay back the investment of £2.5 million each and start generating 'free' energy but with their capacity to supply 1,200 homes, and a commitment by the European Union to increase renewable energy to 10 per cent of overall power generation capacity by 2010, more of these generators are likely to dot the landscape in future.

✎	*Foster & Partners, UK*	306
⚙	*Prototype*	
▣	*Various*	339
♺	*• Wind power renewable energy generation*	329

NSS (Non-Stop Shoes)

Translating the expenditure of human energy into power is well understood in the context of sport, but how much energy expended in everyday activities can be harnessed to power appliances in our daily lives? Emili Padrós suggests that even the process of walking could generate electricity, which could be utilized to power lamps and radios once we return home. Developing the mechanisms to generate and store energy could redefine the shoe of the future.

✎	*Emili Padrós, Barcelona, Spain*	309
⚙	*Conceptual design*	
▬	*Various, battery energy storage*	339
♻	*• Renewable (human) energy generator*	329

GFX

The heat within waste water from domestic showers, baths and sinks can be reclaimed to heat the incoming cold-water supply to the hot-water tank. GFX is an insulated spiral coil of copper tubing carrying the cold supply, which is in intimate contact with a falling-film heat exchanger through which the waste hot water

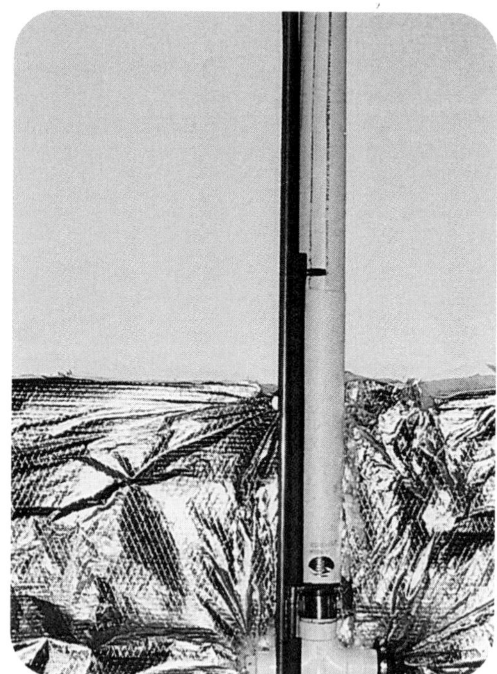

travels by gravity. The system is capable of saving up to 2kW of power from each shower.

✎	*WaterFilm Energy, USA*	326
⚙	*WaterFilm Energy, USA*	326
▬	*Copper, insulation*	295
♻	*• Energy conservation*	329

Computer-keyboard generator

Laptop computers used away from power sources quickly drain the power from batteries, but if an electrical current can be generated during normal keyboard use it is possible to recharge the batteries as the computer is being used. Magnets attached to each key move over a wire coil shaft, generating the current. This patented technology could either make laptops much lighter and/or extend the working time away from a mains power source.

✎	*Adrian Crisan, Compaq, USA*	314
⚙	*Prototype, Compaq, USA*	314
▬	*Plastics, wire coils, electronics, battery*	295
♻	*• Human power*	329

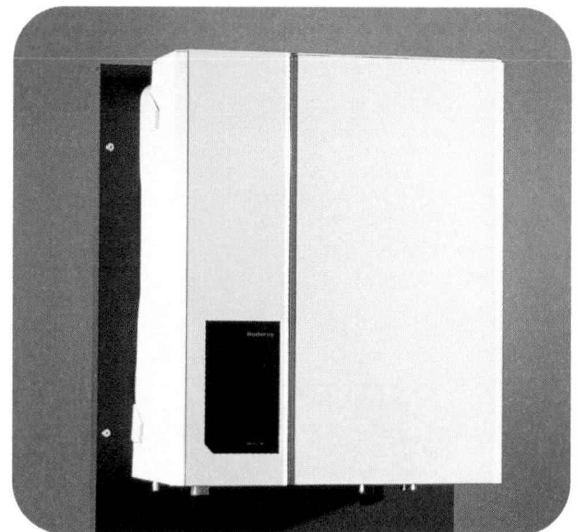

Logamax plus GB112-19 (Linea)

This wall-mounted boiler unit offers an output capacity of between 9.6kW and 19.1kW. It uses an efficient ceramic burner to provide more complete combustion of the gas fuel, resulting in emission levels well under those specified in the German Blue Angel eco-label scheme.

✎	*Buderus Heiztechnik GmbH, Germany*	313
⚙	*Buderus Heiztechnik GmbH, Germany*	313
▬	*Steel, various metals including aluminium-silicon alloy, ceramics (burner unit)*	295
♻	*• Energy efficient • Blue Angel eco-label*	329

Logano G124

This free-standing boiler unit offers an output capacity of between 9kW and 34kW, making it suitable for heating single or multiple dwellings. A key feature is the efficient ceramic burner, which provides more complete combustion of the natural or liquid gas fuel, reducing emission levels of nitrous oxides and carbon monoxide below the levels set by the German Blue Angel eco-label scheme.

✎	*Buderus Heiztechnik GmbH, Germany*	313
⚙	*Buderus Heiztechnik GmbH, Germany*	313
▬	*Cast iron, various metals including aluminium-silicon alloy, ceramics (burner unit)*	295
♻	*• Energy efficient • Blue Angel eco-label*	329

NSD (Non-Stop Doors)

Any repetitive human movement in our everyday lives expends energy, some of which can be captured and stored for later use. In public buildings the act of opening and passing through doors is repeated hundreds of times each day. This human energy is transferred to stored energy, which lights up the frame of the door. Potentially this improves the eco-efficiency of each individual as some of the energy acquired from primary food reserves is recycled. But the real advantage of this concept is that renewable energy is generated without requiring any behavioural or cultural changes

✎	*Emili Padrós, Barcelona, Spain*	309
⚙	*Conceptual design*	
▬	*Various, battery energy storage*	339
♻	*• Renewable (human) energy generator*	329

Multibrid wind energy converter

This wind turbine is designed to work offshore exposed to high-speed, salt-laden winds, so all components are sealed to prevent ingress of water. Unique aspects of the design include slow rotational movement to ensure that the unit can be operated without maintenance for the first three years. This massive generator, with individual blades spanning 50 metres (164ft), is an innovative rotor with excellent aerodynamics.

✎	*Bartsch Design Industrial Design Gbr, Germany*	304
⚙	*aerodyn Energiesysteme GmbH, Germany*	312
	Various	340
	• Source of renewable energy	329

Paradigma CPC Star

This solar collector is based upon a modular design allowing easy separation of components and materials and facilitating almost 100 per cent recycling. Material usage has been kept to a minimum, giving a lightweight structure with a high efficiency in low sunlight and at ambient temperatures below freezing point.

✎	*Büro für Produktgestaltung, Germany*	305
⚙	*Ritter Energie- und Umwelttechnik GmbH KG, Germany*	323
	Aluminium, glass	295
	• Design for disassembly and recycling	328
	iF Ecology Design Award, 2000	332

POWER Cell

Over 16 per cent of incident sunlight is converted into electrical power with these Sunway solar cells, a very efficient ratio compared with conventional solar cells. Various versions of the POWER cells are manufactured, including those offering up to 30 per cent transparency. The transmitted light is white, yet there is a range of external colours for the cells, using a process of texturing that avoids the use of chemicals. Now solar cells can be integrated into any aperture intended to introduce light into a building, such as windows and roof lights, thereby reducing overall construction costs.

✎	*Roland Burkhardt, Sunways, Germany*	305
⚙	*Sunways, Germany*	324
▮	*Silicon polycrystalline wafers*	295
♻	*• Dual-function solar-power generator and window material*	328, 329

Solar Homes Systems

The archipelago of Indonesia comprises over 13,000 islands, so nationwide distribution of electricity by a conventional overland 'grid' is not feasible. Invented in 1988, the Solar Homes Systems concept is an inexpensive solar generator, capable of generating up to 250W per day and suitable for powering lighting, radio and TV. Hessels has designed lighting specifically for the system as well as a TV table-cum-battery holder. Lampu Lita are hanging lamps made of plastic. Systems can be purchased under a monthly payment scheme.

	Paul Hessels, unknown	
	PT Sudimar Energi Surya, Indonesia	321
	Various plastics, photovoltaics	295
	• *Low-cost solar systems for remote households and communities*	329

The Solar Shingle SHR-17

Why install a photovoltaic panel on top of an existing roofing surface when the job of keeping out the weather and generating energy can be combined in one product – the Solar Shingle? These 2m-long (7ft), 30cm-wide (12in), photovoltaic panels can be simply nailed on to the roofing substructure instead of roofing shingles, slates or tiles. Each panel is subdivided into 12 x 30cm (5 x 12in) sections that visually mimic traditional roofing materials. Generating 17W each at 6V, panels can be wired together to produce the required capacity.

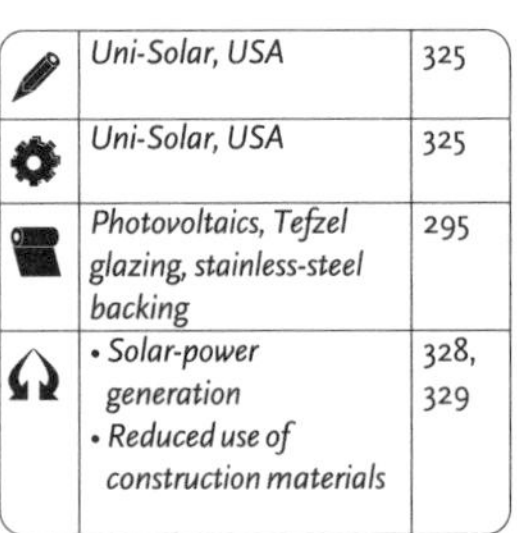

	Uni-Solar, USA	325
	Uni-Solar, USA	325
	Photovoltaics, Tefzel glazing, stainless-steel backing	295
	• *Solar-power generation* • *Reduced use of construction materials*	328, 329

Solar Moon portable renewable energy unit

The lid of this briefcase is a photovoltaic panel capable of recharging AA batteries to operate the appliances stored inside the case – radio, torch and emergency light. Included in the kit is a 10W high-efficiency bulb capable of providing light for up to ten hours.

	MSK Corporation, Japan	320
	MSK Corporation, Japan	320
	Photovoltaics, metal, batteries, circuit boards	295
	• *Solar power*	329

Tedlar™ laminate

BP Solarex, the world's largest manufacturer of photovoltaic cells and laminates, constructed the G8 Solar house to demonstrate the efficacy of low-energy solar-powered houses and offices. The system uses a curving, south-facing photovoltaic array of 176 laminate modules connected to a 240V inverter wired to the local network. This array can meet the needs of four energy-efficient houses. BP Solarex produce a diverse range of photovoltaic options including: screen-printed cells capable of converting 12-14 per cent of incident sunlight into electrical energy; high-efficiency Laser Grooved Buried Grid (LGBG) cells, in which a very thin copper grid is etched into the surface of the silicon wafer, resulting in a 20 per cent increase in efficiency over 'normal' cells; and thin film cells using amorphous silicon at two-thousandths of a millimetre rather than crystalline silicon, which must be about one-third of a millimetre to absorb the full spectrum. Efficiency in the thin film cells does drop but high-volume manufacturing compensates in terms of cheapness. BP Solarex are also now able to produce semi-transparent photovoltaic modules, in a special laminate called Tedlar™, in which the density of the PV cells per square metre can be customized to meet particular architectural requirements.

✎	*BP Solarex, worldwide*	313
⚙	*BP Solarex, worldwide*	313
▮	*Silicon, semi-conductor materials, copper, glass*	295
♺	• *Dual-functional PV units for solar-power generation and glazing*	328, 329

Solar-powered service station canopy

Forecourts of most service stations protect customers from the weather by means of a canopy. BP Amoco plc, in line with their long-term objectives to become a clean and responsible energy company, have designed special photovoltaic arrays for installation on canopies to generate all the electricity needed to pump fuel and for lighting and so on. This energy-neutral installation will eventually be incorporated into all new service stations.

✎	*BP Amoco, UK*	313
⚙	*BP Amoco, UK*	313
▮	*Photovoltaic panels*	339
♺	• *Conversion of specialist building to energy-neutral status*	328

Solar roof tiles

Solar roof tiles, which are a similar size to conventional tiles or slates, can be attached to a building instead of conventional photovoltaic penals, enabling the user to renew the actual protective roofing layer and install a solar-powered energy generator in one operation. Each solar tile is a special photovoltaic cell that is connected to a battery storage system and/or the local electricity supply network. On a typical British day a Victorian terraced house that has

been totally reroofed with an installed capacity of 2kW would generate enough capacity to burn the toast 800 times and brew 350 cups of tea. Householders can become suppliers of green electricity, although a long view is needed to make the payback on capital investment.

✎	*Solar Century, UK*	310
⚙	*Uni-Solar, USA*	325
▤	*Special photovoltaic panels*	339
♻	• *Multifunctional* • *Solar-powered*	329

Thermomax®

Flat-plate solar collectors show a reduction in efficiency from 60 per cent at an operating temperature of 20°C down to about 40 per cent as the temperature doubles. Not so with vacuum-tube solar collectors, which can maintain efficiencies of over 60 per cent at temperatures of 80°C. A semi-conductor absorber plate sits within an evacuated glass tube. The special liquid-filled heat pipe is in intimate contact with the absorber plate where heat from the sun causes the liquid to evaporate to the top of a condenser unit. Between the pipe and the condenser sits a spring made of shape-memory metal, which limits heat transfer through the pipe when pre-set temperatures are reached, so preventing overheating. Water surrounding the condenser absorbs heat as it flows. Energy conversion even on cloudy days is very efficient, with an overall annual efficiency of over 70 per cent. The reduction of gas or electricity heating costs for an average household is about 40 per cent. All Thermomax manufacturing plants comply with ISO 9001.

✎	*Rayotec Ltd, UK*	322
⚙	*Rayotec Ltd, UK*	322
▤	*Low-iron soda glass, copper, shape-memory metal*	295 339
♻	• *High-efficiency solar-powered hot water system*	329

Sun Catcher

Fitting neatly inside a standard carrying case for a laptop PC, these twin solar panels can triple the run time of your PC or be used independently to recharge your spare battery. The device is compatible with over three hundred models.

✎	*Kyocera Corporation, Japan*	319
⚙	*Kyocera Corporation, Japan*	319
▬	*Photovoltaic cells*	339
♻	• *Renewable power*	329

Topolino

Traditional wood-burning stoves are stoked with timber in a haphazard fashion, causing rapid, uncontrolled combustion with significant heat loss up the chimney stack. GAAN's range of wood-burning heaters encourage optimal combustion because wood is stacked vertically and burns from the top, like the wick of a candle, producing a fuel efficiency of 85 per cent. As the warm combustion gases rise they are forced through a double swan-necked constriction where heat is absorbed into the surrounding materials. Immediate space heating is provided by radiated heat from the toughened glass door, while the remaining heat passes into the surrounding cast stone/granite or steatite body panels, where 60 per cent of the total combustion energy is stored and emitted over the next six to eight hours. Emissions are significantly lower than required under existing EU and Swiss regulations.

✎	*GAAN GmbH, Switzerland*	306
⚙	*Tonwerk Lausen AG, Switzerland*	325
▬	*Steel, glass, granite*	295, 339
♻	• *Improved energy generation* • *Durable construction*	329

Axor Starck

This functional, easy-to-clean mixer tap limits water output to 7.2 litres (1.6gal) a minute, eliminates limescaling and has a special stop valve. It combines low maintenance with good looks.

✎	*Philippe Starck, France*	310
⚙	*Hans Grohe, Germany*	317
▬	*Chromium-plated steel*	295
♲	*• Reduces water consumption*	330
✿	*iF Design Award, 1999*	332

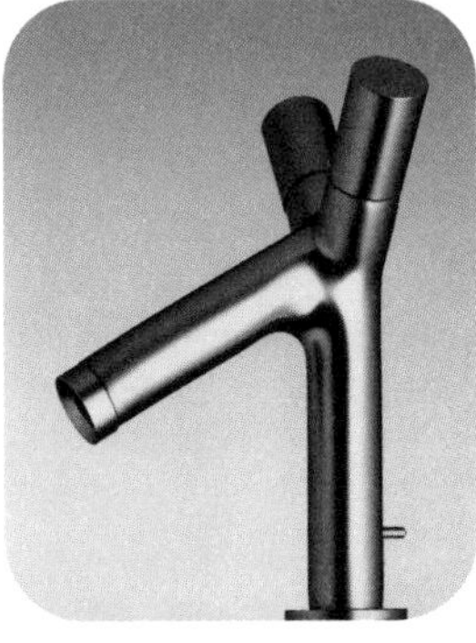

Axor Starck showerhead

This free-standing shower unit is sparing in its use of materials as parts of the frame also act as hot- and cold-water pipes to deliver to the overhead and hand-held roses. Pleating the polyester curtain prevents it from clinging to the user. The unit is easily plumbed in, provides excellent access for maintenance and can be repositioned when moving house. Stainless steel would be a preferred substitute for the chromium-plated steel to minimize the impacts of this unit even further.

✎	*Philippe Starck, Agence Philippe Starck, France*	310
⚙	*Hans Grohe AG, Germany*	317
▬	*Enamelled and chromium-plated steel, polyester, polymer base*	295
♲	*• Economy of materials usage*	328
✿	*iF Ecology Design Award, 2000*	332

Clivus Multrum 2 composter

This company has been manufacturing composting toilets since 1939. This particular model, made of 100 per cent-recycled polyethylene, provides adequate sanitation for a three-bedroomed house.

An integral moistening system ensures biomass volume reductions of 95 per cent. Water vapour and carbon dioxide are the only emissions.

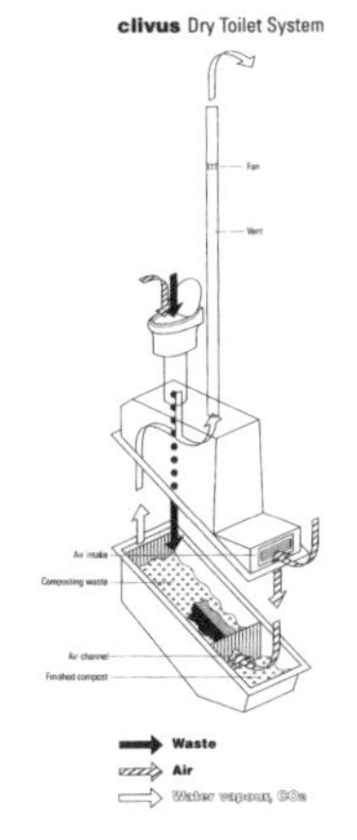

	Clivus Multrum Canada, Canada	314
	Clivus Multrum Canada, Canada	314
	Recycled polyethylene	341
	• *Zero water consumption* • *Recycled materials* • *Compost generator* • *Canadian eco-label Environmental Choice EcoLogo M certified*	327, 328

Columbia emergency water system

A triple in-line filter system on the inlet hose removes particles greater than or equal to 1 micron and provides filtration of lead, chlorine, nitrates, radon, mercury and various toxic chemicals and pesticides as the water is hand-pumped to the storage container. Filtration of Giardia, cysts, E-coli, cryptosporidium and other bacteria ensures protection against water-borne disease. The whole system is highly portable and can also be fitted to static water supplies.

	Water Tech Industries, USA	326
	Water Tech Industries, USA	326
	Plastic, metal, filters	295
	• *Emergency provision of clean, safe, drinking water*	329

Ifö Cera range

The humble toilet bears the hallmark of a couple of hundred years of traditional industrial design but few people know what happens inside the water cistern. In traditional toilet designs extravagant volumes of water are used to flush even small quantities of human effluent. Today, to meet the need for water conservation, sanitary-ware manufacturers such as Ifö Sanitar have introduced dual-flush cisterns offering two- or four-litre (0.4–0.9gal) water delivery and, more recently, adjustable flushing volumes, from three to eight litres (0.7–1.8gal) in the Ifö Cera range. Polypropylene or duroplastic seating is available, ergonomically designed to fit a huge variety of posteriors, and with hygienic surfaces in a typically clean, sculptural, Scandinavian form.

✎	*Ifö Sanitar AB, Sweden*	318
⚙	*Ifö Sanitar AB, Sweden*	318
▮	*Ceramics, polypropylene or duroplastic*	295
♻	*• Encourages water conservation* *• Improved ergonomics*	329, 330

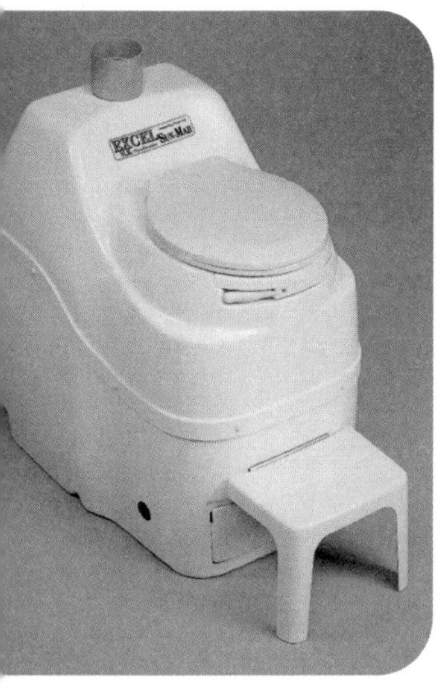

Excel NE

With over twenty-five years' experience of designing composting, waterless toilets, Sun-Mar Corporation have developed a range of self-contained and central composting toilet systems. Most models are equipped with an electrically driven fan to provide an odour-free atmosphere but the Excel NE is totally non-electric, using a vent chimney instead. The operating principle in all Sun-Mar toilets is identical. A mixture of peat, some topsoil and/or 'Microbe Mix' is added to the Bio-drum™ and a cupful of peat bulking mix is added per person per day. After use the Bio-drum is mechanically turned between four and six revolutions every third day or so to aerate the mixture. Fully degraded compost is removed from a bottom finishing drawer as required. An evaporating chamber at the rear of the drum ensures excess moisture is removed. So confident are the manufacturers in the robust design of their toilets that they offer free parts for three years and a twenty-five year warranty on the fibreglass body.

✎	*Sun-Mar Corporation, Canada*	324
⚙	*Sun-Mar Corporation, Canada*	324
▮	*Fibreglass*	295, 340
♻	*• Reduction in water consumption* *• Recycling of human waste*	330

Mister Sunnyboy

Designed for ease of assembly, this modular construction uses sand-blasted plexiglass to create a water distiller driven by the passive energy of the sun. It can be suspended or placed in the ground and provides fresh, treated water from a deceptively simple yet functional design.

Designer	*FrogDesign, Germany*	306
Manufacturer	*Prototype, 1997*	
Materials	*Plexiglass, plastics*	295
Eco-features	*• Passive solar power* *• Provision of safe drinking water*	328, 329

Plush tap

Conservation of resources in public buildings ought to be a high priority but it often needs an innovation to encourage capital investment before tangible results can be achieved.

Plush Tap is such an innovation. It allows existing cross-head taps to be converted into push taps by using an adaptor to fit on the old tap body. Water is conserved, as taps cannot be accidentally left running. The advantages of push taps are especially felt where water is metered.

Designer	*Flow Control Water Conservation, UK*	316
Manufacturer	*Flow Control Water Conservation, UK*	316
Materials	*Brass, seals, stainless steel*	295
Eco-features	*• Encourages water conservation*	330

Oxfam bucket

Jerrycans holding about 22 or 45 litres (5 or 10gal) are the normal means of providing water carriers for aid or disaster relief work by agencies such as Oxfam. But rigid jerrycans take up a lot of valuable payload space on aid work planes, so Core Plastics developed a stackable bucket with a removable lid, which incorporates a filler hole/spout with snap-on top. An indentation in the base helps reduce the risk of spinal injuries when the bucket is carried on the head. The bucket design improves the efficacy of relief efforts.

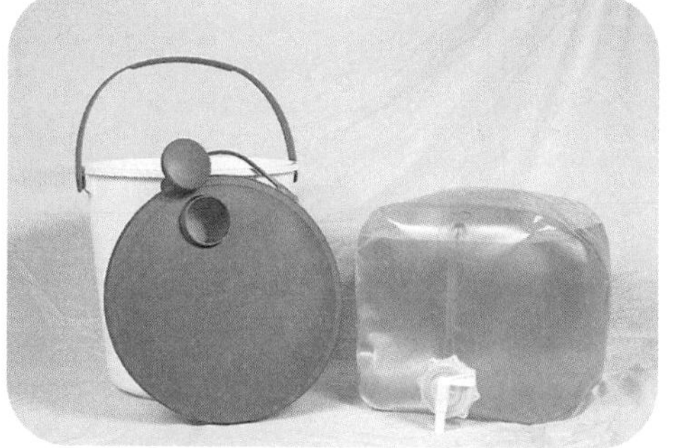

Designer	*Oxfam/Core Plastics, UK*	309
Manufacturer	*Core Plastics, UK*	309
Materials	*Lightweight, UV-resistant plastic*	295
Eco-features	*• Reduction in transport energy per unit water carrier*	328

Safe Tap

As more households install systems for recycling water the risk of accidental usage of greywater (waste water from washing, bathing, etc.) for drinking will increase. This tap can be opened only when a special garden hose connector is inserted into the greywater faucet.

✎	*WeLL Design Associates, Netherlands*	311
⚙	*Flamco, Netherlands*	316
▬	*Recyclable materials*	341
♻	• *Safety feature for greywater systems* • *Recyclable materials*	327, 340

Water harvester

In a Chilean fishing village called Chungungo a stunningly simple system helps mitigate water supply problems. Local conditions give rise to fog where the air is saturated with moisture. The airborne water particles are encouraged to condense on fine nylon mesh screens, providing up to 10,000 litres (2,200gal) of water a day.

✎	*Ad-hoc system*	
⚙	*Ad-hoc system, Chile*	
▬	*Nylon net*	295
♻	• *Water collection and conservation*	330

Orso rain collector

Water is the resource of the twenty-first century. Both industrial and domestic use is increasing in most nations. Storage of this precious commodity is essential but many solutions for small-volume storage consist of little more than cylindrical plastic containers with a tap. Marc De Jonghe's Rain Column has an attachment point for a faucet and garden hose. A standard connector allows any number of columns to be connected to one another to provide increased storage capacity.

✎	*Marc De Jonghe, Orso Design, Belgium*	305
⚙	*Prototype*	
▬	*Plastics*	295
♻	• *Encourages water conservation* • *Flexible storage system*	329, 330

Rainwater storage tanks

Wagner & Co. fabricate a range of rainwater storage tanks from 750 to 2,000 litres (165–440 gallons) capacity, which, when fitted to a pump and filtration system, supply water for washing machines, toilets, gardening and for general cleaning purposes. Potentially reductions of up to 50 per cent of normal mains water consumption can be achieved. At the same time there is a concomitant saving in the energy and chemicals that the water utility companies use to deliver drinking-quality water – much of which ends up being used for cleaning rather than drinking. The company is registered to both ISO 14001 and EMAS.

✎	*Wagner & Co. Solartechnik GmbH, Germany*	326
⚙	*Wagner & Co. Solartechnik GmbH, Germany*	326
▬	*Polyethylene, various other materials*	341
♻	• *Conservation and utilization of rainwater*	330

Waterless urinal system

To avoid the build-up of odours, public urinals tend to use a lot of water to flush the problem away. Waterless UK think they have come up with a solution by using water-repellent gels on the inside of the bowl and a special filter to absorb the urine solids and let the remaining aqueous waste enter the greywater system. A floating gel on top of the filter prevents any smelly vapours from polluting the local atmosphere. Filters last up to six months and are replaced under a maintenance contract. The full environmental costs of this waterless system must include the embodied energy in the manufacture of the system components, the transport energy of the installation and maintenance and the disposal option when the filters are no longer usable. Saving money on water may be possible with this system but the full environmental costs must be computed.

✎	*Waterless UK, UK*	326
⚙	*Waterless UK, UK*	326
▮	*Water-repellent gel, filter cartridge*	341
♻	*• Reduces water consumption*	328

Vulcan Ram

A ram is a water-driven pump using a natural head of water to force water in a small-diameter pipe uphill. Water flows through a pipe taken from a stream or lake feed and is accelerated as it passes through a pulse valve. This valve snaps shut when sufficient pressure builds up in the 'input' chamber in the ram, with the result that a proportion of the water is forced through a delivery valve into the 'output' chamber. Typically there are between forty and ninety open/shut cycles in the pulse valve each minute. Air under pressure in the output chamber converts the pulsing water through the delivery valve into a steady flow to a header tank. Rams are capable of raising water up to 100 metres (330ft) above the ram and pumping 250,000 litres (55,000gals) in twenty-four hours. Using traditional cast-iron and gunmetal production techniques, Green & Carter have been manufacturing rams since 1928 and export worldwide. They still repair rams designed and made by Josiah and James Easton, who installed water-pumping schemes for many eighteenth- and nineteenth-century landowners. The ram is an example of Industrial Revolution technology still proving durable, reliable and economical.

✎	*Originally patented by Pierre Montgolfier in 1816*	
⚙	*Green & Carter, UK*	317
▮	*Cast iron, metals, rubber*	295, 340
♻	*• Energy and water conservation • Durability*	328, 329

Kolaps-A-Tank

This collapsible 1,340 US gallon (1,116 imperial gal) water bag is a portable cubic package measuring just 45cm (18 in) on each side. Made of tough, food-grade vinyl, approved by the US Food and Drugs Administration, it is ideal for relief work in drought zones, being easily transportable by road.

✎	*Burch, USA*	313
⚙	*Burch, USA*	313
▮	*Food-grade vinyl*	295
♻	*• Facilitates emergency water distribution*	328

APT battery adapter

A series of cylindrical sleeves permits rechargeable AA- and C-type battery cells to be used instead of D-type cells.

✎	*Unknown*	
⚙	*Unknown; retailer Jade Mountain, USA*	335
▮	*Card, plastic, metal*	295, 340
♻	*• Reduction in raw materials during production* *• Encourages use of rechargeable batteries*	328, 329

Eco Charger

Battery life of NiMH, Nicad and Alkaline AA, AAA, C and D cells is generally shortened by overcharging but the Eco Charger's LCD allows monitoring of the state of the charge and so extends the number of possible recharges.

✎	*Saitek, USA*	323
⚙	*Saitek, USA*	323
▮	*Plastic, metal, LCD*	295
♻	*• Reuse and extended life for consumables*	328

Trojan L-16

This 360Ah (amp hour), 6V-capacity battery is suitable for trickle charge from photovoltaic generating systems but will also accept a rapid charge from a fossil fuel, wind or water generator. This makes it ideal for domestic renewable energy systems. All the lead is from recycled sources and 80 per cent of the plastic Polyon casing is also recyclate. A lifespan of ten years is guaranteed and thereafter many of the components can be once again recycled.

✎	*Trojan Battery Company, USA*	325
⚙	*Trojan Battery Company, USA*	325
▮	*Recycled plastic, recycled lead*	295
♻	*• High percentage of recyclates used in manufacturing*	327

Savaplug

This 13-amp, three-pin plug will adjust the electricity supply to match the load requirements of the motor on a refrigerator and so reduce consumption, especially on older models or large motors.

✎	*Unknown*	
⚙	*SAVAWatt (UK) Ltd*	323
▮	*Plastic, brass, electronics*	295
♻	*• Reduction in energy consumption*	328

Scimat 700/30 and 700/35

Rechargeable nickel metal hydride batteries (NiMH) don't use any cadmium, which is a highly toxic ingredient of nickel-cadmium (NiCad) batteries. When NiMH batteries were introduced they used the same nylon material to separate the positive and negative electrodes and the electrolyte as NiCads but this separator resulted in loss of charge and degraded chemically. Scimat found that if polypropylene was exposed to an ultraviolet grafting technique it could absorb water and became hydrophilic. This improved penetration of the electrolyte into the separator, improving charge retention and efficiency of NiMH batteries.

✎	*SciMAT, UK*	323
⚙	*SciMAT, UK*	323
▮	*UV-treated polypropylene*	341
♻	*• Improves efficiency and lifetime of rechargeable batteries*	329

AccuPlus Ultra

Varta were one of the first battery manufacturers to abandon the use of mercury with the introduction of rechargeable nickel cadmium (NiCad) batteries for portable appliances in the mid-1990s. Continuing their quest to reduce the environmental impact of their products, Varta now offer 1.2V AA, C and D and 8.4V PP3 rechargeable nickel metal hydride (NiMH) batteries. These batteries are totally free of mercury and cadmium and offer a longer life than NiCads with, typically, up to a thousand charge/discharge cycles.

	Varta, Germany	325
	Varta, Germany	325
	Nickel, metal hydride, metal	295
	• *Reduction in materials usage* • *Reduction in toxic emissions following disposal* • *Reuse by recharging*	328, 329

W high-efficiency motor

Brook Hansen is a major supplier of heavy-duty electric motors to UK industry. The 'W' High-Efficiency Motor uses a new type of steel with improved magnetic characteristics, which increases electrical efficiency by 3 per cent. Electric motors account for over 65 per cent of the energy usage by UK industry, so this new motor can potentially reduce carbon dioxide emissions in the UK by up to 2.5 million tonnes per annum as existing motors are replaced. Use of this special steel also allows a reduction of 30 per cent by weight compared with conventional steels.

	Brook Hansen with Sheffield and Cambridge Universities, UK	313
	Brook Hansen, UK	313
	Steel, copper, various others	295
	• *Reduction in energy and materials usage*	327, 328

eNDOSeAL

The debate about ozone-depleting gases such as CFCs in refrigeration units overshadowed other necessary innovations to tackle this problem. Leakage of gas from flare joints on old and new units with CFCs, HCFCs or other gases still makes a significant contribution to ozone depletion. eNDOSeAL is a special PTFE seal that can be easily fitted to provide a 100 per cent gas-tight seal, as the material extrudes into cavities and is not corroded by the refrigerant. Preventing leakage of refrigerant also improves refrigeration efficiency and reduces consumption of electric power.

Universal Master Products, UK	325
Universal Master Products, UK	325
PTFE	341
• Reduction in ozone-depleting gases • Reduction in energy consumption	328, 340

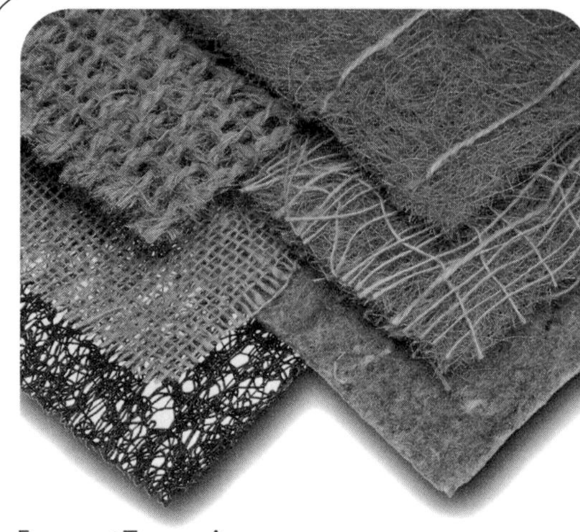

Erosamat Type 1, 1A, 2

Woven mats of natural fibres placed on the surface of the soil absorb raindrop impact and significantly reduce water runoff and consequent soil erosion. Erosamat Type 1 and 1A are made from jute fibres while Erosamat Type 2 is a heavier duty geotextile of coir fibres extracted from the husks of coconuts. The latter takes longer to decompose but affords greater protection to soils more at risk from erosion.

All types of mat can be seeded to create a dense sward of vegetation, which further bonds the surface of the soil.

Unknown	
Various for ABG Ltd, UK	312
Jute, coir	281
• Renewable materials • Prevention of soil erosion	327, 330

3M Serie 9300

If masks are uncomfortable, wearers tend to discard them, so compromising their individual protection against fine dust in the workplace. This new mask from 3M has a rigid centre section and flexible upper and lower flaps to provide a better individual fit and make speaking easier. This three-section design also allows the mask to be folded flat and the interior kept dirt-free when not in use.

3M New Products Development Team, Germany	312
3M, Germany	312
Various	339
• Improved personal health equipment	328
iF Design Award, 1999	332

BioAcoustic Fish Fence (BAFF)

Industrial and hydroelectric water intakes are usually protected by a physical grille or barrier to prevent fish from being drawn in with the water. However, these conventional barriers reduce water flow, need maintenance and can kill the fish they are designed to protect. The BAFF is a patented technology for creating a curtain of sound using air bubbles. The sonic barrier warns fish to avoid the area and diverts them elsewhere.

Fish Guidance Systems, UK	316
Fish Guidance Systems, UK	316
Various	339
• Protection of fish stocks	33[illegible]

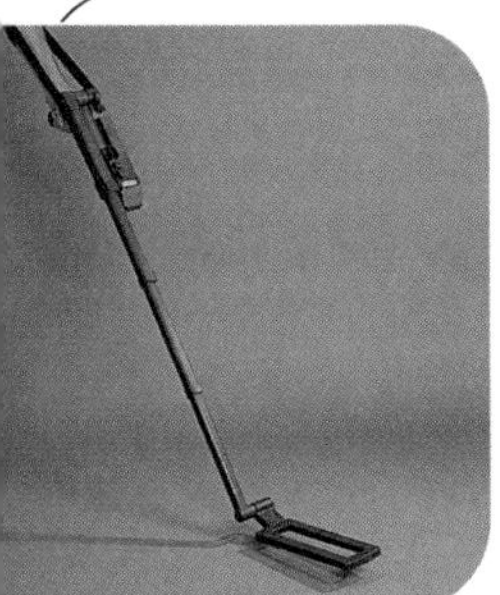

Mimid

Land mines planted during military and civil conflicts during the twentieth century kill or maim innocent civilians every day. An estimated 100 million undiscovered mines form a lethal legacy for future generations, so this portable, compact mine detector is a useful addition to the tools available to mine-clearance personnel.

✎	*Prof. Gerhard Heufler, Germany*	307
⚙	*P Schiebel Elektronische Geräte AG, Germany*	321
▤	*Various*	339
♻	• *Contributes to a healthier environment*	328

ExoFly Trap™

Control of the common house fly is essential in food-manufacturing plants. ExoSect has developed a method of killing flies without using insecticides and with a self-contained system of disposal of the dead flies. A cardboard box is marked with visual stimuli and doused with the female fly's sex hormone. Once enticed inside the box, the victims cannot take a direct flight path out and so try and alight on the inside surface of the box. This is coated with an inert powder which they cannot grip, so they fall to the bottom of the box where they suffocate in a layer of the same powder. Boxes can be disposed of by incineration or removal to a landfill.

✎	*Xo2 Limited t/as Exosect, UK*	326
⚙	*Exosect, UK*	326
▤	*Electrostatic powder, cardboard, hormones*	288-9
♻	• *Avoidance of toxic substances* • *Control of pests in food manufacturing*	329

Pureprint

Conventional web-offset printing processes use water with about 10 per cent industrial alcohol, such as IPA, to ensure the plates stay wet so the inks can flow. IPA is highly mobile as it readily evaporates and 'dissolves' in water. It is also a carcinogen and therefore creates a potentially toxic environment for workers. Beacon Press avoid using water or alcohol and instead use silicon rubber to ensure appropriate 'wetting' of the plates and sharper resolution. Nor are any chemicals used in preparation of filmwork, and a strong corporate environmental policy ensures that Beacon Press operate a clean technology printing plant in all aspects, from supply-chain management to car-sharing for employees.

✎	*Originally developed in Japan and USA*	
⚙	*Beacon Print, UK*	313
▤	*Silicon rubber*	283
♻	• *Reduction in water consumption* • *Avoidance of use of toxic substances*	329, 330

Stairmate

Working up ladders on slopes or stairs can be hazardous. The Stairmate, a folding foot to use on the base of the ladder, can improve matters. It is adjusted to give a stable base from which any conventional ladder can be safely climbed.

✎	*John Sandham and Stan Lewis, UK*	310
⚙	*Lew San Ltd*	310
	Metal, plastic	295
	• *Adding multifunctionality to existing design*	329

TRISIT 2000

An estimated 90 million square metres (108 million sq yds) of waste seating fabric was generated by the automobile industry. Trisit have patented a method of fabricating a multilayered textile to three-dimensional patterns without generating waste from cutting and sizing. The system can be modified to bespoke designs and is suitable for automobile seating and general-purpose furniture.

✎	*Trisit Design, Germany*	325
⚙	*Trisit Textiltechnologie GmbH, Germany*	325
	Flame-resistant fabric	300-1
	• *Reduction in waste output* • *Reduction in materials and energy consumption*	328, 329
	iF Ecology Design Award, 2000	332

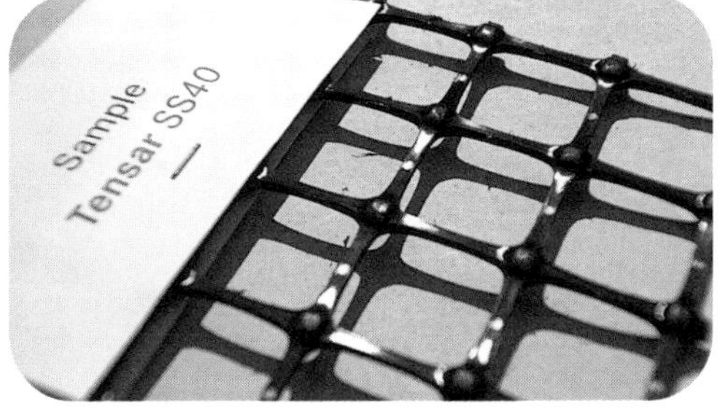

Tensar® range

Steep construction slopes can be reinforced with Tensar® 80RE, a uni-axial grid of polypropylene with elongated apertures, which improves the shear strength of the exposed surface layers. Extruded sheets of special polyethylene are punched with regularly shaped apertures, then stretched under heat to create a high-strength grid. When this geomat is laid on the surface it reduces soil erosion by absorbing the energy of raindrop impact and providing an anchor for plant roots.

✎	*Netlon, UK*	321
⚙	*Netlon, UK*	321
	Polypropylene or polyethylene	341
	• *Protection against soil erosion and slope failure*	330

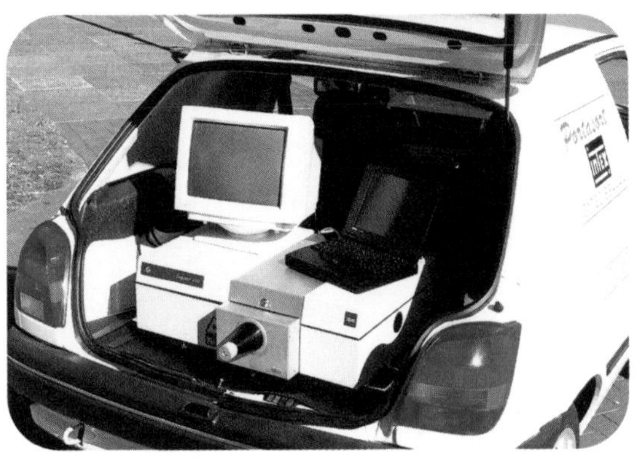

Polyana® 420

Although there is an internationally recognized system of labelling plastics to facilitate recycling, many products and components are not suitably embossed or labelled. A typical car can contain as many as thirty different plastics. So any device that can help identify plastics facilitates recycling. The Tribopen is a hand-held pen device with a brass tip that accurately measures the electrostatic surface charge and is calibrated to read the charge from polycarbonates and polypropylenes. A light then comes on to indicate which of these two plastics has been identified. Polyana is a portable detector, which uses infrared beams and an electronic chip to match the reflected infrared profile of the plastic being tested against a series of known profiles to determine its exact type. Both these devices speed up the process of plastics identification and permit more efficient recycling, thus also assisting with supply-chain management.

✎	*Southampton Innovations, University of Southampton and Ford Motor Company, UK*	310, 316
⚙	*Southampton Innovations, UK*	310
▬	*Various*	341
♻	• *Facilitates plastics recycling*	328

Tree masts

As the telecommunications industry extends its networks in response to public demand for more mobile phones, Internet connections and other pay-as-you-go services, there is a demand for greater network coverage. This means installing new transmitter (and receiver) masts. The masts are visually intrusive, so Orange, the UK's largest mobile phone network provider, has created a mast that mimicks the look of a Scots pine tree. Tree Masts are made of galvanized-steel 'stem' and 'branches' painted to look like bark and covered with UV-resistant plastic foliage. Although this product deals with the question of visual intrusion, the real debate should be about the environmental health aspects of the massive network expansion of telecoms companies.

✎	*Orange, UK*	321
⚙	*Orange, UK*	321
▬	*Galvanized steel, paint, UV-resistant plastic*	295
♻	• *Reduction of visual intrusion in the landscape*	329

3.0 Materials

It's A Material World

People first developed methods to synthesize materials from nature at the time of the earliest civilizations in Mesopotamia. The Industrial Revolution and two world wars accelerated the synthesis of new manmade materials. Today the designer is faced with a mind-boggling array of hundreds of thousands of materials, some of which have no or little impact on the environment while others generate a rucksack of environmental impacts including depletion of non-renewable resources, toxic or hazardous emissions to air, water or land, and the generation of large quantities of solid waste.

While designers have traditionally selected materials on the basis of their physical, chemical and aesthetic properties, as well as by cost and availability, other parameters, such as resource depletion, are now proving important. Designers are now obliged to observe legal restrictions on the use of materials from endangered species, as listed in the 1973 Convention on International Trade in Endangered Species (CITES). Various voluntary certification schemes, such as the Forest Stewardship Council and SmartWood schemes, ensure that materials originate from sustainably managed forests. Unfortunately, designers have few published guidelines about criteria for selecting materials in relation to environmental, social and ethical issues. The checklist in Table 1 offers a method of considering the potential impacts of a material.

Ecomaterials

An ecomaterial is one that has a minimal impact on the environment but offers maximum performance for the required design task. Ecomaterials are easily reintroduced into cycles. Ecomaterials from the biosphere are recycled by nature and ecomaterials from the technosphere are recycled by manmade processes.

Embodied energy

One measure of eco-efficiency is the degree of efficiency of use of energy within an ecosystem, that is, the energy captured, energy flows within the ecosystem and energy losses. All materials represent stored energy, captured from the sun or already held in the lithosphere of the earth. Materials also represent or embody the energy used to produce them. One tonne of aluminium takes over a hundred times more energy to produce than one tonne of sawn timber, so the embodied energy of aluminium is comparatively high. Materials with a low embodied energy are generally those with a smaller rucksack of environmental impacts. Materials extracted directly from nature and requiring little processing tend to be low-embodied-energy materials, while manmade materials tend to possess medium to high embodied energy (Table 2).

In complex products, such as a car, involving application of many materials, the calculations of embodied energy are more involved. For instance, using lightweight aluminium as opposed to steel in the chassis of a car will ensure greater fuel efficiency and so reduce the total energy use over the lifetime of the product. Selection of high-embodied-energy materials, which are durable and extend product life, may be preferred to lower-embodied-energy materials, which have a short product life. So a very important consideration is the embodied energy of the material over the lifespan of the product.

Materials from the biosphere and lithosphere

Materials derived from the living components of the planet, the biosphere, are renewable and originate from plants, animals and micro-organisms. Biosphere materials include special groups of manmade materials such as compostable biopolymers and biocomposites derived from plant matter. Such materials are readily returned to the cycles of nature. Materials derived from the lithosphere (geological strata of the earth's crust) fall into two main categories. The first category is widely distributed or abundant materials such as sand, gravel, stone and clay, while the second category includes materials whose distribution is limited, such as fossil fuels, metal ores and precious metals/stones. Materials

Table 1: A checklist for selecting materials

Material attribute	Low environmental impact	High environmental impact
Resource availability	Renewable and/or abundant	Non-renewable and/or rare
Distance to source (the closer the source the less the transport energy consumed) km	Near	Far
Embodied energy (the total energy embodied within the material from extraction to finished product) MJ per kg	Low	High
Recycled fraction (the proportion of recycled content) per cent	High	Low
Production of emissions (to air, water and/or land)	Zero/Low	High
Production of waste	Zero/Low	High
Production of toxins or hazardous substances	Zero/Low	High
Recyclability, reusability	High	Low
End-of-life waste	Zero/Low	High
Cyclicity (the ease with which the material can be recycled)	High	Low

from the biosphere or lithosphere are often processed by synthesis or concentration to create technosphere materials.

Materials from the technosphere
Technosphere materials are generally non-renewable. Synthetic polymers (plastics, elastomers and resins) derived from oil, a fossil fuel, are technosphere materials. Embodied-energy values tend to be much higher than in biosphere materials. Most technosphere materials are not readily returned to the cycles of nature and some, such as plastics, ceramics (glass, glass/graphite/carbon fibres) and composites (ceramic, metal), are inert to microbial decomposition and will never re-enter the biosphere. In a world of finite resources we need to be aware of the need to recycle technosphere materials.

Table 2: Embodied energy values for common materials

Material type	Typical embodied energy (MJ per kg)
Biosphere and lithosphere materials	
Ceramic minerals, e.g., stone, gravel	2–4
Wood, bamboo, cork	2–8
Natural rubber (unfilled)	5–6
Cotton, hemp, silk, wool	4–10
Wood composites, e.g., particleboards	6–12
Technosphere materials	
Ceramics – bricks	2–10
Ceramics – glass	20–25
Ceramics – glass fibre	20–150
Ceramics – carbon fibre	800–1,000
Composites – titanium-carbide matrix	600–1,000
Composites – alumina fibre reinforced	450–700
Composites – polymer – thermoplastic – Nylon 6 (PA)	400–600
Composite – polymer – thermoset – epoxy matrix – Kevlar fibre	400–600
Foam – metal – high-density aluminium	300 –350
Foam – polymer – polyurethane	140–160
Metal – ferrous alloys – carbon steel	60–72
Metal – ferrous alloys – cast iron – grey (flake graphite)	34–66
Metal – light alloys – aluminium – cast	235–335
Metal – non-ferrous alloys – copper various alloys	115–180
Metal – non-ferrous alloys – lead various alloys	29–54
Metal – precious metal alloys – gold	5,600–6,000
Polymer – elastomer – butyl rubber	125–145
Polymer – elastomer – polyurethane	90–100
Polymer – thermoplastic – ABS	85–120
Polymer – thermoplastic – nylon	170–180
Polymer – thermoplastic – polyethylene	85–130
Polymer – thermoplastic – polypropylene	90–115
Polymer – thermoset – melamine	120–150
Polymer – thermoset – epoxy	100–150

Adapted from Cambridge Engineering Selector, version 3.0, Granta Design Ltd, UK

Recycling
Three exhibitions in the 1990s encouraged designers to focus on the potential of using recycled materials from the technosphere. Rematerialize (1994), collated by Jakki Dehn of Kingston University, UK, displayed a diverse selection of contemporary materials made using recycled content. 'Mutant Materials', curated by Paola Antonelli at the Museum of Modern Art (MoMA) in New York in 1997, examined the application of recycled thermoplastics alongside new material developments such as specialist polymers, foamed alloys, foamed ceramics and unusual composites.

An exhibition called Recycling, organized by Craftspace Touring in the UK in 1996, revealed the beauty of hand-crafted products made from recycled materials.

Materials from the biosphere are readily taken back into nature's cycles by the process of biodegradation, or composting, by the action of microbes and by water and weather. Nature recycles all its materials but humans recycle only certain manmade materials. Materials of low monetary value tend to have low volumes of recycling. Thus relatively expensive ferrous metal and light alloys often include a recycle fraction of between 70 and 80 per cent, non-ferrous metals between 10 and 80 per cent and precious metal alloys (gold, platinum, silver) between 90 and 98 per cent. Relatively inexpensive polymers (plastics), on the other hand, exhibit recycle fractions of between zero and 60 per cent, the most commonly recycled plastics being PET (20-30 per cent recycle fraction), polypropylene (25-35 per cent), polyethylene as LDPE or HDPE (typically 50-60 per cent) and polystyrene (35-40 per cent). Specialist technosphere materials, especially composites, for example, thermosets and reinforced thermoplastics, often have less than 1 per cent recycle fraction.

Closed-loop recycling of materials from the technosphere significantly reduces environmental impacts. Metals made entirely of recycled content and recycled plastics have an embodied energy that is often only half or even as little as 10 per cent of that of virgin metals. Increasing the recycle fraction in more materials, by re-evaluating the idea of 'waste', will bring savings in energy.

Green procurement
Designers can also reduce the impacts of materials they use if they specify sources of materials and minimum recycle fractions and if they insist on compliance with certain standards, such as eco-labels or voluntary industry schemes (see Green Organizations, p. 331). Specifiying suppliers or manufacturers that comply with internationally recognized environmental management systems, such as ISO 14001 or EMAS, is also desirable.

General-purpose panels

Agricultural residues, such as wheat and rice straw, cotton stalks and bagasse, sugar cane waste, are bonded with formaldehyde-free resins into sheeting and panels.

⚙	*Compak Systems Ltd, UK*	314
♲	*• Renewable materials*	327

DuraCane

Bagasse, the plant-fibre residue from sugar cane, is formed into a tough board, DuraCane, suitable for a variety of indoor uses from furniture to built-in units and flooring.

⚙	*Acadia Board Company, USA*	312
♲	*• Renewable materials*	327

Eco Panel

This lightweight board comprises a layer of Gridcore, a board made from a honeycomb of mixed waste paper, sandwiched between layers of veneer manufactured from timber harvested from sustainably managed forests.

✎	*Buchner Design Studio, USA*	313
⚙	*Gridcore Systems International, USA*	317
♲	*• Renewable materials • Recycled materials • Low embodied energy*	327, 328

Elastic wood

Thin sheets of plywood are curved laterally to create a 'wave' profile, then bonded together to form a springy, flexible sheeting suitable for a wide range of applications. Varying the thickness of each layer and amount of curve changes the degree of elasticity.

⚙	*Prototype designed by Nickie Kieboom, graduate student 2000, Design Academy Eindhoven, Netherlands*	308
♲	*• Renewable materials*	327

Environ™

Environ™ is possibly the first example of a mass-produced biocomposite using a plant-based resin to bond recycled materials. It is manufactured from recycled paper and soy flour into sheets and floor strips to provide a material, which, it is claimed, is harder than oakwood and suitable for interior decoration and furniture.

✎	*Phenix Biocomposites, USA*	322
⚙	*Phenix Biocomposites, USA*	322
♲	*• Renewable and recycled materials*	327

Findlay-Form®

Jute, sisal and kenaf fibres are the raw ingredients for Findlay-Form®, a natural fibre-based composite, which is suitable for detailed moulding especially for automobile components.

⚙	*Findlay Industries, USA*	316
♲	*• Renewable materials*	327

FlexForm™

This company is part of the Kafus Environmental Industries group, which manufactures materials from alternative crops and recycled waste streams. FlexForm™ is made from kenaf and hemp fibres mixed with synthetic polymers and is particularly suited to moulded panels for the automobile and construction industries.

⚙	*Kafus Bio-Composites, USA*	318
♲	*• Renewable materials*	327

Gridcore™

Gridcore™ is a lightweight, chemical-free, honey-combed solid panel made from 100 per cent-recycled fibres such as used cardboard, newsprint and jute, kenaf and wood waste. The panels can be curved to compound or custom radii, making the material suitable for interior design and furniture.

⚙	*Gridcore Systems International (GSI), USA*	317
♲	*• Recycled content • Toxin-free*	327, 329

N.C.F.R. Homasote®

Homasote claim to be the oldest manufacturer of building board from 100 per cent-recycled post-consumer paper in the USA, with a pedigree stretching back to 1909. All the products in their range are free of asbestos and formaldehyde additives. For each tonne of recycled paper there is a net reduction of 73 per cent emissions to air, 40 to 70 per cent less water consumption and 70 per cent less energy than virgin wood pulp fibre. N.C.F.R. Homosote®, a multipurpose interior or exterior board, is a good insulator and a barrier to moisture, noise and fire (when impregnated with fire retardants).

Homasote Company, USA	318
• *Recycled materials* • *Low embodied energy*	327, 328

Isobord

Straw is an annual agricultural residue that causes environmental problems when burnt and can lock up soil fertility upon decomposition. But it can provide secondary income for farmers when it is used as the raw material in composite board manufacturing. Isobord is an alternative to conventional particle boards. It is made under high pressure and temperature by combining straw fibres with non-toxic isocyanurate resins to provide a resilient high-density board that can be surface-finished by painting or laminating. Isobord is suitable for building, exhibition and furniture purposes.

Isobord Enterprises, USA	318
• *Renewable materials* • *Non-toxic manufacturing*	327, 329

Kronospan®

This Swiss company manufactures a diverse range of particle boards, T & G panels, MDF, Kronoply (an orientated strand board, OSB), laminate flooring and post-formed panels and surfaces for interior use. Laminated flooring sheets are FSC certified, the formaldehyde-free, panel-type 'Hollywood' qualifies for a Blue Angel eco-label and the company is certified to ISO 14001. Timber is generally sourced locally.

Kronospan AG, Switzerland	319
• *Renewable materials* • *Clean production* • *Certification of various products to FSC or Blue Angel eco-label*	327, 328, 333

Kucospan Life

Kucospan Life is a formaldehyde-free chipboard formed with conifer wood thinnings and bound with up to 5 per cent by weight Polycarbamide (PMDI), a polyurethane resin.

Kucospan, UK	319
• *Renewable waste content* • *Reduction of toxicity and emissions*	328, 329

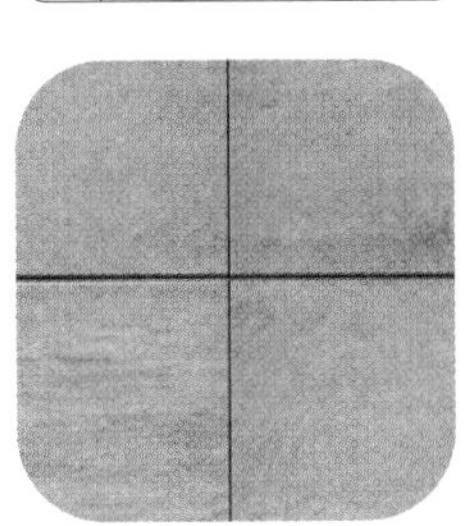

Lignasil®

Lignasil® is made from 100 per cent natural fibre held in a patented bio-alloy structure. It is an extremely tough material and is the primary component of Madera® floor tiles.

Matrix Composites, Inc., Canada	320
• *Renewable materials*	327

Maderón

Ground waste shells from the almond-growing industry are mixed with resins to form a hard, durable composite suitable for furniture and panel manufacturing.

Lignocel SA, Spain	319
• *Renewable material* • *Recycled content*	327

Masonite CP

This tough, dense board is made from long-fibre wood compressed to attain a very high density of 940kg/sq m (192lb/sq ft), which makes it especially suitable where structural strength is required. It is manufactured to ISO 9001 and guaranteed and approved by the Swedish National Board of Housing.

Masonite Corporation, USA	320
• *Renewable materials content*	327

Meadowood panels and sheeting

Compressed panels of ryegrass straw are suitable for all interior design, exhibition and furniture production.

Meadowood Industries, Inc., USA	320
• *Renewable material*	327

Medite ZF

Medite ZF is the trade name for an interior-grade, medium-density fibreboard (MDF) manufactured using softwood fibres bonded with formaldehyde-free synthetic resin. Free formaldehyde content of Medite ZF is less than 1.0mg/100g (one part in 100,000), which is equivalent to or less than natural wood, and formaldehyde emissions are well below general ambient outdoor levels. All other Medite MDF boards are manufactured to Class A EN622 Part 1, complying with free formaldehyde content of less than 9.0mg/100g (nine parts per 100,000). The company has applied for FSC certification for Medite.

⚙	*Willamette Europe Ltd, UK*	326
♻	• *Renewable materials* • *Reduction in toxic ingredients and emissions*	327, 329

Oil-tempered hardboard

Natural cellulose fibres are the primary constituents of this type of hardboard, in which the natural glues from the fibres, rather than synthetic adhesives, bond the fibres together.

⚙	*Masonite CP, UK*	320
♻	• *Renewable materials*	327

Pacific Gold Board

This is a straw-based building board suitable for interior uses.

⚙	*BioFab LLC, USA*	313
♻	• *Renewable resources*	327

Easiboard and Easiwall

A range of wall panels is manufactured with wheat straw.

⚙	*Pierce International, Inc., USA*	322
♻	• *Renewable material*	327

Pacific board™

Wheat straw and Kentucky bluegrass are the main fibre constituents of the particleboard manufactured by this company.

⚙	*Pacific Northwest Fiber, USA*	321
♻	• *Renewable material*	327

General-purpose particleboard

Some 14,000 tonnes of waste wheat straw annually go to make this half-inch-thick (1-cm), wheat-based particleboard suitable for furniture, construction and interior design.

⚙	*Prairie Forest Products, USA*	322
♻	• *Renewable material*	327

Resincore

Resincore is a formal-dehyde-free particleboard composed of sawdust, phenolic resin and wax.

⚙	*Rodman Industries, USA*	323
♻	• *Renewable and recycled materials*	327

Schauman Wisa® plywoods

Birch, spruce and pine from managed forests in Finland are used to manufacture a range of plywoods suitable for interior, exterior and concrete formwork and as laminboard. Special tongue-and-groove panel plywood laminated floorings include Schauman Birchfloor, Sprucefloor and Spruce Dek. The company is certified to ISO 14001.

⚙	*Schauman Wood Oy, Finland*	323
♻	• *Renewable materials* • *Stewardship sourcing*	327

ShetkaBoard

This range of sheeting materials made from recycled waste paper is suitable for construction and interior design work.

⚙	*All Paper Recycling, Inc., USA*	312
♻	• *Recycled materials*	327

Stramit

This composite fibreboard panel is made of 100 per cent wheat straw sandwiched between a recycled paper facing.

⚙	*Stramit USA, USA*	324
♻	• *Renewable and recycled materials*	327

Wood composite

Thin strands of aspen pulpwood are rebonded in moulds for furniture and automobile parts such as legs, shells and seat backs.

⚙	*Strandwood Molding, Inc., USA*	324
♻	• *Renewable materials*	327

Thermo-ply

These fibreboards are made of 100 per cent-recycled materials including cardboard, office waste, mill waste and production scrap.

⚙	*Simplex Products, USA*	324
♻	• *Renewable and recycled materials*	327

Wheatboard™

This is a strong particleboard using bonded, cross-linked fibres of wheat straw. It is suitable for diverse construction and interior uses, furniture and kitchen fixtures.

⚙	*Primeboard, Inc., USA*	322
♲	*• Renewable material*	327

Bamboo

Bamboo sourced from Vietnam is the principal material for strip and laminated flooring manufactured by the company, but poles and bamboo for structural purposes can also be supplied.

⚙	*Bamboo Hardwoods, Inc., USA*	313
♲	*• Renewable material*	327

Certified timber

This company supplies high-density prepared boards from sustainably harvested palm trees. The timber is guaranteed 100 per cent chemical-free and is suitable for structural, flooring and furniture applications. A wide range of North American and tropical hardwoods is supplied from certified sources.

⚙	*Eco Timber International, USA*	315
♲	*• Renewable materials • Toxin-free • SmartWood or FSC certified*	327, 329, 333

Timber from sustainable sources

Harwood Products supplies timber and products from sustainably managed forests certified by the FSC. A member of CERES.

⚙	*Harwood Products, USA*	317
♲	*• Renewable materials • Certified materials*	327

Microllam® and Intrallam®

With minimal wastage from the forest roundwood, TJM bond layers of aspen wood with resin to form high-strength timber composites – Microllam™ comprising thin even layers and Intrallam™ formed from more irregular layers and chips.

⚙	*Trus Joist MacMillan, USA*	325
♲	*• Reduction of waste output • Efficient use of resources*	327, 328

Rubberwood

There are over 7.2 million hectares (17.8 million acres) of cultivated rubber trees worldwide, of which over 5.2 million hectares (12.8 million acres) are in Malaysia, Indonesia and Thailand. Declining latex yields normally occur twenty-five to thirty years after planting. These older trees are now being harvested to provide a growing supply of Hevea, or rubberwood, the dominant species being Hevea braziliensis. In 1990 the ASEAN (the Association of South-east Asian Nations) produced about 17 million cubic metres (600 million cubic ft) of rubberwood. The timber is suitable for a wide range of applications such as flooring, particle boards, kitchen utensils and general furniture woodworking.

⚙	*Numerous manufacturers in tropical countries*	
♲	*• Renewable resource*	327

THL Iron Woods®

Diniza, Purpleheart, Greenheart and Macaranduba are very tough, exceptionally dense, tropical hardwoods. Promoted under the brand name THL Iron Woods®, these sawn and planed woods are certifed by the FSC and the Rain Forest Alliance's SmartWood® schemes as originating from sustainably managed forests. All these iron woods are extremely durable and do not require any chemical treatments to prolong life.

⚙	*Timber Holdings Ltd, USA*	325
♲	*• Renewable materials • Certified sources*	327

Timberstrand® LSL

TJM produce a range of engineered timbers composed of strands or sheets of veneer bonded with adhesives or resins at high pressure and heat. Timberstrand® TSL is a general-purpose structural timber. TJM products encourage better resource usage than sawn timber since almost all the sawn log is used in the composite timber.

⚙	*Trus Joist MacMillan, USA*	325
♲	*• Renewable material • Efficient use of resources*	327

Willows

This nursery specializes in the cultivation of willow species and cultivars suited to the climate of the UK and Europe. Over 135 species, subspecies and varieties of willow are listed in the catalogue. Advice is also given on bulk supplies of cut osiers and willows.

⚙	*The Willow Bank, UK*	326
♲	*• Renewable materials*	327

BioFoam

BioFoam is a loose-fill packaging made of pure starch and is biodegradable.

Johnson Corrugated Products, USA	318
• *Renewable materials*	327

Biocorp: biopolymer

Corn starch is the main ingredient of the compostable biopolymers made by Biocorp. Products include plastic bags and cutlery.

Biocorp, USA	313
• *Renewable materials* • *Compostable*	327

Bioplast® and Biopur®

Biotec specializes in biodegradable plastics using vegetable starch as the raw ingredient. Trade products include Bioplast® and Biopur®. They have similar properties to polystyrene, so they are suitable for making disposable cups for vending machines and catering companies.

Biotec, Germany	313
• *Renewable materials* • *Compostable*	327

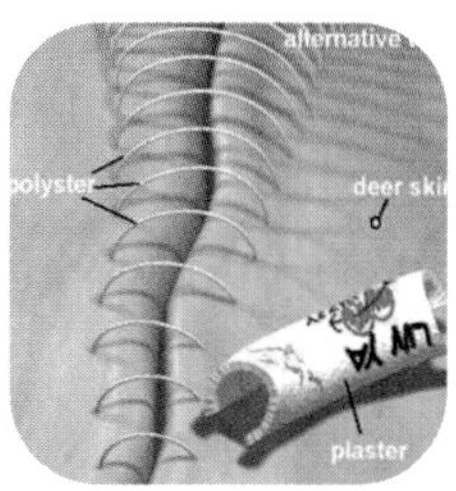

Capa®

Capa® is a thermoplastic made of polycaprolactones, which are biodegradable.

Solvay Plastiques, Belgium	324
• *Renewable material* • *Compostable*	327

Biopolymers

Biopolymers and industrial starches are extracted and processed from the corn (maize) plant.

Cerestar USA, USA	314
• *Renewable material* • *Compostable*	327

depart®

Derived from polyvinyl alcohol, depart® is a water-soluble and biodegradable plastic.

Environmental Polymers Group plc, UK	316
• *Compostable*	327

Biopolymers

Eastman manufactures a range of biodegradable polymers from cellulose acetate.

Eastman Chemical Company, USA	315
• *Renewable materials* • *Compostable*	327

Eco-Flow

Eco-Flow is an extruded packaging material primarily composed of wheat starch.

American Excelsior Company, USA	312
• *Renewable material* • *Compostable*	327

Eco-Foam®

Polystyrene chips, often made by injecting chorofluorocarbon (CFC) gases, can now be substituted with biodegradable chips of foamed starch polymer, Eco-Foam®, where steam is used as the blowing agent. This biopolymer is made of 85 per cent corn starch, so it is biodegradable, water-soluble and reusable. It is also free of static, which makes the packaging process easier.

National Starch & Chemical Co., USA	320
• *Renewable materials* • *Reusable* • *Avoidance of CFC emissions*	327, 329

EnPol

Enpol is a fully biodegradable plastic, which is similar to polyethylene (polythene) but uses two and a half times less material to achieve the same strength properties.

Polyval plc, UK	322
• *Potential reduction in materials usage for applications using the biopolymer* • *Compostable*	327

EnviroFill

EnviroFill is an extruded, biodegradable, starch-based, loose-fill packaging material.

⚙	*Norel/Unisource, USA*	321
♺	• *Renewable material* • *Compostable*	327

Flo-Pak Bio 8

Corn, wheat or potato starch is the raw material for Flo-Pak Bio 8 loose-fill packaging.

⚙	*Free-Flow Packaging International, Inc., USA*	316
♺	• *Renewable materials* • *Compostable*	327

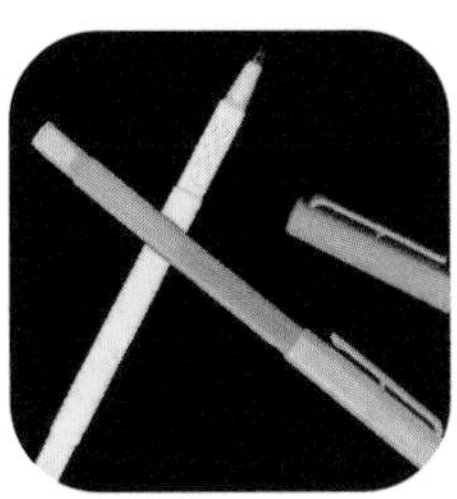

Mater-Bi

Mater-Bi is a biodegradable plastic film manufactured by Novamont in Italy and under licence by EnPac in a joint venture between DuPont and ConAgra in the USA. It is derived from corn starch and is suitable for a wide range of applications from packaging to refuse disposal bags.

⚙	*Novamont SpA, Italy/EnPac, USA*	316, 321
♺	• *Renewable material* • *Compostable*	327

MAZIN

This compostable biopolymer is derived from polymers extracted from corn (maize). It is produced in extruded sheets for phone and ID cards and similar printed products.

⚙	*Corn Card International, Inc., USA*	314
♺	• *Renewable materials* • *Compostable*	327

Natural rubber (NR)

The history of rubber cultivation can be traced back to early civilizations in Central and South America but it wasn't until the nineteenth century that a native species, Hevea braziliensis, was commercially exploited and became a major export for Brazil. The process of vulcanization, discovered by Charles Goodyear in 1839, rapidly expanded the applications for natural latex in the Industrial Revolution. Today over 70 per cent of rubber production, 5.2 million hectares of a world total of 7.2 million hectares (12.8 million acres and 17.8 million acres respectively), centres around Malaysia, Indonesia and Thailand. Trees have a productive lifetime of up to thirty years, after which latex production declines. Plantations also act as a sink for absorbing carbon dioxide. Natural rubber is used pure or mixed with synthetic rubbers and fillers to manufacture a huge range of products from tyres and tubes, industrial components and medical goods to footwear and clothing. Special grades of NR produced by Malaysia include SUMAR (Non-Smelly Rubber), ENR (Epoxidized NR), DPNR (Deproteinized NR), and PA/SP (Superior Processing Rubber).

⚙	*Many in tropical countries*	
♺	• *Renewable material* • *Versatile natural polymer*	327

Novon®

This is a thermoplastic starch, containing up to 90 per cent starch derived from plants. Additives control the rate of decomposition, which varies from five to forty-five days depending on ambient moisture and temperature conditions and microbial activity.

⚙	*Novon International, USA*	321
♺	• *Renewable material* • *Compostable*	327

PHA

PHAs are biodegradable plastics derived from plants or bacteria that are water-soluble and easily recycled. PHAs are suitable for medical and food-packaging uses.

⚙	*Metabolix, Inc., USA*	320
♺	• *Renewable materials* • *Compostable and recyclable*	327

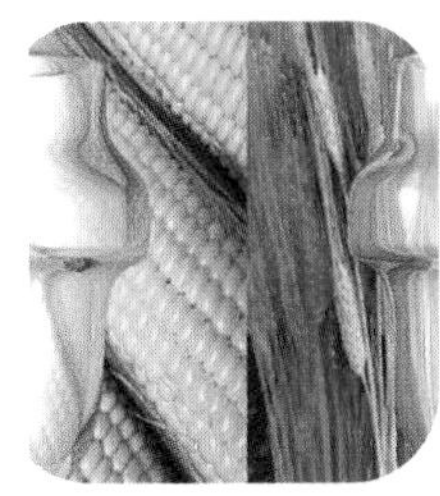

PLA, EcoPLA

Plastics manufacturers all over the world are examining the commercial viability of making plastics using renewable resources. In 2000 Cargill Dow Polymers announced that their 'NatureWorks Technology' had created a new bioplastic called polyactide (PLA), derived from the maize plant. A new factory is scheduled to open in Blair, Nebraska, to supply initially up to 150,000 tonnes per annum. Some of the world's largest manufacturers of plastic food packaging, such as TetraPak, Autobarr, Bimo and Treopaphan, are interested in producing PLA products in the future.

⚙	*Cargill Dow Polymers, USA*	314
♺	*• Renewable materials • Compostable*	327

Polymeric resins

This company specializes in developing engineered polymers for the medical, personal care and agro-technology markets. Their polymeric resins are degradable.

⚙	*Plant Polymer Technologies, Inc., USA*	322
♺	*• Degradable materials*	327

Biopolymers and resins

This company specializes in the manufacture of starch-based biopolymers and resins suitable for injection moulding. Clean Green is loose-fill packaging that is water-soluble.

⚙	*Starch Tech, Inc., USA*	324
♺	*• Renewable materials • Compostable*	327

Chanvrisol, Chanvrilaine, Méhabit

Loose-fill and blanket insulation is made by combining cellulose (wood) fibres with hemp fibre. Chanvrisol is loose-fill insulation, Chanvrilaine a blanket insulation and Méhabit a flooring underlay.

⚙	*LCDA (La Chanvrière de l'Aube), France*	319
♺	*• Renewable materials*	327

Insulation

Recycled textile waste is reprocessed into insulation materials.

⚙	*Greenwood Cotton Insulation Products, Inc., USA*	317
♺	*• Recycled content*	327

Heraflax

Long and short flax plant fibres are separated; the former are used for weaving linen and the latter are manufactured into insulation battens and quilts. In the Heraflax WP battens and Heraflax WF quilt the fibres are integrated with polyester fibres to form standard 60mm- or 80mm-thick (1/4- or 1/3-inch) products. Both materials are good insulators with a thermal conductivity of 0.42 W/sq m.

⚙	*Deutsche Heraklith GmbH, Germany, and Österreichische Heraklith Gmbh, Austria*	315, 321
♺	*• Renewable materials • Energy-saving product*	327, 329

Hypodown

Fibres from the milkweed plant provide the raw materials for this company's range of hypoallergenic down products, Hypodown, suitable for use in bedding and upholstery.

⚙	*Natural Fibers Corporation, USA*	320
♺	*• Renewable materials • Non-allergenic*	327, 329

Thermo-Hanf®

Hemp is an ideal crop for all aspiring organic farmers. It does not require the application of any herbicides or insecticides, it is a good weed suppressant, helping to clean the land, and it is a prolific producer of biomass and fibre, growing up to 4 metres (13ft) high in 100 days. Hemp cultivars with minimal active 'drug' chemicals have been grown in Germany since 1996 specifically for the production of this new insulation material. Fibres are extracted from the harvested plants and reworked into panels using 15 per cent polyester for support and 3-5 per cent soda for fireproofing. It is suitable for insulating between stud walls and roofing timbers. Thermo-Hanf® (Thermo Hemp) conforms to all DIN-Norm standards and has a thermal conductivity of 0.039W/mk for DIN 52612. It also has in-built resistance to insect attack from the plant's own natural defences.

⚙	*Hock Distribution/ Swabian ROWA, Germany*	318
♺	*• Renewable material • Clean production*	327

Woolbloc

Sheep's wool is combined with an acrylic solution and natural boron salts to make low thermal-conductivity (0.038W/mk) insulation batts, of 50mm, 75mm and

100mm thickness (0.2, 0.3 and 0.4 inch), with square-cut ends. Manufacturing typically consumes less than one-fifth of the energy required to make glass-fibre insulation, so the embodied energy of woolbloc is less than 150 MJ/square metre. Woolbloc is hydroscopic, so it can absorb excess moisture vapour but, being also breathable, it permits evaporation of this moisture. Tests have also proven that it absorbs formaldehyde released from other building materials, is a good acoustic barrier and is fire-resistant.

⚙	*Klober, UK*	319
♻	• *Energy conservation* • *Clean production* • *Renewable, recyclable and biodegradable primary material*	327, 329

Papers, panels, composites

Kenaf plant fibre is grown and processed by Arizona Fibers Marketing ready for a variety of commercial uses for the paper and construction industries.

⚙	*Arizona Fibers Marketing, USA*	312
♻	• *Renewable materials*	327

Packaging

Agricultural fibres and residues are formed into a diverse range of food packaging and disposable cutlery.

⚙	*Enbiomass Group, Inc., USA*	316
♻	• *Renewable materials* • *Compostable*	327

Nativa Rubber

Latex is harvested from wild trees in the Amazon rather than commercial plantations. This helps support local cultures and economies and encourages rainforest conservation.

⚙	*Deep E Company, USA*	315
♻	• *Renewable material* • *Ethical production* • *Encourages nature conservation*	327, 330

Sundeala and Celotex Sealcoat

Sundeala is a soft board manufactured from unbleached recycled newsprint available in a range of natural colours. Celotex Sealcoat Medium Board is also made from recycled newsprint and is coloured with natural mineral pigments. Both boards are suitable for interior applications, pinboards, noticeboards, exhibition displays and furniture.

⚙	*Celotex Ltd, UK*	314
♻	• *Recycled materials* • *Clean production*	327

Sustana® leather

Claimed to be the most exclusive 'eco-leather' in the world, Sustana® originates from cattle managed on sustainable and humane principles, without the use of growth hormones, steroids or antibiotics, on the Coleman ranch in Colorado. Tanning is undertaken by Cudahy Tanning in Wisconsin using low-toxicity trivalent chromium and chorine-free water-based dyes and finishes. Protein wastes are recycled and water effluents treated by biological purifying systems. Sustana® is the primary leather source for shoes made by the Deep E Company.

⚙	*Deep E Company, USA*	315
♻	• *Renewable materials* • *Clean production* • *Ethical production*	327, 330

Auro paints, oils, waxes and finishes

Auro manufactures an extensive range of 'organic' paints, oils, waxes, stains and other finishes without the use of fungicides, biocides or petrochemicals including white spirit (an isoaliphate). Oils originate from renewable natural sources such as ethereal oils, balm oil of turpentine or oil from citrus peel, so waste from the manufacturing process is easily recycled and the potential health hazard of the finished products is less than in petrol or isoaliphatic-based manufacturing systems. Emulsion paints for interior use include white chalk and chalk casein paints, which can be tinted using pigments from a range of 330 colours. Exterior-grade gloss paints and stain finishes are suitable for applying to wood, metal, plaster and masonry.

Auro Pflanzenchemie AG/Auro GmbH, Germany	312
• Non-toxic ingredients • Clean production	327

BioShield paints, stains, thinners, waxes

BioShield Paint Company manufactures a diverse range of paints, stains, thinners and waxes from natural ingredients such as oils from linseed, orange peel and soybean.

BioShield Paint Company, USA	313
• Renewable materials	327

Adhesives, paints, varnishes, oils

Natural organic constituents and abundant minerals are the basis for the entire range of Holzweg products for timbers and masonry surfaces including adhesives, primers, paints, varnishes and oils.

Holzweg, Germany	318
• Renewable materials • Non-toxic	327

Livos

In 1975 Livos developed techniques for dispersing ingredients in natural resins. The company has continued to develop its range of natural-based primers (with linseed oil), hardening floor agents (pine tree resins), transparent glazes (phytochemical oils such as citrus), wood polishes (beeswax), wall glazes (beeswax and madder root) and varnishes pigmented with natural soil pigments. Livos URA Pigment Paint comprises organically sourced beeswax, linseed/stand oil, orange-peel oil and dammar mixed with water, methylcellulose, isoaliphate, ethanol, iron oxide, mineral pigments, borax and boric acid. The amount of pigment can be adjusted to give the desired strength of colour.

Livos Pflanzenchemie, Germany	319
• High content of natural, renewable materials • Low or nil VOC content • EU eco-label for some products	327, 339, 341

The Natural Choice

All paints and finishes in The Natural Choice collection utilize natural oils and solvents, originating from citrus peel or seeds, resins from trees, waxes from trees and bees, inert mineral fillers and earth pigments. Oils are extracted by cold pressing or with low heat and all products are packaged in biodegradable or recyclable containers with an emphasis on keeping packaging to a minimum.

The Natural Choice, USA	320
• Renewable materials • Minimal pollution manufacturing • Minimal packaging	327

Nutshell®

Nutshell produces a full range of adhesives, paints, herb and resin oils, varnishes and stains with natural pigments.

Nutshell Natural Paints, UK	321
• Renewable materials • Non-toxic • Clean production	327

Milk-based paints

Traditional milk-based paints, suitable for interior design/restoration and furniture production, are made by this company. These paints follow authentic recipes and are free of synthetics.

Old Fashioned Milk Paint Company, USA	321
• Renewable materials	327

OS Color

Waxes from canauba and candelilla plants and oils

from sunflower, soybean, linseed and thistle are the raw ingredients of a wide range of natural stains and protective finishes for exterior and interior wood surfaces. For example, OS Color Wood Stain and Preservative is a natural oil-based, microporous, water-repellent treatment for timber exposed to the weather. The natural oils, water-repellent additives and lead-free siccatives (drying agents) form the binder, which comprises almost 85 per cent of the solids content. This binder is mixed with the active (bacteria and fungi) protective ingredients, alipathic low-odour solvents (benzole-free, diaromatized, medical-grade white spirit) and pigments (iron oxide, titanium dioxide). Floor treatment, such as the OS Color Hardwax-Oil, is an oil-based application, which gives a durable, washable, surface. It doesn't contain biocides or preservatives. Manufacturing plants are covered by ISO 9001 and ISO 14000.

Ostermann & Scheiwe, Germany	321
• *Low in solvents and free VOCs, biocides, preservatives and citrus oils* • *Natural, renewable raw materials*	327, 341

Bio T®

Bio T® is a general-purpose cleaner derived from terpene, which is suitable for use in the manufacturing industries and public-sector maintenance.

BioChem Systems, USA	313
• *Derived from renewable materials*	327

BioForm®

This biodegradable release agent is made from canola oil and is suitable for use with concrete, plastic, PVC, silicone rubber, steel, styrofoam and wood.

Leahy Wolf Company, USA	319
• *Renewable material*	327

Natural colourants and dyes

This company bulk-manufactures dyes from natural sources to supply other industries with alternatives to synthetic colourants.

Color Trends, Inc., USA	314
• *Renewable materials*	327

GlueMate™

Dry and green timber can be finger-jointed using the PRF/Soy 2000 adhesive system, which uses GlueMate™, a protein-based gel derived from soybeans.

Hopton Technologies, USA	318
• *Renewable material*	327

Adhesives, paints

Potmolen make a traditional range of cabinetmakers' glues and adhesives derived from casein, together with gloss paints based on linseed oil and other natural ingredients.

Potmolen Paints, UK	322
• *Renewable materials* • *Toxin-free*	327

Rilsan

Rilsan resins are derived from castor beans and are often used in the powder coating of metals.

Elf Atochem, USA	316
• *Renewable materials*	327

Soy Clean

Soy Clean is a range of biodegradable, non-toxic cleaners and paint removers derived from soybeans.

Soy Environmental Products, Inc., USA	324
• *Renewable materials* • *Toxin-free*	327

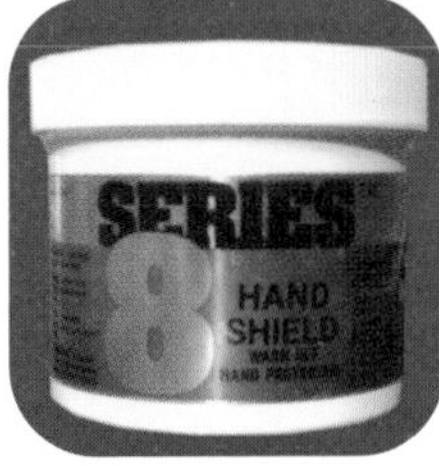

Bean-e-clean™

Franmar Chemical manufacture a multipurpose, industrial-strength cleaner, Bean-e-doo™, and a waterless hand cleaner, Bean-e-clean™, both derived from soybeans.

Franmar Chemical, Inc., USA	316
• *Renewable materials* • *Reduction in toxic chemicals and VOCs*	327, 341

Continuum

Old denim jeans, worn-out money notes and industrial cotton waste are recycled in a diverse range of papers. Zenus Crane's mill has been recycling waste textiles and paper since 1801. The tradition continues with the Continuum brand of tree-free papers using 50 per cent cotton fibre and 50 per cent hemp fibre.

⚙	*Crane & Company, USA*	314
♻	*• Renewable resources* *• Conservation of forest resources*	327, 330

Conservation, Retreeve

The Conservation range includes 100 per cent-recycled wove and laid papers suitable for ink-jet and laser printing, corporate stationery and general-purpose office use. It consists of 25 per cent mill waste, 50 per cent pre-consumer and 25 per cent post-consumer waste and meets all the requirements of NAPM and Eugropa recycled marks. Retreeve is a range of quality text and cover papers, which (excluding Brilliant White) is 100 per cent recycled. The company has an environmental policy and is certified to ISO 14001 and EMAS.

⚙	*Curtis Fine Papers Ltd, UK*	314
♻	*• Recycled content* *• NAPM certified*	327, 334

Tree-free paper

A range of papers is made from natural plant fibres, such as cotton and hemp, and post-consumer paper waste.

⚙	*Green Field Paper Company, USA*	317
♻	*• Renewable and recycled materials* *• Encourages forest resource conservation*	327, 330

Multiboard Kraft, Offset, Ecofrost

Composite sheeting and boards are made from a diverse range of recycled materials, of which 55 per cent originates from used PE-coated milk cartons, newsprint and corrugated paper, the remaining 45 per cent from the industrial or production waste streams. This company is registered to ISO 9001, ISO 14001 and EMAS.

⚙	*Fiskeby Board Ltd, UK*	316
♻	*• Recycled materials* *• EMS policy*	327, 340

Index paper, board for folders

Hurum takes back used laminated drinks cartons made of paper, plastic and aluminium. The cartons are shredded and separated into the component waste streams, then the recovered paper is used to make recycled paper for index-card systems and board for folders. The aluminium fraction is sent to another manufacturer for reprocessing. The company is certified to ISO 9001, ISO 14001 and EMAS.

⚙	*Hurum Fabrikker AS, Norway*	318
♻	*• Recycled content* *• Recycling of recovered metal*	327, 328

Office and sanitary paper

Over four hundred tree-free papers, made from plant fibres and recycled waste paper, are available from this manufacturer.

⚙	*New Leaf Paper, USA*	321
♻	*• Renewable and recycled materials* *• Conservation of forest resources*	327, 330

'Context' and other Paperback papers

There are tens of paper manufacturers and distributors in the UK who offer recycled papers in their range but Paperback offers the most extensive range of gloss and matt coated papers, uncoated offsets, letterheads and speciality grades manufactured from recycled waste paper. This process consumes less than half the energy required to make paper from virgin wood pulp. The company was set up in 1983 when use of recycled paper was a fringe activity in both the consumer and commercial markets. It is committed to encouraging use of recycled paper to decrease the disposal of six million tonnes of waste paper annually in the UK. Boards range in weight from 225gsm up to 300gsm with a variety of finishes from smooth white watermarked up to natural-coloured micro-fluting. All 'context' papers and boards contain 75 per cent-de-inked used waste to a NAPM approved grade and 'context FSC' is made from 75 per cent-de-inked fibre and 25 per cent-FSC-endorsed pulp.

⚙	*Paperback, UK*	322
♻	• *Recycled materials* • *Reduction in embodied energy* • *NAPM approved* • *Stewardship sourcing, FSC*	327, 328, 333, 334

Savatree

This company produces a vast range of kraft, packaging grade and printing papers. The Savatree range uses 100 per cent-waste paper to create recycled papers such as MG Greentreesaver Kraft, MG Green Envelope and MG Treesaver Plus Kraft used in the manufacture of envelopes.

⚙	*Smith Anderson & Co. Ltd, UK*	324
♻	• *Recycled content*	327

Vanguard Ecoblend™

This tree-free, bond-quality paper is manufactured from 25 per cent agricultural crops and 75 per cent post-consumer waste paper.

⚙	*Living Tree Paper Company, USA*	319
♻	• *Renewable and recycled materials* • *Conservation of forest resources*	327, 330

Vision™ and Re-vision™ printing paper

Kenaf fibre is the principal raw material for the manufacture of a range of 100 per cent tree-free and chlorine-free printing papers.

⚙	*Vision Paper, KP Products, USA*	319
♻	• *Renewable materials* • *Conservation of forest resources*	327

Printing inks

Alden & Ott manufacture a range of heat-set soy-based inks with about 20-25 per cent soy content and colour pigments avoiding the use of heavy metals.

⚙	*Alden & Ott, USA*	312
♻	• *Renewable material* • *Cleaner production*	327

EcoPure

EcoPure is a range of inks derived from soybeans. The company also produces a diverse range of water-based flexographic inks and specialist inks for printing on metal.

⚙	*Inx International Ink Co., USA*	318
♻	• *Renewable materials*	327

Printing inks

An extensive range of vegetable-based inks is available for offset and lithographic printing.

⚙	*Flint Ink, USA*	316
♻	• *Renewable materials*	327

Soybean inks

Manufacturer of a diverse range of inks derived from soybeans.

⚙	*Ron Ink, USA*	323
♻	• *Renewable materials*	327

Argyll CF727

Designer Jasper Morrison has built on a long Scottish tradition of weaving woollen textiles by creating a new range of furnishing fabrics for Bute Fabrics in vibrant, contemporary colours, yet the durability and warm surface textures associated with traditional crafted products are retained. Bute Fabrics source much of their raw materials locally and adopt clean production, minimizing the use of harmful substances during processing, as an integral part of their environmental policy. These fabrics are suitable for restoration projects and for new furniture.

Bute Fabrics, UK	313
• *Renewable materials* • *Clean production*	327

Cantiva™

Hemp is a very strong natural fibre, naturally resistant to salt water, mould, mildew and UV light, and its use in China is documented through ten thousand years. Tens of different pure hemp or hemp/natural-fibre fabrics are designed by Hemp Textiles International using the Cantiva™ brand hemp fibre. Fabrics range from heavy-duty pure hemp canvas weighing 620g/square metre (18.3 oz/sq yd) to lightweight hemp/silk or hemp/cotton mixtures weighing between 92 and 193g/square metre (2.7 and 5.7 oz/sq yd). Bulk or wholesale orders are produced in contractual arrangements with a Chinese mill.

Hemp Textiles International, USA	317
• *Renewable materials*	327

Furrows, Carnegie and Wintex fabric from Climatex® Lifecycle™ yarn

DesignTex commissioned McDonough Braungart Design Chemistry to create a new biodegradable fabric for their office furniture systems. The new fabric, Climatex® Lifecycle™, was designed by William McDonough and Professor Dr Michael Braungart, McDonough Braungart Design Chemistry, USA/Germany, with Susan Lyons, DesignTex, and Lothar Pfister and Fabiola Fornasier, Rohner Textil. After screening over 8,300 chemicals used in conventional textile manufacturing, the design consultancy concluded that only thirty-eight were really safe, being completely non-toxic and non-hazardous. Two natural fibres were selected, wool for its warmth and water-absorption properties, and ramie, a flax-like fibre produced in Indonesia, for its coolness and water-repellent properties. Ciba Geigy assisted with the development of natural dyes and the methods of processing and manufacture of the textile at Rohner Textil's mills. Apparently, the effluent water from the factory was cleaner after treatment than the original imported water source.

Rohner Textil, Switzerland, for DesignTex, USA	315, 323
• *Durable, recyclable and compostable materials* • *Non-toxic and non-hazardous manufacturing* • *Reduction in water consumption during manufacturing*	327, 328

Yarns and textiles

Wool from rare breeds of animals is spun and woven into a range of high-performance yarns and fabrics.

Dalton Lucerne Rare Fibres Ltd, UK	315
Various manufacturers	
• *Renewable resources* • *Encouraging animal conservation*	327, 330

FoxFibre®

FoxFibre® is made from organic sources of natural-coloured cotton that don't require dyeing and so significantly reduce water usage and effluent production during processing.

Natural Cotton Colours, Inc., USA	320
• *Renewable materials* • *Clean production*	327

Unbleached textiles

Dyeing and bleaching both generate emissions to water and air during textile manufacturing, so Junichi Arai borrowed from the traditions of jacquard woven fabrics to create a striking series of heavily textured, undyed, unbleached textiles. 'Basket Weave Pockets' uses fine cotton yarn and knitted tapes to create a densely woven fabric, while 'Korean Carrot' is an undyed wool weave with a felt-like finish.

⚙	*Junichi Arai, c/o Nuno Corp., Japan*	321
♻	*• Renewable materials • Clean production*	327

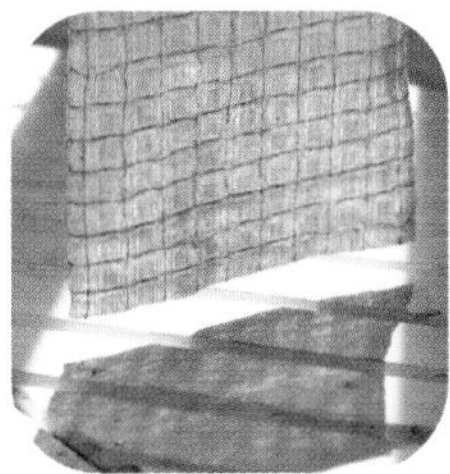

Recycled yarn textiles – wool, cotton

Mollsjö produces a range of fabrics by weaving recycled yarns of wool and cotton from reclaimed denim jeans. Each fabric run is unique and depends on the mixture of yarns and warp and weft settings.

⚙	*One-offs, small batch production by designer-maker Carina Mollsjö, Sweden*	308
♻	*• Recycled content*	327

Green Cotton®

Well before 'organic' became the adjective of the late 1990s, companies such as Novotex were re-examining the sustainable features of their business. Sources of raw materials were analyzed and it was discovered that hand-picked cotton from pesticide-free South American sources required less cleaning than intensively grown 'commercial' cotton. Long-fibre cottons were selected to provide a yarn that could be woven to facilitate dyeing with water-based dyes and reduce chemical additives throughout the production process. As a result Green Cotton is free of chlorine, benzidine and formaldehyde. Waste water generated in processing is chemically and biologically cleaned in situ. Supply chain management, cleaner production and dust and noise control have also created a healthier environment for employees at Novotex.

⚙	*Novotex, Denmark*	321
♻	*• Clean production of 'organic' natural-fibre textiles*	327

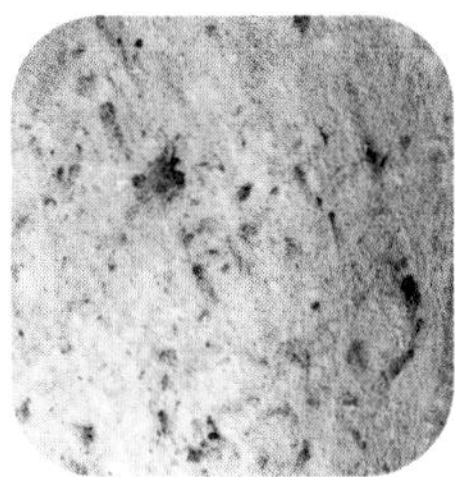

TENCEL®

TENCEL® is a modern textile that uses natural raw materials in the form of 'lyocell' cellulose fibre derived from wood pulp harvested from managed forests. This lyocell fibre is processed through the unique TENCEL® 'closed loop' solvent spinning process, which is economical in its use of water and energy and uses a non-toxic solvent that is continuously recycled. The resultant TENCEL® fibre is soft, breathable, absorbent and fully biodegradable. Luxurious surface finishes are achieved by abrading the wet fibres, a technique called fibrillation. A wide variety of fibrillated or non-fibrillated (TENCEL A100) finishes is achievable. TENCEL® filament is suitable for knitted and woven fabrics, is softer in feel yet stronger than cotton and provides a good surface for printing and dyeing. Many of the world's leading fashion designers have taken advantage of the versatility of fabrics woven with TENCEL® yarn.

⚙	*Acordis Fibres (Holdings) Ltd, UK*	312
♻	*• Renewable, compostable materials • Clean production • Energy-efficient production*	327, 328

Terrazo Felt 'Colour Chips'

This non-woven, needle-punched, blanket-type fabric fuses dye-chips into a 100 per cent-natural-coloured alpaca-wool felt over a core of polyester organdy to produce unique pieces of material.

⚙	*Nuno Corporation, Japan*	321
♻	*• Renewable and recyclable materials*	327

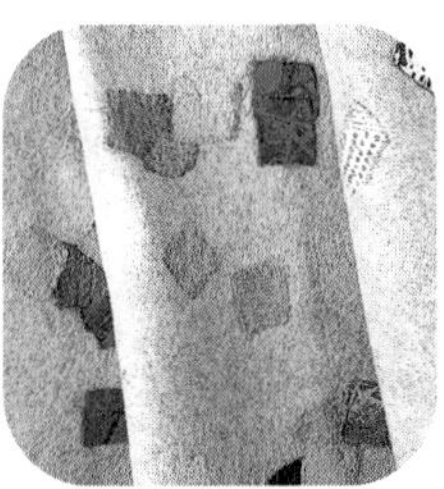

Terrazo Felt 'Nuno'

Industrial-waste snippets of various Nuno fabrics and 'outtakes' in raw wool are combined in a needle-punched technique to create an interesting textured terazzo effect. The constituents are 85 per cent alpaca wool with 15 per cent Nuno production waste.

⚙	*Nuno Corporation, Japan*	321
♻	*• Renewable and recycled materials*	327

ACAT fibre board

The sourcing of this fibre board, made from 90 per cent waste fibre from paper, wood and plastics with 10 per cent adhesives, makes its manufacture a viable proposition and reduces waste disposal while minimizing embodied energy of manufacturing.

⚙	*Alaska Center for Appropriate Technology, USA*	304
♻	• *Recycled materials locally sourced* • *Reduction in embodied energy*	327, 340

AERT LifeCycle, ChoiceDek and MoistureShield

AERT's products are manufactured from a mixture of recycled polyethylene (HDPE and LDPE) plastics and waste wood fibre. LifeCycle and ChoiceDek are plank sections suitable for decking while MoistureShield is suitable for door, window and furniture construction.

⚙	*Advanced Environmental Recycling Technologies (AERT), USA*	312
♻	• *Recycled materials*	327

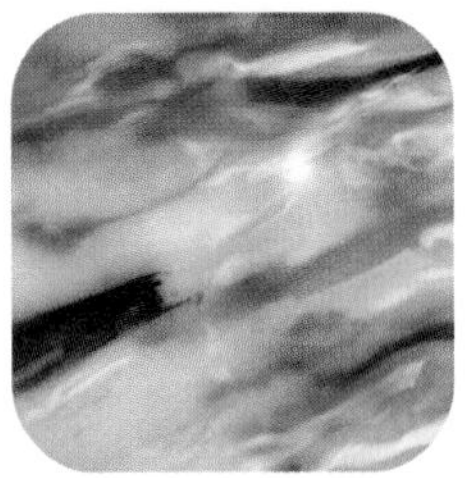

Eco Panel

RPI's Eco Panel is made from HDPE recycled plastics and is available in ten sample mixes and patterns ranging from neutral greys to mixed primary colours.

⚙	*Recycled Plastics, Inc., USA*	323
♻	• *Recycled content*	327

Duraplast

Recycled mixed polyethylene (HDPE and LDPE) is bound with resin to form general-purpose boards and sheets.

⚙	*EnviroSafe Products, Inc., USA*	316
♻	• *Recycled materials*	327

Plastic recyclate

MAP manufactures a range of mixed ABS/polycarbonate recyclates, which are suitable for injection- or blow-moulding of furniture components.

⚙	*MAP (Merchants of Australia Products) Pty/Wharington International Pty, Australia*	320, 326
♻	• *Recycled content*	327

Stokbord™ and Centriboard

Stokbord™ is a smooth or embossed low-density polyethylene (LDPE) sheet available in standard sheets in a thickness of 6, 9, 12 and 14mm (between about 1/5 and 1/2in). It is constituted from 40-50 per cent post-consumer waste and 50-60 per cent industrial/commercial waste. Centriboard is available in three grades: L – a smooth LDPE sheet, 1.5mm to 18mm thick (about 1/20 to 7/10in); H – smooth HDPE sheet, 2mm to 6mm thick (about 1/12 to 1/4in); and P – smooth polypropylene sheet, 2mm to 6mm thick.

⚙	*Centriforce, UK*	314
♻	• *Recycled materials* • *Reduction in embodied energy (compared with virgin plastics)* • *Encouraging conservation of timber resources*	327, 330, 340

Tectan

Used drinks cartons are mixed with industrial scrap from the carton-manufacturing plants under the Duales System Deutschland scheme to provide the ingredients for this tough, water-resistant board. The raw material is shredded, then compressed under heat and pressure, causing the polyethylene fraction to melt and bond the particles. It is suitable for building and furniture manufacturing.

⚙	*Tetrapak, UK*	325
♻	• *Recycled materials*	327

Unicor

Unicor panel comprises 90 per cent-recycled wood fibres and particles sandwiched between surface layers of polyethylene. It is used in coach building in the recreational vehicle industry.

⚙	*Unicor Corporation, USA*	325
♻	• *Recycled content*	327

Wood-Com

Wood-Com is a mixture of recycled plastic and waste wood particles and dust. It is easily moulded into panels suitable for interior design and automotive fittings.

⚙	*North Wood Plastics, Inc., USA*	321
♻	*• Renewable and recycled materials*	327

Frostex

Commingled, recycled plastics are extruded into sheets suitable for a wide range of uses from packaging to surface laminates and for general product-design applications.

⚙	*Yemm & Hart, USA*	326
♻	*• Recycled content*	327

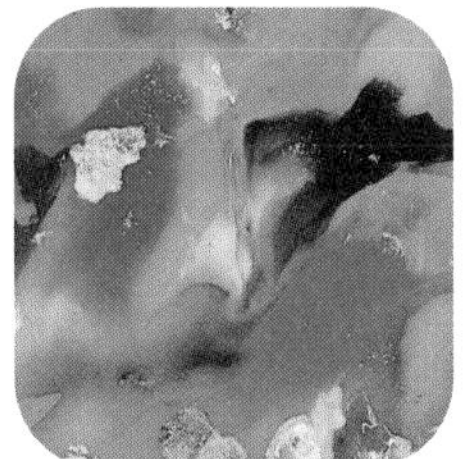

Plastic board

Recycled HDPE is used to manufacture new plastic boards suitable for a wide variety of applications.

⚙	*Yemm & Hart, USA*	326
♻	*• Recycled content*	327

Recycled plastic

Stakes and posts are made from post-consumer and production waste.

⚙	*Cabka Plast Kunststoffverarbeitungs GmbH, Germany*	313
♻	*• Recycled materials*	327

Durawood

Durawood is a high-density material available in a range of rectangular profiles, which is made entirely from recycled plastics. It is especially suited to the manufacture of street and outdoor furniture.

⚙	*Save Wood Products Ltd, UK*	323
♻	*• Recycled content*	327

Epoch

Commingled, recycled HDPE plastics are extruded to form rectangular, square or plank sections suitable for a multiplicity of uses in street and garden furniture.

⚙	*Environmental Polymer Products Ltd, UK*	316
♻	*• Recycled content*	327

Govaplast®

A range of square, round, rectangular and tongue-and-groove profiles is produced using recycled polyethylene and polypropylene plastics. A range of colours includes charcoal grey, grey-green and mid-brown. The T & G is used in everything from fabrication of equestrian buildings to outdoor planters.

⚙	*Govaerts Recycling NV, Belgium*	317
♻	*• Recycled and recyclable content*	327

Plastic profiles

A variety of round and square profiles and stakes are made from recycled plastics.

⚙	*Hahn Kunststoffe GmbH, Germany*	317
♻	*• Recycled content*	327

Plastic planks, profiles, stakes

Plastic lumber in the form of planks, profiles and stakes is manufactured from recycled plastics for indoor and outdoor use.

⚙	*Henne Kunststoffe GmbH, Germany*	318
♻	*• Recycled content*	327

Holloplas

To date Centriforce has supplied more than 150,000 tonnes of recycled finished products to construction, industrial, agricultural and recreational markets in over thirty countries. It offers an extensive range of hollow extruded profiles using a blend of recycled plastic from waste from retail distribution (40-50 per cent) and industrial/commercial waste including film, pipe and packaging (50–60 per cent). Standard sections are suitable for decking, T & G flooring, fencing, railings and street furniture.

⚙	*Centriforce, UK*	314
♺	• *Recycled materials* • *Reduction in embodied energy (compared with virgin plastics)* • *Encouraging conservation of timber resources*	327, 330, 340

Plastic profiles

A range of profiles is manufactured from recycled plastics.

⚙	*Josef Meeth Fensterfabrik GmbH & Co. KG, Germany*	318
♺	• *Recycled content*	327

Plastic sheeting, tubing and profiles

This company makes a range of sheeting for construction and other uses, tubing and round profiles from recycled plastics.

⚙	*MGSL GmbH, Germany*	320
♺	• *Recycled content*	327

Partek

Partek manufacture profiles and decking made from recycled plastics.

⚙	*Partek Insulations, Inc., USA*	322
♺	• *Recycled content*	327

Plastic profiles

Round and square profiles are manufactured from recycled plastics.

⚙	*Planex GmbH, Germany*	322
♺	• *Recycled content*	327

Plaswood

Reclaimed polythene and polypropylene – 30 per cent waste from supermarkets and 70 per cent production factory waste – are reblended into extruded profiles suitable for uses requiring tough, rot-free materials.

⚙	*Dumfries Plastics Recycling*	315
♺	• *Recycled materials* • *Reduction in embodied energy (compared with virgin plastics)* • *Encouraging conservation of timber resources*	327, 330, 340

Plastic profiles

Planks, stakes and square profiles are made from recycled plastics.

⚙	*Poly-Beek-Kunststoff-Handels-GmbH, Germany*	322
♺	• *Recycled materials*	327

Plastic stakes

Round profiles and stakes are manufactured from recycled plastics.

⚙	*PURUS Kunststoffwerke GmbH, Germany*	322
♺	• *Recycled content*	327

Recydur®

Square profiles and stakes are made entirely from recycled plastics.

⚙	*LSR GmbH Recycling-Zentrum, Germany*	320
♺	• *Recycled content*	327

Plastic profiles and stakes

Planks, square profiles and stakes are fabricated from recycled plastics.

⚙	*Re-Reluma GmbH, Germany*	323
♺	• *Recycled content*	327

Plastic profiles

Consumer waste is the primary constituent of a range of plastic profiles suitable for furniture.

⚙	*Transform Plastics Ltd, UK*	325
♺	• *Recycled content*	327

Plastic profiles

Profiles and stakes in a variety of round and square shapes are manufactured from recycled plastics.

⚙	*WKR Altkunststoffproduktions- u. Vertriebsgesellschaft mbH, Germany*	326
♺	• *Recycled content*	327

Plastic lumber

Commingled, recycled plastics are extruded into a variety of rectangular sections, making an alternative material for traditional uses such as decking and outdoor furniture.

⚙	*Yemm & Hart, USA*	326
♺	• *Recycled content*	327

Environmental stone

Floor tiles, wall panelling and paving stones are fabricated from 100 per cent-recycled glass.

⚙	*Environmental Stone Products, USA*	316
♻	• *Recycled materials*	327

Faswall

Waste wood dust and particles are combined with concrete to create high-density panels, tiles and ready-made wall sections.

⚙	*Insulholz-Beton International, Inc./K-X Industries, Inc., USA*	318, 319
♻	• *Recycled content*	327

High-performance ceramics

Advances in ceramics technology have enabled fine-tolerance manufacturing of everything from parts for car engines to superconductors and fibres for reinforcement. Alumina, titanium, carbide and rare earth minerals such as zirconia bond with the clay particles to form very tough composites. The composites can be formed by slip casting, sintering and even a form of injection-moulding, so they can be applied to diverse manufacturing ends. Some ceramic composites are lightweight and so offer potential savings in energy consumption when applied to power units and/or mobility or transport products.

⚙	*Various*	
♻	• *Very durable and inert* • *Potential energy savings in the usage phase of a product*	328, 329

Ecoplast

Europol manufactures a range of recycled plastics entirely from material discarded by consumers to create injection-moulding grades of HDPE, LDPE, PP, HIPS and ABS and a blow-moulding grade of HDPE.

⚙	*Europol, UK*	316
♻	• *Recycled content*	327

First Glow

These glass beads shed a luminous glow after the illuminating light source has been switched off. Road markings and lighting systems are suitable applications of this new materials technology.

⚙	*Product 2000 Ltd, UK*	322
♻	• *Energy-efficient lighting material*	329

Lightweight metals – metal matrix composites, metal foams, light alloys

With advances in technology it is now possible to produce very lightweight but strong metals. The first group, light alloys, such as aluminium, magnesium, titanium and beryllium, are well known and available in a diverse selection of profiles, sheets and cast forms. The second group, metal foams, are specialist foamed aluminium, varying in density from high to ultra-low, which are suitable for applications where weight-saving is critical to a product's performance. The final group, metal matrix composites, includes substances such as alumina (fibre- or particulate-reinforced), boron, carbon, iron or silicon carbide bonded in a matrix of aluminium or magnesium. All these lightweight metals are high-embodied-energy materials but can potentially significantly improve energy efficiency in the usage phase of a product by reducing the amount of mass that has to be moved.

⚙	*Various*	
♻	• *Strong, lightweight, tough* • *Potential energy savings in the usage phase of a product*	328, 329

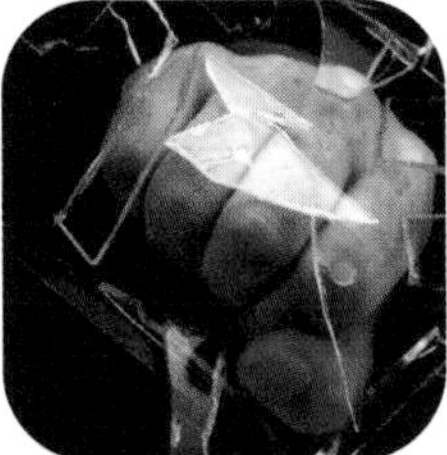

Safeglass

This special glass breaks into harmless pieces when shattered, making it ideally suited to any application where there is a risk of impact.

⚙	*Safeglass (Europe) Ltd, UK*	323
♻	• *Improved health and safety*	328

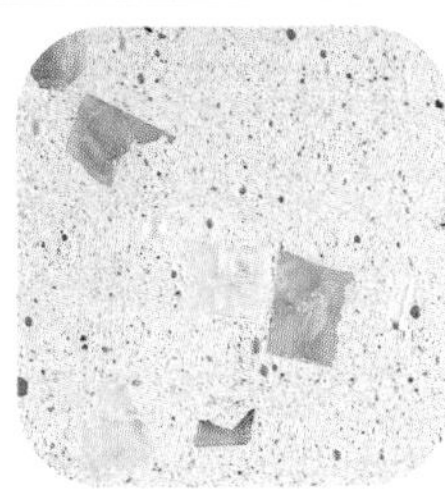

Syndecrete®

Syndecrete® is a chemically inert, zero out-gasing, concrete-like material composed of cement and up to 41 per cent recycled or recovered materials from industrial or consumer waste. Typical wastes include HDPE, crushed recycled glass, wood chips and brass screw shavings. Pulverized fly ash (PFA), a waste residue from coal-fired power stations, is added to reduce the cement requirement by up to 15 per cent and recovered polypropylene fibre scrap provides a 3-D matrix to increase the tensile strength of this composite recyclate concrete. It is easily worked and polished to create a contemporary terrazzo look.

⚙	*Syndesis, Inc., USA*	324
♻	• *Recycled materials usage* • *Reduction in embodied energy of manufacture* • *Certified as a recycled product by the Californians Against Waste Foundation*	327, 340

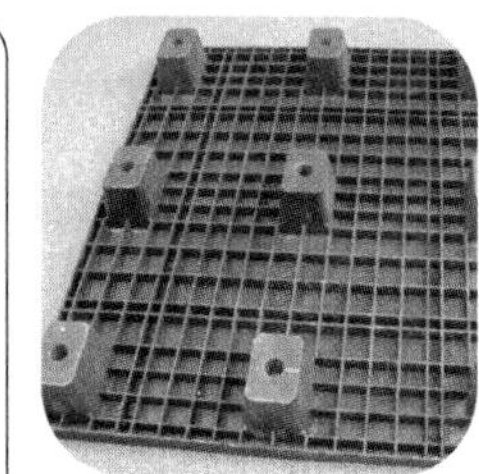

Agro Plastic

Agro Plastic is polypropylene or polyethylene manufactured using a filler derived from wheat straw. It was jointly developed by PTI and the USDA Forest Products Laboratory.

Pinnacle Technology, Inc. (PTI), USA	322
• Renewable and biodegradable components	327

Bionelle®

Bionelle® polymer is physically degraded by the action of ultraviolet light and mechanical agents.

Showa Highpolymer Co., Japan	324
• Degradable	327

Biopol™

The polymer structure of Biopol™ breaks down when exposed to ultraviolet light. The actual material is PHBV, which is not a biodegradable polymer since it is not compostable by biological agents and when it degrades remains as fine particles.

ICI Americas, USA	318
• Rapid physical degrading of material at the end of its life	330

Rubber granulate

This company manufactures rubber granulate, 0.5mm to 30mm (0.02 to 0.1in) diameter particles, from 100 per cent-reclaimed scrap tyres. The granulate can be bonded with virgin natural or synthetic rubber and elastomers and is ideal for play surfaces or other uses to reduce impact damage.

Charles Lawrence Recycling Ltd, UK	314
• Recycled materials	327

Correx

This lightweight twin-walled PP sheet is made from 100 per cent production and customers' returned waste. It is utilized for packaging, self-assembly storage systems and tree shelters.

Correx Plastics, UK	314
• Recycled materials	327

EcoClear®

EcoClear® is a resin and film made from recycled PET, which is suitable for beverage and food packaging.

Wellman Inc., USA	326
• Recycled content	327

NH001

NH001 fabric has similar performance characteristics to PVC (polyvinyl chloride) but there are no emissions of chlorides, phthalates or other toxic compounds during the manufacture or use of NH001. For this reason it replaced PVC as the roofing material for the Millennium Dome, London.

Carrington Performance Fabrics, UK	314
• Cleaner production	327

Plastic sheeting

This sheeting is manufactured from recycled plastics and is a suitable grade for construction use.

ORBITA Film GmbH, Germany	321
• Recycled content	327

Santoprene®

Santoprene® is cross-linked polypropylene (PP) and ethylene-polypropylene-diene-monomer (EPDM) rubber with a soft, yielding texture suitable for moulding components for hand-held equipment. Its inherent qualities improve usability in items ranging from cameras to ski sticks but its specialist nature means disassembly of Santoprene® parts is essential to prevent contamination of pure-grade waste streams.

⚙	*Advanced Elastomer Systems L.P., USA*	312
☊	• *Improved user comfort*	329

Styradex, Propadex

Syradex is made from recycled polystyrene (PS); Propadex uses recycled polypropylene (PP). Most materials are sourced from production waste (98 per cent) and small quanities from post-consumer waste (2 per cent).

⚙	*Styradex Plastics Recycling, UK*	324
☊	• *Recycled content*	327

Biosynthetic polymers

USSC manufactures a range of specialist polyurethane foams using soybean oil. Like synthetic PU, the USSC foams are suitable for everything from loose-fill packaging and furnishing to panels and shoe components.

⚙	*Urethane Soy Systems Company (USSC), USA*	325
☊	• *Renewable content*	327

Biora

Biora is a range of water-based acrylic resins suitable for application to walls, ceilings and other interior surfaces. Qualifying for the EU eco-label, these eight paints and varnishes offer a reduction in a variety of environmental impacts of conventional paints, especially VOCs and toxic ingredients. Teknos Tranemo are also certified to ISO 9001 and ISO 14001 and are working with the Swedish Paint Makers Organization to develop tools, such as lifecycle analysis, to make further improvements.

	Teknos Tranemo, Sweden	325
	• Cleaner production *• EU eco-label ensuring low toxicity of constituents*	327, 339

Ecos

This company claims to manufacture the only solvent-free odourless paints and varnishes in the world, with zero VOC content, independently tested by the US EPA and the Swedish National Testing & Research Institute. The Ecos range is, however, based upon synthetic resins, albeit non-allergenic, harmless resins, processed from crude oil, so it is not from a renewable source.

	Lakeland Paints, UK	319
	• Free of VOCs and vinyl chloride	341

Innetak and Bindoplast

At the paint manufacturing plant at Malmö, Sweden, Akzo Nobel produce over 30 million litres (6.6 million gallons) of decorative coatings and 16 million litres (3.5 million gallons) of industrial coatings. Since 1995 the company has set itself a series of environmental targets, such as reducing the emissions of solvents to the air by 50 per cent between 1995 and 1999 and reducing the total energy consumption per litre of paint manufactured by 5 per cent between 1995 and 2000. Innetak and Bindoplast are decorative, water-based emulsion paints, which were the first brand in Europe to receive the EU eco-label.

	Nordsjö (Akzo Nobel Dekorativ), Sweden	321
	• EU eco-label ensuring low VOCs and general reduction in toxicity *• Manufactured with clean technology/eco-efficiency practices*	328, 339, 341

Keim paints

All the paints manufactured by Keim use inorganic materials that are abundant in the geosphere, including potassium silicate binders, mineral fillers and earth oxide colour pigments. Granital is an exterior paint with a range of 350 colours suitable for all mineral substrates, Concretal protects concrete against corrosion and Biosil is a water-borne, silicate-based paint suitable for interior applications. Ecosil is a recently introduced interior-quality paint, which is water-based, contains no chemical solvents and is VOC-free. Keim are certified to ISO 14001 and ISO 9001.

	Keim Mineral Paints Ltd, UK	319
	• Use of abundant inorganic materials *• Non-toxic*	327

Pinturas Proa

A range of water-borne, vinyl polymer interior paints containing less than 45 per cent volatiles is certified with an EU eco-label. The company is also registered with the Spanish eco-label certification authority, AENOR, and participates in the Punto Verde (Green Dot) packaging disposal scheme.

	Pinturas Proa, Spain	322
	• EU eco-label *• Reduction in volatiles* *• Recycled and recyclable packaging*	327, 328, 339, 341

Chapco® Safe-Set

The adhesives in this professional range are low in VOCs, non-flammable, non-toxic and anti-microbial and contain no hazardous ingredients as defined by the Occupational Safety and Health Administration (OSHA) Regulations. All products are packaged in recycled plastic containers with printed labels on recycled paper including OSHA data on safety.

	Chicago Adhesive Products Company, USA	314
	• *Non-toxic and safe* • *Recycled packaging materials*	327, 328

Dasic Aerostrip 323

This water-based paint stripper was developed specifically for the aeronautics industry but is suitable for removal of paint from metals and metal alloys.

	Dasic International Ltd, UK	315
	• *Reduction in emissions of VOCs* • *Improved health and safety*	329, 341

Home Strip

Powerful solvents, usually methylene chloride (dichloromethane or DCM), are used in conventional paint strippers. DCM is a skin irritant and is highly volatile, the fumes inducing narcotic effects, and it has recently been classified as a Category 3 carcinogen by the EU. Home Strip is DCM- and solvent-free, is water-based and doesn't give off fumes, yet is just as effective at removing layers of paint or varnish.

	Eco Solutions, UK	315
	• *Reduction of toxicity and emissions*	327

Laybond Quickstick Green

This synthetic rubber/resin emulsion is a general-purpose contact adhesive suitable for wall or floor coverings and other applications where a bond is required to aluminium, concrete, plaster, steel and timber. Quickstick Green is water-based, non-flammable and is much safer to handle than solvent-based adhesives with VOCs.

	Laybond Products Ltd, UK	319
	• *Non-toxic*	327

Brass Cloth

Woven textiles combining metals and natural or synthetic yarns are texturally and visually striking and offer the designer new possibilities with shapes and tailoring. Brass Cloth, designed by Reiko Sudo, Japan, is part of the Metal series manufactured by Nuno and consists of 40 per cent cotton and 60 per cent brass from recycled wire.

⚙	*Nuno Corporation, Japan*	321
♻	*• Metal component is recyclable*	327

ComforTemp

'Phase Change' technology is used in space applications to control temperatures. Microcapsules woven into fabrics moderate temperatures by changing from solids to liquids. As they convert from solids to liquids they absorb body heat and, conversely, when they solidify they release heat, which is reabsorbed by the body. ComforTemp fabric is pleasantly tactile, comfortable to wear and illustrates possible developments in textiles that can respond intelligently to their surroundings.

⚙	*Scholler Textil, Switzerland*	323
♻	*• Potential health and safety improvements*	329

EcoSpun®

Wellman is one of the world's leading manufactures of yarn and textiles using PET from recycled drinks bottles. Wellman supply the furnishing and clothing industries, including Patagonia, the outdoor clothing company. Ecospun® is a specialist fibre made using recycled plastics.

⚙	*Wellman, Inc., USA*	326
♻	*• Recycled content*	327

Elex Tex™

Conductive fibres are woven with traditional, natural yarns to create a flexible textile suitable for a variety of applications such as electronic clothing, roll-up keyboards and so on.

⚙	*Electrotextiles Ltd, UK*	315
♻	*• Dual-function material*	329

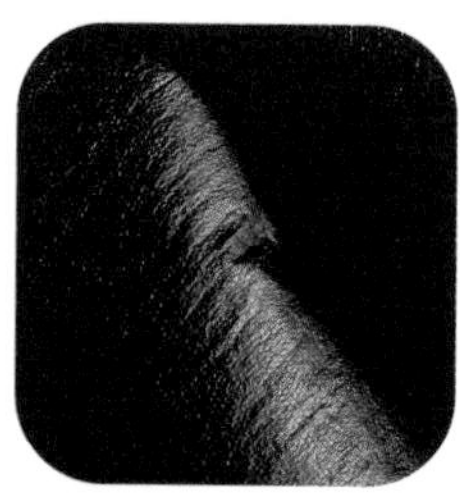

Otterskin

This 100 per cent-polyester, non-woven, needle-punched fabric is made from recycled PET bottles. A surface coating of polyurethane provides wind- and water-proofing, yet the material is breathable and retains body heat.

⚙	*Nuno Corporation, Japan*	321
♻	*• Recycled materials*	327

Play It Again Sam

DesignTex is a leading manufacturer of furnishing fabrics. Play It Again Sam is a polyester fabric made entirely of fibres from recycled PET bottles.

⚙	*DesignTex, Inc., USA*	315
♻	*• Recycled materials*	327

Stomatex

Stomatex is a breathable fabric made of a combination of neoprene and polyethylene, which mimics transpiration, the process of evaporation of moisture from leaves. Perspiration vapour generated by the activity of the wearer is collected in small depressions on the inside of the fabric. At each depression a tiny pore provides an exit for the vapour to the external environment. Stomatex is activated only when sufficient body perspiration is generated, so this is a responsive, 'smart' textile.

⚙	*Micro Thermal Systems, UK*	320
♻	*• Improved personal health with breathable fabric*	329

Terratex

Made entirely of recycled PET recycled plastic bottles, Terratex is a tough, versatile, recyclable fabric for furnishing and similar applications.

✿	*Interface Fabrics International, UK/USA*	318
↻	• *Recycled and recyclable materials*	327

Therma-Pore, Therma-Float, Therma-Foil

This company produces a range of specialist breathable fabrics suitable for sports applications and survival in extreme conditions. Therma-Pore is a breathable fabric, Therma-Float a high-buoyancy insulating material and Therma-Foil a lightweight foam insulator bonded to foil.

✿	*Therma-Float Ltd, UK*	325
↻	• *Improved health and safety*	329

Trevira NSK/Trevira CS

This is a fabric made from two types of polyester yarn, Trevira NSK, which gives strength, and Trevira CS, which acts as a flame retardant. Being 100 per cent polyester, it can be reworked by pleating, dyeing and printing but has the in-built advantage of not requiring a flame-proof coating. It is entirely recyclable.

✿	*Trevira GmbH & Co. KG, Germany*	325
↻	• *Recyclable* • *Cleaner technology*	327
🔍	*iF Design Award, 2000*	332

Tyvek

With its durability and high chemical resistance, Tyvek was originally developed by DuPont for protective clothing but has since been used for haute-couture fashion and as a paper substitute for envelopes, stationery and various printed media. Tyvek is fully recyclable.

✿	*DuPont, USA*	315
↻	• *Recyclable synthetic material*	327

Velcro®

Velcro® is a combination of two nylon fabrics, one woven with a surface of hooks and the other with a smooth surface with loops. When juxtaposed the two fabrics adhere as the hooks take up in the loops, creating a strong 'adhesive' bond.

✿	*Velcro, USA*	325
↻	• *Temporary bonding system allowing reuse of textiles*	330

4.0 Resources

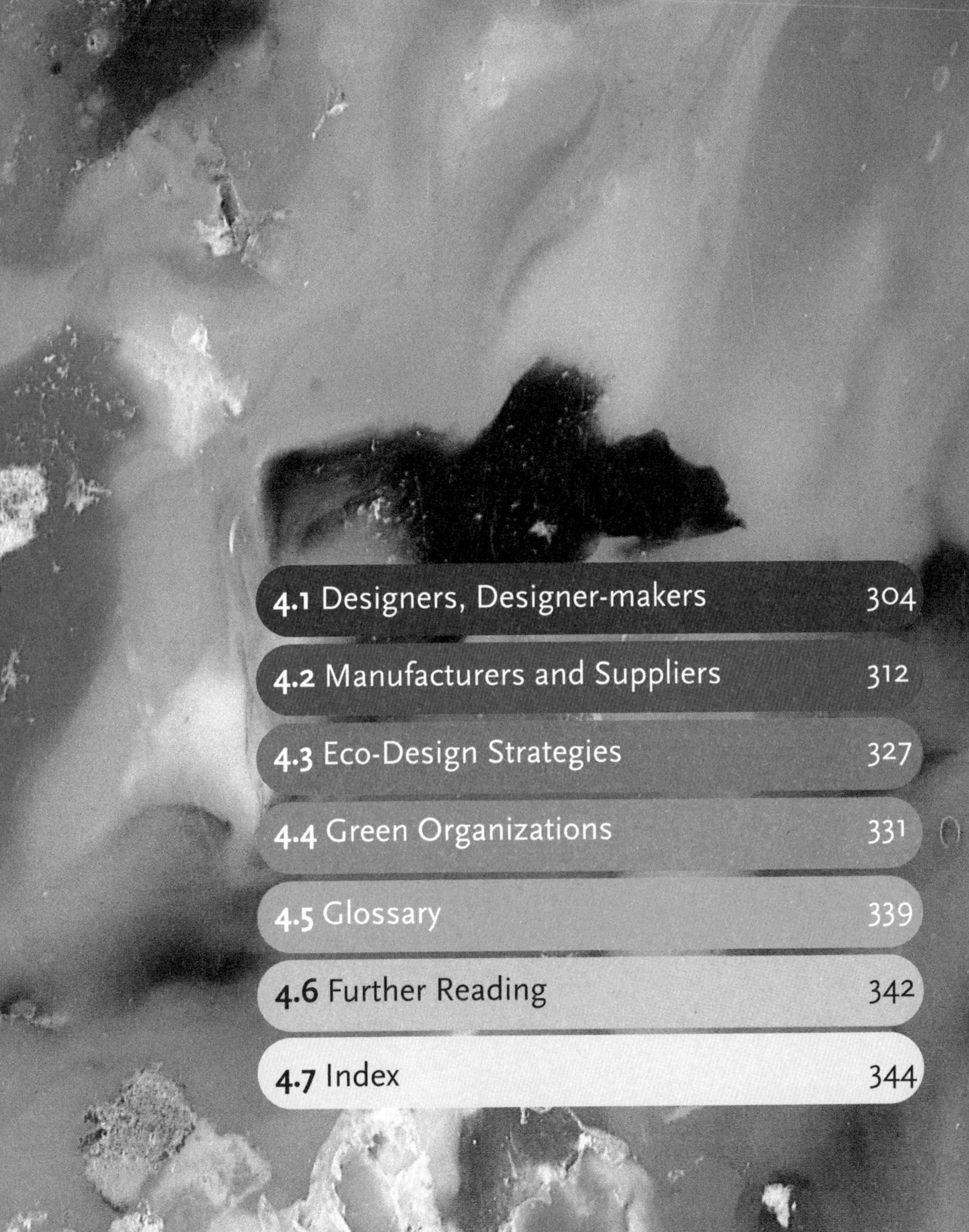

Abbate Cinzia
for the Italian Energy Authority: Officine di Architettura di Cinzia Abbate
Piazza S. Anastasia 3
00186 Rome, Italy
T +39 (0)6 679 6498
F +39 (0)6 697 83038
E cinzia.abbate@flashnet.it

Ackon, Gabriele
see David Zyne Productions, UK

Ad Rem Design
Industriestrasse 25
CH 3076 Worb, Switzerland
T +41 (0)31 832 07 10
F +41 (0)31 832 07 14

AeroVironment
Corporate HQ
825 S. Myrtle Dr.
Monrovia, CA 91016, USA
T +1 626 357 9983
F +1 626 359 9628
www.aerovironment.com

Akeler Developments plc
20 Berkeley Square
London W1X 5HD, UK
T +44 (0)20 7864 1800
F +44 (0)20 7864 1801/2
www.akeler.co.uk

Alaska Center for Appropriate Technology
851 E. West Point Drive
#206
Wasilla, AK 99654, USA

Amato, John; Meta Morf Design
2700 4th Avenue South
Seattle, WA 98134, USA
T +1 206 903 6332
F +1 206 223 0853
E colin@metamorfdesign.com

Andringa, Jacqueline
Design Academy Eindhoven
Emmasingel 14
PO Box 2125
5600 CC Eindhoven
Netherlands
T +31 (0)40 239 3939
F +31 (0)40 239 3940
E info@designacademy.nl
www.designacademy.nl

Anthologie Quartett
49152 Bad Essen, Germany
T +49 (0)5472 94090
F +49 (0)5472 940940
www.anthologiequartett.de

Apotheloz, Christophe
Industrial Designer
Lörgernstrasse 27
CH 8037 Zurich, Switzerland
T +41 (0)1 361 51 47
F +41 (0)1 361 51 97

Arai, Junichi
see Nuno Corporation

Arosio, Pietro
Studio Pietro Arosio
Via Gaetano Giardino 2/A
20053 Muggio (MI)
Italy
T +39 (0)39 793 237
F +39 (0)39 278 1088
E studio@pietroarosio.it

Arzuaga, Amaya
Irun Km 2025
09340 Lerma Burgos
Madrid, Spain
E info@amayaarzuaga.com
www.amayaarzuaga.com

Atfield, Jane
244 Grays Inn Road
London WC1X 8JR, UK
T +44 (0)20 7278 6971
F +44 (0)20 7833 0018

Azumi, Shin and Tomoko
Ground Floor
953 Finchley Road
London NW11 7PE, UK
T +44 (0)20 8731 9057
F +44 (0)20 8731 7496
E shin.tomoko.azumi@nifty.ne.jp
http://member.nifty.ne.jp/AZUMI/

Baccarne Design
Baccarne bvba
Gentbruggekouter
9050 Gent, Belgium
T +32 (0)9 232 44 21
F +32 (0)9 232 44 30
E baccarne@planet_internet.be

Bakker, Erik
Design Academy Eindhoven
Emmasingel 14
PO Box 2125
5600 CC Eindhoven
Netherlands
T +31 (0)40 239 3939
F +31 (0)40 239 3940
E info@designacademy.nl
www.designacademy.nl

Bally, Boris
Atelier Boris Bally
The Rug Building
3421 Bigelow Blvd
Pittsburgh, PA 15213
USA
T +1 412 682 8118
F +1 412 682 7244
E Bad4Borr@aol.com

Ban, Shigeru
5-2-4 Matsubara Ban Bldg
1Fl, Setagaya
Tokyo 156, Japan
T +81 (0)3 3324 6760
F +81 (0)3 3324 6789
www.dnp.co.jp/millennium/sb/van.html

Bansod, Abhijit
Titan Industries Ltd
Tower A, Golden Enclave
Airport Road
Bangalore 560017, India
T +91 80 526 8551

Bär + Knell
7 Untere Turmgasse
74206 Bad Wimpen
Germany
T +49 (0) 7063 6891
F +49 (0) 7063 6980
E Baerknell@aol.com
www.baer-knell.de

Barlow-Lawson, Stephen
Ground Support Equipment (US) Ltd
11 Broadway, Room 1010
New York, NY 10004, USA
T 888 302-DESK/
+1 212 809 4323
F +1 212 809 4324
E steve@biomorph.com
www.biomorphdesk.com

Baroli, Luigi
c/o Baleri Italia
Via F. Cavallotti 8
20122 Milan, Italy
T +39 (0)2 76 01 46 72
F +39 (0)2 76 01 44 19
E info@baleri-italia.com

Bartsch Design
Industrial Design GbR
Philipp-Müller-Strasse 12
23966 Wismar
Germany
T +49 (0)3841 758 160
F +49 (0)3841 758 161

Bergne, Sebastian
Bergne Design for Manufacture
2 Ingate Place
London SW8 3NS
UK
T +44 (0)20 7622 3333
F +44 (0)20 7622 3336
E bergne.dfm@mailbox.co.uk

Berkowitz, Adam
c/o Arbor Vitae (see p. 312)
www.time.com/time/reports/environment/heroes/gallery

Bernabei, Rina
52 Regent Street
Paddington, NSW 2021
Australia

Bernard Kerr and Pejack Campbell
c/o Solar Cookers International
1919 21st St, Suite 101
Sacramento, CA 95814
USA
T +1 916 455 4498
F +1 916 455 4498
E sbci@igc.apc.org
www.solarcooking.org

Bernett, Jeffrey
c/o Cappellini Arte/Capellini SpA (see p. 314)

Berthier, Marc
Design Plan Studio
141 Bd St Michel
75005 Paris
France
T +33 (0)143 26 49 97
F +33 (0)143 26 54 62
E dpstudio@wanadoo.fr

Besse, Hedda
see IDEO Product Development for BP Solar International

BEST
Büro für Produktgestaltung
Am Brögel 19
42283 Wuppertal
Germany
T +49 (0)202 88 595
F +49 (0)202 899 355

Bey, Jurgen
Passerelsstraat 44A
13023 ZD Rotterdam 1
Netherlands
T +31 (0)10 425 8792
F +31 (0)10 425 9437
E bey@luna.nl

Bill Dunster Architects
Zedfactory
Hope House
Molember Road
East Molesey
Surrey KT8 9NH, UK
T +44 (0)20 8339 1242
F +44 (0)20 8339 0429
E bill.dunster@btinternet.com
www.zedfactory.com

BioRegional Development Group
The Ecology Centre
Honeywood Walk
Carshalton
Surrey SM5 3NX, UK
T +44 (0)20 8773 2322
F +44 (0)20 8773 2878
E info@bioregional.com
www.bioregional.com

Blanca, Oscar Tusquets
c/o Escofet 1886 SA
Ronda Universitat 20
E 08007 Barcelona, Spain
T +34 (0)93 318 5050
F +34 (0)93 412 4465
E escofet@escofet.com
www.escofet@escofet.com

Blejer, Danilea, and Bostelmann, Saskia
148 Salvador Arditti
Sierra Chalchihie 175
IBIsA 501
Lomas de Cahpultepec C.P.
11000 Mexico City, Mexico

Boeri, Cini
c/o Fiam Italia SpA
Via Ancona 1/B
61010 Tavullia, Pesoro, Italy
T +39 (0)721 200 51
F +39 (0)721 202 432
E fiam@fiamitalia.it
www.fiamitalia.it

Boner, Jörg
N2 Switzerland
T/F +41 (0)61 693 4015
E n2@n2design.ch
www.n2design.ch

Boontje, Tord
tranSglass, Studio 19
33 Rushworth Street
London SE1 ORB, UK
T/F +44 (0)20 7261 9315

Bredahl, Pil, and Risell, Liselotte
Denmark
E pilbredahl@get2net.dk

Bristow, Stuart
c/o Designed to a 't' Ltd
11 Maxwell Gds
Orpington
Kent BR6 9QR, UK
T +44 (0)1689 831 400
F +44 (0)1689 609 301
www.d2at.demon.co.uk

Broess, Alfons
Design Academy Eindhoven
Emmasingel 14
PO Box 2125
5600 CC Eindhoven
Netherlands
T +31 (0)40 239 3939
F +31 (0)40 239 3940
E info@designacademy.nl
www.designacademy.nl

Brown, Julian
Studio Brown
6 Princes Buildings
George Street
Bath BA1 2ED, UK
T +44 (0)1225 481 735
F +44 (0)1225 481 737
E julian@studiobrown.com

Buchner Design Studio
1030 Quesada Avenue
San Francisco, CA 94124, USA

Burkhardt, Roland
c/o Sunways Gesellschaft
für Solartechnik mbH
Macairestrasse 5
78467 Konstanz, Germany
T +49 (0)7531 99677 0
F +49 (0)7531 99677 10
E info@sunways.de
www.sunways.de

Büro für Form
Hans-Sachs-Strasse 12
80469 Munich, Germany
T +49 (0)89 2694 9000
F +49 (0)89 2694 9002
E meek@bürofürform.de
www.bürofürform.de

Büro für Produktgestaltung
Brendstrasse 83
75179 Pforzheim, Germany
T +49 (0)7231 442 115
E f-neubert@s-direktnet.de

Cahen, Antoine
Les Ateliers du Nord/
Antoine Cahen
Pl. du Nord 2
CH 1005 Lausanne
Switzerland
T +41 (0)21 320 58 07
F +41 (0)21 320 58 43
E antoine.cahen@atelierdunord.ch

Campana, Fernando and Humberto
Campana Objetos Ltda
Rua Barão de Tatui 219
São Paulo 01226030
Brazil
T +55 (0)11 825 3 408
+55 (0)11 366 7 4317
F +55 (0)11 825 3408

Carrasco, Pedro
Rua da Liberdade 37
10 Esq 2800
Cova da Piedade, Portugal

Chadwick, Don, and Stumpf, Bill
Herman Miller, Inc.
855 East Main Ave
PO Box 302
Zeeland, MI 49464-0302, USA
www.hermanmiller.com

Chalayan, Hussain
Studio B, 1st Floor
71 Endell Street
London WC2H 9AJ, UK
F +44 (0)20 7240 5220

Champian, Brian
c/o International Design
Resource Awards (IDRA)
Design Resource Institute
7406A Greenwood Avenue
Seattle, WA 98177, USA
T +1 206 289 0949
F +1 206 789 3144
www.designresource.org

Clerkin, Carl
Domestic Hardware
F1 2-4 Southgate Road
London N1 3JJ, UK
T/F +44(0)20 7249 2021

Coates, Nigel
Branson Coates Architecture
23 Old Street
London EC1V 9HL, UK
T +44 (0)20 7490 0343
F +44 (0)20 7490 0320

Colwell, David
c/o Trannon Furniture
Limited
Chilhampton Farm
Wilton, Salisbury
Wilts SP2 OAB, UK
T +44 (0)1722 744 577
F +44 (0)1722 744 477
E info@trannon.com
www.trannon.com

Connell, Christopher
c/o MAP (Merchants of
Australia Products) Pty Ltd
570 Chapel Street
Sth Yarra, Melbourne
Victoria 3141, Australia

Constansia, Gonnie
Design Academy Eindhoven
Emmasingel 14
PO Box 2125
5600 CC Eindhoven
Netherlands
T +31 (0)40 239 3939
F +31 (0)40 239 3940
E info@designacademy.nl
www.designacademy.nl

Conti, Jean-Remi
Design Academy Eindhoven
Emmasingel 14
PO Box 2125
5600 CC Eindhoven
Netherlands
T +31 (0)40 239 3939
F +31 (0)40 239 3940
E info@designacademy.nl
www.designacademy.nl

Corkran, Julius T, and Harp, Alan
Center for Rehabilitation
Technology
College of Architecture
Georgia Institute of
Technology
USA

Cramer, Dan
Golden Valley, Minnesota
c/o International Design
Resource Awards (IDRA)
Design Resource Institute
7406A Greenwood Avenue
Seattle, WA 98177, USA
T +1 206 289 0949
F +1 206 789 3144
www.designresource.org

Culpepper, Michael
Michael Culpepper
Architect
2216 West Addison Street
Chicago, IL 60618, USA

da Silva, Ronaldo Edson
c/o Papa-papel, Brazil

De Denktank
(Design Studio) Rotterdam
Netherlands

de Haas, Marit
c/o Design Academy
Eindhoven
Emmasingel 14
PO Box 2125
5600 CC Eindhoven
Netherlands
T +31 (0)40 239 3939
F +31 (0)40 239 3940
E info@designacademy.nl
www.designacademy.nl

De Jonghe, Marc
Orso Design
Antwerp, Belgium
www.orso.be

de Klerk, Sander
c/o Design Academy
Eindhoven
Emmasingel 14
PO Box 2125
5600 CC Eindhoven
Netherlands
T +31 (0)40 239 3939
F +31 (0)40 239 3940
E info@designacademy.nl
www.designacademy.nl

de Leede, Annelies
Oak Product Design,
Netherlands
c/o International Design
Resource Awards (IDRA)
Design Resource Institute
7406A Greenwood Avenue
Seattle, WA 98177, USA
T +1 206 289 0949
F +1 206 789 3144
www.designresource.org

Deka Research & Development (USA)
www.indetech.com

Design Academy Eindhoven
Emmasingel 14
PO Box 2125
5600 CC Eindhoven
Netherlands
T +31 (0)40 239 3939
F +31 (0)40 239 3940
E info@designacademy.nl
www.designacademy.nl

Designed to a 't'
11 Maxwell Gardens
Orpington
Kent BR6 9QRUK
T +44 (0)1689 831 400
F +44 (0)1689 609 301
www.d2at.demon.co.uk

Designteam, Hameln
c/o Vorwerk & Co.
Teppichwerke GmbH
& Co. KG
Kulhmanstrasse 11
31785 Hameln
Germany
T +49 (0)5151 103 0
F +49 (0)5151 103 377
www.vorwerk-teppich.de

Deuber, Christian
N2 Büro
Breisacherstr. 64
CH 4057 Basel, Switzerland
T +41 (0)61 693 4011

Ditzel, Nanna
c/o Fredericia Furniture A/S
Treldevej 183
7000 Fredericia, Denmark
T +45 (0)75 92 33 44
F +45 (0)75 92 38 76
E ml@fredericia.com
www.fredericia.com

Dixon, Robert
c/o Advanced Vehicle Design
L&M Business Park
Norman Road
Altrincham, Cheshire
WA14 4ES, UK
T +44 (0)161 928 5575
F +44 (0)161 928 5585
E sales@windcheetah.co.uk
www.windcheetah.co.uk

Dixon, Tom
c/o Cappellini
Arte/Capellini SpA
Via Marconi 35
22060 Arosio, Italy
T +39 (0)31 759 111
F +39 (0)31 763 322/763 333
E cappellini@cappellini.it
www.cappellini.it

Dolphin-Wilding, Julienne
34 Cecil Rhodes House
Goldington Street
London NW1 1UG, UK
T +44 (0)20 7380 0950
F +44 (0)20 7252 1778
E dolphin@julienne.demon.co.uk
www.julienne.demon.co.uk

Domus Academy
Via Savona 97
20144 Milan
Italy

Dougan, Brian
Dept of Industrial Design
University of Southwest
Louisiana
Lafayette, Louisiana, USA
c/o International Design
Resource Awards (IDRA)
Design Resource Institute
7406A Greenwood Avenue
Seattle, WA 98177, USA
T +1 206 289 0949
F +1 206 789 3144
www.designresource.org

Dougherty, Brian
Celery Design Collaborative
2315B Prince Street
Berkeley, CA 94715
USA
T +1 510 649 7155
T +1 510 848 6716
E info@celerydesign.com
www.celerydesign.com

Douglas-Miller, Edward
c/o Remarkable Pencils Ltd
Worlds End Studios
134 Lots Road
London SW10 ORJ
UK
T +44 (0)20 7351 4333
T +44 (0)20 7352 4729
E info@re-markable.com

Dranger, Jan
Dranger Design AB
Stora Skuggans Väg 11
115 42 Stockholm
Sweden
T +46 (0)8 153 929
F +46 (0)8 153 926
E jan.dranger@newsab.se

Droog Design
Keizersgracht 518
1017 EK Amsterdam
Netherlands
T 031 (0)20 626 9809
F 031 (0)20 638 8828
E gbakker@xs4all.nl

Dryden Research Center
USA
www.dfre.nasa.gov

Dyson, James
Dyson Appliances
c/o 20 Shawfield Street
London SW3 4BD, UK
T +44(0)20 7883 8244
www.dyson.com

E+Z Design
at Retrospace
1824 Grand Blvd
Kansas City, MO 64108, USA

Ecke: Design
Albrecht Ecke
Am Neuen Markt 10
14467 Potsdam, Germany
T +49 (0)331 280 3885
F +49 (0)331 280 3890
E eckedesign@snafu.de
www.eckedesign.de

El Ultimo Grito
Studio 8
23-28 Penn Street
London N1 5DL, UK
T +44(0)20 7739 1009
F +44(0)20 7739 2009
E grito@btinternet.com

Enlund, Teo
c/o Simplicitas
Grevgatan 19
114 52 Stockholm, Sweden
T +46 (0)8 661 00 91
F +46 (0)8 661 00 97
www.simplicitas.se

Erik Krogh Design
Denmark
E erkr@dk-designskole.dk

Espmark, Erik
c/o Royal Institute
of Technology (KTH)
Nada
100 44 Stockholm
Sweden
www.nada.kth.se

Ettenheim Design (George Ettenheim)
41 Market Street
Venice, CA 90291, USA

Feilden Clegg Architects
Bath Brewery
Toll Bridge Road
Bath BA1 7DE, UK
T +44 (0)1225 852 545
F +44 (0)1225 852 528

Feo, Roberto
El Ultimo Grito
Studio 8
23-28 Penn Street
London N1 5DL, UK
T +44(0)20 7739 1009
F +44(0)20 7739 2009
E grito@btinternet.com

Fleetwood, Roy
Roy Fleetwood Ltd
Office for Design Strategy
1 St John's Innovation Park
Cowley Road
Cambridge CB4 4NS, UK
T +44 (0)1223 240 074
E roy.fleetwood@fleetwoodinc.com

FortuneCookies (Jacob Jürgensen Ravn)
Denmark
E jacob@fortunecookies.dk

Foster and Partners
Riverside Three
22 Hester Road
London SW11 4AN, UK
T +44 (0)20 7738 0455
www.fosterandparters.com

Fritsch, Antoine
c/o Hermès
28 Rue du Faubourg
St Honoré
75008 Paris, France
T +33 (0)1 42 65 03 37/
+33 (0)1 40 17 47 17

FrogDesign
Torstrasse 105-107
10119 Berlin
Germany
T +49 (0)30 41714 0
F +40 (0)30 41714 36
www.frogdesign.com

GAAN GmbH
Sonneggstrasse 76
CH 8006 Zurich
Switzerland
T +41 (0)1 363 52 00
F +41 (0)1 363 52 05
E info@gaan.ch
www.gaan.ch

Gardère, Adrien
Gardère Design
49 Rue au Maire
75003 Paris
France

Gasser, Danny and Michael Hort, Ben Sheperd and Quisinh Tran
c/o 5/60c Raglan Street
Mosman NSW 2088,
Australia

Gehry, Frank O.
Frank O. Gehry &
Associates Inc
1520-B Cloverfield
Boulevard
Santa Monica, CA 90404
USA
T +1 310 828 6088
F +1 310 828 2098

Girand, Ann and Champian, Brian
730 East 8th, #3
Moscow, ID 83843, USA

gmp-Architekten
von Gerkan Marg und Partner
Elbchaussee 139
22763 Hamburg, Germany
T +49 (0)40 88 151 0
F +49 (0)40 88 151 177
E hamburg-e@gmp-architekten.de
www.gmp-architekten.de

Grcic, Konstantin
Konstantin Grcic
Industrial Design
Schillerstrasse 40/11 Rgb
80336 Munich, Germany

Griffiths, Jason
Higher Tideford Cornworthy
Totnes, Devon
TQ9 7HL, UK
T +44 (0)1803 712 387
F +44 (0)1803 712 388

Gröne, Ralf and Dallas Grove
Palo Alto Products International
567 University Avenue
Palo Alto, CA 94301
USA
T +1 650 327 9444
F +1 650 327 9446

Grunert, Pawel
c/o Alicja Trusiewicz
Via Bramante 22/L
06100 Perugia, Italy
T/F +39 (0)75 572 6470
E alicjet@tin.it

Guixé, Martí
Calabria 252
8029 Barcelona, Spain
T/F +34 (0)93 322 5986
E info@guixe.com
www.guixe.com

Häberli, Alfredo, and Marchand, Christophe
c/o Danese srl/Alias srl
Via dei Videttei 2
Grumello del Monte
24064 Bergamo, Italy
T +39 (0)35 442 0240
F +39 (0)35 442 0996

Hatton, Pamela
58 Hardel Walk
London SW2 2QE, UK
T +44 (0)20 8674 9618

Hereford & Worcester County Council
Technical Services Department
County Hall
Spetchley Road
Worcester WR5 2NP, UK
T+44 (0)1905 766 422

Hermann, Anette, Designer MDD
Dampfærgevej 27-305
DK 2100 Copenhagen
Denmark
T/F +45 (0)35 55 11 64
E info@plana.nu
www.plana.nu

Hertz, David
SENSORY (design agency)
Syndesis, Inc.
2908 Colorado Ave
Santa Monica, CA 90403-3616, USA
T +1 310 829 9932
F +1 310 829 5641
www.syndesisinc.com

Heufler, Prof. Gerhard
Koröisistrasse 5
A 80101 Graz, Austria
T +43 (0)316 672 258
F +43 (0)316 672 258 4

Hofmann, Alfred
(Denmark)
c/o Fritz Hansen A/S
Fritz-Hansen UK
20-22 Rosebery Avenue
London EC1R 4SX, UK
T +44 (0)20 7837 2030
F +44 (0)20 7837 2040
E roh@fritzhansen.co.uk
www.fritzhansen.co.uk

Hoogendijk, Martin
c/o Droog Design
Keizersgracht 518
1017 EK Amsterdam
Netherlands
T +31 (0)20 62 69 809
F +31 (0)80 63 88 828
E gbakker@xs4all.nl

Hooke Forest (Construction) Ltd
Parnham House
Beaminster
Dorset DT8 3NA, UK
T +44 (0)1308 862 204
F +44 (0)1308 863 494
E info@hookepark.com
www.hookepark.com

Human Factors
c/o Oxo International
230 Fifth Avenue, 2nd floor
New York, NY 10001, USA
T +1 212 242 3333
F +1 212 242 3336

Hutasoit, Renaldi
c/o Meta Morf, Inc.
c/o Colin Reedy
2700 4th Avenue South
Seattle, WA 98134, USA
T +1 206 903 6332
F +1 206 223 0853
E colin@metamorfdesign.com
www.metamorfdesign.com

Hutten, Richard
52 Marconistraat
3029 AK Rotterdam
Netherlands
T +31 (0)10 477 0665
F +31 (0)10 425 7603
E reeel@planet.nl

IBM Personal Systems Group Design
IBM Corporation
3039 Cornwallis Road
Research Triangle Park
NC 27709, USA
T +1 919 254 8650
F +1 919 254 8385
E HDavid@us.ibm.com
www.ibm.com

Ichi, Yoshihiro
Industrial Design Division
Minolta, Japan
www.minolta.com

IDEO Japan
413 Axis Building
5-17-1 Roppongi
Minato-ku, Tokyo, Japan
T +81 (0)3 5570 2664
F +81 (0)3 5570 2669
E kaoru@ideojapan.co.jp

IDEO Product Development
1033 University Place
Chicago, IL 60201, USA
T +1 847 570 4350
F +1 847 570 4351

IDEO Product Deveopment
Pier 28 Annex
The Embarcadero
San Francisco, CA 94105, USA
T +1 415 778 4700
F +1 415 778 4701
E jlevin@ideo.com

ijs designers
7 Edis Street
London NW1 8LG, UK
T +44 (0)20 7916 6708
F +44 (0)20 7916 6709

Independence Technology
a Johnson & Johnson Company, USA
www.indetech.com

Interform Design
Am Wenderwehr 3
38114 Braunschweig
Germany
T +49 (0) 531 233 7810
www.interform-design.de

Ito, Setsu/Studio I.T.O. Design
Via Brioschi 54
20141 Milan, Italy
T/F +39 (0)2 8954 6007
E setsuito@micronet.it

Jacobs, Camille
100 Taman Nakhoda
Villa delle Rose
257793 Singapore
T/F +65 475 3581
E a_cordenier@pacific.net.sg
alain.cordenier@bbl.be

Jakobsen, Hans Sandgren
Færgevej 3
DK 8500 Grenaa
Denmark
T +45 (0)86 32 00 48
F +45 (0)86 32 48 03
E mail@hans-sandgren-jakobsen.com
www.hans-sandgren-jakobsen.com

Jam Design & Communications Ltd
1 Goods Way, 2nd Floor
London NW1 1UR, UK
T +44 (0)20 7278 3263
F +44 (0)20 7278 5567
E jamdesign@compuserve.com

Jerome, Mike
c/o Philips Electronics NV
Building HWD
PO Box 218
5600 MD Eindhoven
Netherlands
T +31 (0)40 275 9066
F +31 (0)40 275 9091
E annemieke.froger@philips.com
www.philips.com

John Makepeace and others
see Hooke Forest (Construction) Ltd, UK

Jongerius, Hella
Schietbaanlaan 75b
3021 LE Rotterdam
Netherlands
T +31 (0)10 477 0253
E jongeriuslab@hotmail.com

Jurinec, Ksenkja and Grupa Dizajnera
Grupa Dizajnera
Baruna Trenka 5
Zagreb, Croatia

Kant, Judith
c/o Design Academy Eindhoven
Emmasingel 14
PO Box 2125
5600 CC Eindhoven
Netherlands
T +31 (0)40 239 3939
F +31 (0)40 239 3940
E info@designacademy.nl
www.designacademy.nl

Karpf, Peter
Glentevej 8
3210 Vejby, Denmark
T +45 (0)48 70 63 73
F +45 (0)48 70 63 79

Kartono, Singh S
Aruna Arutala
P O Box 187
Temanggung 56200
Central Java, Indonesia

Katayanagi, Tomu (Japan)
c/o Fiam Italia SpA
Via Ancona 1/B
61010 Tavullia
Pesoro, Italy
T +39 (0)721 200 51
F +39 (0)721 202 432
E fiam@fiamitalia.it
www.fiamitalia.it

KFN Kaufmann Produkt GmbH
Sagerstrasse 4
A 6850 Dornbirn, Austria
T +43 (0)5572 26283
F +43 (0)5572 262834
E kfn.product@gmbh.vol.at

Kieboom, Nickie
c/o Design Academy Eindhoven
Emmasingel 14
PO Box 2125
5600 CC Eindhoven
Netherlands
T +31 (0)40 239 3939
F +31 (0)40 239 3940
E info@designacademy.nl
www.designacademy.nl

Killaars, Remko
c/o Design Academy Eindhoven
Emmasingel 14
PO Box 2125
5600 CC Eindhoven
Netherlands
T +31 (0)40 239 3939
F +31 (0)40 239 3940
E info@designacademy.nl
www.designacademy.nl

Klug, Ubald
33 Rue Croulebarbe
75013 Paris, France
T +33 (0)1 44 33 13 882
F +33 (0)1 45 35 31 54

Konings, Jan
c/o Droog Design
Keizersgracht 518
1017 EK Amsterdam
Netherlands
T +31 (0)20 626 9809
F +31 (0)20 638 8828
E gbakker@xs4all.nl

Korb & Korb
Schösslistrasse 36A
CH 5408 Ennetbaden
Switzerland
T +41 (0) 56 222 81 20

Kotkas, Aki
Hamentie 130E
00560 Helsinki, Finland
T +358 50 5879077
E akotkas@uiah.fi

Kuckuck, Henner
Nana Design
11–55 45th Avenue
Long Island City, NY 11101
USA

Kwakkel, Eric-Jan
c/o REEEL
52 Marconistrat
3029 AK Rotterdam
Netherlands
T +31 (0)10 925 4612
F +31 (0)10 925 7603

Laing, Patrick
ADAPT=REACT
57 Holmesdale Road
London N6 5TH, UK
T +44 (0)20 8374 6665
F +44 (0)20 8245 3153
E patrick.adapt-react@virgin.net

Landmark Design Switzerland
Glärnischstrasse 8
CH 8640 Rapperswil
Switzerland
T +41 (0)55 211 84 25
F +41 (0)55 211 84 28
E landmark.ch@bluewin.ch
www.landmark.nl

Les Ateliers Du Nord/Antoine Cahen
Pl. du Nord 2
CH 1005 Lausanne
Switzerland
T +41 (0)21 320 58 07
F +41 (0)21 320 58 43
E antoine.cahen@atelierdunord.ch

Lewis, David (UK)
c/o Vestfrost A/S
Spangsbjerg Møllevej 100
Postbox 2079
DK-6705 Esbjerg Ø, Denmark
T +45 (0)79 14 22 22
F +45 (0)79 14 23 55

Looker, Philip
c/o Plastics fth Industry Ltd
The Stables
Sandholme Mill
Commercial Street
Todmorden
Lancs OL14 5RH, UK
T +44(0)1706 817 784
F +44(0)1706 817 227
E plasfth@msn.com

Lovegrove, Ross
Lovegrove Studio X
21 Powis Mews
London W11 1JN, UK
T +44 (0)20 7229 7104
F +44 (0)20 7229 7032
E lovegroves_rmr@compuserve.com

Macchioni, Sergio/SMAC
Via Tombetto 40
37135 Verona, Italy
T/F +39 (0)45 8200 279
E smac@iol.it

Maier-Aichen, Hansjerg
Authentics artipresent GmbH
Max Eyth Strasse 30
71088 Holzerlingen
Germany
T +49 (0)7031 6805 0
F +49 (0)7031 6805 99
www.authentics.de

Marczynski, Mike
Business Lines Ltd
Harcourt Street
Walkden, Worsley
Manchester M28 3GN, UK
T +44 (0)1204 576 334
E info@checkpoint-safety.com
www.checkpoint-safety.com

Mari, Enzo
c/o Alessi SpA
Via Privata Alessi 6
28882 Crusinallo (VB), Italy
T +39 (0)323 868 611
F +39 (0)323 866 132
E pub@alessi.it

Marinho, Reginaldo (Brazil)
T +39 (0)338 124 6641
E inventor_br@hotmail.com

Marriott, Michael
Unit F2, 2-4,
Southgate Road
London N1 3JJ, UK
T/F +44 (0)20 7923 0323
E marriott.michael@virgin.net

Martin, Guy
Crown Studios
Old Crown Cottage
Greenham, Crewkerne
Somerset TA18 8QE, UK
T +44 (0)1308 868122

McCrady, Paul
AeroVironment
825 S. Myrtle Drive
Monrovia, CA 91016, USA
T +1 626 357 9983
F +1 626 359 9628
www.aerovironment.com

McDermott, Ruth
52 Regent Street
Paddington, NSW 2021
Australia

McDonagh, Julie
The Inner Tube Ltd
Unit B1, The Wren Centre
Westbourne Road
Emsworth, Hampshire, UK
T +44 (0)2392 433 433

McDonough Braungart Design Chemistry, LLC
401 East Market St, Suite 201
Charlottesville, VA 22902, USA
T +1 804 295 111
F +1 804 295 1500
E info@mbdc.com
www.mbdc.com

Meller Marcovicz, Gioia
102 Newark Street
London E1 2ES, UK
T +44 (0)20 7247 1282
F +44 (0)20 7375 2668
E gmm@mrac.demon.co.uk
www.mrac.demon.co.uk/designgmm

Miles, J R
c/o Retail Place Ltd
34A Campden Hill Gardens
London W8 7AZ, UK
T +44 (0) 20 7727 0486
F +44 (0) 20 7221 7012

Miyashita, Shin
c/o Sony Corporation Design Center
6-7-35 Kitashinagawa
Shinagawa-ku
Tokyo 141, Japan
T +81 (0)3 5448 7758
F +81 (0)3 5448 7822
www.sony.co.jp *and*
www.sony.co.uk

Moerel, Marre
182 Hester Street No. 13
New York, NY 10013, USA
T +1 212 219 8965
F +1 212 925 2371
E marremoerel@rcn.com

Moinat, Christophe
Pré-du-Marché 23
CH 1004 Lausanne
Switzerland
and
71 Northwold Road
London E5 8RN, UK
T +44 (0)20 7502 0511

Mollsjö, Carina
yxhammarsgatan 28
503 31 Borås, Sweden
T +46 (0) 33 10 27 25
E mollsjo@hotmail.com

Moore, Isabelle (UK)
22257 NE Inglewood
Hill Road
Redmond, WA 98053, USA

Morrison, Jasper (UK)
c/o Cappellini Arte/
Capellini SpA
Via Marconi 35
22060 Arosio, Italy
T +39 (0)31 759 111
F +39 (0)031 763 322/763 333
E cappellini@cappellini.it
www.cappellini.it

Mr Toyozo/Nifty Palmtop Users Group (Japan)
http://member.nifty.ne.jp/toyozou/palmpc/release_English.html
www.morphyone.org

N2 (Switzerland)
T/F +41 (0)61 693 4015
E n2@n2design.ch
http://www.n2design.ch

NASA (USA)
www.dfre.nasa.gov

Naur, Mikala
Gammel. Mont 37
DK 1117 Copenhagen
Denmark
T/F +45 (0)33 11 95 20
E mikalanaur@hotmail.com

Nervo, Paulo
c/o Design Academy
Eindhoven
Emmasingel 14
PO Box 2125
5600 CC Eindhoven
Netherlands
T +31 (0)40 239 3939
F +31 (0)40 239 3940
E info@designacademy.nl
www.designacademy.nl

Niemeir, Tim
c/o International Design
Resource Awards (IDRA)
Design Resource Institute
7406A Greenwood Avenue
Seattle, WA 98177, USA
T +1 206 289 0949
F +1 206 789 3144
www.designresource.org

Nijland, Paul
c/o Design Academy
Eindhoven
Emmasingel 14
PO Box 2125
5600 CC Eindhoven
Netherlands
T +31 (0)40 239 3939
F +31 (0)40 239 3940
E info@designacademy.nl
www.designacademy.nl

Oak Product Design
see de Leede, Annelies

Ohlsson, Daniel
cbi, BirgerJarlsgatan
Stockholm, Sweden
T +46 (0)8 611 5252
F +46 (0)8 611 7565
E daniel.ohlsson@konstfack.se

Øhre, Janne, and Hermann, Anette
MC Arkitekter a/s
Esplanaden 8 A
DK 1263 Copenhagen K
Denmark
T +45 (0)33 43 30 30
F +45 (0)33 43 30 40
E jo@mc-arch.dk

Oslapas, Arunas
c/o International Design
Resource Awards (IDRA)
Design Resource Institute
7406A Greenwood Avenue
Seattle, WA 98177, USA
T +1 206 289 0949
F +1 206 789 3144
www.designresource.org

Oxfam/Core Plastics
274 Banbury Road
Oxford OX2 7DZ, UK
T +44 (0)1865 311 311/312 498
www.oxfam.org.uk

Padrós, Emili
c/o Escola Superior de
Disseny Elisava
Carrer Ample 11-13
08002 Barcelona, Spain
T +34 (0)93 317 47 15
F +34 (0)93 317 83 53
E Elisava@seker.es

Palo Alto Products International
567 University Avenue
Palo Alto, CA 94301, USA
T +1 650 327 9444
F +1 650 327 9446

Paton, Charlie
Light Works Ltd
2A Greenwood Road
London E8 1AB, UK
T +44 (0)20 7249 3627
F +44 (0)20 7254 0306

Pellone, Giovanni, and Means, Bridget, Benza, Inc.
413 W 14 Street, #301,
New York, NY 10014, USA
T +1 212 243 4047
F +1 212 243 4689
E help@benzadesign.com
www.benzadesign.com

Pesavento, Luciano, and Pezzetta, Roberto
c/o Zanussi Electrolux
Electrolux Group
Environmental Affairs
105 45 Stockholm, Sweden
T +46 (0)8 738 76 66
F +46 (0)8 738 05 98
E environmental.affairs@electrolux.se

Philips, Stephen
Stephen Philips Design
52 Park Street, Thame
Oxon OX9 3HS, UK
T/F +44 (0)1844 214 897
E sphilips@madasafish.com

Philips Corporate Design
Building HWD
PO Box 218
5600 MD Eindhoven
Netherlands
T +31 (0)40 275 9066
F +31 (0)40 275 9091
E annemieke.fröger@philips.com

Philips Lighting BV
Haarmanweg 25
4538 AN Temeuzen
Netherlands
T +31 (0)115 684 318
F +31 (0)115 684 448
E rene.abein@philips.com

Pillet, Christopher (France)
c/o Cecotti Aviero SpA
Viale Sicilia 4
Cascina 56021, Pisa, Italy

Polvara, Giulio
c/o Kartell SpA
Via delle Industrie 1
Naviglio, 20082 Milan, Italy
T +39 (0)2 90 001 21
F +39 (0)2 90 533 16
www.kartell.it

Porsche, F A (Porsche Design Management GmbH & Co. KG)
Giselakai 37
A 5020 Salzburg, Austria
T +43 (0)662 887 4880
E office@porsche-design.com
www.porsche-design.com

Premsela & Vonk
Nieuwe Herengracht 89
1018 VR Amsterdam
Netherlands
T +31 (0)20 626 20 30

Pret à Porter
Paris, France
E comdept@pretparis.com
www.pretaporter.com

Priestman, Paul
Priestman Goode
4 & 5 Broadstone Place
London W1H 3FJ, UK
T +44 (0)20 7935 6665
F +44 (0)20 7935 0668
E design@priestmangoode.com
www.priestmangoode.com

Prins Dokkum BV
Rondweg 35
PO Box 4
9100 AA Dokkum
Netherlands
E prinsdokkum@niv-webhosting.com
www.prins-dokkum.nl

Produkt Entwicklung Roericht
c/o Wilkhahn GmbH & Co.
Postfach 2035
31844 Bad Münder, Germany
T +49 (0)5042 9990
F +49 (0)5042 999 226
E info@wilkhahn.de
www.wilkhahn.com

PROFORM Design
Lener + Rossler +
Hohannismeier Gbr
Seehalde 16
71364 Winnenden, Germany
T +49 (0)7195 919100
F +49 (0)7195 919108
E proform_design@t-online.de
www.industriedesign.com

Puotila, Ritva
Finland
c/o Woodnotes Oy
Tallberginkatu 8
00180 Helsinki
Finland
T +358 694 2200
F +358 694 2221
E woodnotes@woodnotes.fi
www.woodnotes.fi

R+r Sustainable Design
610 Wilson Street #5
Lafayette, LA 70503
USA

Reedy, Colin
Metamorf Design
2700 4th Avenue South
Seattle, WA 98134
USA
T +1 206 903 6332
F +1 206 223 0853
E colin@metamorfdesign.com

Remy, Tejo
Netherlands
c/o Droog Design
Keizersgracht 518
1017 EK Amsterdam
Netherlands
T +31 (0)20 62 69 809
F +31 (0)20 63 88 828
E gbakker@xs4all.nl

Rogers, Mark
BUT
81 Lothair Road North
London N4 1ER, UK
T +44 (0)20 8341 7776

Ruano, Maria
c/o Bedrock Industries
Seattle, WA, USA

Sadler, Marc
see Domus Academy, Italy, and American Hardwoods Export Council, USA

Sams Design
103 Friern Barnet Road
London N11 3EU, UK
T +44 (0)20 8361 8845
F +44 (0)20 8361 4305
E info@samsdesign.co.uk

Sanders, Mark
c/o Roland Plastics
Strida Limited
Wickham Market
Woodbridge
Suffolk IP13 0QZ, UK
T +44 (0)1728 747 777
F +44(0)1728 748 222
E strida@rolandplastics.co.uk

Sandham, John, and Lewis, Stan
c/o Lew San Limited
3 Sutton Gardens
Hornchurch
Essex RM12 4LD, UK
T +44 (0)1708 473 842
F +44 (0)1708 524 389
E stmate@dircon.co.uk
www.stairmate.co.uk

Sant, Roy
67 Wilberforce Road
London N4 2SP, UK
T/F +44 (0)20 7704 1592

Schneider, Wulf, Prof., and Partners
Schellbergstrasse 62
70188 Stuttgart, Germany

Schreuder, Hans
MOY Concept & Design
Arnhem, Netherlands
E info@moy.nl

Seiko Epson Corporation
(Japan)
www.epson.co.jp/e/

Seymour Powell Limited
The Chapel
Archel Road
London W14 9QH, UK
T +44 (0)20 7381 6433
F +44 (0)20 7381 9081
E design@seymourpowell.co.uk

Shetka, Stanley
All Paper Recycling, Inc.
10247 40th Street West
Webster, MN 55088, USA

Shiotani, Yasushi
c/o Canon, Inc.
Design Centre
3-30-2 Shimomaruko
Ota-ku, Tokyo 146-8501
Japan
T +81 (0)3 3758 2111
F +81 (0)3 5482 9711
E fukujr@drc.canon.co.jp

Shumacher, Sheri
Topos
426 N. Gay Street
Auburn, AL 36830, USA

Simmons, Roland
PO Box 3396
Santa Rosa, CA 95402, USA

Smart Design in co-development with Oxo International
Oxo International
230 Fifth Avenue, 2nd Floor
New York, NY 10001, USA
T +1 212 242 3333
F +1 212 242 3336
E info@oxo.com
www.oxo.com

Smith, Janice
University of Kansas
Art and Design Building
Room 300,
Lawrence, KS 66045, USA

Solar Century Holdings Ltd
Unit 5, Sandycombe Centre
1-9 Sandycombe Road
Richmond, Surrey, UK
T +44 (0)870 735 8100
F +44 (0)870 735 8101
E jl@solarcentury.co.uk
www.solarcentry.co.uk

Southampton Innovations Limited
University of Southampton
Highfield, Southampton
Hampshire SO17 1BJ, UK
T +44 (0)23 8059 2035
F +44 (0)23 8059 3585
E info@sil-uk.com
www.southamptoninnovations.com

Stachowicz, Wojtek
2416 54th Place SW #15
Seattle, WA 98116, USA

Starck, Philippe
Agence Philippe Starck
27 Rue Pierre Poli
92130 Issy-les-Moulineaux
France
T +33 (0)1 41 08 82 82
F +33 (0)1 41 08 96 65
E starck@starckdesign.com
www.philippe-starck.com

Stark, Herbert, Dr, Kopf AG
Stutzenstrasse 6
72172 Sulz-Borgfelden
Germany
T +49 (0)7454 75285
E h.stark@kopf-ag.de
www.kopf-ag.de

Startup, Jasper
Startup Design, No. 4
126A Albion Road
London N16 9PA, UK
T +44 (0)20 7923 1223
E jasper@startupdesign.co.uk

Staton, John M
Anderson Design Associates, Inc.
175 New Britain Ave
Plainville, CT 06062, USA

Steinberg, Erez, and Giasullo, Gia
Studio eg
2431 Peralta Street
Suite 2437A
Oakland, CA 94607, USA

Steinmann, Peter, and Schmid, Herbert
c/o Atelier Alinea AG
Zähringerstrasse 14
CH 4007 Basel
Switzerland
T +41 (0)61 690 97 97
F +41 (0)61 690 97 90

Stichting Art Depot
Frans Halsstraat 3
5062 LJ Oisterwijk
Netherlands

Sugasawa, Mitsumasa
(Japan)
E suga@tendo-mokko.co.jp

Suppanen, Ilkka
Studio Ilkka Suppanen
Punavuorenkatu 1 A 7 b
00120 Helsinki, Finland
T +358 9622 78737
F +358 9622 3093
E suppanen@kolumbus.fi

Sylvania Design Team
Sylvania Lighting International
20 Route de Pré-Bois
1215 Geneva 15
Switzerland
T +41 (0)22 717 0895
www.sylvania.com

Tam, Roy
c/o Trannon Furniture Limited
Chilhampton Farm
Wilton, Salisbury
Wilts SP2 0AB, UK
T +44 (0)1722 744 577
F +44 (0)1722 744 477
E info@trannon.com
www.trannon.com

Teams Design
Hollwitzstrasse 1
73728 Esslingen, Germany

Teppich-Art-Team
Untere Gasse 1
CH 7012 Ferlsberg
Switzerland
T +41 (0)81 252 86 89

Thomas, Deborah
323(B) Grove Green Road
Leytonstone
London E11 4EB, UK

Thorp, Ian, and Morris, Steve
c/o Slough Rubber Company, UK
T +44 (0)1753 570 438

Thorpe, Clarkson, and Beukema, Steve
c/o Haworth, Inc.
One Haworth Center
Holland, MI 49423, USA
T +1 616 393 3000
www.haworth.com

Thun, Matteo
c/o Domus Academy
Via Savona 97
20144 Milan, Italy

Tilder, Henk
c/o Municipality of Almere, Flevoland, Netherlands

Titan Design Studio
see Bansod, Abhijit

Tolstrup, Nina
47 Warwick Mount
Montague Street
Brighton, East Sussex
BN2 1JY, UK
T/F +44 (0)1273 570 179
E tolstrup@studiomama.com
www.studiomama.com

Topen, Paul
c/o Designed to a 't' Ltd
11 Maxwell Gds, Orpington
Kent BR6 9QR, UK
T +44 (0)1689 831 400
F +44 (0)1689 609 301
www.d2at.demon.co.uk

Trachsel, Sonja
Av. de Jurigoz 2
CH 1006 Lausanne
Switzerland
T +41 (0)21 601 38 94

Trubridge, David
44 Margaret Avenue
Havelock North
New Zealand
T/F +64 (0)6 877 46 84
E trubridge@clear.net.nz
http://home.clear.net.nz/pages.trubridge

University of Eindhoven (Building Initiative Environmental Standards)
c/o Design Academy
Eindhoven
Emmasingel 14
PO Box 2125
5600 CC Eindhoven
Netherlands
T +31 (0)40 239 3939
F +31 (0)40 239 3940
E info@designacademy.nl
www.designacademy.nl

University of Technology Delft
Jaffalaan 9
2628 BX Delft, Netherlands

van de Voorde, Patrick
c/o Philips Lighting BV
Haarmanweg 25
4538 AN Temeuzen
Netherlands
T +31 (0)115 684 318
F +31 (0)115 684 448
E rene.abein@philips.com

van Maanen, Martijn
c/o Design Academy
Eindhoven
Emmasingel 14
PO Box 2125
5600 CC Eindhoven
Netherlands
T +31 (0)40 239 3939
F +31 (0)40 239 3940
E info@designacademy.nl
www.designacademy.nl

van Severen, Martin
Galgenberg 25
9000 Gent, Belgium
T +31 (0)2 92 33 89 99

VarioPac Disc Systems GmbH
Hangbaumstrasse 13
32257 Bünde, Germany
T +49 (0)5221 7684 17
F +49 (0)5221 7684 20
www.variopac.com

Varney, James
c/o International Design
Resource Awards (IDRA)
Design Resource Institute
7406A Greenwood Avenue
Seattle, WA 98177, USA
T +1 206 289 0949
F +1 206 789 3144
www.designresource.org

Veloland Schweiz
Stiftung Veloland Schweiz
Postfach 8275
CH 3001 Bern, Switzerland
T +41 (0)31 307 47 40
E info@veloland.ch
www.veloland.ch

Velthuizen, A J
European Design Centre
PO Box 6279
5600 HG Eindhoven
Netherlands
T +31(0) 40 848 4848
F +31(0) 40 848 4844
E info@edc.nl

Vink, Frits, Ing
Eusebiusbuitensingel 37
6828 NX Arnhem
Netherlands
T/F +31 (0)26 168 420
E vink.design@atagmail.nl

VK & C Partnership (Ian Cardnuff and Hamid von Koten)
2/2 248 Woodlands Road
Glasgow G3 6ND, UK
T/F +44 (0)141 332 2049

Vogelzang, Marije
c/o Design Academy
Eindhoven
Emmasingel 14
PO Box 2125
5600 CC Eindhoven
Netherlands
T +31(0)40 239 3939
F +31(0)40 239 3940
E info@designacademy.nl
www.designacademy.nl

Vuarnesson, Bernard
Sculptures-Jeux
18 Rue Domat
75005 Paris
France
T +33 (0)1 43 54 20 39
F +33 (0)1 43 54 83 32
E sculptures.jeux@wanadoo.fr

Walpole, Lois
100 Fairhurst Road
London E3 4EH, UK
T/F +44 (0)20 7515 6014

Wanders, Marcel
Van Diemenstraat 296
1013 CR Amsterdam
Netherlands
T +31 (0)20 422 1339
F +31 (0)20 422 7519

Wannet, Edwin
c/o Design Academy
Eindhoven
Emmasingel 14
PO Box 2125
5600 CC Eindhoven
Netherlands
T +31 (0)40 239 3939
F +31 (0)40 239 3940
E info@designacademy.nl
www.designacademy.nl

Warren, William
ww.modcons
Units 2b + 2c
Vanguard Court
36 Peckham Road
London SE5 8QT, UK
T/F +44 (0)20 7708 4154

WeLL Design Associates
Huis ter Heideweg 56
3705 LZ Zeist
Netherlands
T +31 (0)30 692 5544
E info@welldesign.nl
www.welldesign.nl

Wettstein, Robert A
Structure Design
Josefstrasse 188
CH 8005 Zurich, Switzerland
T +41 (0)1 272 9725
F +41 (0)1 272 0717
E robert.wettstein@gmx.ch
www.change.to/comfort

Wiegand, Lorenz
Pool Products
Metzerstrasse 19
10405 Berlin, Germany
T +49 (0)30 440 555 16
E POOL-products@t-online.de

Wiesendanger, Köbi
Avant de Dormir
Via Turato 3
20121 Milan, Italy
T +390 (0)2 659 9990
F +390 (0)2 657 1058
E marina wiesendanger marina@avantdedormir.com

Willat, Boyd
see Willat Writing Instruments

Williamson, Damian
Björneborgsvägen 13
122 63 Enskede
Stockholm, Sweden
T +44 (0)20 8874 4046 (UK)
T +46 (0)8 649 1131 (Stockholm)

Wilson, Neil
180 Sackville Road
Heaton
Newcastle-upon-Tyne
NE6 5TD, UK
T/F +44 (0)191 224 3850

Wurz, Gerard
Teschniergasse 17
A 1170 Vienna, Austria
T +43 (0)407 21 25

Yamanaka, Kazuhiro
27 Burnley Road
London NW10 1EE, UK
T +44 (0)20 8452 3018
E kaz@ma.kew.net

Yurkievich, Gaspard
(Paris) c/o Tencel
Acordis Fibres
(Holdings) Ltd, UK
www.acordis.com
www.tencel.com

Zanussi Industrial Design Centre (Italy)
Electrolux Zanussi
c/o AB Electrolux
Electrolux Group
Environmental Affairs
105 45 Stockholm
Sweden
T +46 (0)8 738 76 66
F +46 (0)8 738 05 98
E environmental.affairs@electrolux.se

Zbryk, Burges
c/o International Design
Resource Awards (IDRA)
Design Resource Institute
7406A Greenwood Avenue
Seattle, WA 98177, USA
T +1 206 289 0949
F +1 206 789 3144
www.designresource.org

Zillig, Michel
c/o Design Academy
Eindhoven
Emmasingel 14
PO Box 2125
5600 CC Eindhoven
Netherlands
T +31 (0)40 239 3939
F +31 (0)40 239 3940
E info@designacademy.nl
www.designacademy.nl

2pm Limited
2 Shelford Place
London N16 9HS
UK
T +44 (0)20 7923 0222
F +44 (0)20 7923 2467
www.2pm.co.uk

3M Deutschland GmbH
Carl-Schurz-Strasse 1
41453 Neuss
Germany
T +49 (0)2131 14 3461
F +49 (0)2131 14 3695
E DSTRUWE@mmm.com

ABG Ltd
Unit E7, Meltham Mills Rd
Meltham
West Yorkshire HD7 3AR
UK
T +44 (0)1484 852 096

Acadia Board Company
518 Iberia Parkway
New Iberia, LA 70563
USA
T +1 318 367 8542
E duracane@bellsouth.net

Acordis Speciality Fibres/Acordis Fibres (Holdings) Ltd (UK)
www.acordis.com
www.specialityfibres.com
www.tencel.com

Advanced Elastomer Systems L P
388 S. Main St
Akron, OH 44311
USA
T +1 800 305 8070
F +1 330 849 5599
E contact@aestpe.com
www.aestpe.com

Advanced Environmental Recycling Technologies, Inc.
801 N. Jefferson Street
PO Box 1237
Springdale, AR 72765
USA
T +1 501 750 1299
F +1 501 750 1322
E aertsales@sat.net
www.choicedek.com

Advanced Vehicle Design
L&M Business Park
Norman Road
Altrincham
Cheshire WA14 4ES, UK
T +44 (0)161 928 5575
F +44(0)161 928 5585
E sales@windcheetah.co.uk
www.windcheetah.co.uk

AEG Hausgeräte GmbH
Muggenhofer Strasse 135
90429 Nuremberg
Germany
T +49 (0)911 323 1/0
F +49 (0)911 323 2283/1770
E info@aeg.hausgeraete.de
www.aeg hausgeraete.de

aerodyn Energiesysteme GmbH
Provianthausstrasse 9
24768 Rendsburg
Germany
T +49 (0)4331 12750
F +49 (0)4331 127555

AeroVironment, Inc.
Corporate HQ
825 S. Myrtle Dr
Monrovia CA 91016
USA
T +1 626 357 9983
F +1 626 359 9628
www.aeroevironment.com

Aga-Rayburn
PO Box 30
Ketley, Telford
Shropshire TF1 4DD
UK
T +44 (0)1952 642 000
F +44 (0)1952 641 961
www.aga-rayburn.co.uk

Air Packaging Technologies, Inc.
25620 Rye Canyon Road
Valencia, CA 913555
USA
T +1 800 424 7269
F +1 661 294 2222
E info@airbox.com

Akzo Nobel Decorative Coatings AB
205 17 Malmö
Sweden
T +46 (0)40 35 50 00
F +46 (0)40 601 52 23

Alden & Ott
616 E. Brook Drive
Arlington Heights
IL 60005-4622
USA
T +1 800 552-INKS
F +1 708 956 6909
www.aldenottink.com

Alessi SpA
Via Privata Alessi 6
28882 Crusinallo (VB)
Italy
T +39 (0)323 868611
F +39 (0)323 866132
E pub@alessi.it

Alfred Kärcher GmbH & Co.
Alfred Kärcher Strasse 28-40
71364 Winnenden
Germany
T +49 (0)711 142310
F +49 (0)711 142981

Alinea Atelier, AG
Zähringerstrasse 14
CH 4007 Basel
Switzerland
T +41 (0)61 690 97 97
F +41 (0)61 690 97 90

All Paper Recycling, Inc.
502 4th Avenue NW
New Prague, MN 56071-1141
USA
T +1 612 758 6577
F +1 612 758 6751

Amasec Airfil
Unit 1, Colliery Lane
Exhall, Coventry
Warwickshire CV7 9NW
UK
T +44 (0)1203 367 994
F +44 (0)1203 644 325

American Excelsior Company
PO Box 5067
850 Ave H East
Arlington, TX 76011
USA
T +1 817 640 3563 *and*
T +1 800 777 7645
F +1 817 640 3570/1555
www.amerexcel.com

Ampair Ltd
17 Windermere Road
West End
Southampton
Hampshire SO18 3PE
UK
T +44 (0)23 80 474 243
F +44 (0)23 80 476 821
E interworld@cwcom.net

Amtico Company Ltd, The
Kingfield Road
Coventry
Warwickshire CV6 5AA
UK
T +44 (0) 24 7686 1400
F +44 (0) 24 7686 1552
Ecustomer.services
@amtico.co.uk
www.stratica.com
www.amtico.com

Anstalten Thorberg
Postfach 1
CH 3326 Krauchtal,
Switzerland
T +41 (0)34 411 1417
F +41 (0)34 411 0019

Arbor Vitae
see Berkowitz, Adam
Brooklyn, New York
USA

Arizona Fibers Marketing
9393 N. 90th #102-159
Scottsdale, AZ 85258-5040
USA
T +1 602 443 5615
F +1 602 443 4917

Armstrong World Industries, Inc.
2500 Columbia Ave
PO Box 3001
Lancaster, PA 17603
USA
T +1 717 397 0611
F +1 717 396 2787
www.armstrong.com

Artemide SpA
Via Bergamo 18
20010 Pregnana Milanese
Italy
F +39 (0)2 9359 0254

AstroPower, Inc.
Corporate HQ
461 Wyoming Road
Solarpark
Newark, DE 19716-2000
USA
T +1 302 366 0400
F +1 302 368 6087
E Sales@astropower.com
www.astropower.com

Auro Paints Ltd
Unit 2, Pamphillions Farm
Purton End, Debden
Saffron Walden
Essex CB11 3JT
UK
T +44 (0)1799 543 077
F +44 (0)1799 542 187
E sales@auroorganic.co.uk
www.auroorganic.co.uk

Auro Pflanzenchemie AG
Alte Frankfurter Str. 211
8122 Braunschweig
Germany
T +49 (0)531 2 81 41 41
F +49 (0)531 2 81 41 61
E info@auro.de
www.auro.de

Authentics artipresent GmbH
Max Eyth Strasse 30
71088 Holzerlingen
Germany
T +49 (0)7031 6805 0
F +49 (0)7031 6805 99
www.authentics.de

Avant de Dormir
Via Turati 3
20121 Milan, Italy
E info@avantdedormir.com
www.avantdedormir.com

Baccarne bvba
Baccarne Design
Gentbruggekouter
9050 Gent
Belgium
T +32 (0)9 232 44 21
F +32 (0)9 232 44 30
E baccarne@planet_internet.be

Baleri Italia
Via F. Cavallotti 8
20122 Milan, Italy
T +39 (0)2 76 01 46 72
F +39 (0)2 76 01 44 19
E info@baleri-italia.com

Bamboo Hardwoods, Inc.
3834 4th Ave South
Seattle, WA 98134, USA
T +1 206 264 2414/3610
E doug@bamboohardwoods.com
www.bamboohardwoods.com

Beacon Print Limited
Brambleside
Bellbrook Park
Uckfield
East Sussex TN22 1PL, UK
T +44 (0)1825 76811
F +44 (0)1825 7680342
E print@beaconpress.co.uk

Bedrock Industries
1401 West Garfield
Seattle, WA 98119, USA
T +1 206 283 7625
F +1 206 283 0497
E bedrockind@uswest.net
www.bedrockindustries.com

Benza, Inc.
413 W. 14 St #301
New York, NY 10014, USA
T +1 212 243 4047
F +1 212 243 4689
E help@benzadesign.com
www.benzadesign.com

BioChem Systems
3511 N. Ohio
Wichita, KS 67219
USA
T +1 316 838 4739
F +1 316 832 1211
E khobbs@biochemsys.com
www.biochemsys.com

Biocorp
2619 Manhattan
Beach Blvd
Redondo Beach, CA 90278
USA
T +1 888 206 5658
F +1 310 643 1622
E info@biocorpusa.com
www.biocorpusa.com

BioFab LLC/Pacific Gold Board
PO Box 990556
Redding, CA 96099-0556
USA
T +1 530 243 4032
F +1 530 244 3241
E info@ricestraw.com
www.strawboard.com

Bioshield Paint Company
1365 Rufina Circle
Santa Fe, NM 87505
USA
T +1 505 438 3448
F +1 505 438 0199
E edesignco@aol.com
www.bioshieldpaint.com

Biotec
Biologische
Naturverpackungen GmbH
Blinder Weg 30
Emmerich
PO Box 100220
Germany
T +49 (0)2822 92310
F +49 (0)2822 537265
E biotecgmbh@t-online.de

Blackwall Ltd
10 Glover Way
Parkside, Leeds
W. Yorks LS11 5JP, UK
T +44 (0)113 276 1646
F +44 (0)113 271 3083
E blackwall.ltd@virgin.net

BMW AG
BMW-Haus Petuelring 130
80788 Munich
Germany
T/F +49 (0)89 3820/
T +49 (0) 89 382 24272
E bmwinfo@bmw.de
www.bmw.com

BMW (GB) Ltd
Ellesfield Avenue
Bracknell
Berkshire RG12 8TA, UK
T +44 (0)1344 480 320
F +44 (0)1344 480 306
E press.bmw@bmwgroup.co.uk
www.press.bmwgroup.com

BOC
Michael House
47 Baker Street
London W1A 1DN, UK
T +44 (0)20 7935 4422

Body Shop International plc
Watersmead
Littlehampton
West Sussex BN17 6LS, UK
T +44 (0)1903 731 500
F +44 (0)1903 726 250
www.bodyshop.com

Bopp Leuchten GmbH
Postfach 1160
74835 Limbach
Germany
T +49 (0)62 87 92 06 0

BP Amoco plc
Britannic House
1 Finsbury Circus
London EC2M 7BA, UK
www.bp.com

BP Solar International
PO Box 191
Chertsey Road
Sunbury-on-Thames
Middlesex TW16 7XA, UK
T +44(0) 1932 779 543
F +44(0) 1932 762 686
www.bpsolar.com

BP Solarex
630 Solarex Court
Frederick, MD 21703, USA
T +1 301 698 4200
F +1 301 698 4201

BREE Collection GmbH & Co. KG
Gerberstrasse 3
30916 Isernhagen/Kirchorst
Germany
T +49 (0)5136 8976 0
F +49 (0)5136 8976 229
E bree.collection@bree.de
www.breecollection.de

Brompton Bicycle Ltd
Kew Bridge Distribution Centre
Lionel Road, Brentford
Middlesex TW8 9QR, UK
T +44 (0)20 8232 8484
F +44 (0)20 8232 8181
www.bromptonbicycle.co.uk

Brook Hansen
St Thomas Road
Huddersfield
West Yorkshire HD1 3DU, UK
T +44 (0)1484 422 150

Bruggli Produktion & Dienstleistung
Hofstrasse 5
CH 8590 Romanshorn
Switzerland
T +41 (0)71 466 94 94
F +41 (0)71 466 94 95

BTM International Ltd
Fosseway
Midsomer Norton
Bath BA3 4AY, UK
T +44 (0)1761 414 824
F +44 (0)1761 419 472
E btm@jarvis-uk.com
www.btminternational.co.uk

Buchner Design Studio
1030 Quesada Avenue
San Francisco, CA 94124
USA
T +1 415 822 7300

Buderus Heiztechnik GmbH
Sophienstrasse 30-32
35576 Wetzlar
Germany
T +49 (0)6441 418
F +49 (0)6441 456 02

Bulo Office Furniture
Industriezone Noord B6
2900 Mechelem, Belgium
T +32 (0)15 28 28 28
F +32 (0)15 28 28 29
E infor@bulo.be

Burch
c/o Domestic Growers Supply
Cave Junction, OR, USA
T +1 541 592 3615

Business Lines Ltd
Harcourt Street
Walkden, Worsley
Manchester M28 3GN
UK
T +44 (0)1204 576 334
E infor@checkpoint-safety.com
www.checkpoint-safety.com

BUT
81 Lothair Road North
London N4 1ER, UK
T +44 (0)20 8341 7776

Bute Fabrics Ltd
c/o Caro Communications
First Floor
49-59 Old Street
London EC1V 9HX, UK
T +44 (0)20 7251 9112
F +44 (0)20 7490 5757
E pr@carocom.demon.co.uk

Cabka Plast Kunststoffverarbeitungs GmbH
Neue Weinsteige 71
70180 Stuttgart, Germany
T +49 (0)711 2489980
F +49 (0)711 248998 18
E cabka@recover-group.de
www.recover-group.de

Campana Objetos
Rua Barão de Tatui 219
São Paulo 01226030
Brazil
T +55 (0)11 36 66 41 52
F +55 (0)11 82 53 408

Canon, Inc.
Design Centre
3-30-2 Shimomaruko
Ota-ku
Tokyo 146-8501
Japan
T +81 (0)3 3758 2111
F +81 (0)3 5482 9711
E fukujr@drc.canon.co.jp

Canon (UK) Limited
Woodhatch
Reigate, Surrey RH2 8BF
UK
T +44 (0)1737 220 000
F +44 (0)1737 220 022
www.canon.co.uk

Cappellini Arte/Capellini SpA
Via Marconi 35
22060 Arosio, Italy
T +39 (0)31 759 111
F +39 (0)31 763 322/763 333
E cappellini@cappellini.it
www.cappellini.it

Cargill Dow Polymers – EcoPLA Business Unit
PO Box 5698
Minneapolis
MN 55440-5698, USA
T +1 612 742 6194
F +1 612 475 6208
E Public_Relations@cargill.com
www.cargill.com

Carrington Performance Fabrics
Calder Works
Thornhill Road
Dewsbury
West Yorkshire
WF12 9QQ, UK
T +44 (0)1924 465 161
F +44 (0)1924 457 596
www.carrington-pf.co.uk

Ceccotti Collezioni srl
PO Box 90
Viale Sicilia 4
Cascina
56021 Pisa, Italy
T +39 (0)50 701 955
F +39 (0)50 703 970
E info@ceccotti.it
www.ceccotti.it

Celotex Ltd
Warwick House
27/31 St Mary's Road
Ealing, London W5 5PR, UK
T +44 (0)20 8579 0811
F +44 (0)20 8579 0106
www.celotex.co.uk

Centriforce Products– Chisholm Plastics Ltd
14-16 Derby Road
Liverpool
Merseyside L20 8EE
UK
T +44 (0)151 207 6221
F +44 (0)151 298 1319
E sales@centriforce.co.uk
www.centriforce.com

Centriforce Products – Plastic Recycling Ltd
86 Blackpole Trading Estate
Worcester
Worcs WR3 8SQ, UK
T +44 (0)1905 455 410
F +44 (0)1905 754 708
E sales@centriforce.co.uk
www.centriforce.com

Cerestar USA, Inc.
110 Indianapolis Blvd
Hammond
IN 46320-1019, USA
T +1 219 659 2000
F +1 219 473 6607
www.cerestar.com

Charles Lawrence Recycling Ltd
Jessop Way
Newark Industrial Estate
Newark, Nottinghamshire
NG24 2ER, UK
T +44 (0)1636 610 680
F +44 (0)1636 610 222
E recycling@clgplc.co.uk

Chicago Adhesive Products Company
4658 West 60th Street
Chicago, IL 60629, USA
T +1 773 581 1300

ClassiCon
8 Perchtingger Strasse
81379 Munich
Germany
E info@classicon.com
www.classicon.com

Clearvision Lighting Limited
Unit 2
Elliott Park Industrial Estate
Eastern Road
Aldershot
Hampshire GU12 4TF, UK
T +44 (0)1252 344 011
F +44 (0)1252 344 066
E sales@clearvisionlighting.co.uk

Clivus Multrum, Kingsley Clivus
Kingsley House
Woodside Road
Boyatt Wood Trading
Estate Eastleigh
Hampshire SO50 4ET, UK
T +44 (0)1703 615 680
F +44 (0)1703 642 613

Color Trends, Inc.
5129 Ballard Ave NW
Seattle, WA 98107
USA
T +1 206 789 1065

Columbia, USA/Comarco Wireless Technologies, Inc.
2 Crowell Street
Irvine, CA 92618, USA
T +1 949 599 7400
F +1 949 599 1415
E callinfo@comarco.com

Compak Systems Ltd
Toor Street
Gainsborough
Lincolnshire DN21 2EG, UK
T +44 (0)1427 616 927

Compaq Computer Corporation
PO Box 692000
Houston, TX 77269-2000
USA
T +1 281 370 0670
F +1 281 514 1740
www.compaq.com

Concord Lighting
Avis Way
Newhaven
East Sussex BN9 0ED, UK
T +44 (0)1273 515 811
F +44 (0)1273 512 688
E concord.intsales@sylvania-lighting.com

Corbin Motors, Inc.
2350 Technology Parkway
Hollister, CA 95023
USA
T + 1 831 635 1033
F +1 831 635 1039
www.corbinmotors.com

Corn Card International, Inc.
PO Box 239
Chapman, NE 68827
USA
T +1 308 946 3662
www.corncard.com

Correx Plastics
Madleaze Industrial Estate
Bristol Road
Gloucester
Gloucestershire, GL1 5SG, UK
T +44 (0)1452 316 500
F +44 (0)1452 300 436

Crane & Company
30 South Street
Dalton, MA 01226
USA
T +1 413 684 6495
www.crane.com

Crowe Building Products
116 Burris Street
Hamilton
ONT L8M 2Js, Canada
T +1 905 529 6818
F +1 905 529 1755
www.authentic-roof.com

Curtis Fine Papers
Guardsbridge
St Andrews
Fife KY16 0G9
UK
T +44 (0)1334 839 551
www.curtisfinepapers.com

Cutouts
11A Lower Boston Road
Hanwell
London W7 3SF, UK
T +44 (0)20 8567 2847
F +44 (0)20 8579 7374
E cutouts.london@virgin.net

Daimler Chrysler
Epplestrasse 225
70546 Stuttgart, Germany
T +49 (0)711 170
F +49 (0)711 17 222 44
E diaolog@daimlerchrysler.com
www.daimlerchrysler.com

Daimler Chrysler (Japan)
www.daimlerchrysler.co.jp

Daimler Chrysler UK Ltd
Tongwell
Milton Keynes
Bedfordshire MK15 8BA, UK
T +44 (0)1908 301 000
F +44 (0)1908 664 351
www.daimlerchrysler.co.uk

Daimler Chrysler Corporation
Auburn Hills, MI 48326-2766
USA
T +1 248 576 5741
F +1 248 576 4742
www.daimlerchrysler.com

Dalsouple Direct Limited
PO Box 140
Bridgewater
Somerset TA5 1HT
UK
T +44 (0)1984 667 233
F +44 (0)1984 667 366
E info@dalsouple.com

Dalton Lucerne Rare Fibres Ltd
The Homestead Farm
Bakestonedale Road
Potts Shrigley

Macclesfield
Cheshire SK10 5RU, UK
T +44 (0)1625 572 381
F +44 (0)1625 572 381

Danese srl
see Alias srl
Via dei Videttei 2
Grumello del Monte
24064 Bergamo, Italy
T +39 (0 35 442 0240
F +39 (0)35 442 0996

Dasic International Ltd
Winchester Hill
Romsey
Hampshire
SO51 7YD, UK
T +44 (0)1794 512 419
F +44 (0)1794 522 346

David Zyne Productions
c/o 100% Rubber
Dalsouple Direct Limited
PO Box 140
Bridgewater
Somerset TA5 1HT, UK
T +44 (0)1984 667 233
F +44 (0)1984 667 366
E info@dalsouple.com

Deep E Company
404 NW 10th Ave
Suite 201
Portland, OR 97209, USA
T +1 888 233 3373
F +1 503 299 628
E info@deepeco.com
www.deepeco.com

DEKA Research & Development Corporation
340 Commercial Street
Manchester, NH 03101
USA
T +1 603 669 5139
F +1 603 624 0573
www.dekaresearch.com

Design Academy Eindhoven
Emmasingel 14
PO Box 2125
5600 CC Eindhoven
Netherlands
T +31 (0)40 239 3939
F +31 (0)40 239 3940
E info@designacademy.nl
www.designacademy.nl

Designed to a 't' Ltd
11 Maxwell Gds
Orpington
Kent BR6 9QR, UK
T +44 (0)1689 831 400
F +44 (0)1689 609 301
www.d2at.demon.co.uk

DesignTex, Inc.
200 Varick St, 8th floor
New York, NY 10014
USA
T +1 212 886 8100
+1 800 221 1540
www.dtex.com

Deutsche Bahn AG
Metropolitan Express Train GmbH, gmp
von Gerkan Marg und Partner Architeken
Elbchaussee 139
22763 Hamburg, Germany

Deutsche Heraklith GmbH
Heraklith Strasse 8
84359 Simach/Inn
Germany
E m.hohmann-maier@heraklith.com

DMD
Parkweg 14
2271 AJ Voorburg
Netherlands
T +31 (0)70 386 4038
F +31 (0)70 387 3975

Domus Academy
Via Savona 97
20144 Milan, Italy
T +39 (0)242 4 14001
F +39(0)242 2 2525
E info@domusacademy.com
www.domusacademy.com

Driade SpA (Aleph)
Via Ancona 1/1
20121 Milan, Italy
T +39 (0)2 720 23 203
F +39 (0)2 720 02 434

Dumfries Plastics Recycling Ltd
College Road
Dumfries DG2 OBU, UK
T +44 (0)1387 247 110
F +44 (0)1387 247 109

DuPont (UK) Limited
Wedgewood Way
Stevenage
Hertfordshire SG1 4QN
UK
T +44 (0)1438 734 000
F +44 (0)1438 374 836

DuPont (USA)
E info@dupont.com
www.dupont.com

Duralay Ltd
Broadway
Haslingden
Rossendale
Lancashire BB4 4LS, UK
T +44 (0)1706 213 131
www.duralay.co.uk

Durex
SSL International
Toft Hall
Toft Road, Knutsford
Cheshire WA16 9PD, UK
T +44 (0)1565 624 000
F +44 (0)1565 624 099
www.durex.com

Dyes dLW Büroeinrichtungen GmbH
Am Deisterbahnhof 6
Bad Münder
Germany
T +49 (0)5042 501 0
F +49 (0)5042 501 117

Dyson Appliances
c/o 20 Shawfield Street
London SW3 4BD, UK
T +44 (0)20 7883 8244
www.dyson.com

Earth Chair (USA)
E vp@earthchair.com
www.earthchair.com

Eastman Chemical Company
100 North Eastman Road
PO Box 511
Kingsport, TN 37662-5075
USA
T +1 423 229 2000
F +1 615 229 1193
www.eastman.com

eco-ball
Birchwood House
Briar Lane, Croydon
Surrey CRO 5AD, UK
T +44 (0)20 8777 3121
F +44 (0)20 8777 3393
E info@ecozone.co.uk
www.ecozone.co.uk

Eco Solutions Ltd
Summerleaze House
Church Road
Winscombe
North Somerset
BS25 1BH, UK
T +44 (0)1934 844 484
F +44 (0)1934 844 119
E homestrip@ecosolutions.co.uk
www.ecosolutions.co.uk

Eco Timber International
1020 Heinz Avenue
Berkeley, CA 94710, USA
T +1 510 549 3000
E ecotimber@igc.apc-org
www.ecotimber.org

EcoDesign (The Natural Choice)
1365 Rufina Cir
Santa Fe, NM 87505-2964
USA
T +1 505 438 3448
F +1 505 438 0199
E ecodesign@aol.com

Ecole cantonale d'art de Lausanne
46 Rue de l'Industrie
CH 1030 Bussigny
Switzerland
T +41 (0)21 702 91 11
F +41 (0)21 702 91 00

Ecologic, Inc.
1140 Elizabeth Avenue
Waukegan, IL 60085
USA
T +1 800 899 8004
+1 847 244 4466
F +1 847 244 5977
E info@ecologic.com
www.ecologicfurniture.com

Ecostar, Inc.
230 Center Drive #201
Vernon Hills, IL 60061
USA
T +1 800 211 7170
F +1 800 780 9870
www.ecostarinc.com

Ecover
UK Promotions
21 Castle Street
Brighton
East Sussex BN1 2HD, UK
T +44 (0)1273 206 997
F +44 (0)1273 206 973
E beasley@pavilion.co.uk

Ecover Products NV
Industrieweg 3
2390 Malle, Belgium

Ehlebracht AG
Werkstrasse 7
32130 Enger, Germany
T +49 (0)5223 185 192
F +49 (0)5223 185 193
E info@ehlebracht-ag.com
www.ehlebracht-ag.com

Electrolux
AB Electrolux
Electrolux Group
Environmental Affairs
105 45 Stockholm, Sweden
T +46 (0)8 738 76 66
F +46 (0)8 738 05 98
E environmental.affairs@electrolux.se

Electrotextiles Ltd
Pinewood Studios
Pinewood Road
Iver, Bucks SLO ONH, UK
T +44 (0)8700 727 272
F +44 (0)8700 727 273
E incoming@electrotextiles.com
www.electrotextiles.com

Elf Atochem
2000 Market St
Ste 2200
Technical Polymers Division
Philadelphia, PA 19103-3399
USA
T +1 800 225 7788
F +1 215 419 7400
www.elf-atochem.com

Enbiomass Group, Inc.
2229 Mason Point Place
Wilmington, NC 28405-5276
USA
T +1 910 256 3998

EnPac
34355 Vokes Drive
Eastlake, OH 44095-0047
USA
T +1 800 936 7229
F +1 440 975 0047
E info@enpak.com
www.enpac.com

Environmental Polymers Group plc
4 Cranford Court
Hardwick Grange
Warrington
Cheshire WA1 4RX
UK
T +44 (0)1925 859 300
F +44 (0)1925 859 311
E info@epgplc.com
www.epgplc.com

Environmental Stone Products
PO Box 904
6600 Midland Court
Allenton, WI 53002
USA
T +1 888 629 1629
E webmaster@environmentalstone.com
www.environmentalstone.com

EnviroSafe Products, Inc.
81 Winant Place
Staten Island
New York, NY 10309-1311
USA
T +1 718 984 7272
F +1 718 984 1083
www.voicenet.com/~rusw/prc/rpg/plaslumb.htm

Epson Deutschland GmbH
Zülpicher Strasse 6
40549 Düsseldorf
Germany
T +49 (0)211 5603 0
F +49 (0)211 5047787
www.epson.de

Erlus Baustoffwerke AG
Hauptstrasse 106
84088 Neufahrn
Germany
T +49 (0)8773 18 133
F +49 (0)8773 18 140
E info@erlus.de
www.erlus.de

Escofet 1886 SA
Ronda Universitat 20
E 08007 Barcelona
Spain
T +34 (0)93 318 5050
F +34 (0)93 412 4465
E escofet@escofet.com
www.escofet@escofet.com

Europol
Unit 19A
Hilton Industrial Estate
Sutton Lane, Hilton,
Derbyshire
DE65 5FE
UK
T +44 (0)1283 730 355/730 354
E tjackson@polytec.co.uk

FanWing
P. Pebbles
Via Mandriola 10
00193 Rome
Italy
T/F +39 (0)67 136 263
E info@fanwing.com
www.fanwing.com

Feldmann & Schultchen
7 Timmermannstrasse
22299 Hamburg
Germany
T +49(0)40 510000
F +49 (0)40 517000
www.fsdesign.de

Festo AG & Co.
Corporate Design
KC-C1, Heugasse 1
73726 Esslingen
Germany
T +49 (0)711 347 3880
F +49 (0)711 347 3889
E tem@festo.com
www.festo.com

Fiam Italia SpA
Via Ancona 1/B
61010 Tavullia
Pesoro
Italy
T +39 (0)721 200 51
F +39 (0)721 202 432
E fiam@fiamitalia.it
www.fiamitalia.it

Fiat Auto Spa
Corso G Agnelli
10010 Tonno, Italy
T +39 (0)11 685 1111
F +39 (0)11 683 7591

Fiat Auto UK
Fiat House
266 Bath Road, Slough
Berkshire SL1 4HJ, UK
T +44 (0)1735 511 431
F +44 (0)1735 511 471

Filsol Limited
Unit 15, Ponthenri
Industrial Estate
Ponthenri
Carmarthenshire SA15 5RA
UK
T +44 (0)1269 860 229
F +44 (0)1269 860 979
E info@filsl.co.uk

Findlay Industries
4000 Fostoria Ave
Findlay, OH 45840
USA
T +1 419 422 1302

Fingermax Gbr
Pestalozzistrasse 54
80469 Munich
Germany
T/F +49 (0)89 267417
www.fingermax.de

Fish Guidance Systems
Chase Mill
Winchester Road
Southampton
Hampshire SO32 1AH
UK
T +44 (0)1489 893 323
F +44 (0)1489 893 831
E fgs@fish-guide.com
www.fish-guide.com

Fiskeby Board Ltd
Lloyd Berkeley Place
Pebble Lane
Aylesbury
Buckinghamshire HP20 2JH
UK
T +44 (0)1296 426 219
F +44 (0)1296 482 682
www.fiskeby.com

Flamco
PO Box 115
2800 AC Gouda
Netherlands
T +31 (0)182 591800
F +31 (0)182 522557

Flint Ink
245 East Marie Ave
West St Paul, MN 55118
USA
T +1 651 552 3217
F +1 651 455 2611
E sfield@flintink.com
www.flintink.com

Float Up VP
244 Grays Inn Road
London WC1X 8JR, UK
T +44 (0)20 7278 6971
F +44 (0)20 7833 0018
E floatupvp@BTinternet.com

Flow Control Water Conservation
Conservation House
Brighton Street
Wallasey
Merseyside CH44 6QJ
UK
T +44 (0)151 638 8811
F +44 (0)151 638 4137

Forbo-Nairn Ltd
PO Box 1
Kirkcaldy
Fife KY1 2SB
Scotland, UK
T +44 (0)1592 643 111
F +44(0)1592 643 999

Ford Motor Company
Customer Relationship Center
PO Box 6248
Dearborn, MI 48126
USA
www.ford.com

Frandsen Lyskilde AS
8-10 Industrivej
DK-8740 Braedstrup
Denmark
T +45 (0)76 58 18 18
F +45 (0)76 58 18 19
www.frandsen-lyskilde.dk

Franmar Chemical, Inc.
105 East Lincoln
PO Box 92
Normal, IL 61761
USA
T +1 309 452 7526
T +1 800 538 5069
www.franmar.com

Fredericia Furniture A/S
Treldevej 183
DK-7000 Fredericia
Denmark
T +45 (0)75 92 33 44
F +45 (0)75 92 38 76
E ml@fredericia.com
www.fredericia.com

Free-Flow Packaging International, Inc.
1090 Mills Way
Redwood City, CA 94063
USA
T +1 800 888 3725
T +1 650 361 1771
E tsutton@fpintl.com
www.fpintl.com

Freeplay Energy Europe Limited
Cirencester Business Park
Love Lane
Gloucester
GL7 1XD
UK
T +44 (0)1285 659 559
F +44 (0)1285 659 559
E freeplay@lineone.net
www.freeplay.net

Freudenberg Building Systems (Division of Freudenberg Nonwovens LP)
Lutterworth
Leicestershire
LE17 4DU
UK
T +44 (0)1455 261 240
F +44 (0)1455 556 529
E norauk@freudenberg.com

Fritz Hansen A/S
Fritz-Hansen UK
20-22 Rosebery Avenue
London EC1R 4SX
UK
T +44 (0)20 7837 2030
F +44 (0)20 7837 2040
E roh@fritzhansen.com.uk
www.fritzhansen.com.uk

Front Corporation
3-13-1 Takadanokata
Shinjuku-ku 169
Tokyo
Japan
T +81 (0)3 3360 3391
F +81 (0)3 3362 6363

Galleri Stolen AB
Birger Jarlsgatan 57
113 56 Stockholm
Sweden
T +46 (0)8 442 9150
F +46 (0)8 442 9151
E info@galleristolen.se
www.galleristolen.se

Gebrüder Thonet GmbH
Michael Thonet Strasse 1
35066 Frankenberg
Germany
T +49 (0)6451 508 0
F +49 (0)6451 508 108
E info@thonet.de
www.thonet.de

General Motors (USA)
www.gm.com

Gervasoni SpA
Zona Industriale Udenese
33050 Pavia di Udine
Italy
T +39 (0)432 675377
F +39 (0)432 675755
E gervasoni@ud.nettuno.it
www.infotech.it/gervasoni

Gibson Guitars
309 Plus Park Blvd
Nashville, TN 37217
USA
T +1 615 871 4500
F +1 615 889 5509
www.gibson.com

Glas Platz
Eckenhagener Strasse 16
51580 Reichshof-Allenbach
Germany
T +49 (0)2261 55557
F +49 (0)2261 56717
E glas-platz@mail.oberberg.de

Glindower Ziegelei GmbH
Alpenstrasse 47
14542 Glindow
Germany
T +49 (0)3327 66490
F +49 (0)3327 42662
E info@glindower-ziegelei.de
www.glindower-ziegelei.de

Gloria-Werke
see H. Schulte-Frankenfeld GmbH & Co.

Goods
218 Prinsengracht
1016 HD Amsterdam
Netherlands
T +31 (0)20 638 5908
F +31 (0)20 620 4457
E goods@goods.nl

Govaerts Recycling NV
Kolmenstraat 1324
Industriepark Kolmen
3570 Alken
Belgium
T +32 (0)11 59 01 60
F +32 (0)11 31 43 03

Grammer AG
Postfach 14 54
922204 Amberg
Germany
T +49 (0)9621 880 216
F +49 (0)9621 880 387
E info@grammer.de
www.grammer.de

Green & Carter
Vulcan Works
Ashbrittle
Near Wellington
Somerset TA21 0LQ
UK
T +44(0)1823 672 365
F +44(0)1823 672 950

Green Field Paper Company
1330 G St
San Diego, CA 92101
USA
T +1 651 552 3217
E jeff@greenfieldpaper.com
www.greenfieldpaper.com

GreenDisk
16398 NE 85th Street
Suite 100
Redmond, WA 98052
USA
T +1 425 883 9165
+1 800 305 3475
F +1 425 883 0425
www.greendisk.com

Greenwood Cotton Insulation Products, Inc.
PO Box 1017
Greenwood, SC 29648-1017
USA
T + 1 800 546 1332
F +1 800 942 4814

Gridcore Systems International (GSI)
1400 Canal Avenue
Long Beach, CA 90813
USA
T +1 562 901 1492

Ground Support Equipment (US)
11 Broadway, Room 1010
New York, NY 10004
USA
T +1 212 809 4323
F +1 212 809 4324
E biomorph@walrus.com
www.biomorphdesk.com

Grundig AG
Kurgartenstr. 37
90762 Fürth
Germany
T +49 (0)911 703 8149
F +49 (0)911 708 736
E lessmann.lennart@grundig.com
or nandzik.andreas@grundig.com

H. Schulte-Frankenfeld GmbH & Co.
Diestedder Strasse 39
59329 Wadersloh
Germany
T +49 (0)2523 77 0
F +49 (0)2523 77 295
E dgoetze@gloria.de
www.gloria.de

Haasa
Biopac GmbH
Ebrichsdorfer Strasse 18
A 2512 Tribuswinkel
Austria
T +43 (0)2252 803 4723

Habitat
196 Tottenham Court Road
London W1P 9LD, UK
T +44 (0)20 7255 3636
F +44 (0)20 7255 6002
E press@habitat.co.uk

Hahn Kunststoffe GmbH
Flugplatz Hahn
Gebäude 1027
55483 Lautzenhausen
Germany
T +49 (0)6543 9886 0
F +49 (0)6543 9886 97
E info@hahnkunststoffe.de

Hans Grohe GmbH & Co. KG
Auestrasse 5-9
77761 Schiltach
Germany
T +49 (0)7836 51 1211
F +49 (0)7836 51 1170
E pressestelle@hansgrohe.com
www.hansgrohe.com

Harwood Products
PO Box 224
Branscomb, CA 95417
USA
T +1 707 984 6181
F +1 707 984 6631
www.harwoodproducts.com

Haworth, Inc.
One Haworth Center
Holland, MI 49423
USA
T +1 616 393 3000
www.haworth.com

Hawtal Whiting Environmental
Phoenix House
Christopher Martin Road
Basildon
Essex SS14 3EZ
UK
T +44 (0)1268 531 155
F +44 (0)1268 273 555
E sb30@dial.pipex.com
www.hawtalwhiting.com

Hemp Textiles International Corporation (HTI)
3200 30th St
Bellingham, WA 98225-8360
USA
T +1 360 650 1684
F +1 360 650 0523
E hti@cantiva.com
www.cantiva.com

Henne Kunststoff GmbH
Am Bahnhof 2
17291 Gollmitz
Germany
T +49 (0)3 98 52 700 50
F +49 (0)3 98 52 700 51

Herman Miller, Inc.
855 East Main Ave
PO Box 302
Zeeland, MI 49464-0302
USA
www.hermanmiller.com

Hermès (France)
www.hermes.com

Hess Naturtextilien GmbH
Marie-Curie Str. 7
35510 Butzbach, Germany
E hess@hess-natur.com
www.hess-natur.com

Hock Vertriebs GmbH & Co. KG
Industriestrasse 7
76297 Stutensee-Spöck
Germany
T +49 (0)7249 94 71 0
F +49 (0)7249 94 71 25
E hock@thermo-hanf.de

Holzweg (Germany)
c/o Construction Resources Ltd
16 Great Guildford Street
London SE1 0HS, UK
T +44 (0)20 7450 2211

Homasote Company
PO Box 7240
West Trenton
NJ 08628-0240, USA
T +1 609 883 3300
F +1 609 883 3497
www.homosote.com

Honda (Japan)
www.honda.com

Hoover Group
Pentrebach, Merthyr Tydfil
Mid Glamorgan CF48 4TU
UK
T +44 (0)1685 721 222
F +44 (0)1685 725 696

Hopton Technologies
Albany, OR, USA
T +1 800 346 5251
E jeffr@hoptontech.com
www.hoptontech.com

Hülsta-Werke
Hüls GmbH & Co. KG
Postfach 1212
48693 Stadtlohn
Germany
T +49 (0)22 63 86 1273
F +49 (0)22 63 86 1400
E info@huelsta.de
www.huelsta.de

Hunton Fiber (UK) Ltd
22A High Street
Irthlingborough
Northants NN9 5TN, UK
T +44 (0)1933 651 811
F +44 (0)1933 652 747
E hunton@compuserve.com

Hurum Fabrikker AS
Postboks 133
3481 Tofte, Norway
T +47 (0)32 79 95 00

Husqvarna
see Electrolux

Iain Sinclair Design
Willow House
Hildersham
Cambridge CB1 6BV
UK
T +44 (0)1223 803 363
F +44 (0)1223 892 611
E kam75@dial.pipex.com

IBM Corporation
IBM Personal Systems
Group Design
3039 Cornwallis Road
Research Triangle Park
NC 27709
USA
T +1 919 254 8650
F +1 919 254 8385
E HDavid@us.ibm.com

ICI Americas
Concord Plaza
3411 Silverside Rd
Wilmington, DE 19810
USA
T +1 302 887 5858
F +1 302 887 5857
E ct_antonelli@ici.com
www.ici.com

IFCO, International Food Container Organisation GmbH
Zugspitzstrasse 15
82049 Pullach
Germany
T +49 (0)89 74 49 13 11
F +49 (0)89 74 49 13 92

Ifö Sanitär AB
295 22 Bromölla
Sweden
T +46 (0)456 480 00
F +46 (0)456 480 48
E info@ifo.se
www.ifo.se

Iform AB/ Inredningsform
PO Box 5055
Davidshallsgatan 20
200 71 Malmö, Sweden
T +46 (0)40 303610
F +46 (0)40 302288
E info@iform.net
www.iform.net

IKEA of Sweden
Box 702, Älmhult
343 81 Småland
Sweden
T +46 (0)47 68 10 00
F +46 (0)47 61 51 23
www.ikea.com

Induced Energy Ltd
Souldern Manor
Bicester
Oxfordshire OX27 9JT, UK
T +44 (0)1869 345 746
F +44 (0)1869 346 051

Inner Tube Ltd
Unit B1
The Wren Centre
Westbourne Road
Emsworth
Hampshire
UK
T +44 (0)2392 433 433

Insulholz-Beton International, Inc.
571 Oak Ridge Club Rd
Windsor, SC 29856-2146
USA
T +1 803 642 9346
F +1 803 642 6361
E faswall@faswall.com
www.faswall.com

Interface, Inc.
Corporate Headquarters
2859 Paces Ferry Road
Suite 2000
Atlanta, GA 30399
USA
T +1 770 437 6800
www.interfaceinc.com

Interfold
PO Box 3396
Santa Rosa, CA 95402
USA

Inx International Ink Co.
651 Bonnie Lane
Elk Grove Village, IL 60007
USA
T +1 847 981 9399
F +1 847 981 9447
E moravec@inxintl.com
www.inxink.com

Isobord Enterprises
1300 SW Fifth Avenue
Suite 3030
Portland, OR 97201
USA
T +1 503 242 7345
E isobord@isobord-sales.com
www.isobord.com
www.isobordenterprises.com

Jiffy Packaging Company Ltd
Road Four Industrial Estate
Winsford
Cheshire CW7 3QR, UK
T +44 (0)1606 551 221
F +44 (0)1606 592 634

Johnson Corrugated Products
Box 246, Rte 193
Thompson, CT 06277
USA
T +1 860 923 9563
F +1 860 923 2531
E info@jcpc.com
www.jcpc.com

Johnson Matthey
Catalytic System Division
Orchard Road
Royston
Hertfordshire SG8 9HE, UK
T +44 (0)1763 253 370
F +44 (0)1763 253 011
www.matthey.com

Josef Meeth Fensterfabrik GmbH & Co. KG
Montreal
54533 Laufeld, Germany
T +49 (0)6572 81 0
F +49 (0)6572 81 148

Junghans Uhren GmbH
Geisshaldenstrasse 49
78713 Schramberg
Germany
T +49 (0)7422 18 360
F +49 (0)7422 18 667
E birgit.binder@junghans.de
www.junghans.de

Kafus Bio-Composites
4955 Beck Dr.
Elkhart, IN 46516, USA
T +1 219 295 3777
E gbalthes@kafus.com
www.kafus.com/divisions/biocomposites.html

Kafus Environmental Industries
270 Bridge Street
Dedham, MA 02026
USA
T +1 888 333 5377
F +1 781 326 5105
E tfrancel@kafus.com
www.kafus.com

Kartell SpA
Via delle Industrie 1
Noviglio
20082 Milan, Italy
T +39 (0)2 9000121
F +39 (0)2 9053316
www.kartell.it

Kautzky Mechanik
Schöffelgasse 26-28
A 1180 Vienna
Austria
T +43 (0)1 4724252

Kayserberg Packaging SA
ETS Plastiques
Route de Lapoutroie
BP 27
68240 Kayserberg
France
T +33 (0)3 89 78 30 00
F +33 (0)3 89 47 18 56
www.kpsa-plastics.com

Keim Mineral Paints
Muckley Cross, Morville
Near Bridgend
Shropshire MV16 4RR
UK
T +44 (0)1746 714 543

KFN Kaufmann Produkt GmbH
Sägerstrasse 4
A 6850 Dornbirn
Austria
T +43 (0)5572 26 2 83
F +43 (0)5572 26 2 83-4
E office@kaufmannkaufmann.com
www.kfnproduct.com

Klober Limited
Pear Tree Industrial Estate
Upper Langford
North Somerset BS40 5DJ
UK
T +44 (0)1934 853 224/5
F +44 (0)1934 853 221
E support@klober.co.uk
www.klober.co.uk

Kopf AG
Stutzenstr. 6
72172 Sulz-Borgfelden
Germany
T +49 (0)7454 75285
E h.stark@kopf-ag.de
www.kopf-ag.de

KP Products
PO Box 20399
Albuquerque
NM 87154-0399
USA
T +1 505 294 0293
E kenafman@aol.com
www.visionpaper.com

Kronospan AG
Dekorative Holzwerkstoffe
CH 6122 Menznau
Switzerland
T +41 (0)41 494 94 94
F +41 (0)41 494 04 49
E s.wiederkehr@kronospan.ch
www.kronospan.ch

Kucospan Sales UK Ltd
Peverel House
The Green
Hatfield Peverel
Essex CM3 2JF, UK
T +44 (0)1245 382 168
F +44 (0)1245 382 207
E pjcarter@kucospan.co.uk

K-X Faswall Corp
PO Box 180
Windsor, SC 29856
USA
T +1 800 491 7891
F +1 803 642 6361
www.faswall.com

Kyocera Corporation
Japan and UK
www.kyocera.com

La Chanvrière de l'Aube (LDCA matériaux)
Rue du Général de Gaulle
10200 Bar sur Aube
France
T +33 (0)3 25 92 31 95
F +33 (0)3 25 27 35 48
E chanvrière.aube@wanadoo.fr
www.chanvre.com

Lakeland Paints
Unit 19
Lake District Business Park
Kendal
Cumbria LA9 6NH
UK
T +44 (0)1539 732 866
F +44 (0)1539 734 400

Lampholder 2000 plc
Unit 8, Express Park
Garrard Way
Telford Way Industrial Estate (South)
Kettering
Northamptonshire
NN16 8TD
UK
T +44 (0)1536 520 101
F +44 (0)1536 523 014

Laybond Products Ltd
Riverside
Saltney
Chester CH4 8RS
UK
T +44 (0)1244 674 774
F +44 (0)1244 681 601

Leahy Wolf Company
1951 North 25th Avenue
Franklin Park
IL 60131-3595
USA
T +1 888 873 5327
F +1 847 455 5700
www.ia-usa.org/a0014.htm

Leclanché
48 Avenue de Grandson
CH 1401 Yverdon
Switzerland
T +41 (0)24 447 22 72
F +41 (0)24 445 24 42

Ledtronics
USA
www.ledtronics.com

Levi Strauss & Co.
Global Headquarters
1155 Battery Street
San Francisco, CA 94111
USA
www.levistrauss.com
www.levi.com

Lew San Limited
3 Sutton Gardens
Hornchurch
Essex RM12 4LD
UK
T +44 (0)1708 473 842
F +44 (0)1708 524 389
E stmate@dircon.co.uk
www.stairmate.co.uk

Lexon Design Concepts
98 ter. Boulevard Héloïse
BP 103
95103 Argenteuil Cedex
France
T +33 (0)1 39 47 04 00
F +33 (0)1 39 47 07 59
E world@lexon-design.com
www.lexon-design.com

Light Corporation
14800 172nd Avenue
Grand Haven, MI 49417
USA
T +1 616 842 5100
F +1 616 846 2144
E info@lightcorp.com
www.lightcorp.com

Ligne Roset SA
Serrières de Briord
01471 Briord
France
T +33 (0)4 74 36 17 00
F +33 (0)4 74 36 16 95

Lignocel SA
c/o Officina de Promocion
Maderon Ronda
San Pedro 58 3-2
E 08010 Barcelona
Spain

LINPAC Environmental
Leafield Way
Leafield Industrial Estate
Corsham
Wiltshire SN13 9UD
UK
T +44 (0)1225 816 500
F +44 (0)1225 816 501
www.linpac-environmental.com

Living Tree Paper Company
1430 Willamette St
Ste 367
Eugene, OR 97401-4049
USA
T +1 800 309 2974
F +1 541 687 7744
E info@livingtreepaper.com
www.livingtreepaper.com

Livos Pflanzenchemie
Auengrund 10
29568 Weisen
Germany
T +49 (0)5825 880
F +49 (0)5825 8860

Lloyd Loom of Spalding
Wardentree Lane
Pinchbeck, Spalding
Lincs PE11 3SY
UK
T +44 (0)1775 712 111
F +44 (0)1775 710 571
E info@lloydloom.com
www.lloydloom.com

LRC Products
c/o Durex
SSL International
Toft Hall
Toft Road
Knutsford
Cheshire WA16 9PD
UK
T +44 (0)1565 624 000
F +44 (0)1565 624 099
www.durex.com

LSK Industries Pty
92 Woodfield Boulevard
Caringbah
NSW 2229
Australia
T +61 (0)2 9525 8544
+61 (0)2 9525 7601

LSR GmbH Recycling-Zentrum
Wachstedter Str. 1-5
37351 Dingelstädt
Germany
T +49 (0)36075 381 0
F +49 (0)36075 381 18
E lsr-dingelstaedt@t-online.de
www.lsr-recydur.de

Luceplan SpA
Via E.T. Moneta 44/46
20161 Milan
Italy
T +39 (0)2 662 42 1
F +39 (0)2 662 03400
E luceplan@luceplan.it
www.luceplan.it

Lumatech Corporation
41636 Enterprise Circle
North, Suite C
Temecula, CA 92590
USA
T +1 800 932 0637
F +1 800 345 5862
www.lumatech.com

LUMINO Licht Elecktronik GmbH
47799 Krefeld
Germany
T +49 (0)2151 819625
F +49 (0)2151 819659
E mfullert@lumino.de
www.lumino.de

MAN B & W Diesel AG
MAN Nutzfahrzeuge
Aktiengesellschaft
Postfach 50 06 20
80976 Munich
Germany
T +49 (0)89 15 08 01
www.man-nutzfahrzeuge.de
www.mbd.man.de

MAP (Merchants of Australia Products) Pty Ltd
570 Chapel Street
Sth Yarra
Melbourne, Victoria 3141
Australia

Marlec Engineering Co. Ltd
Rutland House
Trevithick Road
Corby
Northamptonshire
NN17 5XY
UK
T +44 (0)1536 201 588
F +44 (0)1536 400 211
E sales@marlec.co.uk
www.marlec.co.uk

Masonite Corporation
1 South Wacker Drive
36th floor
Chicago, IL 60606
USA
T +1 312 750 0900
F +1 312 750 0958
E comm@ipaper.com

Masonite CP
West Wing
Jason House
Kercyhill
Hosforth
Leeds
West Yorkshire LS18 4JR
UK
T +44 (0)1132 587 689
F +44 (0)1132 590 015

Massachusetts Institute of Technology
77 Massachusetts Avenue
Cambridge, MA 02139
USA
T +1 617 253 1000
http://web.mit.edu

Matrix Composites, Inc
6310 Shawson Drive
Mississauga
ONT L5T 1H5
Canada
T +1 800 767 4495
www.maderatile.com

MDD (Denmark)
www.mdd.dk

Meadowood Industries, Inc.
33242 Red Bridge Rd SE
Albany, OR 97321-9769
USA
T +1 541 259 1303
F +1 541 259 1355
E strawboard@proaxis.com
www.meadowoodindustries.com

Meta Morf, Inc.
c/o Colin Reedy
2700 4th Avenue South
Seattle, WA 98134
USA
T +1 206 903 6332
F +1 206 223 0853
E colin@metamorfdesign.com
www.metamorfdesign.com

Metabolix, Inc.
303 3rd St
Cambridge, MA 02142-1126
USA
T +1 617 492 0505
F +1 617 492 1996
E info@metabolix.com

Metpost Limited
Mardy Road
Cardiff CF3 8EX
UK
T +44 (0)2920 777 877
F +44 (0)2920 779 295
www.metpost.com

MGSL GmbH
Deichstrasse 6
25335 Elmshorn
Germany
T +49 (0)4121 2607 17
F +49 (0)4121 2607 79
E steffens@mgsl.de

Michael Kaufmann Zimmerei
Baien 116
A 6870 Reuthe
Austria
T +43 (0)5514 2209
F +43 (0)5514 3275

Micro Thermal Systems
Tregonce Cliff
St Issey
Wadebridge
Cornwall
PL27 7Q3
UK
T +44 (0)1208 813 028
F +44 (0)1208 813 026
E stomatex@compuserve.com

Milliken & Co.
Carpet Division
USA
T +1 706 880 5511
www.millikencarpet.com

Minolta (Japan)
www.minolta.com/japan/

Monodraught
Halifax House
Cressex Business Park
High Wycombe
Buckinghamshire
HP12 3SE
UK
T +44 (0)1494 897 700
F +44 (0)1494 532 465
E info@monodraught.com
sunpipe@monodraught.com

Monotub Industries
212 Piccadilly
London W1V 9LD
UK
T +44 (0)20 7917 1863
F +44 (0)20 7917 1883
www.monotub.com

Moonlight Aussenleuchten GmbH
Gewerbegebiet Hemmet
79664 Wehr
Germany
T +49 (0)7762 1018
F +49 (0)7762 2203
www.moonlight.outdoorlighting.de

Moormann Möbel
An der Festhalle 2
83229 Aschau im Chiemgau
Germany
T +49 (0)8052 40 01
F +49 (0)8052 43 93

MSK Corporation
Japan
www.si.edu/ndm/exhib/sun/4/kk.html

Muscle Power, MOY Concept and Design
Netherlands
E info@moy.nl

National Starch & Chemical Company
10 Finderne Ave
Bridgewater, NJ 08807-3300
USA
T +1 800 797 4992
F +1 908 417 5696
E bill.greenhalgh@nstarch.com
www.nationalstarch.com

Natural Choice, The
USA
www.oikos.com/naturalchoice/index.htm

Natural Cotton Colors, Inc.
PO Box 66
Wickenburg, AZ 85358
USA
T/F +1 520 684 7199
E nodyes@foxfibre.com
www.foxfibre.com

Natural Fibers Corporation
Airport Road
Box 830
Ogallala, NE 69153
USA
T +1 308 284 8403
E ogallala@megavision.com
www.ogalladown.com

NEC Deutschland GmbH
Steinheilstrasse 4-6
85737 Ismanin
Germany
T +49 (0)89 96274 376
F +49 (0)89 96274 547
www.nec.com

Netlon Group Limited, The
New Wellington Street
Blackburn
Lancashire BB2 4PJ
UK
T +44 (0)1254 262 431
F +44 (0)1254 266 868
E customerservices@tensar.co.uk

New Leaf Paper
215 Leidesdorff St
Suite 4
San Francisco, CA 94111
USA
T +1 415 291 9210
F +1 415 291 9353
E info@newleafpaper.com
www.newleafpaper.com

News Design DfE AB
Stora Skuccanas V. 11
115 42 Stockholm
Sweden
T +46 (0)8 15 39 29
F +46 (0)8 15 39 26

N Fornitore
Italy
c/o Purves and Purves
220-224 Tottenham
Court Road
London W1T 7QE
UK
T +44 (0)20 7580 8223

Nighteye GmbH
Daimlerstrasse 13-15
73249 Wernau
Germany
T +49 (0)7153 937833
F +49 (0)7153 937832
E info@nighteye.de
www.nighteye.de

Nils Holger Moormann Möbel Produktions- und Handels GmbH
Kirchplatz
83229 Aschau
Germany
T +49 (0)8052 9045
F +49 (0)8052 4393
E infor@moormann.de
www.moormann.de

Nisso Engineering Co Ltd (NSE)
Nobuhiro Saito
Tokyo Takii Bldg.
6-1, 1-Chome, Kanda
Kinbo-cho, Chiyoda-ku
Tokyo 101
Japan
T +81 (0)3 3296 9313/9204
F +81 (0)3 3296 9250

Nordsjö (Akzo Nobel Dekorativ)
205 17 Malmö
Sweden
T +46 (0)40 35 50 00
F +46 (0)40 601 52 23

Norel/Unisource
223 Gates Road
Little Ferry, NJ 07643
USA
T +1 201 440 4400
F +1 201 440 9292
E sales@norel.com
www.norel.com

North Wood Plastics, Inc.
103 Water Street
Baraboo, WI 53913-2446
USA
T +1 608 355 4100

Nova Cruz Products LLC
537 Hamilton Avenue
Palo Alto, CA 94301
USA
T +1 603 868 3708/
+1 888 353 4464
E sales@novacruz.com
www.xootr.com

Nova Form
Schörgelgasse 21
A-8010 Graz
Austria
T +43 (0)316 82 2263
F +43 (0)316 82 23 34
E novaform@novaform.com
www.novaform.com

Novamont SpA
Novara, Italy
T +39 (0)321 699611
E relazioni.esterne@novamont.com
www.novament.com

Novon International
181 Cooper Avenue
Tonawanda, NY 14150-664
USA
T +1 716 874 8696
F +1 716 874 8699
E info@novonintl.com
www.novonintl.com

Novotex A/S
Ellehammervej 8
7430 Ikast
Denmark
T +45 (0)96 60 68 00
F +45 (0)96 60 68 10
E novotex@green-cotton.dk
www.green-cotton.dk

Nuno Corporation
Axis Building B1F
5-17-1 Roppongi
Minato-ku
Tokyo 106
Japan
T +81 (0)3 3582 7997
F +81 (0)3 3589 3439

Nutshell Natural Paints
Hamlyn House
Mardle Way
Buckfastleigh
Devon TQ11 0NR, UK
T +44 (0)1364 73801
E nuts@nutshellpaints.freeserve.co.uk

NuvoMedia, Inc.
310 Villa Street
Mountain View
CA 94041 USA
T +1 650 314 1200
F +1 650 314 1201
E info@nuvomedia.com
www.nuvomedia.com

Ocean Kayak (USA)
www.oceankayak.com

Old Fashioned Milk Paint Company
436 Main St
Groton, MA 01450-1232
USA
T +1 978 448 6336
F +1 978 448 2754
www.milkpaint.com

Optare International
Manstone Lane
Leeds
W. Yorks LS15 8SU
UK
T +44 (0)113 264 5182
F +44 (0)113 260 6635

Orange
Orange Media Centre
50 George Street
London W1H 5RF
UK
T +44 (0)20 7984 2000
F +44 (0)20 7984 2001
E media.centre@orange.co.uk
www.media.orange.net

ORBITA Film GmbH
Köthner Str. 11
06369 Weissandt-Gölzau
Germany
T +49 (0)340 78 27 0
F +49 (0)340 78 27 376

Osram Sylvania
North America HQ
100 Endicott Street
Danvers, MA 01923
USA
T +1 978 777 1900
E +1 978 750 2152
www.sylvania.com

Ostermann & Scheiwe
Hafenweg 31
48155 Münster
Germany
www.ostermann-scheiwe.com

Ostermann & Scheiwe UK Ltd
Osmo House
Unit 2
Pembroke Road
Stocklake Industrial Estate
Aylesbury
Bucks HP20 1DB, UK
T +44 (0)1296 481 220
www.ostermann-scheiwe.com

Österreichische Heraklith AG
Postfach 31
A 9586 Furnitz, Austria
T +49 (0)4257 3370 0
F +49 (0)4257 3370 57

Oxo International
230 Fifth Avenue
2nd Floor
New York, NY 10001, USA
T +1 212 242 3333
F +1 212 242 3336
E info@oxo.com
www.oxo.com

P T Sudimar Energi Surya
Jalan Banyumas 4
Jakarta 10310
Indonesia
T +62 (0)21 390407
F +62 (0)21 361639

P. Schiebel Elektronische Geräte AG
Margaretenstrasse 112
A 1050 Vienna
Austria
T +43 (0)1 548260
F +43 (0)1 5452339

Pacific Northwest Fiber
PO Box 610
Plummer, ID 83851
USA
T +1 208 686 6800
F +1 208 686 6810
E contact@pacificfiber.com
www.pacificfiber.com

Palluco Italia SpA
Via Azzi 36
Castagnole de Paese
31040 Treviso
Italy
T +390 (0)422 438800

Papa-Papel
c/o Endereço da
Fiesp/Ciesp
Av. Paulista, 1.313
Cerqueira Cesar
São Paulo/SP-CEP
01 311-923
Brazil
T +55 (0)11 252 4499

Paperback
Unit 2
Bow Triangle
Business Centre
Eleanor Street
London E3 4NP
UK
T +44 (0)20 8980 5580
F +44 (0)20 8980 2399

Partek Insulations, Inc.
401 Westpark Drive 202
Peachtree City, GA 30269
USA

Patagonia
239 W. Santa Clara Street
Ventura, CA 93001
USA
T +1 805 643 8616
www.patagonia.com

P.C.D. Maltron Ltd
15 Orchard Lane
East Molesey
Surrey KT8 0BN
UK
T +44 (0)20 8398 3265
E sales@maltron.com
www.maltron.com

Pendlewood
The Old Officers Mess
Barton Aerodrome
Barton
Salford
Manchester M30 7SA
UK
T +44 (0)161 789 4441
F +44 (0)161 787 7400

Peugeot
France
www.psa.fr

Peugeot Motor Co. Plc
Aldermore House
PO Box 227
Aldermore Lane
Coventry
Warwickshire CV3 1LT
UK
T +44 (0)24 7688 4212
F +44 (0)24 7688 4122
www.peugeot.co.uk

Phenix Biocomposites
PO Box 609
Mankato, MN 56002-0609
USA
T +1 507 931 9787
+1 800 324 8147
F +1 507 931 5573
E sales@phenixllc.com
www.phenixbiocomposites.com

Philips Electronics NV
Building HWD
PO Box 218
5600 MD Eindhoven
Netherlands
T +31 (0)40 275 9066
F +31 (0)40 275 9091
E annemieke.froger@philips.com
www.philips.com

Pierce International, Inc.
PO Box 4871
Englewood, CO 80155
USA
T +1 303 792 0719
F +1 303 799 6469

Pinnacle Technology, Inc. (PTI)
619 East 8th, Suite D
Lawrence, KS 66044
USA
T +1 785 832 8866
F +1 785 749 9214
E info@pinnaclet.com
www.pinnaclet.com

Pinturas Proa
Industrias Proa SA
San Salvador de Budiño
Gánderas de Prado
36475 Porriño (Pontevedra)
Spain
T +34 (0)986 34 6525
F +34 (0)986 34 6589

Planet
c/o Creative Energy
Technologies
Main St
Summit, NY 12175
USA
www.cetsolar.com/planetdc.htm

Planex GmbH
Steinauer Weg
91589 Aurach
Germany
T +49 (0)9804 1780
F +49 (0)9804 7207
E rost@planex.com

Plant Polymer Technologies, Inc.
9985 Businesspark
Ave, Suite A
San Diego, CA 92131-1102
USA
T +1 619 549 5130
F +1 619 549 5133

Plastics Fth Industry Ltd
The Stables
Sandholme Mill
Commercial Street
Todmorden
Lancashire OL14 5RH
UK
T +44 (0)1706 817 784
F +44 (0)1706 817 227
E plasfth@msn.com

Polti SpA
Via Verloni 83
22070 Bulgarograsso (CO)
Italy
T +39 (0)31 939 111
F +39 (0)31 890 513
E contabilita@polti.it
www.polti.it

Poly-Beek-Kunststoff-Handels GmbH
Schmidestr. 34
26629 Grossefehn
Germany
T +49 (0)4943 91990
F +49 (0)4943 4744
E info@polybeek.de

Polyval plc
Priors Hall
Stebbing
Dunmow
Essesx CM6 3SW
UK
T +44 (0)1371 856 791
F +44 (0)1371 856 791

Porous Pipe Ltd
Standroyd Mill
Cottontree, Colne
Lancashire
BB8 7BW
UK
T +44 (0)1282 871 778
F +44 (0)1282 871 785

Potmolen Paints
27 Woodcock
Industrial Estate
Warminster
Wiltshire BA12 9DX
UK
T +44 (0)1985 213 931
F +44 (0)1985 213 960

Powabyke Ltd
6 Riverside Business Park
Bath BA2 3DW
UK
T +44 (0)1225 443 737
F +44 (0)1225 446 878
E sales@powabyke.com
www.powabyke.com

PowerMakers Plus Limited
Croft Business Park
Bromborough
Wirral
Cheshire CH62 3RB
UK
T +44 (0)151 343 0080
F +44 (0)151 343 0081

Prairie Forest Products
200 S Obee Rd
Hutchinson, KS 67501
USA
T +1 316 665 7000

Primeboard, Inc.
2111 North 3M Drive
Wahpeton, ND 58075-3019
USA
T +1 701 642 1152
F +1 701 642 1154
E sales@primeboard.com
www.primeboard.com

Prins Dokkum BV
Rondweg 35
PO Box 4
9100 AA Dokkum
Netherlands
E prinsdokkum@niv-webhosting.com
www.prins-dokkum.nl

Product 2000 Ltd
Archfarm Industrial Estate
Whitsbury Road
Fordingbridge
Hampshire SP6 1NQ
UK
T +44 (0)1425 652 226
F +44 (0)1425 657 288

PURUS Kunststoffwerke GmbH
Am Blätterrangen 4
95659 Arzberg, Germany
T +49 (0)9233 7755 0
F +49 (0)9233 7755 50
E purus-kunststoffwerke@purus-arzberg.de

Radius GmbH
145 Weisser Strasse
50999 Cologne
Germany
T +49 (0)2232 7636 32
F +49 (0)2232 7636 30
E radius.design@netcologne.de

Rayotec Limited
London Road
Sunningdale
Berkshire SL5 0DJ
UK
T +44 (0)1344 874 747
F +44 (0)1344 872 030

Recycled Plastics, Inc.
609 Co. Rd 82 NW
Garfield, MN 56332
USA
T +1 320 834 2293
F +1 320 834 2290
E gipo@gctel.com
www.gipo-rpi.com

Red Bank Manufacturing Ltd
Atherstone Road
Measham
Swadlincote
Derbyshire DE12 7EL
UK
T +44 (0)1530 270 333/542

Reed Corrugated Cases
see Sams Design

REEEL
52 Marconistrat
3029 AK Rotterdam
Netherlands
T +31 (0)10 925 4612
F +31 (0)10 925 7603

Reln
(Australia with Wiggly Wigglers, UK)
Lower Blakemere Farm
Blakemere
Herefordshire
HR2 9PX, UK
T +44 (0)1981 500 391
F +44 (0)1981 500 108
www.wigglywigglers.co.uk

Remarkable Pencils Ltd
Worlds End Studios
134 Lots Road
London SW10 ORJ, UK
T +44 (0)20 7351 4333
F +44 (0)20 7352 4729
E info@re-markable.com

Re-New Wood
104 N. 8th
PO Box 1093
Wagoner, OK 74467, USA
T +1 800 420 7576
F +1 918 485 5803
www.renewwood.com

Re-Reluma GmbH
Bahnhofstr. 32a
09518 Grossrückerswalde/
Steckewalde, Germany
T +49 (0)37369 136 0
F +49 (0)37369 136 66
E reluma.t-online.de

Retail Place Ltd
34A Campden Hill Gardens
London W8 7AZ, UK
T +44 (0)20 7727 0486
F +44 (0)20 7221 7012

Rexam
c/o Recycled UK
Gate House
Castle Estate
Turnpike Road
High Wycombe
Buckinghamshire
HP12 3NR, UK

Rexite SpA
Via Edison 7
20090 Cusago
Milan, Italy
T +39 (0)2 9039 0013
F +39 (0)2 9039 0018

riese und müller GmbH
Erbacher Strasse 123
64287 Darmstadt
Germany
T +49 (0)6151 424034
F +49 (0)6151 424036
E team@r-m.de
www.r-m.de

Ritter Energie und Umwelttechnik GmbH & Co. KG
Ettlinger Strasse 30
76307 Karlsbad
Germany
T +49 (0)7202 922 0
F +49 (0)7202 922 100
E ritter@paradigma.de
www.paradigma.de

Robert Cullen & Sons Limited
10 Dawsholm Avenue
Glasgow G20 OTS, UK
T +44 (0)141 945 2222
F +44 (0)141 945 3567
E sales@cullen.co.uk
www.cullen-packaging.co.uk

Rodman Industries
PO Box 76
Marinette, WI 54143
USA
T +1 715 735 9500

Rohner Textil AG
CH 9435 Heerbrugg
Switzerland
T +41 (0)61 722 2218
F +41 (0)61 722 7152

Roland Plastics
Strida Limited
Wickham Market
Woodbridge
Suffolk IP13 0QZ, UK
T +44 (0)1728 747 777
F +44 (0)1728 748 222
E strida@rolandplastics.co.uk

Rolls Royce
PO Box 31
Derby
Derbyshire DE24 8BJ, UK
T +44 (0)1332 242 424
F +44 (0)1332 249 936
www.rolls-royce.com

Ron Ink Company
200 Trade Court
Rochester, NY 14624-4771
USA
T +1 800 833 7383
F +1 716 529 3519

Rothlisberger Schreinerei AG
Dorfstrasse 73
CH 3073 Gümligen
Switzerland
T +41 (0)31 951 41 17
F +41 (0)31 951 16 52/35 63

Safeglass (Europe) Ltd
James Watt Building
Scottish Enterprise
Technology Park
East Kilbride
Glasgow G75 0QD, UK
T +44 (0)1355 272 438
F +44 (0)1355 272 555
E info@safeglass.co.uk
www.safeglass.co.uk

Saitek Industries Ltd
2295 Jefferson Street
Torrance, CA 90501
USA
T +1 310 212 5412
F +1 310 212 0866
E info@saitekusa.com
www.saitekusa.com

Sanford UK
Berol House
Oldmeadow Road
King's Lynn
Norfolk PE30 4JR, UK
T +44 (0)1553 761 221
F +44 (0)1553 766 534
E mail@sanford.co.uk

SAVAWatt (UK) Ltd
SAVA Building
Waterloo Industrial Estate
Bidford on Avon
Warwickshire B50 4JH, UK
T/F +44 (0)1789 490
E enquiries@savawatt.com
www.savawatt.com

Save A Cup Recycling Company
Suite 2, Bridge House
Bridge Street
High Wycombe
Buckinghamshire
HP11 2EL, UK
T +44 (0)1494 510 167
F +44 (0)1494 510 168

Save Wood Products Ltd
Amazon Works
Three Gates Road, Cowes
Isle of Wight PO31 7UT, UK
T +44 (0)1983 299 935
F +44 (0)1983 299 069
E AAaxylon@aol.com

Schäfer Werke GmbH
Pfannenbergstrasse 1
57290 Neunkirchen
Germany
T +49 (0)2735 787 273
F +49 (0)2735 787 284
E h.schlabach@schaefer-werke.de
www.schaefer-werke.de

Schauman Wood Oy
Niemenkatu 16
PO Box 203
15141 Lahti
Finland
T +358 204 15 113
F +358 20415 112
E schaumanwood@upm-kymmene.com

Scholler Textil AG
Bahnhofstrasse
CH 9475 Sevelen
Switzerland
T +41 (0)81 786 08 35

SciMAT Limited
Dorcan 200
Murdock Road
Dorcan
Swindon
Wiltshire SN3 5HY, UK
T +44 (0)1793 511 160
F +44 (0)1793 533 352
E sales@scimat.co.uk
www.scimat.co.uk

Sculptures-Jeux
18 rue Domat
75005 Paris, France
T +33 (0)1 43 54 20 39
F +33 (0)1 43 54 83 32
E sculptures.jeux@wanadoo.fr

sdb Industries BV
PO Box 2197
5202 CD 's-Hertogenbosch
Netherlands
T +31 (0)73 6333 91 33
F +31 (0)73 631 33 85
E info@sdb-industries.nl
www.sdb-industries.nl

Sensor Systems Watchman
Shaerf Drive
Lurgan, Craigavon
County Armagh
Northern Ireland
BT66 8DE, UK
T +44 (0)1762 321 111
F +44 (0)1762 324 444
E sales@sensor-systems.com
www.sensor-systems.com

Showa Highpolymer Co.
Kanda Chuo Bldg
3-20 Kanda Nishiki-cho
Chiyoda-ku
Tokyo 101, Japan
T +81 (0)3 3293 8844
F +81 (0)3 3233 0137

Simplex Products
PO Box 10
Adrian, MI 49221-0010
USA
T +1 517 263 8881

Simplicitas
Grevgatan 19
114 52 Stockholm
Sweden
T +46 (0)8 661 00 91
F +46 (0)8 661 00 97
www.simplicitas.se

Skoot International Limited
24 Peartree Business Centre
Peartree Road
Stanway
Essex CO3 5JN, UK
T +44 (0)1206 542 542
F +44 (0)1206 542 543

Skystreme UK Ltd
367 High Street
Brentford
Middlesex TW8 0BD, UK
T +44 (0)20 8560 6872
F +44 (0)20 8569 8581
E kas09@dial.pipex.com
www.skystreme.uk.net

SLI Lighting Ltd
Otley Road
Charlestown
Shipley, West Yorkshire
BD17 7SN, UK
T +44 (0)1274 537 777
F +44 (0)1274 597 683

Slough Rubber Company Ltd
441 Perth Avenue
Slough Trading Estate
Slough
Berkshire SL1 4TS, UK
T +44 (0)1753 570 438
F +44 (0)1753 530 178
www.sloughrubber.co.uk

SmartDeck Systems
2600 W. Roosevelt Road
Chicago, IL 60608
USA
E info@smartdeck.com
www.smartdeck.com

Smith & Fong Company
Plyboo Bamboo Products
601 Grandview Drive S.
San Francisco, CA 94080
USA
T +1 650 872 1184
F +1 650 872 1185
E info@plyboo.com
www.plyboo.com

Smith Anderson & Co. Ltd
Fettykil Mills
Leslie
Fife KY6 3AQ, UK
T +44 (0)1592 746 000

Snow
Finland
c/o Studio Ilkka Suppanen
Punavuorenkatu 1 A 7 b
00120 Helsinki, Finland
T +358 9 622 78737
F +358 9 622 3093
E suppanen@kolumbus.fi

Solar Century Holdings Ltd
Unit 5
Sandycombe Centre
1-9 Sandycombe Road
Richmond, Surrey, UK
T +44 (0)870 735 8100
F +44 (0)870 735 8101
E jl@solarcentury.co.uk
www.solarcentry.co.uk

Solar Cookers International
1919 21st St, Suite 101
Sacramento, CA 95814
USA
T +1 916 455 4498
F +1 916 455 4498
E sbci@igc.apc.org
http://solarcooking.org

Solar Solutions (UK) Ltd
Unit D6
Capel Hendre
Industrial Estate
Capel Hendre
Ammanford
Carmarthenshire
SA18 3SJ
UK
T/F +44 (0)1269 844 670
E sunset@connect-wales.co.uk

Solvay Plastiques SA
Rue du Prince Albert 33
1050 Brussels
Belgium
T 32 (0)2 509 61 11
F 32 (0)2 509 69 18

Sony Corporation Design Center
6-7-35 Kitashinagawa
Shinagawa-ku
Tokyo 141, Japan
T +81 (0)3 5448 7758
F +81 (0)3 5448 7822
www.sony.co.jp and
www.sony.co.uk

Southampton Innovations Limited
University of Southampton
Highfield, Southampton
Hampshire SO17 1BJ, UK
T +44 (0)23 8059 2035
F +44 (0)23 8059 3585
E info@sil-uk.com
www.southamptoninnovations.com

Soy Environmental Products, Inc.
8855 N. Black Canon Fwy
Ste 2000
Phoenix, AZ 85021, USA
T +1 602 674 5500
www.soyclean.com

SRAM Corporation
Global Headquarters
361 West Chestnut St
Chicago, IL 60610, USA
T +1 312 664 8800
F +1 312 664 8826
E davidz@sram.com or
E ksolberg@sram.com

Staber Industries, Inc.
4800 Homer Ohio Lane
Groveport, OH 43125
USA
T +1 614 836 5995
F +1 614 836 9524
www.staber.com

Starch Tech, Inc.
720 Florida Ave S.
Golden Valley
MN 55426-1704, USA
T +1 612 545 5400
F +1 612 545 9450
E sti@starchtech.com
www.starchtech.com

Steelcase, Inc.
6100 E Paris Ave SE
Caledonia, MI 49316-9790
USA
www.steelcase.com

sTRAKA sPORTs
Niebuhrstrasse 62
10629 Berlin, Germany
T +49 (0)30 327016 16
F +49 (0)30 327016 17
E s.straka@ciro.de
www.ciro.de

Stramit
East Loop 143
Perryton, TX 79070, USA
T +1 806 435 9303

Strandwood Molding, Inc.
531 Highway M-26
PO Box 360
Hancock, MI 49930-0360, USA
T +1 906 487 9768
F +1 906 487 9770
www.strandwood.com

Studio eg
2431 Peralta Street
Suite 2437A
Oakland, CA 94607, USA

Styradex Plastics Recycling
Unit A, Burnfoot Industrial Estate
Hawick TD9 8SL, UK

Sun-Mar Corporation
600 Main Street
Tonawanda, NY 14150-0888
USA
T +1 905 332 1314
F +1 905 332 1315
E compost@sun-mar.com
www.sun-mar.com

Sunways Gesellschaft für Solartechnik mbH
Macairestrasse 5
78467 Konstanz, Germany
T +49 (0)7531 99677 0
F +49 (0)7531 99677 10
E info@sunways.de
www.sunways.de

Supercool AB
Banehagsgatan 1 B
414 51 Gothenburg
Sweden
T +46 (0)31 42 05 30
F +46 (0)31 24 79 09
www.supercool.se

Sutton Vane Associates
Britannia House
1 Glenthorne Road
London W6 0LH, UK
T +44 (0)20 8563 9370
F +44 (0)20 8563 9371
www.sva.co.uk

Syndesis, Inc.
2908 Colorado Ave
Santa Monica
CA 90403-3616, USA
T +1 310 829 9932
F +1 310 829 5641
www.syndesisinc.com

Tectan
Entwicklungsgesellschaft
für Verbundmaterial
Diez GmbH
Industriestrasse 17-2
65582 Diez, Germany

Teisen Products Limited
Bradley Green
Redditch
Worcestershire
B96 6RP, UK
T +44 (0)1527 821 488
F +44 (0)1527 821 665

Teknos Tranemo AB
Limmaredsvägen 2
Box 211
514 24 Tranemo
Sweden
T +46 (0)325 707 70
F +46 (0)325 767 54
www.teknos.se

Tendo Co. Ltd
1-3-10 Midarekawa
Tendo 994
Yamagata
Japan
T +81 (0)236 53 3121
F +81 (0)236 53 3454
www.tendo-mokko.co.jp/

Tetrapak Ltd
1 Longwalk Road
Stockley Park
Uxbridge
Middlesex UB11 1DL
UK
T +44 (0)870 442 6000
F +44 (0)870 442 6001
www.tetrapak.com

Therma-Float Ltd
PO Box 8
Beech Lane House
Alderly Edge
Cheshire SK9 5ES
UK
T +44 (0)1625 251 000
F +44 (0)1625 524 584
E therma-float.ltd@dial.pipex.com

TH!NK Nordic AG
Norway/Ford Motor Company, USA
TH!NK Mobility, LLC
5920 Pasteur Court
Carlsbad, CA 92008
USA
www.thinkmobility.com

Timber Holdings Ltd
2400 W. Cornell
Milwaukee, WI 53209
USA
T +1 414 445 8989
F +1 414 445 9155
E info@ironwoods.com
www.ironwoods.com

Tonwerk Lausen AG
CH 4415 Lausen
Switzerland
T +41 (0)61 927 95
F +41 (0)61 927 95

Toyota (GB) plc
The Quadrangle
Redhill
Surrey RH1 1PX, UK
T +44 (0)1737 768 585
F +44 (0)1737 771 728
www.toyota.co.uk

Toyota Motor Corporation
1 Toyota-cho
471-8571 Toyota City
Aichi Prefecture
Japan
www.toyota.com

Trannon Furniture Limited
Chilhampton Farm
Wilton
Salisbury
Wilts SP2 0AB, UK
T +44 (0)1722 744 577
F +44 (0)1722 744 477
E info@trannon.com
www.trannon.com

Transform Plastics Ltd
Potter Place
West Pimbo
Industrial Estate
Skelmersdale
Lancashire
WN8 9PW
UK
T +44 (0)1695 51399
F +44 (0)1695 51393

Traveller
Germany
c/o Feldmann & Schultchen
7 Timmermannstrasse
22299 Hamburg
Germany
T +49 (0)40 510000
F +49 (0)40 517000
www.fsdesign.de

Trevira GmbH & Co. KG
Lyoner Strasse 38A
60528 Frankfurt
Germany
T +49 (0)69 305 5756
F +49 (0)69 305 1642

Trisit Textiltechnologie GmbH
Trisit Design
Stuttgarter Strasse 73
73230 Kirchheim
Germany
T +49 (0)7021 935175
F +49 (0)7021 935339
E roellf@recaro.de

Trojan Battery Company
USA
T +1 800 423 6569
+1 562 946 8381
F +1 562 906 4033
E marketing@trojanbattery.com
www.trojanbattery.com

TrusJoist MacMillan (TJM)
Corporate Headquarters
200 East Mallard Drive
Boise, ID 83706
USA
T +1 208 364 1200
F +1 208 364 1300
www.tjm.com

TRW Lucas Varity Electrical Steering (UK)
c/o TRW, Inc.
USA
www.trw.com

Unicor Corporation
24271 Larkwood Lane
Lake Forest, CA 92630
USA
T +1 714 770 8494

Uni-Solar
1110 West Maple Road
Troy, MI 48084
USA
T +1 248 362 4170
F +1 248 362 4442
E unisolarinfo@ovonic.com
www.uni-solar.com

Universal Master Products
23 Station Approach
Hayes, Bromley
Kent BR2 7EQ
UK
T +44 (0)20 8462 0222
F +44 (0)20 8462 7746

Universal Pulp Packaging
Milton of Campsie
Glasgow G65 8EE
UK
T +44 (0)1360 310 322
F +44 (0)1360 311 975
E pulppack@aol.com
www.pulppack.co.uk

Urethane Soy Systems Company (USSC)
PO Box 569
Princeton, IL 61356
USA
T +1 888 514 9096
F +1 815 643 2998
E johnwawak@yahoo.com

US Plastic Lumber Ltd
Smartdeck Systems
2600 W. Roosevelt Road
Chicago, IL 60608
USA
T +1 888 733 2546
E techsupport@smartdeck.com
www.smartdeck.com

Uwe Braun GmbH
Herr Braun Lange Felder
19309 Lenzen (Elbe)
Germany
T +49 (0)38792 9850
E info@uwe-braun.de

Vaccari Limited
27 Prospect Way
Lapford, Crediton
Devon EX17 6QB
UK
T +44 (0)1363 83115
F +44 (0)1363 83849
E info@vaccari.co.uk
www.vaccari.co.uk

VarioPac Disc Systems GmbH
Hangbaumstrasse 13
32257 Bünde
Germany
T +49 (0)5221 7684 17
F +49 (0)5221 7684 20
www.variopac.com

Varta Batteries AG/Varta AG
Press and Public Relations
Sven Kremser
Am Leineufer 51
30419 Hannover
Germany
T +49 (0)511 79 03 8 21
F +49 (0)511 79 03 7 17
E press@varta.com
www.varta.com

Vauxhall Motors Limited/General Motors
Griffin House
Osborne Road
Luton
Bedfordshire LU1 3YT
UK
T +44 (0)1582 721 122
F +44 (0)1582 427 400

Velcro (USA)
www.velcro.com

Veloland Schweiz
Stiftung Veloland Schweiz
Postfach 8275
3001 Bern
Switzerland
T +41(0)31 307 47 40
F +41(0)31 307 47 48
E info@veloland.ch

Vestfrost A/S
Spangsbjerg Møllevej 100
Postbox 2079
DK-6705 Esbjerg Ø
Denmark
T +45 (0)79 14 22 22
F +45 (0)79 14 23 55

Vetropack
Schützenmattstr. 266
CH 8180 Bülach
Switzerland
T +41 (0)1 863 33 73
F +41 (0)1 863 34 35

Vision Paper
see KP Products

Vitra (International) AG
22 Klünenfeldstrasse
CH 4127 Birsfelden
Switzerland
T +41 (0)61 377 15 09
F +41 (0)61 377 15 10
E info@vitra.com
www.vitra.com

VK & C Partnership
2/2 248 Woodlands Road
Glasgow G3 6ND, UK
T/F +44 (0)141 332 2049

Volkswagen AG
Environment Industrial
Safety and Traffic Systems
Letter box 174
38436 Wolfsburg
Germany

Volkswagen (UK)
Yeomans Drive
Blakelands
Milton Keynes
Buckinghamshire
MK14 5AN, UK
T +44 (0)1908 601 777
F +44 (0)1908 663 936
www.volkswagen.co.uk

Vorwerk & Co. Teppichwerke GmbH & Co. KG
Kulhmanstrasse 11
31785 Hameln, Germany
T +49 (0)5151 103 0
F +49 (0)5151 103 377
www.vorwerk-teppich.de

Wagner & Co. Solartechnik GmbH
Ringstrasse 14
35091 Cölbe
Germany
T +49 (0)64 21 8007-0
F +49 (0)64 21 8007-13

Wanders Wonders BV
Jacob Catskade 35
1052 BT Amsterdam
Netherlands
T +31 (0)20 422 1339
F +31 (0)20 422 7519
E joy@wanderswonders.nl

Waterfilm Energy
PO Box 128
Medford, NY 11763
USA
T +1 631 758 6271
F +1 631 758 0438
E GFX-CH@msn.com
www.oikos.com/gfx

Waterless UK Ltd
6 Bladon Close
Woodstock Road
Oxford
Oxfordshire OX2 8AD, UK
www.waterless.co.uk

Water Tech Industries
12665 NE Marx Street
Portland, OR 97230, USA
T +1 888 254 8412
+1 503 254 8412
F +1 503 261 9118
E marketing@watertech.com
www.watertech.com

Wellman, Inc.
212 7th St
Jersey City, NJ 07302
USA
E home@wellmaninc.com
E aboutus@wellmaninc.com
www.wellmanwlm.com

Werth Forsttechnik
Reidelbach 22
66687 Wadern
Germany
T +49 (0)68 712029
F +49 (0)68 715555
E ww@werth-weihnachts-welt.de
www.werth-weihnachts-welt.de

Werzalit AG + Co.
Germany
see Inka Presswood Pallets

Wettstein, Robert A
Josefstr. 188
CH 8005 Zurich
Switzerland
T +41 (0)1 272 97 25
F +41 (0)1 272 07 17

Wharington International Pty Ltd
48-50 Hargreaves Street
Huntingdale
Victoria 3166
Australia
T +61 (0)3 9544 5533
F +61 (0)3 9543 1907
E sales@wharington.com.au
www.wharington.com.au

Whirlpool
see Jam Design & Communications

Wiggly Wigglers
Lower Blakemere Farm
Blakemere
Herefordshire
HR2 9PX, UK
T *(Freephone, UK only)*
0800 216990
F +44 (0)1981 500 108
www.wigglywigglers.co.uk

Wilde & Spieth GmbH & Co
Zeppelinstr. 126
73730 Esslingen
am Neckar, Germany
T +49 (0)711 319710
F +49 (0)711 317111

Wilkhahn + Hahne GmbH & Co.
Postfach 2035
31844 Bad Münder
Germany
T +49 (0)5042 9990
F +49 (0)5042 999 226
E info@wilkhahn.de
www.wilkhahn.com

Willamette Europe Ltd
10th Floor
Maitland House
Warrior Square
Southend-on-Sea
Essex SS1 2JY, UK
T +44 (0)1702 619 044
www.willamette-europe.com

Willat Writing Instruments
8548 Washington Blvd
Culver City, CA 90232
USA
T +1 310 202 6000
F +1 310 202 0405
www.sensa.com

Willow Bank, The
PO Box 17
Machynlleth
Powys SY20 8WR, UK
T +44 (0)1686 430 510
www.telecentre.com/Willow_Bank/willowap.htm

WKR Altkunststoffproduktions- u. Vertriebsgesellschaft mbH
Entenpfuhl 10
67547 Worms, Germany
T +49 (0)6241 43451
F +49 (0)6241 49579
E kontakt.wkr@t-online.de

Woodnotes Oy
Tallberginkatu 8
00180 Helsinki
Finland
T +358 694 2200
F +358 694 2221
E woodnotes@woodnotes.fi
www.woodnotes.fi

ww.modcons
Units 2b-c
Vanguard Court
36 Peckham Road
London SE5 8QT, UK
T +44 (0)20 7708 4154

Xerox Corporation
800 Long Ridge Road
Stamford, CT 06904
USA
T *(Freephone, US only)*
+1 800 334 6200
www.xerox.com

Xerox (UK) Ltd
Bridge House
Uxbridge
Middlesex UB8 1HS, UK
T *(Freephone, UK only)*
0800 787 787
www.xerox.co.uk

XO
RN 19
77170 Servon
France
T +33 (0)1 60 62 60 60
F +33 (0)1 60 62 60 62

XO2 Limited (Trading as Exosect)
Administration
Building (SIL)
University of Southampton
Highfield
Southampton
Hampshire SO17 1BJ, UK
E info@exosectuk.com
www.exosectuk.com

Yemm & Hart Ltd
Green Materials
RR1 Box 173
Marquand, MO 63655, USA
T +1 573 783 5454
F +1 573 783 7544
E info@yemmhart.com
www.yemmhart.com

YKK Architectural Products, Inc.
1, Kanda Izumi-cho
Chiyoda-ku
Tokyo 101-0024
Japan
T +81 (0)3 36258844
F +81 (0)3 56108199

Zanotta SpA
Via Vittorio Veneto 57
20054 Nova Milanese (Mi)
Italy
T +39 (0)362 368 330
F +39 (0)362 451 038
E zanottaspa@zanotta.it

Zanussi
see Electrolux

Zimmerei Michael Kaufmann
see KFN Kaufmann Produkt GmbH

The design strategies described with each product in Objects for Living and Objects for Working are listed below. They are grouped according to one of five lifecycle phases – pre-production, including materials selection; manufacturing/making/fabrication; distribution/transportation; functionality and use; and disposal/end-of-life. Other strategies that do not easily fit into this product lifecycle are described under the heading Miscellaneous. Extended descriptions of each design strategy are given where appropriate. Reference should also be made to the Glossary of eco-design terms (p. 339).

PRE-PRODUCTION PHASE

Anti-fashion – a design that avoids temporary, fashionable styles.

Anti-obsolescence – a design that is easily repaired, maintained and upgraded so it is not made obsolete with changes in technology or taste.

Dematerialization – the process of converting products into services. A good example of dematerialization through timeshare of a product is a local community sharing a car 'pool' in which all individuals have the opportunity to use/hire a car when needed rather than own a car that stands idle for a large part of its life. Other examples include digital cameras where silver halide film is replaced by CCD chips, dematerializing part of the consumables cycle. Designing products used in the context of a dematerialized service may place unusual constraints on the design such as concentration on maintenance and longevity of parts.

Open access design – design that allows other designers to see how software, hardware and other electronic products are coded and constructed.

Product take-back – a system under which manufacturers agree to take back a product when it has reached the end of its useful life so that components and/or materials can be reused or recycled (see also Producer responsibility). This can fundamentally change the essence of the design and engage the designer in examining design for assembly (DfA), disassembly (DfD)and remanufacture.

Reusable product – a product that can be reused at the end of its initial lifespan for an identical, similar or new use.

Universal design – the application of widely accepted practices, components, fixtures, materials and technologies suitable for a wide range of end-uses.

PRE-PRODUCTION: MATERIALS SELECTION

Abundant materials from the lithosphere/geosphere – inorganic materials, such as stone, clay, minerals and metals from the earth's crust.

Biodegradable – decomposed by the action of microbes such as bacteria and fungi.

Biopolymers – plastics made from plants. Biopolymers can be composted and returned to nature.

Certified sources – materials that are independently certified as originating from sustainably managed resources, from recycled materials or conforming to a national or international eco-label.

Compostable – can be decomposed by microbes such as bacteria and fungi to release nutrients and organic matter.

Durable/extremely durable – tough, strong materials that do not break or wear and survive the life of the product or well beyond.

Lightweight – materials with a high strength-to-weight ratio.

Locally sourced materials are those in close proximity to the point of manufacturing or production.

Non-toxic/Non-hazardous – not likely to cause loss of life or ill health to man and/or degradation of living ecosystems.

Reclaimed – materials saved for reuse on demolition of the built environment.

Recyclable components – components of products that can be used in a new product.

Recyclate – material that has been made into a new material comprising wholly or partially recycled materials. An alternative term is 'recycled feedstock'.

Recycled – materials that have been processed (such as cleaned, graded, shredded, blended), then remanufactured

Recycled content – materials that include some recycled and some virgin content. If a material has 100 per cent-recycled content, it is a recycled material.

Renewable – a material that can be extracted from resources which absorb energy from the sun to synthesize or create matter. These resources include primary producers, such as plants and bacteria, and secondary producers, such as fish and mammals.

Single or mono-materials – consist of pure materials rather than mixtures. This facilitates recycling.

Stewardship sourcing – materials from certified sources and supply chain management.

Supply-chain management (green procurement) is the process of specifying that the goods/materials of suppliers meet minimum environmental standards. The specification may be that the goods will come from certified sources (e.g., the Forest Stewardship Council, national or international eco-labels), carry recognized accreditation (e.g. ISO 14001, EMAS) or meet trade association standards (e.g. National Association of Paper Manufacturers' recycled-paper logo in the UK).

Sustainable/from sustainable sources – materials that originate from managed resources which are forecast to last for a very long time and/or are renewable resources (see above).

Waste materials – materials fabricated from production (factory) or consumer waste.

MANUFACTURING/MAKING/FABRICATION PHASE

Production processes

Avoidance of toxic/hazardous substances – avoiding substances liable to damage human health and living ecosystems.

Bio-manufacturing – using nature to help fabricate products in situ. For example, 'manufacturing' natural gourds by training them in special shapes for later use as packaging; growing plants to produce biopolymers (natural plastics).

Clean production systems are put in place to reduce the impact of manufacturing goods by minimizing the production of waste and emissions to land, air and water. Closed-loop recycling (see below) technologies are often incorporated into clean production.

Closed-loop recycling/production is the process of introducing waste streams back into the manufacturing process in a continuous cycle without loss of waste from that cycle. The textile and chemical industries often recycle chemical compounds used in processing their end-products, resulting in cleaner production.

Cold fabrication/manufacturing – methods that require no heat or pressure and hence reduce energy consumption and facilitate disassembly.

Design for assembly (DfA) is a method of rationalizing and standardizing parts to facilitate the fixing together of components during production or manufacture.

Design for disassembly (DfD) is a method of designing products to facilitate cost-effective, non-destructive breakdown of the component parts of a product at the end of its life so that they can be recycled and/or reused.

Efficient use of raw and manufactured materials – reducing materials used and minimizing waste production.

Lightweight construction – reducing materials used but maintaining strength.

Low-energy manufacturing/production/construction techniques/assembly – reducing the energy required to make components and/or products.

Reduced resource consumption – reducing materials used, especially raw materials extracted from the environment.

Reduction in use of consumables – reducing consumables used during the manufacturing process.

Reduction in materials usage – efficient use of materials compared with conventional/traditional designs

Reduction of production waste is achieved by more efficient designs and/or manufacturing processes.

Reusable buildings – demountable, modular buildings, which can be transported and reassembled in new locations.

Self-assembly – the final assembly is done by the consumer, thereby saving energy in the fabrication process.

Simple, low-cost construction – manufacturing with simple, inexpensive tooling and low-energy processes.

Zero waste production – the elimination of waste from the production process.

Recycling and reuse

Design for recyclability (DfR) is a design philosophy that tries to maximize positive environmental attributes of a product, such as ease of disassembly, recyclability, maintenance, reuse or refurbishment, without compromising the product's functionality and performance.

Design for recycling (DfR) considers the best methods to improve recycling of raw materials or components by facilitating assembly and disassembly, ensuring that materials are not mixed and appropriately labelling materials and components.

Materials labelling assists with improved identification of materials for recycling.

Materials recycled at source – use of office, factory or domestic waste to make new products in situ.

Reuse of end-of-life components (remanufacturing) – taking back worn-out or old components/products and refurbishing them to an 'as-new' standard for resale.

Reuse of materials – reusing materials without changing their original state. By comparison, recycling involves some reorganization or partial destruction of the material followed by reconstitution.

Reuse of redundant components – components formally manufactured for another use are re-employed in a new product.

Re-used objects – any complete object reused in a new product.

Single material components – components made of one material (a mono-material component).

Use of ready-mades/ready-made components – components made for one product reapplied to a new or different type of product.

DISTRIBUTION/TRANSPORTATION PHASE

Flat-pack products – products that can be stored flat to maximize use of transport/storage space.

Lightweight products – products that have been designed to be lightweight, yet retain full functionality, and as a result require less energy to transport.

Reduced energy use during transport/reduction in transport energy – this can be achieved by careful design of products to maximize packing per unit area and minimize weight per product.

Reusable packaging – packaging that can provide protection on more than one trip.

Self-assembly – designs that are assembled by the consumer, therefore saving valuable space in transport and storage.

FUNCTIONALITY AND USE PHASE

Socially beneficial designs

Alternative modes of transport for improved choice of mobility – reduces dependency on high-environmental-impact products such as the car and affords improved mobility options for minority groups, such as the disabled.

An aid to reduce population growth – helps keep the balance between population and resource availability and so slows environmental degradation, social exclusion and other problems.

Community ownership – encourages group rather than individual ownership and so improves the efficiency of product usage.

Design for need – A concept that emerged in the 1970s and was promoted by exponents such as the design academic Victor Papanek and by a landmark exhibition at the Royal College of Art, London, in 1976. Design for need concentrates on design for social needs rather than for creating 'lifestyle' products.

Emergency provision/ distribution of clean, safe water – products designed to reduce human mortality and disease.

Encourages recycling – products designed to facilitate recycling.

Equal access for public services – products to enable minority groups, such as the disabled, full access to public services, such as transport.

Hire rather than ownership – products designed for hire rather than for personal ownership, receiving more efficient and economical use.

Equal access to information resources – products to enable minority groups, such as the disabled, to gain access to information resources.

Reduction in noise/noise pollution – products designed to minimize distress and disturbance caused by excessive noise.

Reduction of visual intrusion in the landscape – products designed to minimize the visual impact of technological or manmade products.

Designs to reduce emissions/pollution/toxins

Avoidance/reduction in emissions (to water) – products whose production and use avoids or minimizes emissions of hazardous/toxic substances to water.

Avoidance/reduction in emissions/pollution (to air) – products whose production and use avoids or minimizes emissions of hazardous/toxic substances to air including greenhouse gases, hydrocarbons, particulate matter and cancer-causing substances (carcinogens).

Avoidance/reduction of hazardous/toxic substances – products that are safe for human use because they contain little or no hazardous or toxic substances. There are international and national lists of banned substances including chemicals and pesticides. Some companies produce their own lists, in addition to those substances on lists with which they legally have to comply. Safe for human use does not necessarily mean safe for plant and other wildlife.

Free of CFCs and HCFCs – products, generally associated with the use of refrigerants, that do not use either chlorofluorocarbons (CFCs), which are greenhouse gases, or hydrochlorofluorocarbons (HCFCs), which are greenhouse gases and ozone-depleting gases.

Zero emissions refers to vehicles powered with electric motors or with hydrogen fuel-cell power systems that do not produce exhaust emissions of greenhouse gases (such as carbon dioxide, carbon monoxide, methane or oxides of nitrogen) or particulate matter (such as PM10s). A true zero-emission electric vehicle (EV) is one that uses electricity generated from renewable power rather than fossil fuel or nuclear sources.

Designs for improved functionality

Customizable – describes a product that the consumer can alter to his/her own specification or configuration.

Dual function – one product with two functions.

Improved ergonomics – products that are easier and more comfortable to use.

Improved health and safety – products that don't endanger health or safety or that promote better health.

Improved user-friendliness – products that are easier to understand and more fun to use.

Improved user functionality – products that serve their purpose better than previous designs.

Modular design/modularity – products that can be configured in many ways to suit the user by changing the arrangement of individual modules. Modular design also offers the user the possibility of adding modules as needs require.

Multifunctional – a product capable of more than two functions.

Multi-use space – a space capable of being used for different types of functions.

Portable – a product that is easily transported for use in different locations.

Safe, i.e., non-toxic and non-hazardous – a product without adverse effects on human health.

Upgradable/upgradability – a product that is easy to upgrade by replacing old components/elements with new. This is especially important for technological products.

Designs to increase product lifespan/longevity

Design for ease of maintenance/maintainability – products with good instructions and easy access to maintain or service parts that wear.

Durability – products that are tough, owing to strong materials and high-quality manufacturing, and so resistant to use and wear.

Ease of repair/repairability – products easy to assemble/disassemble to repair worn or broken parts.

Designs to reduce energy consumption

Integrated or intelligent transport systems – transport systems that permit a range of mobility products to be used to offer a choice of mobility paths for the user.

Energy conservation – products designed to prevent loss of energy.

Energy efficiency – products/buildings designed to use energy efficiently.

Energy neutral – products/buildings that generate as much energy as they consume.

Fuel economy – products that use less fossil fuel energy than an earlier generation of products and so cause reduced emissions to air over their lifetime.

Human-powered products – products that need energy supplied by humans.

Hybrid power – products that combine two or more power sources, for example, hybrid electric/petrol or fuel cell/electric cars.

Improved energy efficiency – products with improved usage or output per unit of energy expended.

Low voltage – products capable of operating on 12-volt or 24-volt electricity supply rather than higher voltages.

Natural lighting – products that encourage the use of natural lighting (rather than consuming electricity).

Rechargeable (batteries) – products that encourage repeat battery use by recharging from a mains or renewable power supply, and so reduce waste production.

Renewable power – electricity generated from products that convert the energy of the sun, wind, water or geothermal heat from the earth's crust.

Solar power (passive) – products that produce light or heat by absorbing the energy of the sun.

Solar power (generation) – products that generate electricity by absorbing the energy of the sun. These typically include products equipped with photovoltaic panels.

Recycling and reduction of waste production

Recyclable packaging/containers – packaging and containers made of materials that can be recycled.

Reduction in use of consumables – products that reduce the use of consumables such as paper, inks, batteries, oils and detergents.

Reusable packaging/containers – packaging and containers that can be reused for repeat trips.

Designs to improve water usage

Water conservation – products that reduce water usage, and/or facilitate water collection.

Water generation (freshwater) – products that generate fresh water from contaminated surface or ground water, seawater or water-saturated air.

DISPOSAL/END-OF-LIFE PHASE

Conservation of landfill space – products that decompose to release landfill space or products that can be reycled, reused or remanufactured to avoid being landfilled.

Encouraging local composting/local biodegradation of waste – products that can be locally decomposed by the owner, so saving on the transport energy of waste collection and landfill space.

Product take-back – a system under which manufacturers agree to take back a product when it has reached the end of its useful life so that components and/or materials can be reused or recycled (see also Producer responsibility). This can fundamentally change the essence of the design and engage the designer in examining design for assembly (DfA), disassembly (DfD) and remanufacture.

Recycling – products that are designed to be easily recyclable by being made of single materials or by being easily disassembled into materials or components which can be recycled.

Remanufacture – products that are easily disassembled for refurbishment to remanufacture new products.

Reuse – products that are easily reused for the same or a new purpose or are easily disassembled for the components and/or materials to be reused.

MISCELLANEOUS STRATEGIES

Certification of products (see also Green Organizations, p. 331)

Eco-labels – labels attached to products which confirm that the manufacturers conform to independently certified standards in terms of reduced environmental impacts.

Independently certified labels – a variety of labels applied to products which signify that the products meet specific criteria for reduced environmental impacts, inclusion of recycled materials, and/or materials/products from sustainable sources.

Environmental management and business systems

Corporate environmental policy – a written statement defining a company's position on the environment with an on-going audit of progess over time. Existence of a corporate environmental policy *usually* indicates inclusion of environmental management systems and/or the use of basic ecodesign strategies in everyday business.

Eco Management and Audit Scheme (EMAS) – an independently certified environmental management system, which operates in the European Union. Certification is awarded by national bodies in individual EU countries verified by the EMAS organization.

ISO 14001 – an international standard for environmental management schemes maintained by the International Standards Organization (ISO) in Geneva, Switzerland. New standards are emerging for lifecycle assessment (ISO 14040) and eco-labelling and environmental labels (draft ISO 14021).

ISO 9001 – an international standard for quality assurance maintained by the International Standards Organization (ISO) in Geneva, Switzerland. Certification is granted by independent national organizations accredited by the ISO.

Biodiversity

Animal-friendly products – products that are manufactured without harm to animals.

Encouragement of conservation and biodiversity – products that assist in promoting conservation and diversity as a result of a corporate environmental or supply-chain management policy or by sourcing materials from habitats managed to maintain diversity.

Protection against soil erosion – products used to avoid or reduce soil erosion by water or wind.

Protection of fish stocks – products used to enhance the survival of fish stocks.

ACADEMIC AND RESEARCH

Centre for Design at Royal Melbourne Institute of Technology (RMIT)
GPO Box 2476V
Melbourne
Victoria 3001, Australia
E john.gertsakis@rmit.edu.au
www.cfd.rmit.edu.au

Centre for Environmental Assessment of Product and Material Systems (CPM)
Chalmers University of Technology
Gothenburg, Sweden
T +46 (0)31 772 56 40
F +46 (0)31 772 56 49
E Christian Nanji
chrnan@vset.chalmers.se
www.cpm.chalmers.se/

Centre for Sustainable Design
Surrey Institute of Art & Design
Farnham, Surrey, UK
T +44 (0)1252 892 772
F +44 (0)1252 892 747
E cfsd@surrart.ac.uk
www.cfsd.org.uk

Consortium on Green Design and Manufacturing (CGDM)
Civil and Environmental Engineering Department
215B McLaughlin Hall
University of California at Berkeley
Berkeley, CA 94720-1712
USA
http://greenmfg.me.berkeley.edu/green2/Home/Index.html

DEMI – Design for the Environment Multimedia Implementation Project
c/o Department of Design Studies
Goldsmiths College
13 Laurie Grove
New Cross
London SE14 6NW, UK
T +44 (0)20 7919 7788
E info@demi.org.uk
www.demi.org.uk
DEMI is a consortium of institutions comprising CTI Art & Design, the Design Council, Falmouth College of Arts, Forum for the Future, Goldsmiths College (lead institution), the Open University, the Royal Society for the Encouragement of Arts, Manufacturing and Business, Surrey Institute of Art and Design and the University of Brighton. The aim of the DEMI project is to create a multimedia design and environmental teaching and learning resource for higher education. It is funded by HEFCE, the Higher Education Funding Councils for England, Wales and Northern Ireland.

Design Academy Eindhoven
Emmasingel 14
PO Box 2125
5600 CC Eindhoven
Netherlands
T +31 (0)40 239 3939
F +31 (0)40 239 3940
E info@designacademy.nl
www.designacademy.nl

Design for Environment Research Group (Dfe)
Department of Mechanical Engineering, Design and Manufacture
Manchester Metropolitan University
John Dalton Building
Chester Street
Manchester M1 5GD, UK
E N.Caluwe@mmu.ac.uk
S.J.Poole@mmu.ac.uk
http://sun1.mpce.stu.mmu.ac.uk/pages/projects/dfe/dfe.html

Design for Sustainability Program
TU Delft Subfaculty of Industrial Design Engineering
Jaffalaan
92628 BX Delft
Netherlands
T +31 (0)15 278 2738
F +31 (0)15 278 2956
www.io.tudelft.nl/research/dfs/index.html

Designition
Design Faculty
University of Kingston
Knights Park
Kingston-upon-Thames
Surrey KT1 2QJ, UK
T +44 (0)20 8547 7165
F +44 (0)20 8547 7365
E designition@kingston.ac.uk
www.designition.org

EcoDesign C@mpus
Coordinator, Luigi Bistanino
Politecnico di Torino
Turin, Italy
E lanzavecchia@araxp.polito.it
www.ecodesigncampus.com

Environment Conscious Design and Manufacturing Lab (ECDM)
Department of Industrial & Manufacturing Systems Engineering
University of Windsor, Canada
http://ie.uwindsor.ca/imse/people/ecdm_list.html

European Design Centre
PO Box 6279
5600 HG Eindhoven
Netherlands
T +31 (0)40 239 30 09
F +31 (0)40 239 39 10
E info@edc.nl
www.edc.nl
Promotes high-quality integrated product development by provision of educational facilities, a database and support for engineers, product designers and industrialists.

Institute for Engineering Design – Austrian Ecodesign Information Point
Austrian Ministry of Transport, Innovation and Technology with the Vienna University of Technology
Austria
www.ecodesign.at/ecodesign_eng/

Institute for Sustainable Design
Campbell Hall
University of Virginia
PO Box 400122
Charlottesville
VA 22904-4122
USA
T +1 804 924 6454
F +1 804 982 2678
E uva-isd@virginia.edu
www.virginia.edu

Interduct/Clean Technology Institute (CTI)
Delft University of Technology
Netherlands
www.interduct.tudelft.nl

IVAM Environmental Research
University of Amsterdam
1001 ZB Amsterdam
Netherlands
T +31 (0)20 525 50 80
F +31 (0)20 525 58 50
E office@ivambv.uva.nl
www.ivambv.uva.nl

ARCHITECTURE

American Institute of Architects
1735 New York Avenue NW
Washington, DC 20006
USA
T +1 202 626 7300
www.e-architect.com
The AIA publishes the Environmental Resource Guide, *in cooperation with the US Environmental Protection Agency (US EPA), which includes articles and case studies of the environmental impacts and resource issues for different building methods and materials.*

Association for Environment Conscious Building (AECB)
PO Box 32, Llandysul
Carmarthenshire
SA44 5EJ, UK
E admin@aecb.net
www.aecb.net

Center of Excellence for Sustainable Development: Affordable Housing (USA)
www.eren.doe.gov/buildings
Jumping-off point for information on green housing and building, including the Energy Efficiency and Renewable Energy Network (EREN) 'Buildings of the 21st Century', Office of Building Technology, State and Community Programs.

Centre for Alternative Technology
Machynlleth
Powys SY20 9AZ, UK
T +44 (0)1654 702 400
F +44 (0)1654 702 782
E info@cat.org.uk
www.cat.org.uk
Established in 1975 as a resource centre to encourage a more ecological way of living, CAT now offers substantive physical evidence of ways in which buildings, renewable-energy technology and wastewater treatment can reduce environmental impacts. CAT has also published extensive DIY and professional guides on all aspects of low-impact technology.

Centre for Sustainable Construction (CSC)
BRE – Building Research Establishment
Garston, Watford
Hertfordshire, WD2 7JR, UK
T +44 (0)1923 664 000
T (Howard at CSC)
+44 (0)1923 664 462
E enquiries@bre.co.uk
www.bre.co.uk/sustainable/ind ex.html

Community Eco-Design Network (CEN)
PO Box 6241
Minneapolis, MN 55406
USA
T +1 612 722 3260
E erichark@mtn.org
www.cedn.org

Ecological Design Group, The
Scott Sutherland School of Architecture
Faculty of Design
The Robert Gordon University
Garthdee Road
Aberdeen AB9 2QB, UK
T +44 (0)1224 263 713
F +44 (0)1224 263 535
E f.stevenson@rgu.ac.uk
www.rgu.ac.uk/subj/ecoldes/edg1.htm

Environmental Design Research Association (EDRA)
PO Box 7146
Edmond, OK 73083-7146
USA
T +1 405 330 4863
F +1 405 330 4150
E edra@telepath.com
www.telepath.com/edra/home.html
Founded in 1968 for the advancement of the art and science of environmental design research to improve the understanding of interrelationships between people and their built and natural surroundings.

Royal Institute of British Architects
66 Portland Place
London W1N 4AD, UK
T +44 (0)20 7580 5533
F +44 (0)20 7580 1541
E bal@inst.riba.org
www.architecture.com

US Green Building Council
90 New Montgomery St
Suite 1001
San Francisco, CA 94105
USA
T +1 202 429 2081
F +1 202 429 9574
E info@usgbc.org
www.usgbc.org

ASSOCIATIONS – ECODESIGN, GREEN DESIGN, DfE

Alternative Technology Association
PO Box 2001 Lygon St
North Brunswick
Victoria 3057, Australia
T +61 (0)3 9388 9311
F +61 (0)3 9388 9322
E ata@ata.org.au
www.ata.org.au

EcoDesign Association
The British School
Slad Road, Stroud
Gloucestershire
GL5 1QW, UK
T +44 (0)1453 765 575
F +44 (0)1453 759 211
www.edaweb.org

Ecodesign Foundation
PO Box 369, Rozelle
NSW 2039, Australia
T +61 (0)2 9555 9412
F +61 (0)2 9555 9564
E edf@edf.edu.au
www.edf.edu.au

EcoDesign Resource Society
201-225 Smithe Street
Vancouver BC
V6B 4X7, Canada
E edrs@infoserve.net
www.ecodesign.bc.ca/

O2 Network
c/o Netherlands Design Institute
Keizersgracht 609
1017 DS Amsterdam
Netherlands
www.o2.org
O2 Network coordinates participating O2 groups in sixteen countries sharing information and promoting discussion about ecodesign and sustainable design in order to integrate sustainability into the design process.

Scottish EcoDesign Association (SEDA)
The Monastery
Edinburgh EH1 3RG, UK
T +44 (0)131 557 2500
F +44 (0)131 557 2870
E sedainfo@aol.com
E SEDA@inverarc.demon.co.uk
www.inverarc.co.uk/seda/

Society for Responsible Design (SRD)
PO Box 288, Leichhardt
NSW 2040, Australia
T +61 (0)2 9564 0721
F +61 (0)2 9564 1611
E srd@green.net.au
www.green.net.au/srd/

AWARDS

Design Preis Schweiz
c/o Design Center
Postfach 1619
CH 4901 Langenthal
Switzerland
T +41 (0)62 923 03 33
F +41 (0)62 923 16 22
E designpreis@designNet.ch
www.designNet.ch

Design Sense
c/o Design Museum
28 Shad Thames
London SE1 2YD, UK
T +44 (0)20 7940 8790
F +44 (0)20 7378 6540
www.designmuseum.org
Launched in 1999, this award probably offers the best prize money in the world, a total of £40,000 to the winner, for the most outstanding sustainable building or product. Twelve designs are shortlisted, six architectural projects and six products. Design Sense is co-ordinated by the Design Museum and is supported by the Rufford Foundation with sponsorship from Corus plc, the European metals producer, and The Guardian newspaper.

Good Design Award – Ecology Design Prize
Japan Industrial Design Promotion Organization (JIDPO)
G-Mark Division
4th Floor Annex
World Trade Center Building
2-4-1 Hamamatsu-cho
Minato-ku, Tokyo 105
Japan
T +81 (0)3 3435 5626
F +81 (0)3 3432 7346
E g-mark@jidpo.or.jp
www.jidpo.or.jp/gda/index.html
The Good Design Selection System, with its G-Mark logo for winning products, was launched in 1957 and became the Good Design Award from April 1998. Product categories are wide-ranging and attract thousands of entrants from Japan and the international design community. A special category, the Ecology Design Prize, is awarded to products with reduced impact on the environment.

Industrie Forum Design Hannover (iF)
Messegelände
30521 Hannover
Germany
T +49 (0)511 89 32 400
F +49 (0)511 89 32 401
E info@ifdesign.de
www.ifdesign.de
This is one of the most prestigious annual design awards in Germany. Categories include a special Ecology Design Award and Interaction Design Award as well as more traditional themes such as Product Design Awards for office, business, communications, home, household, lighting, consumer electronics, lifestyle, public design, packaging design, textile design, building technology, industry, transport, medical and leisure. Winners of the Ecology Design Award are selected from any of the subcategories in the competition.

International Design Resource Awards (IDRA)
Design Resource Institute
7406A Greenwood Avenue
Seattle, WA 98177, USA
T +1 206 289 0949
F +1 206 7893 144
E JohnsonDesignStudio@compuserve.com
www.designresource.org
Now in its sixth year, the IDRA competition requires that entries have a high degree of post-consumer recycled or sustainably harvested materials and demonstrate added value as a result, be designed for

future reuse or recycling and be suitable for commercial production.

RIBA Sustainability Award 2000
RIBA Journal
2 Harbour Exchange Square
London SE14 2EG, UK
www.ribaawards.co.uk

BUSINESS AND THE ENVIRONMENT

Enviroene
US Environmental Protection Agency (EPA)
http://es.epa.gov
A government web resource for pollution prevention, compliance assurance, enforcement information and databases.

Global Futures Foundation and The Future 500
801 Crocker Road
Sacramento, CA 95864
USA
T +1 916 486 5999
F +1 916 486 5998
E infor@globalff.org
www.globalff.org/

International Institute of Sustainable Development (IISD)
Head Office
161 Portage Avenue East
6th floor
Winnipeg
Manitoba R3B 0Y4, Canada
T +1 204 958 7700
F +1 204 958 7710
E info@iisd.ca
http://iisd.ca/

National Centre for Business and Sustainability
The Peel Building
University of Salford
Greater Manchester
M5 4WT, UK
T +44 (0)161 295 5276
F +44 (0)161 295 5041
E thencbs@thencbs.co.uk
www.thencbs.co.uk

World Business Council for Sustainable Development
160, Route de Florissant
Conches, CH 1231 Geneva
Switzerland
T +41 (0)22 839 3100
F +41 (0)22 839 3131
E elleboode@wbcsd.ch
www.wbcsd.ch

CERTIFICATION, ECO-LABELS AND ENERGY LABELS

British Standards Institute
BSI Quality Assurance
389 Chiswick High Road
London W4 4AL, UK
T +44 (0)20 8996 9000
F +44 (0)20 8996 9001
E info@bsi.org.uk
www.bsi-global.com

Certified Forest Products Council
14780 SW Osprey Drive
Suite 285, Beaverton
OR 97007, USA
T +1 503 590 6600
F +1 503 590 6655
E info@certifiedwood.org
www.certifiedwood.org
Established in 1997, the Certified Forest Products Council is an independent, not-for-profit, voluntary business initiative committed to encouraging responsible forest management and the manufacture of environmentally responsible forest products in North America. The CFPC endorses the 'well-managed' standards defined by the Forest Stewardship Council. Members include suppliers, manufacturers, specifiers and individuals.

Duales System Deutschland AG – The Green Dot (Der Grüne Punkt)
Frankfurter Strasse 720-726
51145 Cologne (Porz Eil)
Germany
T +49 (0)2203 93 70
F +49 (0)2203 93 7190
E pressestelle@gruener-punkt.de
www.gruener-punkt.de
Founded in 1990, this non-profit organization administers Der Grüne Punkt (the Green Dot) packaging recycling scheme to comply with the 1991 German Packaging Ordinance. Any packaging marked with the Green Dot is acceptable for recycling. All types of packaging are accepted including glass, wood, ceramics, ferrous and non-ferrous metals, plastics and paper. This scheme is now licensed to a number of organizations in other EU countries – the ARA System (Austria), Ecoembalajes España (Spain), FOST Plus (Belgium), Repak Ltd (UK), Sociedade Ponto Verde SA (Portugal) and VALORLUX asbl (Luxembourg).

EMAS Eco-Management and Audit Scheme
Department of the Environment, Food and Rural Affairs
Zone 6/E10
Ashdown House
123 Victoria Street
London SW1E 6DE
UK
T +44 (0)20 7890 3052
F +44 (0)20 7890 6559
www.defr.gov.uk/environment/greening/emas/emashome.htm

EMAS, EU
The EMAS Help Desk
The European Commission
Brussels, Belgium
http://europa.int.eu/comm/environment/emas

EU Energy Label Scheme/ The Save Programme
European Commission
Brussels, Belgium
http://europa.eu.int/comm/energy/library/save2000.pdf

FSC Forest Stewardship Council, UK
UK Working Group
Unit D, Station Building
Llanidloes SY18 6EB, UK
T +44 (0)1686 413 916
F +44 (0)1686 412 176
E hannah@fsc-uk.demon.co.uk
www.fsc-uk.demon.co.uk
Founded in 1993, the Forest Stewardship Council (FSC) is an independent, non-profit, non-governmental organization, which is responsible for administering, monitoring and tracking a programme to certify timber produced from well-managed woodlands and labelling for products originating from such timber. It is an international programme implemented by independent organizations that are evaluated, accredited and monitored by the FSC. In the UK the Soil Association Woodmark Scheme and the SGS Forestry QUALIFOR Programme are both accredited. Other accredited organizations include the Rainforest Alliance SmartWood Program and Scientific Certification Systems Forest Conservation Program (USA), Silva Forest Foundation (Canada), Skal (Netherlands) and the Institut für Marktökologie (Switzerland). In the Directory of FSC Endorsed Forests Worldwide, *Spring 2000, a total of 234 forests covering millions of hectares were certified in temperate, subtropical and tropical regions spanning thirty-four countries. A companion* Directory of Manufacturers of FSC Endorsed Products Worldwide, *Spring 2000, includes 825 manufacturers from forty-three countries. Products include sawn timber, veneers and finished products. The chain of custody is also inspected by the FSC, ensuring that the endorsement with the FSC logo is not abused by agents, distributors, wholesalers or retailers. The extent of manufacturers' certification is most advanced in the Netherlands (seventy-five manufacturers), the UK (158) and the USA (185).*

FSC Forest Stewardship Council, USA
1155 30th Street NW
Suite 300
Washington, DC 20007
USA
T +1 877 372 5646 (toll free)
F +1 202 342 6589
E info@foreststewardship.org
www.fscus.org

Global Ecolabelling Network (GEN)
GEN Secretariat

Terra Choice Environmental Services, Inc.
2781 Lancaster Road
Suite 400
Ottawa, ONT KIB 1A7
Canada
T +1 613 247 1900
F +1 613 247 2228
E gensecretariat@terrachoice.ca
www.gen.gr.jp
GEN is not accredited to issue eco-labels but keeps the most up-to-date list of all eco-labelling organizations worldwide on its website and details of the type of products and materials currently covered. GEN links directly with most eco-labelling organizations' websites.

Group for Efficient Appliances (GEA)
www.gealabel.org/
An association of energy labelling authorities in European countries (includes Austria, Denmark, Finland, France, Germany, Sweden, Netherlands and Switzerland), the European Energy Network and the European Association of Consumer Electronics Manufacturers (EACEM). Labels are available for a range of electronic equipment from PCs to TVs.

International Organization for Standardization (ISO)
Central Secretariat
1 Rue de Varembé
Case postale 56
CH 1211 Geneva 20
Switzerland
T +41 (0)22 749 01 11
F +41 (0)22 733 34 30
E central@iso.ch
www.iso.ch

National Association of Paper Merchants (NAPM)
Hamilton Court
Gogmore Lane,
Chertsey
Surrey KT16 9AP, UK
T +44 (0)1932 569797
F +44 (0)1932 569749
E info@napm.org.uk
www.napm.org.uk
NAPM-approved recycled paper and boards are guaranteed to contain a minimum of 75 per cent-recycled fibre content from genuine paper and board waste, not mill waste.

Pan European Forest Certification (PEFC)
PEFC Council asbl
2éme Etage
17 Rue des Girondins
L-1626 Merl-Hollerich
Luxembourg
T +352 (0)26 25 90 59
F +352 (0)26 25 92 58
E pefc@pt.lu
www.pefc.org
The PEFC is a new scheme initiated by the private forestry sector. Forests (and their timber and wood product output) are certified by independent auditors to be managed in accordance with the Pan European Criteria on the Protection of Forests in Europe, which were resolved at the Helsinki and Lisbon Ministerial Conferences in 1993 and 1998. It is a scheme that offers a common European framework, in contrast to the FSC scheme, which is applied to forests worldwide.

ReSy GmbH
Postfach 101541
64215 Darmstadt, Germany
T +49 (0)6151 92 94 22
F +49 (0)6151 92 94 522
www.resy.de/ind-eng.htm
This company certifies that the content of paper and corrugated board packaging is suitable for recycling in the German paper industry. The ReSy logo is used with the international recycling logo of the Mobius loop.

SmartWood® Program
Rainforest Alliance
65 Bleecker Street
New York, NY 10012, USA
T +1 212 677 1900
www.smartwood.org and
www.rainforest-alliance.org
SmartWood is a program of the Rainforest Alliance® which encourages environmentally and socially responsible forestry management. SmartWood has certified up to one hundred operations worldwide, which produce a wide range of certified lumber and products. The Forest Stewardship Council has accredited SmartWood for its certification of forestry operations. The SmartWood Rediscovered Program certifies salvaged or recycled wood from demolished buildings or waste sources.

Soil Association
Bristol House
40-56 Victoria Street
Bristol BS1 6BY, UK
T +44 (0)117 929 0661
F +44 (0)117 925 2504
E info@soilassociation.org
www.soilassociation.org
WoodMark is the name of the Soil Association's international forestry and chain of custody scheme. The Soil Association is an accredited organization to the Forest Stewardship Council and is permitted to inspect and certify forests and their products as sustainably managed under the FSC scheme. It is also the leading organization in the UK that independently certifies farm produce as being organically grown and certified to bear the Soil Association logo.

US EPA Energy Star Office Equipment
USA
E labelling@energystar.gov
www.energystar.gov
Energy Star labels for office equipment, buildings and more.

ECOMATERIALS

Alternative Crops Technology Interaction Network (ACTIN)
Pira House
Leatherhead, Surrey, UK
T +44 (0)1372 802 054
F +44 (0)1372 802 245
E info@actin.co.uk
www.actin.co.uk

ATHENA™ Sustainable Materials Institute
Canada
E wbtrusty@fox.nstn.ca and
E jkmeil@fox.nstn.ca
www.athenasmi.ca

BioComposites Centre, The
University of Wales
Bangor
Gwynedd LL57 2UW, UK
T +44 (0)1248 370 588
F +44 (0)1248 370 594
E biocomposites@bangor.ac.uk
www.bc.bangor.ac.uk
Specializes in industrial contract research on the processing of wood and plant materials to facilitate the production of new materials.

Building Research Establishment (UK)
www.bre.org.uk
The BRE holds the National Database of Environmental Profiles for a wide range of common building and construction materials. These Environmental Profiles document the material's inputs, outputs and lifecycle assessment, enabling architects and their clients, specifiers and manufacturers to assess the impacts of different materials. Full access to the database is subject to a fee.

Carbohydrate Economy Clearinghouse, The
c/o The Institute for Local Self-Reliance
1313 5th Street SE
Minneapolis, MN 55414-1546
USA
T +1 612 379 3815
F +1 612 379 3920
E kmullen@ilsr.org
www.carbohydrateeconomy.org

Center for Environmentally Appropriate Materials
Department of Work Environment
University of Massachusetts Lowell
One University Avenue
Lowell, MA 01854, USA
T +1 978 934 3250
F +1 978 452 5711
E Director, Dr Ken Geiser: kgeiser@turi.org

www.uml.edu/Dept/WE/centers.htm

Certified Forest Products Council
14780 SW Osprey Drive
Suite 285
Beaverton, OR 97007
USA
T +1 503 590 6600
F +1 503 590 6655
E info@certifiedwood.org
www.certifiedwood.org

Co-op America's WoodWise Directory
USA
www.coopamerica.org/woodwise/directory.htm
Aimed at providing information for consumers, the WoodWise Directory publishes an online directory of paper and wood products from certified and recycled sources of 'raw' materials. It also lists suppliers of 'alternative' non-wood and non-paper products.

EcoDesign Resource Society
PO Box 3981
Main Post Office
Vancouver BC V6B 3Z4
Canada
T +1 604 255 2049
F +1 604 255 2079
E penner@infoserve.net
www.ecodesign.bc.ca/product.htm

FSC Forest Stewardship Council, UK
UK Working Group
Unit D, Station Building
Llanidloes SY18 6EB, UK
T +44 (0)1686 413 916
F +44 (0)1686 412 176
E hannah@fsc-uk.demon.co.uk
www.fsc-uk.demon.co.uk

FSC Forest Stewardship Council, USA
1134 29th Street NW
Washington, DC 20007
USA
T +1 877 372 5646
F +1 202 342 6589
E info@foreststewardship.org
www.fscus.org

Harris Directory, The
USA
www.harrisdirectory.com
This directory has been revised annually since 1992 and now lists five thousand recycled products and materials from the USA. Information includes contact details, product or material type, environmental benefits and examples of applications. The publishers of the Directory *work closely with the California-integrated Waste Management Board to revise key words to facilitate identification of products that comply with US government ecological procurement criteria.*

Institute for Local Self Reliance (USA)
www.ilsr.org
The ILSR maintains an online database of materials called The Carbohydrate Economy, which lists state by state the companies in the USA that are manufacturing materials from biological sources. This includes biofuels, biocomposites, biopolymers, paints, finishes and cleaners with examples of the use of waste or recycled raw materials.

Material ConneXion
4 Columbus Circle
New York, NY 10019-1100
USA
T +1 212 445 8825
F +1 212 445 8950
www.materialconnexion.com
Material ConneXion maintains a database of over three thousand materials, including materials derived from or containing recycled content. This privately operated database is available online and can be visited in New York.

New Uses Council
295 Tanglewood Drive
East Greenwich
RI 02818-2210
USA
T +1 401 885 8177
F +1 401 821 5789
E info@newuses.org
www.newuses.org
The New Uses Council is dedicated to developing and commercializing new industrial, energy and non-food consumer uses of renewable agricultural, forestry, livestock and marine products. It publishes an extensive online listing of bio-products, The BioProducts Directory, *such as biofuels, biocomposites and biopolymers.*

Pan European Forest Certification (PEFC)
PEFC Council asbl
2ème Etage
17 Rue des Girondins
L-1626 Merl-Hollerich
Luxembourg
T +352 (0)26 25 90 59
F +352 (0)26 25 92 58
E pefc@pt.lu
www.pefc.org

Proterra BV
PO Box 188
6700 AD Wageningen
Netherlands
T +31 (0)317 467 661
F +31 (0)317 467 660
E info@proterra.nl
www.proterra.nl

Salvo (UK)
www.salvo.co.uk
Established in 1992, Salvo is Europe's only association coordinating the activities of architectural salvage companies and reclaimed building materials suppliers. Although members are predominantly from the UK, listings include companies in Australia, Belgium, Canada, France, Ireland and the USA.

SmartWood® Program
Rainforest Alliance
65 Bleecker Street
New York, NY 10012
USA
T +1 212 677 1900
www.smartwood.org and
www.rainforest-alliance.org

Waste Watch and National Recycling Forum
Europa House
Ground Floor
13-17 Ironmonger Row
London EC1V 3QN, UK
T +44 (0)20 7253 6266
F +44 (0)20 7253 5962
E info@wastewatch.org
www.wastewatch.org.uk/
The UK Recycled Products Guide *was jointly published by the National Recycling Forum and Waste Watch in 1998. It is available as a bound copy or online at www.nrf.org.uk and lists over a thousand products and materials. Data include type of material, percentage of post-consumer waste or recovered material, brand names, accreditation and contact details of suppliers.*

ECO SHOPS

Centre for Alternative Technology
Machynlleth
Powys SY20 9AZ, UK
T +44 (0)1654 702 400
F +44 (0)1654 702 782
E info@cat.org.uk
www.cat.org.uk

EcoMall
New York, USA
E ecomall@ecomall.com
www.ecomall.com

The Green Stationery Company
Studio One
114 Walcot Street
Bath BA1 5BG
UK
T +44 (0)1225 480 556
F +44 (0)1225 481 211
E jay@greenstat.demon.co.uk
http://greenstat.ebusiness.co.uk

Jade Mountain
PO Box 4616
Boulder, CO 80306, USA
T +1 800 442 1972
F +1 303 449 8266
E info@jademountain.com
www.jademountain.com

Millennium Whole Earth Catalog
Whole Earth
PO Box 3000
Denville, NJ 07834-9879
USA
T +1 888 732 6739
E info@wholeearthmag.com
www.wholeearthmag.com

Natural Collection
Eco House
Monmouth Place
Bath BA1 2DQ, UK
T +44 (0)8703 313 333
F +44 (0)1225 469 673
www.naturalcollection.com

Real Goods
USA
www.realgoods.com

Sustainability Souce™, Inc., USA
E info@sustainabilitysource.com
www.sustainabilitysource.com

ENERGY

Amazing Environmental Organization Web Directory – Alternative Energy
California, USA
www.webdirectory.com/Science/Energy/Alternative_Energy

British Wind Energy Association, The
26 Spring Street
London W2 1JA
UK
T +44 (0)20 7402 7402
F +44 (0)20 7402 7407
E info@bwea.com
www.bwea.com
Promotes the use of renewable wind power and has an extensive list of publications for commercial and domestic generation, plus a list of members and suppliers.

Centre for Sustainable Energy
Create Centre
Smeaton Road
Bristol BS1 6XN
UK
T +44 (0)117 929 9950
F +44 (0)117 929 9114
E info@cse.org.uk
www.cse.org.uk
CSE provides research, consultancy, education and training in sustainable energy technology and systems. It also has experience of delivering local and regional initiatives and lobbying to assist development of appropriate energy policies.

Energy Efficiency and Renewable Energy Network (EREN) (USA)
www.eren.doe.gov/buildings/builders.htm

GENERAL

Center for Renewable Energy and Sustainable Technlogy (CREST) and Renewable Energy Policy Program (REPP)
1612 K St NW, Ste 202
Washington, DC 20006
USA
T +1 202 293 2898
F +1 202 293 5857
E mkcampbell@repp
www.CREST.org
CREST operates Solstice, *an Internet information service about renewable energy.*

International Network for Environment Management (INEM)
Osterstrasse 58
20259 Hamburg
Germany
T +49 (0)40 4907 1600
F +49 (0)40 4907 1601
E info@inem.org
www.inem.org/

INTERNATIONAL, NATIONAL AND FEDERAL AGENCIES

Department of the Environment, Food and Rural Affairs
Eland House
Bressenden Place
London
SW1E 5DG
UK
T +44 (0)20 7944 3000
www.detr.gov.uk

Envirowise
UK
www.envirowise.gov.uk
A source of practical environmental advice for business, a government programme run by the Department of the Environment.

European Environment Agency
Kongens Nytorv 6
1050 Copenhagen K
Denmark
T +45 (0)3336 7100
F +45 (0)3336 7199
E eea@eea.eu.int
www.eea.eu.int/

United Nations Environment Programme
Working Group on Sustainable Product Development
UNEP-WG-SPD
Nieuwe Achtergracht 166
J.J. van't Hoff Institute, B-315
1018 WV Amsterdam
Netherlands
E UNEP@UNEP.uva.nl
http://unep.frw.uva.nl
This Working Group has been wound up but an interesting gallery of products is available on the web site.

US Environmental Protection Agency
1200 Pennsylvania Avenue NW
Washington DC, 20460
USA
www.epa.gov

LIFECYCLE ANALYSIS LINKS AND ORGANIZATIONS

Dr Kohmei Halada's LCA and ecodesign links
National Research Institute for Metals, Japan
www.nrim.go.jp:8080/ecomat/LCA/links.htm
An eclectic mixture of links for LCA and ecodesign.

Life-Cycle Links by Thomas Gloria
E tgloria@tufts.edu
www.life-cycle.org/Academia.htm
A comprehensive list of the links for LCA from academia, research institutes, government and international organizations, together with companies applying LCA.

SETAC (Society of Environmental Toxicology and Chemistry), USA
1010 North 12th Avenue
Pensacola, FL 32501-3367
USA
T +1 850 469 1500
F +1 850 469 9778
E setac@setac.org
www.setac.org/

SETAC, Asia/Pacific
CSIRO Centre for Advanced Analytical Chemistry
Private Mailbag 7
Bangor NSW 2234, Australia
F +61 (0)2 9710 6837
E graham-batley@syd.dcet.csiro.au
www.setac.org/

SETAC, Europe
Avenue E Maunier 83
Box 3
1200 Brussels
Belgium
T +32 (0)2 722 72 81
F +32 (0)2 770 53 86
E setac@ping.be
www.setac.org/

Society of the Promotion of Life-Cycle Assessment Development (SPOLD)
SPOLD European Centre
Attn: Peter Hindle
Temselaan 100
1853 Stomberk-Bever
Brussels
F +32 2 456 2849
www.spold.org/FAQ.html

LCA SOFTWARE REVIEWS AND SUPPLIERS

Boustead Consulting
Black Cottage,
East Grinstead, Horsham
West Sussex RH13 7BD, UK
T +44 (0)1403 864 561
F +44 (0)1403 865 284
E info@boustead-consulting.co.uk
www.boustead-consulting.co.uk
Boustead Model version 4 is the most extensive, up-to-date, lifecycle inventory tool on the market today, drawing on over twenty-seven years' experience to define inputs and outputs for thousands of raw and manufactured materials and processes.

Cambridge Engineering Selector (CES3)
Granta Design Ltd
Trumpington Mews
40B High Street
Trumpington
Cambridge CB2 2LS, UK
T +44 (0)1223 518 895
F +44 (0)1223 506 432
E sales@grantadesign.com
www.grantadesign.com
Cambridge Engineering Selector permits simultaneous selection of material, manufacturing process and shape from three interlinked comprehensive databases. An accompanying CD-ROM provides access to online documentation and web links. Recently a new Eco-data module has been developed by researchers at Cambridge University together with connector software, which allows interconnectivity with Boustead Consulting's Version 4 Life Cycle Analysis programme.

DFE Research Group
Department of Mechanical Engineering, Design and Manufacture
Manchester Metropolitan

University
John Dalton Building
Chester Street
Manchester M1 5GD, UK
E N.Caluwe@mmu.ac.uk
http://sun1.mpce.stu.mmu.ac.uk/pages/projects/dfe/pubs/dfe33/list.htm
This is an online eco-tools manual providing a comprehensive review of twenty-six LCA/LCI tools, seven DfE tools and nine Pollution, Prevention and Waste Prevention tools by Nils de Caluwe, July 1997.

PRé Consultants BV
Plotterweg 12
3821 BB Amersfoort
Netherlands
T +31 (0)33 4555022
F +31 (0)33 4555024
E info@pre.nl
www.pre.nl
Suppliers of ECO-it and entry level LCA software and SimaPro, a professional package based upon the Eco-indicator 99 methodology.

TNO Institute of Industrial Technology
PO Box 5073
2500 GB Delft
Netherlands
T +31 (0)15 260 87 45
F +31 (0)15 260 87 56
E ecoscan@ind.tno.nl
www.ind.tno.nl/en/productdevelopment/ecoscan/prodinfo.html
Suppliers of EcoScan3.0 entry level LCA software based upon the Eco-indicator 95 and 99 methodologies.

RECYCLING

Alucan, Aluminium Can Recycling Association (ACRA)
5 Gatsby Court
176 Holliday Street
Birmingham B1 1TJ, UK
T +44 (0)121 633 4656
F +44 (0)121 633 4698
E alucan@dial.pipex.com
www.alucan.org.uk
Alucan is a national organization dedicated to the collection and recycling of aluminium drinks cans. It claims a recycling rate of 36 per cent (1998 data) of all the aluminium cans sold, which means that this material is the most recycled type of packaging in the UK.

Amazing Environmental Organization Web Directory – Recycling
California, USA
www.webdirectory.com/Recycling

American Plastics Council
1300 Wilson Boulevard
Suite 800
Arlington, VA 22209, USA
http://sourcebook.plasticsresource.com
The Council maintains an online database of sources of recycled plastics and plastics feedstock in the USA and Canada in cooperation with the Environment and Plastics Industry Council (EPIC) of Canada.

British Glass, The Manufacturers Confederation
Northumberland Road
Sheffield
South Yorkshire S10 2UA, UK
T +44 (0)114 268 6201
F +44 (0)114 268 1073
E recycling@britglass.co.uk
www.britglass.co.uk
In 1998 glass recycling in the EU exceeded 8 million metric tonnes, of which British glass constituted 6 per cent, or 476,000 tonnes. The Confederation encourages post-consumer collection and recycling of glass.

British Metals Federation and Textile Recycling Association (TRA)
16 High Street
Brampton, Huntingdon
Cambs PE28 4TU, UK
T +44 (0)1480 455 249
F +44 (0)1480 453 680
E admin@britmetfed.org.uk
www.britmetfed.org.uk
The British Metals Federation encourages recycling of ferrous and non-ferrous metals in the UK. It publishes a directory of members and provides links to other associations and organizations in the metals recycling industry worldwide. The TRA coordinates the activities of some forty-four members who specialize in recycling textiles in the UK.

Bureau of International Recycling
24 Avenue Franklin Roosevelt
1050 Brussels, Belgium
T +32 2 627 5770
F +32 2 627 5773
E bir@bir.org
www.bir.org
BIR is an international trade association of the recycling industries.

Deutsche Gesellschaft für Kunststoff-Recycling mbH
Germany
www.dkr.de
DKR recycled around 600,000 tonnes of plastics in 1998 collected from plastic packaging under the Green Dot system (see Duales System Deutschland AG) and encourages recycling and reuse of this waste. DKR maintains an online database of mainly German companies that manufacture materials and products from recycled plastics. The organization works closely with the design agency Bär + Knell and organizes touring exhibitions of their diverse range of furniture, lighting and fittings using recycled plastics.

Industry Council for Electronic Equipment Recycling (ICER)
6 Bath Place
Rivington Street
London EC2A 3JE, UK
T +44 (0)20 7729 4766
F +44 (0)20 7729 9121
E pgibson@bpf.co.uk
www.icer.org.uk
The ICER is a cross-industry group examining the best way to improve recycling and reuse of end-of-life electronic equipment.

RECOUP
9 Metro Centre
Welbeck Way
Woodston
Peterborough
Cambridgeshire
PE2 7WH, UK
F +44 (0)1733 390 031
E enquiry@recoup.org
www.recoup.org
RECOUP is the UK's national plastic-bottle recycling organization with seventy-five members including plastics manufacturers, beverage companies, retailers and local authorities.

Textile Environment Network (TEN)
c/o National Centre for Business Ecology
Peel Building
University of Salford
Greater Manchester
M5 4WT, UK
T +44 (0)161 745 5276
F +44 (0)161 745 5041

Waste Watch and National Recycling Forum
Europa House
Ground Floor
13-17 Ironmonger Row
London EC1V 3QN, UK
T +44 (0)20 7253 6266
F +44 (0)20 7253 5962
E info@wastewatch.org
www.wastewatch.org.uk
Waste Watch publishes an online directory of products and materials in the UK made from recycled materials. Waste Watch also manages the independent National Recycling Forum, which promotes recycling.

SUSTAINABLE DEVELOPMENT

Centre for Environmental Strategy
University of Surrey
Guildford
Surrey GU2 5XH, UK
www.surrey.ac.uk/CES/home.htm

European Foundation for the Improvement of Living and Working Conditions
Ireland
http://susdev.eurofound.ie

International Institute of Sustainable Development (IISD)
Head Office
161 Portage Avenue East,
6th Floor, Winnipeg
Manitoba R3B 0Y4, Canada
T +1 204 958 7700
F +1 204 958 7710
E info@iisd.ca
http://iisd.ca

National Councils for Sustainable Development
The NCSD Network

The Earth Council
Apdo. 2323-1002
San José, Costa Rica
T +506 256 1611
F +506 255 2197
E info@ncsdnetwork.org
www.ncsdnetwork.org

Product-Life Institute, The (Institut de la Durée)
Geneva, Switzerland
www.product-life.org/intro.htm
An independent contract research institute developing innovative strategies and policies to encourage a sustainable society. The Institute provides consultancy services to government, industry and universities.

Rocky Mountain Institute
1739 Snowmass Creek Road
Snowmass, CO 81654-9199
USA
T +1 970 927 3851
F +1 970 927 3420
E info@rmi.org
www.rmi.org

Sustainability Web Ring
Sustainability Development Communications Network (SDCN), c/o IISD
161 Portage Avenue East
6th Floor, Winnipeg
Manitoba R3B 0Y4
Canada
T +1 204 958 7700
F +1 204 958 7710
E sdcn@iisd.ca
http://sdgateway.net

Tellus Institute
11 Arlington Street
Boston, MA 02116-3411, USA
T +1 617 266 5400
F +1 617 266 8303
E info@tellus.org
www.tellus.org

United Nations Sustainable Development
CSD Secretariat
United Nations Plaza
Room DC2-2220
New York, NY 10017, USA
T +1 212 963 3170
F +1 212 963 4260
E dsd@un.org
www.un.org/esa/sustdev/

World Resources Institute
10 G Street, NE, Suite 80
Washington, DC 20002, USA
T +1 202 729 7600
F +1 202 729 7610
E lauralee@wri.org
www.wri.org

Wuppertal Institute
(Wuppertal Institut für Klima, Umwelt, Energie)
PO Box 10 04 80
42204 Wuppertal, Germany
T +49 (0)202 2492
F +49 (0)202 2492 108
E infor@wupperinst.org
www.wupperinst.org

TRADE AND BUSINESS ASSOCIATIONS

Alliance for Beverage Cartons and the Environment
Rue Josep II 36
1000 Brussels,
Belgium
T +32 (0)2 219 06 43
F +32 (0)2 219 02 23
E info@ace.be
www.ace.be
ACE is an association of leading producers of beverage cartons and paperboard, which provides information on the impact of these products on the environment.

American Plastics Council
1300 Wilson Boulevard
Suite 800
Arlington, VA 22209
USA
T +1 800 2 HELP 90
www.americanplasticscouncil.org

Association of Plastics Manufacturers Europe (APME)
Avenue E van Nieuwenhuyse 4, Box 3
1160 Brussels
Belgium
T +32 (0)2 672 82 59
F +32 (0)2 675 39 35
E info@apme.org
www.apme.org
An extensive resource on plastics including information about plastics and the environment together with detailed eco-profiles of common plastics.

British Plastics Federation
6 Bath Place
Rivington Street
London EC2A 3JE, UK
T +44 (0)20 7457 5000
F +44 (0)20 7457 5045
E cparkho@bpf.co.uk
www.bpf.co.uk

Composite Panel Association (CPA) and Composite Wood Council (CWC)
18928 Premiere Court
Gaithersburg
MD 20879-1574, USA
T +1 301 670 0604
F +1 301 840 1252
E info@pdmdf.com
www.pbmdf.com
The CPA is a US and Canadian organization devoted to promoting the use and acceptance of particleboard, MDF and other similar products. Operating from the same headquarters, the CWC is an international organization that provides a forum for members of the particleboard and fibreboard industries and promotes their products.

Corrugated Packaging Association
2 Saxon Court
Freeschool Street
Northampton NN1 1ST, UK
T +1 (0)1604 621 002
F +1 (0)1604 620 636
E postbox@corrugated.org.uk
www.corrugated.org.uk
Members of the Corrugated Packaging Association account for over 95 per cent of the corrugated output in the UK, which in turn is the fourth largest national corrugated industry in Europe. Over 70 per cent of UK goods use corrugated packaging and up to 77 per cent of this packaging is recycled.

Institute of Packaging, The
Sysonby Lodge
Nottingham Road
Melton Mowbray
Leicestershire LE13 0NU, UK
T +44 (0)1664 500 055
F +44 (0)1664 564 164
E info@iop.co.uk
www.iop.co.uk

National Association of Paper Merchants (NAPM)
Hamilton Court
Gogmore Lane, Chertsey
Surrey KT16 9AP, UK
T +44 (0)1932 569 797
F +44 (0)1932 569 749
E info@napm.org.uk
www.napm.org.uk
This is the trade association representing UK paper merchants. It operates the NAPM Approved Recycled scheme, in which use of its logo guarantees a minimum content of 75 per cent paper and board waste.

TRANSPORT AND HUMAN-POWERED VEHICLES

Calstart
California, USA
www.calstart.org
Commercial company with an extensive catalogue of electric and hybrid bicycles, cars and commercial vehicles.

Designition
Kingston-upon-Thames
Surrey, UK
www.designition.org
Excellent range of examples of electric cars in the product database.

International Human Powered Vehicle Association
California, USA
www.ihpva.org

Also refer to Eco-Design Strategies (p. 327)

5Rs is a concept with five cornerstones aimed at reducing the impact of design, manufacturing and products on the environment - to reduce, remanufacture, reuse, recycle and recover (energy by incineration). 'Reduce' implies designing to use fewer raw materials and less energy.

Agenda 21 is a comprehensive blueprint for global action drafted by the 172 governments present at the 1992 Earth Summit organized by the United Nations in Rio de Janiero, Brazil. It is often interpreted and implemented at a local level in 'Local Agenda 21' plans.

Atmosphere refers to the gaseous components at and above the world's surface including the important gases oxygen, hydrogen, nitrogen, carbon dioxide, methane and ozone.

Biosphere is the term for the living components of the world that meet the seven characteristics of life – movement, feeding, respiration, excretion, growth, reproduction and sensitivity.

Carcinogens are chemicals that are definite or potential agents in causing cancer in humans. They are classified by the World Health Organization according to their perceived risk. Group 1 chemicals carry clear evidence of risk, Group 3 chemicals may have some associated risk.

Carrying capacity is a finite quantity (K) that equates to the ecosystem resources of a defined area such as a locality, habitat, region, country or planet. A given carrying capacity can support a finite population of organisms. Stable populations in harmony with the carrying capacity are sustainable, but excessive population growth can lead to sudden decline and/or permanent reduction in the carrying capacity.

Clean design is the systematic incorporation of lifecycle environmental considerations into product design.

Design for environment (DfE) is the analysis and optimization of the environmental, health and safety issues considered over the entire life of the product. DfE permits resource depletion, waste production and energy usage to be reduced or even eliminated during the manufacture, use and disposal or reuse of the product.

Design for manufacturing (DfM) examines the relationship between resource usage and product design using computer-aided design (CAD) and computer-aided manufacturing (CAM) tools for cost-effectiveness and reduced environmental impacts.

Design for manufacturing and assembly (DfMA) is a combination of DfA and DfM thinking and practice.

Design for X (DfX) is a generic term where X denotes the specific focus of a design strategy, such as DfD (Design for Disassembly) or DfE (Design for Environment).

Downcycling refers to the recycling of a waste stream to create a new material that has properties inferior to those of the original virgin materials. A good example is recycled plastic (HDPE) panels made of multicoloured waste sources.

Eco-efficiency embodies the concept of more efficient use of resources with reduced environmental impacts resulting in improved resource productivity, i.e., doing more with less.

Eco-label refers to labels applied to products and materials that conform to standards set by independent organizations to reduce environmental impacts. There are national and international eco-labels – see p. 333 for a detailed listing.

Eco-wheel, or ecodesign strategy wheel, is a means of identifying strategies that will assist in making environmental improvements to existing products. It embraces eight strategies: 1) selection of low-impact materials; 2) reduction of materials usage; 3) optimization of production techniques; 4) optimization of distribution system; 5) reduction of impact during use; 6) optimization of initial lifetime; 7) optimization of end-of-life system; and 8) new concept development.

Eco-tools: A generic name for software or non-software tools that help with the analysis of the environmental impact of products, manufacturing processes, activities and construction projects. Tools generally fall into several main categories: Lifecycle analysis, design or environment, environmental management or eco-audits and energy flow management.

Ecodesign is a design process that considers the environmental impacts associated with a product throughout its entire life from acquisition of raw materials through production/manufacturing and use to end of life. At the same time as reducing environmental impacts, ecodesign seeks to improve the aesthetic and functional aspects of the product with due consideration to social and ethical needs. Ecodesign is synonymous with the terms design for environment (DfE), often used by the engineering design profession, and lifecycle design (LCD) in North America.

Eco-indicator is a single numeric value used to denote the environmental impact of a material, process or product used in specific software applications and their databases. Eco-indicators are calculated in a two-step process, first using empirical data, then applying a weighting calculated by making subjective decisions as to the degree of importance of different types of environmental impact. For example, many software applications rate ozone depletion as more important than acid rain or pesticide pollution. Eco-indicators are very useful for determining the relative environmental impacts of different materials, processes or products, but care must be exercised when comparing eco-indicators originating from different software applications and databases.

Ecomaterials are materials that have minimal impact on the environment at the same time as providing maximum performance for the required design task. Ecomaterials originating from components from the biosphere are biodegradable and cyclic, whereas ecomaterials originating from the technosphere are easily recyclable and can be contained within 'closed-loop' systems.

EcoReDesign (ERD) was first coined by the Royal

Melbourne Institute of Technology, Australia, to denote the redesigning of existing products to reduce the environmental impact of one or more components of the product.

Ecological footprint is a measure of the resource use by a population within a defined area of land, including imported resources. Assessment of the ecological footprints of nation states or other defined geographic areas reveals the true environmental impact of those states and their ability to survive on their own resources in the long term. The term ecologcial footprint can also be applied to products but is more commonly referred to as the environmental 'rucksack' associated with product manufacturing.

Embodied energy is the total energy stored in a product or material and includes the energy in the raw materials, transport to the place of production, energy in manufacturing and (sometimes) transport energy used in the distribution and retail chain. It is measured in MJ per kg or GJ per tonne.

End of life (EoL) describes both the end of the life of the actual product and the cessation of the environmental impacts associated with the product. Disassembly and recycling of components and/or materials at a product's EoL are preferable to disposal via landfill or incineration.

End of pipe (EoP) solution is another term given to pollution control in which the by-products of manufacturing processes that are toxic or hazardous emissions or wastes are treated or neutralized before being released to the wider environment. This is design to correct or minimize a problem.

Environment conscious manufacturing (ECM) is the application of green engineering techniques to manufacturing to encourage greater efficiency and reduction of emissions and waste.

Environmental impact assessment (EIA) is a complex process of predicting and defining the possible environmental effects of public- and private-sector projects in advance of implementation and of examining how to mitigate the predicted impacts. Originating in North America in the 1970s, EIAs are typically applied to construction, forestry, infrastructure and housing projects. In Europe and the UK public enquiries and local government planning department processes generally take the place of EIAs.

Environmental management systems (EMS) are aimed at improving the environmental performance of organizations in a systematic way integrated with legislative and compliance requirements. The international bench-mark for EMS is the International Standard ISO 14001, which more and more organizations each year are meeting, but national EMS standards also play a significant role, such as the British Standard for Environmental Management, BS 7750. Other independently certified systems exist, such as EMAS operated in the European Union.

EU Energy label is a classification applied to domestic appliances such as washing machines and refrigerators according to their energy use, expressed as kWh per year. Group A are the most energy-efficient and Group G are the least efficient. This scheme is due to be expanded to other types of appliances.

Geosphere consists of the inorganic, geological components of the world such as minerals, rocks and stone, sea and fresh water.

Green design is a design process in which the focus is on assessing and dealing with individual environmental impacts of a product rather than on the product's entire life.

Greenhouse gases are any manmade gaseous emission that contributes to a rise in the average temperature of the earth, a phenomenon known as global warming, by trapping the heat of the sun in the earth's atmosphere. The key greenhouse gases include carbon dioxide, mainly from fossil-fuel burning activities; methane from landfill sites, agriculture and coal production; chlorofluoro-carbons (CFCs), hydro-chlorofluorocarbons, (HCFCs) and hydrofluoro-carbons (HFCs), used in refrigerants and aerosols; nitrous oxide from nylon and nitric acid production, fossil-fuel burning and agriculture; and sulphur hexafluoride from the chemical industry.

Greywater is the waste water from personal or general domestic washing activities.

Industrial ecology is a holistic approach that considers the interaction between natural, economic and industrial systems. It is also termed industrial metabolism.

Intelligent transport system (ITS) is a series of inte-grated transport networks in which individual networks use specific transport modes but allow easy interconnection to facilitate efficient movement of people.

Lifecycle analysis or Lifecycle assessment (LCA) is the process of analyzing the environmental impact of a product from the cradle t o the grave in four major phases: production, transport/distribution/packaging, usage, disposal or end of life/design for disassembly/design for recycling.

Lifecycle inventory (LCI) is the practice of analyzing the environmental consequences of inputs required and outputs generated during the life of a product.

Lifecycle matrix is a tool or checklist to analyze potential environmental impacts at each phase in the product's lifecycle. Different types of industry create specific lifecycle matrices related to the peculiarities of the manufacturing process of their products.

Lithosphere is the geological strata that make up the earth's crust.

Mobility path describes a route an individual can take travelling between two points using one or more forms of transport which are, preferably, integrated into a flexible system (see ITS).

Non-renewable resources are those in finite supply that cannot be regenerated or renewed by synthesizing the energy of the sun. Such resources include fossil fuels, metals and plastics. Improving the rate of recycling will extend the longevity of these resources.

Off-gasing is the term for emissions of volatile compounds to the air from synthetic or natural polymers. Emissions usually derive from the additives, elastomers, fillers and residual chemicals from the manufacturing process rather than from the long, molecular-chain polymers.

Post-consumer waste is waste that is collected and sorted after the product has been used by the consumer. It includes glass, newspaper and cans from special roadside 'banks' or disposal facilities. It is generally much more variable in composition than pre-consumer waste (see below).

Pre-consumer waste is waste generated at the manufacturing plant or production facility.

Producer responsibility (PR) prescribes the legal responsibilities of producers/manufacturers for their products from the cradle to the grave. Recent European legislation for certain product sectors, such as electronic and electrical goods, packaging and vehicles, sets specific requirements regarding 'take-back' of products and targets for recycling components and materials.

Product lifecycle (PLC) is the result of a lifecycle assessment of an individual product, which analyzes its environmental impact.

Renewable resources refer to those resources that originate from storage of energy from the sun by living organisms including plants, animals and humans. Providing that sufficient water, nutrients and sunshine are available, renewable resources can be grown in continuous cycles.

Smart products are those with in-built sensors to control the function of the product automatically or to make the user aware of the condition of the product.

Sustainable is an adjective applied to diverse subjects including populations, cities, development, businesses, communities and habitats; it means that the subject can persist a long time into the future.

Sustainable development: According to the most widely quoted definition, published in the 1987 report 'Our Common Future' by the World Commission on Environment and Development chaired by Gro Harlem Brundtland, the Norwegian prime minister, sustainable development is development that meets the needs of the present without compromising the ability of future generations to meet their own needs. The term contains within it two key concepts: the concept of 'needs', in particular the essential needs of the world's poor, to which overriding priority should be given; and the idea of limitations imposed by the state of technology and social organization on the environment's ability to meet present and future needs.

Sustainable product design (SPD) is a design philosophy and practice in which products contribute to social and economic well-being, have negligible impacts on the environment and can be produced from a sustainable resource base. It embodies the practice of eco-design, with due attention to environmental, ethical and social factors, but also includes economic considerations and assessments of resource availability in relation to sustainable production.

Sustainable products serve human needs without depleting natural and manmade resources, without damage to the carrying capacity of ecosystems and without restricting the options available to present and future generations.

Technosphere consists of the synthetic and composite components and materials formed by human intervention in re-ordering and combining components and materials of the biosphere, geosphere and atmosphere. True technosphere materials cannot re-enter the biosphere through the process of biodegradation alone. Synthetic polymers such as plastics are examples of such materials.

Transport energy is the energy expended to transport or distribute a product from the manufacturer to the wholesaler or retailer. Locally manufactured and locally purchased products tend to have much lower transport energies than imported products. The unit of measure is MJ per kilogram.

Use-impact products are consumer products that create (major) environmental impacts, such as cars and electrical appliances.

Volatile organic compounds (VOCs) are natural and synthetic organic chemicals that can easily move between the solid/liquid and gaseous phase.

ACRONYMS AND ABBREVIATIONS

Materials, chemicals

ABS acrylonitrile-butadiene-styrene
CFCs chlorinated fluorocarbons – compounds containing chlorine, fluorine and carbon
CO carbon monoxide
CO2 carbon dioxide
HC hydrocarbon
HCFCs hydrochlorofluorocarbons – compounds containing hydrogen, chlorine, fluorine and carbon
HFCs hydrofluorocarbons – compounds containing hydrogen, fluorine and carbon
HDPE high-density polyethylene
LDPE low-density polyethylene
GRP glass-reinforced plastic (polymer)
NO nitrous oxide
NO_x oxides of nitrogen
NiMH nickel metal hydride
NiCd nickel cadmium
O_3 ozone
PE polyethylene (polythene)
PET polyethylene terephthalate
PP polypropylene
PS polystyrene
PU polyurethane
PVC polyvinyl chloride
VOC volatile organic compound

Miscellaneous

EV electric vehicle
LED light emitting diode
PV photovoltaic
CFL compact fluorescent lamp
UV ultraviolet light
DC direct current
AC alternating current
PM10s particulate matter (dust, acids and other types) suspended in the air and measuring less than 0.00001mm diameter
PV photovoltaic module
PRN packaging recovery note

Books

EARLY VISIONARIES

Carson, Rachel, *Silent Spring* (1962), Hamish Hamilton, UK.

Ecologist, The, editors of, *A Blueprint for Survival* (1972), Penguin Books, UK/Australia.

Fuller, Richard Buckminster, *Operating Manual for Spaceship Earth* (1969), Feffer & Simons, London and Amsterdam.

Meadows, Donella, Dennis Meadows, Jørgen Randers and William Behrens III, *The Limits to Growth, A Report for the Club of Rome's Project on the Predicament of Mankind* (1972), Earth Island, London.

Meller, James (ed), *The Buckminster Fuller Reader* (1970), Jonathan Cape, London.

Packard, Vance, *The Hidden Persuaders* (1957), Penguin Books, UK.

Packard, Vance, *The Waste Makers* (1960), Penguin Books, UK/Australia.

Papanek, Victor, *Design for the Real World, Human Ecology and Social Change*(1972), Thames & Hudson, London.

Wright, Frank Lloyd, *The Natural House* (1963), Horizon Press, New York.

ARCHITECTURE

Baggs, Sydney and Joan, *The Healthy House* (1996), Thames & Hudson, London.

Behling, Sophia and Stefan, *Solar Power: The Evolution of Sustainable Architecture* (2000), Prestel Verlag, Munich.

Howard, Nigel and David Sheirs, *The Green Guide to Specification, An Environmental Profiling System for Building Materials and Components* (1998), BRE Report 351, Building Research Establishment, UK.

Jones, David Lloyd, *Architecture and the Environment: Bioclimatic Building Design* (1998), Lawrence King Publishing, London.

Slessor, Catherine, *Eco-Tech: Sustainable Architecture and High Technology* (1997), Thames & Hudson, London.

Vale, Robert and Brenda, *Green Architecture: Design for a Sustainable Future* (1991), Thames & Hudson, London.

Wines, James (and Philip Jodidio [ed]**)**, *Green Architecture* (2000), Taschen, Cologne.

Woolley, Tom, Sam Kimmins, Paul Harrison and Rob Harrison, *Green Building Handbook, A guide to building products and their impact on the environment* (1997), E & F N Spon, London.

BUSINESS AND SUSTAINABILITY

Allenby, B, and D Richards, (eds), *The Greening of Industrial Ecosystems* (1994), National Academy Press, Washington, D.C.

Charter, Martin and Ursula Tischner (eds), *Sustainable Solutions: Developing Products and Services for the Future* (2001), Greenleaf Publishing, UK.

Datschefski, Edwin, *Sustainable Products: The Trillion Dollar Opportunity* (1999), J L Publishing, Hitchin, UK.

Davis, John, *Greening Business: Managing for Sustainable Development* (1991), Blackwell, Oxford.

Fussler, Claude with Peter James, *Driving Eco-innovation* (1996), Pitman Publishing, London.

Hawken, P A B, Lovins and L H Lovins, *Natural Capitalism: Creating the Next Industrial Revolution* (1999), Little & Brown, Boston, and Earthscan, London.

Institute of Materials and Glasgow Caledonian University, *Manufacturing and the Environment* (1997), Institute of Materials, London.

Kirkwood, R C, and A J Longley, *Clean Technology and the Environment* (1995), Blackie Academic & Professional, London.

ECODESIGN, GREEN DESIGN, DfX, SUSTAINABLE PRODUCT DESIGN

Balcioglu, Tevfik (ed), *The Role of Product Design in Post Industrial Society* (1998), Middle East Technical University Faculty of Architecture Press, Ankara, and Kent Institute of Art & Design, Rochester, UK.

Beukers, Adriaan and Ed van Hinte, *Lightness: The Inevitable Renaissance of Minimum Energy Structures* (1999), 010 Publishers, Rotterdam.

Billastos, Samir and Nadia A Basaly, *Green Technology and Design for the Environment* (1997), Taylor and Francis, Washington D.C.

Brezet, Han and Carolein van Hemel, *Ecodesign. A Promising Approach to Sustainable Production and Consumption* (1997), United Nations Environment Programme, Paris, France.

Burrell, P, *Product Development and the Environment* (1996), Design Council & Gower Publications, London.

Commission of the European Communities, *Green Paper on Integrated Product Policy* (2001), COM, Brussels.

Henstock, M, *Design for Recyclability* (1988), Institute of Metals, London.

Krause, F. and Helmut Jansen (eds), *Life Cycle Modelling for Innovative Products & Processes* (1996), Chapman & Hall, London.

Lyle, John, *Regenerative Design for Sustainable Design*, (1994), Wiley, New York.

MacKenzie, Dorothy, *Green Design: Design for the Environment* (1991), Rizzoli, New York.

Papanek, Victor, *The Green Imperative: Ecology & Ethics in Design and Architecture* (1995), Thames & Hudson, London.

Van der Ryn, Sim & Stuart Cowan, *Ecological Design* (1996), Island Press, Washington D.C.

van Hinte, Ed and Conny Bakker, *Trespassers: Inspirations for Eco-efficient Design* (1999), 010 Publishers, Rotterdam.

Whiteley, Nigel, *Design For Society* (1993), Reaktion Books, London.

ENVIRONMENTAL ISSUES AND DATA

Brundtland, Gro Harlem et al, World Commission on Environment and Development, *Our Common Future* (1987), Oxford University Press, UK/USA.

Curran, Susan, *Environment Handbook* (1998), The Stationery Office, UK.

Lees, Nigel and Helen Woolston, *Environmental Information: A Guide to Sources* (1997), The British Library, London.

McLaren, Duncan, Simon Bullock and Nusrat Yousuf, *Tomorrow's World, Britain's Share in a Sustainable Future* (1998), Earthscan, London.

GENERAL

Antonelli, Paola, *Mutant Materials in Contemporary Design* (1995), Museum of Modern Art, New York.

Counsell, Simon, *The Good Wood Guide* (1996), Friends of the Earth, London.

Elkington, John and Julia Hailes, *The Green Consumer Guide* (1988), Gollancz, London.

National Recycling Forum/ Waste Watch, *UK Recycled Products Guide* (1998), National Recycling Forum/Waste Watch, UK.

Philips Design, *La Casa Prossima Futura (The Home of the Near Future) exhibition* (1999), Royal Philips Electronics, Netherlands.

Philips Design, *Vision of the Future* (1996), Philips Design and V+K Publishing, Netherlands.

Powers, Alan, *Nature in Design* (1999), Conran Octopus, London.

Ramakers, Remy and Gils Bakker (eds), *Droog Design. Spirit of the Nineties* (1998), 010 Publishers, Rotterdam.

Taylor, Louise et al, *Recycling, Forms for the Next Century – Austerity for Posterity* (1996), Craftspace Touring, Birmingham.

Magazines, journals, e-zines and newsletters

ARCHITECTURE

Environmental Design & Construction (USA)
A magazine covering all aspects of environmentally sound building design and construction.
www.edcmag.com

GreenClips: Sustainable Building Design News Digest (USA)
An e-mail newsletter and web resource providing a summary of the latest news on sustainable building design.
www.greendesign.net/greenclips

BUSINESS AND SUSTAINABILITY

Business and the Environment (Cutter, USA)
A hard-copy and online resource for business executives worldwide to keep abreast of the debate on environmental management issues.
http://cutter.com/bate

Greener Management International – The Journal of Corporate Environmental Strategy and Practice
(Greenleaf Publishing, UK)
A quarterly journal, which discusses the developments around key strategic environmental and sustainability issues and their effects on public- and private-sector organizations.
http://www.greenleaf-publishing.com

Sustain
(World Business Council for Sustainable Development, Switzerland)
Quarterly magazine providing examples of how members are tackling the issue of sustainable development and discussing current issues.
www.wbcsd.ch

Tomorrow
(Tomorrow Publishing, Sweden)
A print and web media journal informing about corporate environmental issues, providing analysis and offering practical solutions.
www.tomorrow-web.com

Sustainable Business
(USA)
A monthly online magazine, which collates news, features and regular columns from the growing arena of sustainable business.
www.sustainablebusiness.com

ECODESIGN, GREEN DESIGN, DfX, SUSTAINABLE PRODUCT DESIGN

The Biothinker
(Biothinking International, UK)
A newsletter that promotes the philosophy of cyclic, solar and safe practices in relation to the design of products and services.
www.biothinking.com

Ecocycle
An online newsletter dedicated to product life-cycle management (LCM) and the dissemination of information on policy and technical issues.
www.ec.gc.ca/ecocycle

EcoDesign
(Ecological Design Association,UK)
This is the journal of the Ecological Design Association, serving its membership of over 1,500 in the UK and overseas. Issues tend to be based upon themes such as transport, eco-products and self-build, but each incorporates diverse editorial matter from lifestyle to semi-technical.
www.edaweb.org

International Journal of Environmentally Conscious Design and Manufacturing
(ECDM Lab, University of Windsor, Canada)
Examines the short- and long-term effects of design and manufacturing on the environment and reports recent trends, advances and research results.
www.ijecdm.com

Journal of Life Cycle Assessment
A journal devoted entirely to LCA for practitioners, product managers and all those interested in reducing the ecological burdens of products and systems.
www.ecomed.de/journals/lca/lca.htm

Journal of Industrial Ecology
(Massachusetts Institute of Technology, USA)
A quarterly hard-copy and online journal published by MIT, which encompasses material and energy-flow studies, lifecycle analysis, design for the environment, product stewardship and much more. Although aimed at academia, it is a good source of technical information, statistics and contacts.
http://mitpress.mit.edu/JIE

Journal of Sustainable Product Design
(The Centre for Sustainable Design, UK)
A quarterly publication that includes contributions from academia and industry to encourage business towards sustainable practices, products and services.
www.cfsd.org.uk/journal

ENVIRONMENTAL NEWS, POLICY AND INFORMATION

ENDS Report, The
(Environmental Data Services Ltd, UK)
In continuous publication since 1978, *The ENDS Report* is a comprehensive monthly print and web media journal offering news, analysis and features on environmental policy and business, with a UK focus informed by developments in the EU.
www.endsreport.com

ENDS Environment Daily
(Environmental Data Services Ltd, UK)
A daily electronic news service focusing on environmental policy developments in Europe.
www.environmentdaily.com

GENERAL

Green Futures
(Forum for the Future, UK)
Magazine that focuses on issues of sustainable development illustrated by case studies and initiatives in business, industry and local government.
www.forumforthefuture.org.uk

Itch (magazine)
(Sustainable Solutions Design Association, Denmark)
A quarterly magazine, which focuses on sustainability and fashion for designers of textiles and clothes.
www.psd-dk.com/_psd_htm/info.htm

Recycler's World
(RecycleNet Corporation, Canada)
This is a worldwide trading site for information about reusable and recyclable products, by-products and materials.
www.recycle.net

Recycling World
(Tec Publications, UK)
Trade magazine, which examines the latest developments in recycling technology and new initiatives in the UK and Europe and offers a resource for trading recycled materials called Recyclers' Corner.
www.teeweb.com/recycle

Warmer Bulletin
Focuses on resource recovery and waste management, including reports on legislative, technical and policy developments around the world.
www.residua.com/WB.html

Index

Illustration Credits
t–top; b–bottom; l–left; r–right; c–centre; c1, c2, c3, c4–column 1, column 2, column 3, column 4

1, Keith Parry; 2 Iform; 9 Wharington International Pty Ltd; 16-17, Michael Gerlach; 19bl, Viaduct; 19br, Ceccotti Collezioni; 20 tl, Design Academy Eindhoven; 20 br, Viaduct; 21 tl, br, Meta Morf Inc.; 22 tl, Studio Ilkka Suppanen; 22 tr, International Design Resource Awards (IDRA); 22 bl, Robert A Wettstein; 23 tl, Marre Moerel; 23 bl, David Trubridge; 23 tr, Damian Williamson; 24 tl, Enrique Corrales; 24 br, El Ultimo Grito; 25 tr, cl, Marcel Loermans; 25 b, Carl Clerkin; 26 Michael Gerlach; 27 bl, br, Design Academy Eindhoven; 27 t, IDRA; 28, Mads Flummer; 29 bl, br, Kazuhiro Yamanaka; 29 t, Plastics f'th Industry Ltd; 30 b, Julio Garcia Garate; 30 tr, c, Deutsche Gesellschaft für Kunststoff-Recycling; 31 b, Marino Ramazzotti; 31 t, Tendo Co. Ltd; 32 t, Viaduct; 32 b, Trannon Furniture Ltd; 33 br, Guy Martin; 33 tl, Fernando and Humberto Campana; 34 bl, br, Johan Kalén; 34 tr, Cappellini SpA; 34 cr, Rosenthal; 35 tc, bl, Jane Atfield; 35 tr, Vitra; 36 t, Meta Morf Inc.; 36 c, b, Lloyd Loom of Spalding; 37 t, Pil Bredahl and Liselotte Risell; 37 b, Earth Chair; 38 t, b, Galleri Stolen AB; 39 t, IDRA; 39 cl, br, Julienne Dolphin-Wilding; 40, Iform; 41 tc, bl, IDRA; 41 cr, br, Robert A Wettstein; 42 t, Dalsouple; 42 b, Hans van der Mars; 43 cr, br, Jane Atfield; 43 tl, Cappellini SpA; 44 t, Mads Flummer; 44 b, Cappellini SpA; 45 tr, Jane Atfield; 45 bl, Fiam Italia SpA; 46 t, Dominique Uldry; 46 b, IDRA; 47 IDRA; 48 bl, MetaMorf Inc.; 48 tr, Cappellini SpA; 49 br, Hans Hansen; 49 tr, Authentics artipresent GmbH; 49 tl, Erik Krogh Design; 50 l, Luke Kirwan; 50 cr, Wilde & Spieth GmbH; 51 tl, tr, Viaduct; 51 bc, Cappellini SpA; 52 b, Pawel Grunert; 52 t, Brazilian eco-design awards 1997; 52 b, Pawel Grunert; 53 bl, Miro Zagnoli; 53 tl, Michael Marriott; 53 tr, Julienne Dolphin-Wilding; 54 b, Trannon Furniture Ltd; 54 t, Cappellini SpA; 55 t, Jam Design & Communications; 55 b, Pamela Hatton; 56 t, Wharington International Pty Ltd; 56 bl, br, Front Corporation; 57 tl, Verne/Bulo; 57 tr, MAP; 57 cr, cb, Design Academy Eindhoven; 58 b, IDRA; 58 tl, tr, David Hertz/Syndesis Inc.; 59 tl, IDRA; 59 tr, Cappellini SpA; 59 tl, IDRA; 60 bl, Bob Goedewagen; 60 tr, DMD/Droog Design; 61 t, Avant de Dormir; 61 b, Kartell; 62 t, Roberto Feo; 62 b, Kartell; 63 Jam Design & Communications; 64, Dominique Uldry; 65 tc,br, Dominique Uldry; 65 bl, Condor P.R/IKEA; 66 tc, bl, Jörg Boner, N2; 66 cr, IDRA; 67 Lorenz Wiegand/ POOL-products; 68 t, b, Deutsche Gesellschaft für Kunststoff-Recycling; 69 tl, IDRA; 69 tr, br, Jasper Startup; 70 Design Academy Eindhoven; 71 tl, bl, Thomas Dobbie; 71 cr, Design Academy Eindhoven; 72 t, b, of ClassiCon, Germany; 73 t, Retail Place Ltd; 73 b, Design Academy Eindhoven; 74 tc, tl, Droog Design; 74 cr, Design Academy Eindhoven; 75 Design Academy Eindhoven; 76t, Droog Design; 76 b, N2/sdb industries; 77 b, El Ultimo Grito; 77 tl, tr, of Richard Hutten; 78 b, Ed Reeve; 78 t, Cappellini SpA; 79 Habitat; 80 tr, Jam Design & Communications; 80 c,b, Cappellini SpA, Italy; 81 tl, Design Academy Eindhoven; 81 br, Deutsche Gesellschaft für Kunststoff-Recycling; 81 c, of Robert A Wettstein; 82 tr, Dominique Uldry; 82 tl, Hülsta; 83 tl, Roberto Feo; 83 cr, Tom Vack; 83 tl, El Ultimo Grito; 84 Andrés Otero; 85 tl, Jason Griffiths; 85 br, Atelier Alinea; 86 br, Peter Gabriel; 86 tl, IDRA; 87 V K & C Partnership; 88 t, Dorte Krogh; 88 b, Sergio Macchioni; 89 t, courtesy Sebastian Bergne/Radius GmbH; 89 b, IDRA; 90 t, Polly Farquharson; 90 b, Hans van der Mars; 91 b, Roy Sant; 91 t, Deborah Thomas; 92 t, Dalsouple Ltd; 92 b, Stephen Philips Design; 93 Deutsche Gesellschaft für Kunststoff-Recycling; 94 tl, Sculptures-Jeux; 94 br, Carl Clerkin; 94 tr, Alastair Fuad-Luke; 95 t, Brahl Fotografi; 95 b, IDRA; 96 bl, Jakob Kristensen; 96 tr, IDRA; 97 tl,br, Design Museum, London; 98 tl, Frits Vink; 98 tr, Designed to a 't'; 98 br, N2; 99 t, Cappellini SpA; 99 b Katherine Fawsett; 100 br, Steven Krause; 100 tl, bl, Cappellini SpA; 101 tl, 2pm Limited; 101 cr, IDRA; 101 bl, Lampholder 2000 plc; 102 t, Deutsche Gesellschaft für Kunststoff-Recycling; 102 b, IDRA; 103 t, IDRA; 103 b, Deutsche Gesellschaft für Kunststoff-Recycling; 104 tl, Manuel Baniera and Francisco Paz; 104 br, IDRA; 105, Glas Platz; 106 tr,br, Arnold Photography; 106 cl, Ligne Roset; 107 t, Bär + Knell; 107 b, Moonlight Aussenleuchten; 108 tl, cr, Viaduct; 108 bl, IDRA; 109 tr, bl, Mark Sutton Vane; 109 br, IDRA; 110 bl, Nisso Engineering; 110 tl, Iain Sinclair Design ; 110 br, Freeplay Energy Europe; 111 bl, Dominique Uldry; 111 br, Light Corporation; 111 tl, c, BP Solar Interntional; 112 tl, Philips Lighting; 112 bl, SLI Lighting; 112 cr, Lampholder 2000 plc; 113 t, Philips Lighting; 113 b, Ledtronics; 114 t, Induced Energy; 114b, Aga-Rayburn; 115 tl, bl, Solar Cookers International; 115 tr, Philips Design; 116 Philips Electronics; 117 tl, Gloria-Werke; 117 bl, Alfred Kärcher GmbH; 117 cr, Polti; 118 cr, Polti; 118 tc, bl, Dyson Appliances; 119 t, AEG; 119 b, Monotub Industries; 120 tr, Staber Industries; 120 bl, Hoover Group; 121 tl, bl, Electrolux Zanussi; 121 br, Planet; 122 tr, c, bl, Supercool AB; 122 br, Nicholas Albertus; 123 tl, IDRA; 123 bl, Gianni Antonali/ Gervasoni SpA ; 123 tr, br Keith Parry; 124 Gabriella Dahlman; 125 tl, br, Acordis Fibres (Holdings) Ltd; 126 t, b, Design Museum, London; 127 t, Acordis Fibres (Holdings) Ltd; 127 b, Philips Design; 128 t, Royal Philips Electronics; 128 b, Design Academy Eindhoven; 129 tl, Deep E®; 129 br, Daniel Ohlsson/Klara AB; 130 t, Alastair Fuad-Luke; 130 b, BREE Collection GmbH; 131 t, Dominique Uldry; 131 b, Dalsouple Ltd; 132, BMW (GB) Ltd.; 133, Fiat Auto UK; 134 t, General Motors; 134 b, Honda; 135 t, Chrysler Jeep® Imports UK; 135 b, General Motors/ Vauxhall Motors; 136 Honda; 137 t, Fiat Auto UK; 137 b, Ford Motor Company; 138 Toyota; 139 t, Corbin Motors; 139 b, Daimler Chrysler AG; 140 TH!NK Nordic AG/Ford Motor Company; 141 t, General Motors/Vauxhall Motors; 141b Volkswagen AG; 142, Daimler Chrysler AG; 143 Independence Technology; 144 t, United Nations Environment Programme (UNEP); 144 b, Daimler Chrysler AG; 145 t, Riese und Müller GmbH; 145 br, Dominique Uldry; 145 cl, Seymour Powell; 146 t, Roland Plastics; 146 b, Advanced Vehicle Design; 147 tl, UNEP; 147, br, Brompton Bicycle Ltd; 148 NASA/Dryden Flight Research Station; 149 Advanced Vehicle Design; 150 bl, Straka sPORTs Ciromachines GmbH; 150 tr, Skoot International Ltd; 150 br, Nova Cruz Products; 151 Powabyke Ltd; 152 t, Design Academy Eindhoven; 152 b, SRAM Corporation; 153 cl, Dalsouple Ltd; 153 br, Dominique Uldry; 154 bl, Design Academy Eindhoven; 154 tr, Patagonia; 155 tl, Nighteye GmbH; 155 br, IDRA; 156 tr, IDRA; 156 cr, cb, Skystreme UK Ltd; 156 bl, Verobüro Olten; 157 tl, tc, Purves & Purves, London; 157 b, Husqvarna/The Electrolux Group; 158 tl, Reln/ Wiggly Wigglers; 158 tr, Blackwall Ltd; 158 bl, Metpost; 159 tl, Porous Pipe; 159 cr, Design Academy Eindhoven; 159 br, Husqvarna/The Electrolux Group; 160 tc, bl, Glas Platz; 160 tr, Philips Design; 161 t, Canon Inc. Japan; 161 b, Sony Corporation; 162 Freeplay Energy Europe; 163 bl, IDRA ; 163 tr, Philips Electronics; 163 br, Lexon Design Concepts; 164 t, Grundig AG; 164 b, Philips Electronics; 165 tl, Gibson Guitars; 165 b, Design Academy Eindhoven; 166 Philips Design; 167 Palo Alto Products International; 168 Mr Toyozo and the Nifty Hewlett Packard PC user forum; 169 t, Goods; 169 b, Alessi SpA; 170 cl, Danese srl; 170 br, Camille Jacobs; 170 tr, cr, Pamela Hatton; 171 tr, Wanders Wonders; 171 tl, bl, Feldmann + Schultchen; 172 tc, bl, IDRA; 172 tr, Droog Design; 173 Studio Brown; 174 t, LINPAC Environmental; 174 b, Benza Inc.; 175 tr, Patrick Laing; 175 bl, William Warren; 175 tl, Oxo International; 175 cr, Richard Davies; 176 cl, REEEL; 176 tr, Droog Design; 176 br, Aki Kotkas; 177 tl, Institute of Contemporary Arts (ICA), London; 177 br, Designed to a 't' Ltd; 178 b, Peter Gabriel; 178 t, Christian Stoll//Authentics artipresent GmbH; 179 b, Robert A Wettstein; 179 t, Dominique Uldry; 180 b, courtesyVaccari Ltd; 180 t, Durex; 181 tl, Alastair Fuad-Luke; 181 br, Ecover Products; 182 cl, Fingermax Gbr; 182 tr, Lois Walpole; 183 Feldmann + Schultchen; 184 t, UNEP; 184 b, Mark Rogers; 185 tl, cr, Junghans Uhren GmbH; 185 bl, Benza Inc; 186, SMAC, Sergio Macchioni; 187 t, Vaccari Ltd; 187 b, Feldmann + Schultchen Design; 188 Cutouts; 189 tl, Authentics artipresent GmbH; 189 br, Goods; 190 tl, br, IDRA; 191 t, b, IDRA ; 192-193, Fritz Hansen; 195 bl, Clearvision Lighting; 195 tl, Philips Electronics; 195 cr,br, Concord Lighting; 196 t, Ground Support Equipment (US) Ltd; 196 b, Herman Miller Inc.; 197 tc, br Baleria Italia SpA; 197 cl, Haworth Inc.; 198 r, Haworth Inc; 199 Fritz Hansen; 200 t, Miro Zagnoli; 200 b, Haworth Inc.; 201 t, Steelcase Photo Services; 201 b, Tetra Pak; 202 t, Nova Form; 202 b, Wilkhahn + Hahne GmbH; 203 t, IDRA; 203 b, Celotex; 204 Fritz Hansen; 205 bl, Dominique Uldry; 205 tc, Design Museum, London; 205 br, Sanford UK Ltd; 206 tr, Alastair Fuad-Luke; 206 br, Green Disk; 207 tr, Epson ; 207 cl, PCD Maltron Ltd; 207 br, Canon (UK) Ltd; 208 t, Kyocera; 208 b Xerox Corporation; 209 cl, IDEO Product Development; 209 br, IBM; 210 t, Air Packaging Technologies; 210 b, Amasec Airfil; 211 t, Cargill Dow; 211 b, Robert Cullen & Sons; 212 t, IFCO; 212 b, LSK Industries Pty Ltd; 213 t, Werzalit AG + Co; 213 b, Ehlebracht AG; 214 tl, Alastair Fuad-Luke; 214 cr, bl, Schäfer Werke GmbH; 215 3M Deutschland; 216 bl, Alastair Fuad-Luke; 216 tl, General Motors/Vauxhall; 216 bl, Alastair Fuad-Luke; 216 tr, br, gmp-Architekten; 217 BTM International Ltd; 218 PowerMakers Plus; 219 t, Man Nutzfahrzeuge/APR (Foto); 219 b, Marks & Spencer; 220 t, LUMINO Licht Elecktronik GmbH; 220 b, Peugeot; 221 Optare; 222 NASA/Dryden Research Centre; 223 cl, FanWing; 223 tr, NASA/Dryden Research Centre; 224 tr, br, Rolls Royce; 224 bl, Festo Corporate Design; 225 t, b, Bernd Kammerer/ Kopf AG; 226, Design Museum, London; 227 t, Droog Design; 227 b, Baccarne bvba; 228 bl, Escofet; 228 tr, Pendlewood; 229 t, b, VK & C Partnership; 230 tl, Comarco Wireless Technologies; 230 bl, Environmental Polymers Group; 230 tr, Landmark GmbH; 231 tl, Philips Design; 231 br, Solar Solutions; 232 cl, br, Roy

Illustration Credits

Fleetwood/YKK Architectural Products Inc; 232 tr, Ecke:Design; 233, Design Museum, London; 234 tl, Zimmerei Michael Kaufmann; 234 br, Design Museum, London; 235 tc, tr, Parnham Trust at Hooke Park; 235 b, Zimmerei Michael Kaufmann; 236 tl, cl, Design Museum, London; 236 tr, br, Akeler Developments plc; 237 Hereford County Council; 238 tr, Festo Corporate Design; 238 bl, Ecover; 239 Peabody Trust; 240 tl, cr, K-X Industries; 240 b, Re-New Wood; 241 cl, Glindower Ziegelei GmbH; 241 tc, Red Bank Manufacturing Company; 242 Monodraught Ltd; 243 Regialdo Marinho; 244 TrusJoist MacMillan (TJM); 245 b, Blesius/Vorwerk & Co. Teppichwerke GmbH & Co. KG; 245 t, Alastair Fuad-Luke; 246 tr, cr, Dalsouple Direct; 246 bl, Interface; 247 Matrix Composites Inc.; 248 tl, Dominque Uldry; 248 cr, Alastair Fuad-Luke; 248 tr, Interface Inc.; 248 br, Smith & Fong Company; 249 cl, Alastair Fuad-Luke; 249 tr, br, The Amtico Company; 250, Duralay; 251 tr, Alligator Sunshine Technologies GmbH; 251 bl, Ampair Ltd; 252 Teisen Products; 253 t, Filsol; 253 b, Nigel Young/Foster and Partners; 254 tc, bc, Water Film Energy; 255 tl, r, Buderus Heiztechnik Gmbh, Germany; 256 t, Bartsch Industrial Design Gbr; 256 b, Ritter Energie- und Umwelttechnik GmbH KG; 257 Sunways; 258 Uni-Solar; 259 BP Solar International; 260 t, Solar Century; 260 b, Rayotec Ltd; 261, GAAN GmbH; 262 Hans Grohe; 263 Clivus Multrum Canada; 264 t, Elemental Solutions; 264 b, Sun-Mar Corporation; 265 t, Flow Control Water Conservation; 265 br, Jenny Matthews/Oxfam; 265 bl, Oxfam; 266 t, Flamco; 266 b, Wagner & Co Solartechnik GmbH; 267 Waterless UK; 269 Brook Hansen; 270 t, ABG Ltd; 270 b, 3M; 271 tl, Dominique Uldry; 271 tr, XO2 Limited; 271 b, Beacon Print; 272 tr, Lew San Ltd; 272 c, Alastair Fuad-Luke; 272 br, Netlon; 273 tl, Southampton Innovations; 273 cr, Orange; 274-275 Richard Learoyd; 278 c2t, Design Academy Eindhoven; 278 c2 b, c3, c4t Kingston University, Rematerialise samples Jakki Dehn; 278 c4b, Alastair Fuad-Luke; 279 c4t, Meadwood Industries; 279 c2, Matrix Composites; 279 c3, Masonite Corporation; 279 c4b, Willamette Europe; 280 c1, BioFab LLC; 280 c2, Alastair Fuad-Luke; 280 c4t, Strandwood Molding; 280 c4b, Primeboard Inc.; 281 c1, Eco Timber International; 281 c2, Alastair Fuad-Luke, Rematerialise samples Jakki Dehn; 281 c4, Trus Joist MacMillan; 282 c1t, Johnson Corrugated Products; 282 c1c, Biocorp; 282 c1b, Biotec; 282 c2, Solvay Plastiques; 282 c3, c4, Alastair Fuad-Luke; 283 c1t, Norel; 283 c1b, Novamont SpA; 283 c3, Novon International; 283 c4, Cargill Dow; 284 c1, Starch Tech Inc.; 284 c2t, Alastair Fuad-Luke; 284 c2b, Deutsche Heraklith; 284 c3 Hock Vertriebs-GmbH & Co. KG; 284 c4, Klober; 286 c1, Auro Organic Paint Supplies Ltd; 286 c2, Bioshield Paint Company; 286 c4t, Old Fashioned Milk Paint Company; 286 c4b, Ostermann & Scheiwe; 287 c4 Franmar Chemical Inc.; 288 c1, Crane & Company; 288 c2, Curtis Fine Papers; 288 c3, Fiskeby Board Ltd; 288 c4, Hurum Fabrikker; 289 c1, Alastair Fuad-Luke; 289 c2, Smith Anderson & Co.; 289 c3 KP Products; 290 c1t, Richard Learoyd; 290 c1b, c4t, Alastair Fuad-Luke; 290 c2, DesignTex; 290 c4b, UNEP; 291 c1 Fredrik, Malmlund Reklamfoto AB; 291 c2, Novotex; 291 c4, Nuno Corporation; 292 c1, AERT; 292 c2t, Recycled Plastics Inc.; 292 c2b, Wharington International Pty; 292 c3, c4, Alastair Fuad-Luke; 293 c1t, North Wood Plastics Inc.; 293 c1b, Alastair Fuad-Luke, Rematerialise samples Jakki Dehn; 293 c2, Kingston Univeristy, Rematerialise samples Jakki Dehn; 293 c3t, Alastair Fuad-Luke, Rematerialise samples Jakki Dehn; 293 c3b, Alastair Fuad-Luke; 293 c4t, Hahn Kunststoffe GmbH; 293 c4b, Alastair Fuad-Luke, Rematerialise samples Jakki Dehn; 294 c2, Alastair Fuad-Luke; 294 c4t, WKR Altkunststoffproduktions-u.Vertriebsgesellschaft GmbH; 294, c4b, Alastair Fuad-Luke, Rematerialise samples Jakki Dehn; 295 c3, Safeglass (Europe) Ltd; 295 c4, Kingtson University, Rematerialise samples Jakki Dehn; 296 c1t, Pinnacle Inc. (PTI); 296 c1b, Showa Highpolymer Co.; 296 c3, c4, Alastair Fuad-Luke; 297 Advanced Elastomer Products; 298 c1t, Teknos Tranemo; 298 c1b, Lakeland Paints; 298 c2, Nordsjö; 298 c3, Keim Mineral Paints Ltd; 298 c4, Pinturas Proa; 299 c2, Eco Solutions; 299 c3, Laybond Products Ltd; 300 c1, Dominique Uldry; 300 c2t, Wellman Inc; 300 c2b, Electrotextiles Ltd; 300 c3, Nuno Corporation; 300 c4, Micro Thermal Systems; 301 c1, Interface Fabrics